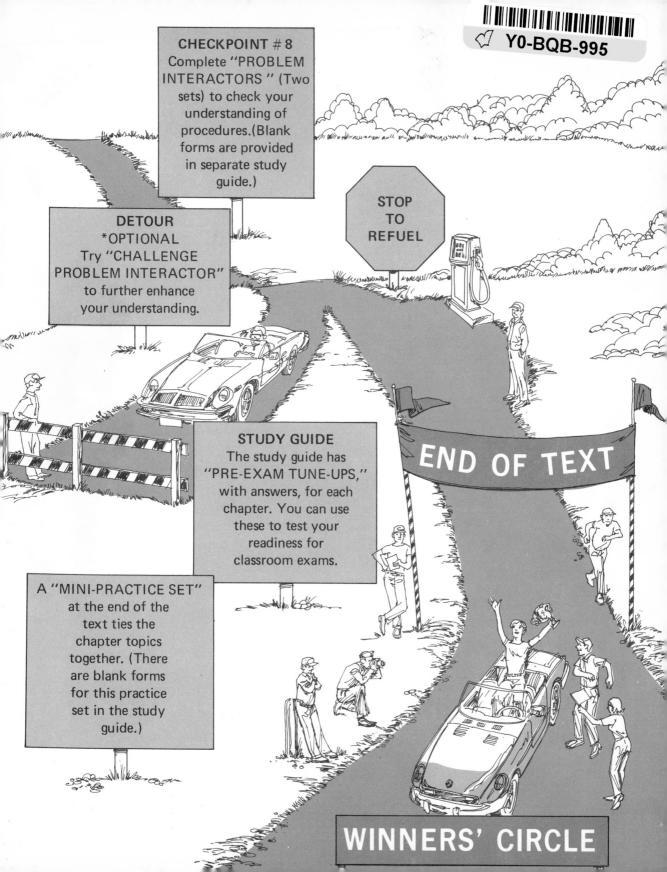

Practical Accounting Procedures

Practical

acco

PRENTICE-HALL INC., Englewood Cliffs, N.J. 07632

unting

Procedures

JEFFREY SLATER

North Shore Community College
Beverly, Massachusetts

Library of Congress Cataloging in Publication Data
Slater, Jeffrey (date)
 Practical accounting procedures.

 Includes index.
 1. Accounting. I. Title.
HF5635.S6315   657   78-15739
ISBN 0-13-688101-7

PRACTICAL ACCOUNTING PROCEDURES
Jeffrey Slater

Editorial/production supervision by Sonia Meyer
Cover and Interior design by Lee Cohen
Cover photograph by John Okladek
Page layout by Gail Cocker and Jayne Conte
Manufacturing buyer: Harry P. Baisley

Printed in the United States of America
10   9   8   7   6   5   4   3   2   1

Prentice-Hall International, Inc., *London*
Prentice-Hall of Australia Pty. Limited, *Sydney*
Prentice-Hall of Canada, Ltd., *Toronto*
Prentice-Hall of India Private Limited, *New Delhi*
Prentice-Hall of Japan, Inc., *Tokyo*
Prentice-Hall of Southeast Asia Pte. Ltd., *Singapore*
Whitehall Books Limited, *Wellington, New Zealand*

acknowledgments

Over the past four years many people have helped in the construction of this total learning package, both by recognizing its strengths and by pointing out areas for improvement. My appreciation must center first around the more than 500 students who have helped shape the final program. Of the many class testers and reviewers, I would like to thank especially Candis Martin, Schoolcraft College; Thomas E. Brown, State University of New York, Alfred Agricultural and Technical College; Robert H. Landry, Massasoit Community College; Stanley Baron, Indiana Vocational College; Ned Perri, Gateway Technical Institute; Jim Humphrey, Hocking Technical College; Steven Baker, Business Consultant; Joe Francis, North Shore Community College; Peter Regan, North Shore Community College; and John Sullivan, North Shore Community College.

Thanks go also to Safeguard Business System, National Blank Book Co., Security National Bank, and Kendall Hunt Publishing (*Simplifying Accounting Language*) for permission to use material for this text.

I am grateful to the entire team at Prentice-Hall who have given of themselves and provided a great deal of assistance over the past several years. The team includes Stephen Cline, Editor, College Division; Sonia Meyer, College Book Production; Lee Cohen, Graphic Designer; Jim Morlock, College Marketing; Robert Lentz, Copy Editor; Esther Koehn, College Book Production; and Ken Cashman, College Book Production.

Most of all, for ''putting up with me,'' I would like to thank my family—Rusty, Abby, and Shelley. Their lovingkindness and their continued support in the making of this book are truly appreciated.

Jeffrey Slater

contents

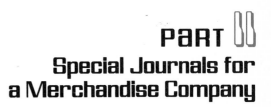

PART II
Special Journals for a Merchandise Company

PART III
The Accounting Cycle
Completed for a Merchandise Firm

 THE ACCOUNTING CYCLE CONTINUED *362*

COMPLETION OF THE ACCOUNTING CYCLE *391*

PART IV
Payroll

 PAYROLL PROCEDURES AND CONCEPTS *426*

preface

PRACTICAL ACCOUNTING PROCEDURES will introduce you to accounting, the most dynamic tool of business.

What is accounting, and why will you find it useful? Accounting is a planned and orderly way of keeping records for the purpose of seeing how a business is performing. It answers such questions as: Is the business profitable, or is it losing money? Which business activities are contributing most to profits, and which to losses? Which resources are well employed, and which are being wasted? Who owes the business money, and how much? What does the business owe? Accounting is also important for regulatory and tax purposes. You will be surprised at how often your understanding of accounting will work for you on the job.

It was once said, "To be complicated is simple, but to be simple is complicated." No better sentiments could express this book's purpose. At first glance, the organization of this book might appear a bit complicated, but once you become familiar with its purpose, you will see that its step-by-step approach is designed to simplify your study of accounting. Learning accounting means familiarizing yourself with many new terms and concepts. Don't let the temptation to cut corners and take shortcuts fool you—you will get the most out of your study of accounting if you follow the detailed, step-by-step directions provided in this text. Once you have learned the basic terms and concepts, the rest will quickly fall into place.

Inside the front cover there is a diagram that illustrates the organization of this text. It outlines the best way to study from the text and its related materials.

By glancing at the chart you'll find that the text is broken down into small segments of material called *Learning Units*. Each one covers an important topic in accounting. Each unit is followed by a list of *Learning Objectives* which indicate the key points you should have learned after studying the unit. At the end of each Learning Unit is something called a *Unit Interactor*. The term *Interactor* is used throughout this text to identify questions, exercises, and problems that allow you to interact with and test your understanding of material already presented. Each Unit Interactor is followed by a detailed solution, so you can identify any difficulties before they cause you problems.

Learning Units combine to make up the chapters of this text. After you have studied each Learning Unit within a chapter, there are several items to help you review and master the chapter material as a whole. They are:

Question Interactors: Provide you with short answer questions that help you to review accounting theory.

Summary of Accounting Terms & Definitions: Help you to develop a clear understanding of the new terms that were introduced in the chapter.

Blueprint Summary: Allows you to visualize the relationships of chapter concepts and important points.

Problem Interactors: Allow you to apply what you have learned by working out a series of exercises and problems. For each learning unit in a chapter there is a related problem in this section. There are also one or more problems that overview the entire chapter. (These are indicated by an asterisk*.)

Additional Problem Interactors: Offer you an alternate set of problems. As these are slightly different from the problem interactors, they will provide you with another opportunity to practice what you have learned.

Challenge Problem: Provides you with a slightly more difficult problem to further reinforce your understanding.

At the end of the text is a Mini-Practice Set, which is a comprehensive exercise based upon the entire text. It shows you how each of the pieces (presented as chapters) fit together to form the accounting process as a whole.

A STUDY GUIDE WITH WORKING PAPERS contains convenient forms for completing all problems in the text. It also includes *Pre-examination Tune-ups* (sample exams with solutions) to help you prepare for classroom exams. *Practical Accounting Procedures* has been designed to help you prepare for your career. It is up to you to make the most of it!

PRACTICAL ACCOUNTING PROCEDURES is a complete learning system to help you teach accounting to non-accounting majors. It was written with an understanding of the time constraints placed on you in trying to meet the needs of a broad spectrum of students—students whose backgrounds vary considerably and whose career aims range from the secretarial/office occupations through entrepreneurship, hotel management, real estate, retailing, and various technical occupations, to name a few, and who bring to your course varying degrees of preparation and learning abilities.

Considerable effort was devoted to providing a wide range and abundance of problems and exercises, many with solutions, which offer immediate feedback and reinforcement. This feedback helps students build confidence. It also helps them to identify their difficulties and formulate their questions. (For a complete description of these and other learning aids, see the preceding section "To the Student.")

Over the past four years, more than 500 students, at several schools, have class-tested this material. Their success has demonstrated the workability of the book's approach—a *think-look-do* approach that offers a gradual and logical buildup of basic concepts through detailed explanations.

A unique feature of this book is the use of Mind-Process Charts, which give students a simplified approach to the analysis of the accounting cycle and the understanding of double-entry bookkeeping. These charts help students to analyze business transactions logically in terms of accounts affected, appropriate categorization, increases and decreases, and applying the rules of debit and credit. Adjustments on the worksheet are introduced at an early stage in the accounting cycle, and the worksheet is reproduced each time a new adjustment is explained. This procedure is further enhanced by Mind-Process Charts.

A "hands on" approach is stressed throughout the book. For example, students complete actual payroll documents, and special emphasis is given to the completion of quarterly reports. The one-write system is illustrated for special journals, and the student learns how to use a combined journal for a small business. The student works through the accounting cycle for both a service and a merchandising company and also gains a strong foundation in payroll, cash, and bank reconciliations.

Many features of this text have been designed to hold student interest. It was written in a lively, narrative style, with down-to-earth examples. Special effort has been made to provide a strong visual appeal throughout the book, with heavy use of colors, charts, diagrams, and marginal aids. All these serve an educational purpose by highlighting and reinforcing important terms and concepts.

**Study Guide/
Working Papers**

Since the student learns accounting by *doing*, the learning package includes a *working* Study Guide. This contains blank forms for all exercises (Unit Interactors) within the text. The Study Guide also provides a comprehensive Pre-examination Tune-up for each chapter, together with all the solutions for students' ready reference. There is a complete set of working papers for all the end-of-chapter problems. There are also working papers for the Mini-Practice Set found at the end of the textbook.

Instructor's Manual	A complete instructor's resource package has been developed to accompany this text. It was designed to cut down on the time you spend in preparing lesson plans, tests, etc., so that you might have more time for individual student needs. This total resource manual not only offers instructional insights but also lists key points/lecture outlines for each chapter. Many questions are provided for each chapter, as well as achievement tests and problem tests. In addition, there are solutions for problems found in the text, and a set of demonstration aid masters.
Practice Set	For those of you who want your students to work through practice set materials, this learning package offers considerable flexibility. A separate practice set, for a service company, covers approximately the first half of the course. It was designed to allow students to work on a practice set without waiting until the final weeks of the course. For an effective "wrap-up" at the end of the course, there is the Mini-Practice Set at the end of the text, which is geared to a merchandise company.

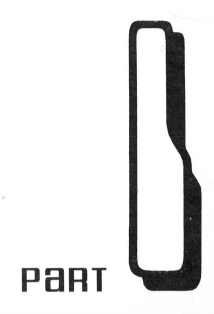

PART 1

The Accounting Cycle

1

introduction to the accounting process

Accounting is a process that *analyzes, records, classifies, summarizes,* and *reports* information.

This process should be familiar to you from your experiences as a student. As you sit in a classroom, you try to *analyze* or understand what an instructor is saying. You decide whether what he says is worth *recording* in your class notes. In recording or reviewing your notes you try to *classify* the information under appropriate headings so as to be able to find groups of related data quickly. Next you try to *summarize* the information so that you can grasp and discuss it better when called upon. And then in class, in quizzes, and especially in the final examination the teacher asks you to *report* on certain information as well as interpret hidden meanings.

As a consequence of your report, decisions are made. What will be your grade on the exam? Will you fail or pass the course? Will you graduate as expected?

If you are studying for more than mere marks—if you are studying in order to learn things—then you report your ultimate findings to yourself. On the basis of your results you may decide to pursue further study in specific directions or you may decide to take other possible actions.

A process like the one you use in mastering course material is used in business, industry, and government to supply timely information for decision making. Accounting—the language of business—provides information to managers, owners, customers, investors, and other decision makers within and outside an organization. Accounting involves analyzing business transactions or events (such as making sales, paying salaries, purchasing equipment) and systematically recording these events so that the information can be classified and summarized in reporting business results. The term bookkeeping is often used to represent the recording function of the accounting process. The accountant's financial statements will answer many vital questions: What is our cash balance? Did we show a profit? Will we be able to pay back some of our debts? And it provides the basis for vital decisions: Do we need a loan? Should we expand our production? Increase our research and development? Raise the product selling price? It is crucial that accounting not only supply such information but supply it in time to allow decision makers to take appropriate action.

In summary, both the student and the business person need a system that analyzes, records, classifies, summarizes, and reports information. The interpretations and uses of the information depend on the situation. As an example, let's see how this process can be applied in a small business: the Russell Smith law practice.

LEARNING UNIT 1

The Accounting Equation: A Basic Approach

ASSETS, EQUITIES, LIABILITIES

At the end of August, Russell Smith decided to open up his own law practice. His accountant told him that all business transactions could be analyzed by the basic accounting equation.

Russell had never heard of the basic accounting equation. He listened carefully as the accountant explained it:

Who supplies the assets?

a. Cash, land, supplies, office equipment, building, and other properties of value owned by your firm will be called *assets*.

b. These rights or financial claims to the assets are called *equities* and they belong to those who supply the assets. For example, if you were the only one to supply assets to the firm, you would have the sole rights or financial claims to them. Therefore, if you supplied the law firm with cash of $2,000 and office equipment of $1,000, your equity in the firm would be $3,000.

c. The relationship between assets and equities is:

$$ASSETS = EQUITIES$$
$$(A) \qquad (B)$$

The total dollar value of the assets of the law firm will be equal to the total dollar value of financial claims or rights to those assets—that is, to the total dollar value of the equities. The dollar values are broken down on the left-hand side to show what specific items comprise them and on the right-hand side to show who supplied them and thus who has claim to them.

d. The law firm, in the future, may have to borrow money or possibly buy more assets *on credit* (buy now, pay later.) For example, if the firm purchases a desk for $100 from Joe's Stationery and Joe's Stationery is willing to wait ten days for a payment, the firm has created a *liability*—an obligation due in the future. The stationery store is the *creditor*. This liability or the amount *owed* to Joe's Stationery gives the store the right or financial claim to $100 of assets of the law firm. When Joe's Stationery is paid, the store's rights to the assets of the law firm will decrease, since the obligation has been reduced. To take account of such actions, equities are usually divided into two parts:

$$ASSETS = EQUITIES$$

1. Liabilities—rights of creditors
2. Owner's equity—rights of owner

The *expanded equation:*

$$ASSETS = LIABILITIES + OWNER'S\ EQUITY$$

Elements of the basic accounting equation

The total value of all the assets of the law firm will be equal to the combined total value of the financial claims or interest of the creditors and the claims of the owner. This is known as the *basic accounting equation.*

**Assets
— liabilities
= owner's equity**

Another way of stating the same equation, Russell discovered, is:

$$ASSETS - LIABILITIES = OWNER'S\ EQUITY$$

Purpose of the accounting equation

This equation emphasizes the importance of the creditors. The owner's rights to the assets of a business are determined by first subtracting the rights of the creditor(s). Creditors have first claim to assets. If a firm has no liabilities and therefore no creditors, the owner has the total rights to the asset.

As the Russell Smith law firm engages in business transactions (paying bills, servicing customers, and so on), changes take place in the assets, liabilities, and owner's equity. Let us analyze some of these.

AUGUST 28: Smith invests $10,000 into law practice

On August 28 Russell Smith withdraws $10,000 from his personal bank account and deposits the money in the newly opened bank account of the law firm. With the help of his accountant, Russell begins to prepare his accounting records. Plans are to *open* the law office on September 1, 19XX.

Based upon the basic accounting equation, on August 28 (1) the law practice owns $10,000 worth of assets in the form of cash, and (2) Smith has the rights to the $10,000 worth of assets, since no liabilities were created. Remember, assets minus liabilities equals owner's equity. The basic accounting equation is as follows:

Increase in assets

	RUSSELL SMITH ATTORNEY AT LAW	
ASSETS	= LIABILITIES +	OWNER'S EQUITY
(1) Cash		(2) R. Smith Investment
$10,000 =		$10,000

Notice that the total value of all the assets (all we have is cash so far), $10,000, is equal to the combined total value of liabilities, plus owner's equity. No liabilities have been created. *Remember, Smith supplies the cash; therefore, he has the financial claim or rights to the asset(s) of the law firm.*

AUGUST 29: Law practice buys equipment for $500 cash

Taking part of the initial investment of $10,000 cash, the law firm buys $500 worth of equipment for cash from Doran Stationery. This equipment has to be bought before the practice can begin. (In using the diagram below to analyze this transaction, keep in mind that if a number has no sign in front, it is assumed to be +.)

Actually, the business receives $500 worth of a new asset (equipment) and reduces its other asset (cash) by $500. The *composition* of assets is now cash and equipment. Notice in the diagram below that the total of the assets remains at $10,000 ($9,500 + $500). The right-hand side of the equation has not been changed; it remains at $10,000. No liabilities have been created, because the business paid for the equipment in cash.

RUSSELL SMITH
ATTORNEY AT LAW

	ASSETS		= LIABILITIES +	OWNER'S EQUITY
	Cash	+ Equipment =		+ R. Smith Investment
BEGINNING INVESTMENT	$10,000		+	$10,000
NEW ASSET PURCHASED (3)		+ $500 (3)		
DECREASE IN CASH (4)	(4) − 500			
ENDING BALANCE	$9,500	+ $500	=	$10,000

Shift in assets

Once again, the total of all the assets ($9,500 + $500) is equal to the *combined* total of all the liabilities and the owner's equity. Many beginning accounting students think incorrectly that *both sides* of an accounting equation have to be changed in order for it to remain in balance. Remember, all we are interested in is having the *total of assets equal to the combined total of liabilities and owner's equity*.

For example, suppose you go food shopping at the supermarket with $100 in your pocket and spend $60. Now you have two assets, food and money. The composition of the assets has been shifted—you have more food than you did and less money—but the *total* of assets has not been increased or decreased. The total value of the food, $60, plus the cash, $40, is still $100.

Business entity

Please keep in mind that we are analyzing the law practice as a business *entity*—an organization or unit that requires the recording of its business transactions as well as the other accounting functions. We are not concerned about Russell Smith's personal assets, such as his car, home, and personal bank account; these are separate and distinct from the operations and business transactions of the law practice. In the same way, we might analyze the business transactions of a school, church, hospital, or baseball team; each of these is an entity that requires the functions of accounting. The personal assets of the school principal, the church custodian, the doctors or nurses at the hospital, or the members or the manager or the owner of the ball team are separate and distinct from the assets and transactions of the business entities with which these individuals are associated.

Cost principle
Before proceeding further, we should take note of the *cost principle* in accounting. This principle states that all assets when bought are recorded *at cost*, not at what you think they may be worth. In the last transaction the equipment cost was recorded at $500. It doesn't matter whether it was really "worth" $1,000 or $100; the firm paid $500; this represented the cost to Russell Smith's law practice, and this was what was recorded. *Remember, record at the transaction price.* This is an objective value, verified by a bill of sale or an amount on a sales tag and agreed upon by both a willing buyer and a willing seller.

AUGUST 30: Bought equipment on account $100.

In preparing to open his law office, Russell Smith has ordered an additional $100 worth of chairs and desks from Doran Stationery. Instead of demanding cash, Doran agrees to deliver the equipment and to allow up to sixty days for the law practice to pay the invoice (bill).

Creation of a liability
This *liability* or obligation to pay in the future to Doran Stationery (creditor) has some interesting effects on the basic accounting equation. Doran Stationery has accepted a partial claim against the assets of Smith's law practice, until Smith is able or wishes to pay off the bill. This unwritten promise to pay the creditor (Doran Stationery) is a liability of a kind called *accounts payable*.

RUSSELL SMITH
ATTORNEY AT LAW

	ASSETS	=	LIABILITIES	+	OWNER'S EQUITY
	Cash + Equipment =		Accounts Payable	+	R. Smith Investment
CARRY OVER BALANCE	$9,500 + $500 =				$10,000
ADD (5) ASSET	+ 100 (5)				
AND (6) AMOUNT OWED			+ $100 (6)		
ENDING BALANCE	$9,500 + $600 =		$100	+	$10,000

In analyzing the above information, notice that the law practice has increased what it *owes* Doran (accounts payable) as well as increased an asset (equipment) by $100. The law practice gains an asset but has an obligation to pay Doran the $100 at a future date.

Notice that the sum of all the individual assets, cash plus equipment ($10,100), is now equal to the combined total of the liability plus owner's equity ($100 + $10,000). *Once again, after each transaction is analyzed, the accounting equation remains in balance.*

Now to review the objectives of Unit 1. At this time, in your own words, you should be able to:

1. List the functions of accounting.
2. List and define the three elements of the accounting equation.
3. State the purpose of the accounting equation.
4. Differentiate between liabilities and owner's equity.
5. Differentiate between a shifting of assets and an increase in assets.
6. Define business entity and cost principle.
7. List four examples of assets.

Now test and confirm your understanding by filling out the following unit interactor. The blank forms you need are in the study guide: the solution follows the interactor in the text below. If you are having difficulties with the problem, review the first learning unit until you have mastered it.

UNIT INTERACTOR 1

Based on the following three transactions, fill out the chart below:

1. Bill Ralph invests $6,000 to begin a real estate office.
2. The real estate office buys $500 equipment on account.
3. Additional equipment is bought for $300 cash.

RALPH REAL ESTATE

	ASSETS	=	LIABILITIES	+ OWNER'S EQUITY
	Cash + Equipment	=	Accounts Payable +	Ralph Investment
TRANSACTION (1) NEW BALANCE		=		
TRANSACTION (2) NEW BALANCE		=		
TRANSACTION (3) ENDING BALANCE		=		

SOLUTION to Unit Interactor 1

RALPH REAL ESTATE

	ASSETS		=	LIABILITIES	+	OWNER'S EQUITY
	Cash	+ Equipment	=	Accounts Payable	+	Ralph Investment
TRANSACTION 1	$6,000				+	$6,000
NEW BALANCE	6,000		=		+	6,000
TRANSACTION 2*		+ $500		+ $500		
NEW BALANCE	6,000 +	500	=	500	+	6,000
TRANSACTION 3†	−300 +	300				
ENDING BALANCE	$5,700 +	$800	=	$500	+	$6,000

*Represents an increase in assets
†Represents a shift in assets

Total Assets	=	$6,500
Total Liabilities	=	$500
Total Owner's Equity	=	$6,000
Total Liabilities + Owner's Equity	=	$6,500

LEARNING UNIT 2

Financial Position of Smith's Law Practice as of August 31: A Balance Sheet Primer

THE BALANCE SHEET

Purpose of balance sheet: a report as of a particular date

In Unit 1 we developed the accounting equation. Russell Smith, in preparing to open his law practice, went through several business transactions. The transactions are reproduced for your convenience.

AUGUST 28: Smith invested $10,000 in business.
29: Bought equipment for $500 cash.
30: Bought equipment on account, $100.
(Before opening practice)

Remember, the law practice plans to begin formal operation on September 1. We now want to develop a *report* that will show us, as of August 31, a history or status of:

1. The amount of assets *owned* by the law practice.
2. The amount of claims (liabilities and owner's equity) against these assets.

Elements making up a balance sheet

This report is called a *balance sheet* or statement of financial position. The balance sheet statement (a report) presents the informa-

10

tion found in the basic accounting equation. The following is the balance sheet of Russell Smith's law practice for August 31, 19XX.

who

what

when

RUSSELL SMITH
ATTORNEY AT LAW

Balance Sheet
August 31, 19XX

Assets		Liabilities and Owner's Equity	
		Liabilities	
➤Cash	$ 9,500	Accounts Payable	$ 100
Equipment	600		
		Owner's Equity	
		R. Smith Investment	10,000
	_____	*Total Liabilities and*	
Total Assets	$10,100	*Owner's Equity*	$10,100

These figures came from the ending balances of the accounting equation shown earlier, as of August 31:

ASSETS	=	*LIABILITIES*	+	*OWNER'S EQUITY*
Cash + Equipment	=	Accounts Payable	+	R. Smith Investment
ENDING BALANCE $9,500 + $600	=	$100	+	$10,000

Notice that the assets *owned* by Smith's practice are listed on the left side and the liabilities and owner's equity (the ones who are responsible for supplying the assets) are listed on the right side. Both sides equal $10,100. It makes sense to call it a balance sheet. When the assets are listed on the left side and liabilities and owner's equity on the right side, as above, the balance sheet is called an *account form.**

POINTS IN PREPARING THE BALANCE SHEET

POINT 1. Notice the heading of the balance sheet. It answers three questions:

1. The company's name (who)—Russell Smith, Attorney at Law.
2. Name of report (what)—Balance Sheet.
3. Date for which the report is prepared (when)—August 31, 19XX.

*Other ways of preparing a balance sheet will be shown later.

Remember:
the balance sheet
is a formal report.

POINT 2. In the balance sheet of Smith's law practice the dollar sign is not repeated each time a figure is written. Usually, it is placed to the left of each column's top figure as well as its total.

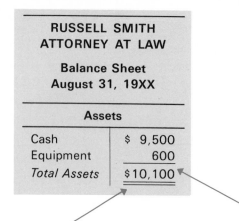

RUSSELL SMITH
ATTORNEY AT LAW

Balance Sheet
August 31, 19XX

Assets	
Cash	$ 9,500
Equipment	600
Total Assets	$ 10,100

POINT 3. When adding numbers together, the use of a single line is appropriate. A double line indicates the numbers are totaled. Most *students' errors* occur because the figures are not lined up carefully, so that mistakes are made in adding.

A SUMMATION. This financial report gives Russell Smith the information he needs to see what position the law firm is in before it opens. *It is impossible from this information to project whether the firm will make money or not.*

Now to review the objectives of Unit 2. At this time, in your own words, you should be able to:

1. Define and state the purpose of a balance sheet.
2. Identify and define the elements making up a balance sheet.
3. Given a balance sheet, show how the accounting equation holds true.
4. Prepare a balance sheet in proper form from information provided.

Now complete the unit interactor. As usual, the solution is provided. Remember that the study guide has forms for you to use in completing the interactor.

UNIT INTERACTOR 2

PREPARATION OF A BALANCE SHEET

Prepare a balance sheet (what) for the Robinson Company (who) for October 31, 19XX (when) using the following information:

Accounts Payable	$25
Cash	3
Robinson Investment	8
Equipment	30

This information has come from the *ending balances* of the accounting equation for the Robinson Company.

SOLUTION to Unit Interactor 2

ROBINSON COMPANY

Balance Sheet
October 31, 19XX

Assets		Liabilities and Owner's Equity	
		Liabilities	
Cash	$ 3	Accounts Payable	$25
Equipment	30		
		Owner's Equity	
		Robinson Investment	8
		Total Liabilities and	
Total Assets	$33	*Owner's Equity*	$33

LEARNING UNIT 3

Analysis of September Transactions:
The Accounting Equation Expanded

TERMINOLOGY PRIMER

As we saw in Unit 2, the accounting equation and the balance sheet have a close relationship. The balance sheet let Russell Smith see how his business stood before opening on September 1. It provided an update of what was *owned* by the business, as well as who had the rights to the *assets*.

Revenue creates an inward flow of assets.

Since Russell was in business to make money, he asked his accountant how he could *measure* the law practice's *performance* for the month of September and each subsequent month. His accountant explained it to him as follows:

1. When the law practice *performs* a legal service, revenue* is recognized. The revenue for the law firm is *earned* whether or not cash is immediately received.

* Many texts refer to revenue as income or sales. We will be using legal *fees* to represent the *revenue* of Russell Smith's law firm.

2. When this revenue is earned, cash (an asset) may be increased (if the customer pays) and/or an amount may be owed to the firm by the client for payment at a future time. If that happens, the law practice creates another asset called *accounts receivable*. Accounts receivable will show the amount of earned revenue the firm has the right to collect for legal service for which payment has not yet been received. Accounts receivable will hopefully be turned into cash.

3. When revenue is earned, whether cash is received or not, the end result will be to increase the law firm's assets, cash, and/or accounts receivable and increase owner's equity.

Remember, revenue (legal fees) creates an inward flow of assets—cash and/or accounts receivable. As the cash and/or accounts receivable increases, the owner's (Smith's) equity will increase.

**Expenses create an outward
or a potential outward
flow of assets.**

Think back to your first paycheck. That was an inward flow of assets. Did that inward flow quickly become an outward flow? Of course—to buy food, new clothes, and entertainment, meet medical bills and car payments, and many other things. In business these outward flows, called *expenses*, represent sacrifices made or costs incurred in attempting to create additional inward flows of assets (revenue). Russell Smith's law practice also will be faced with inward and outward flows of assets.

Let's continue to analyze the inward and outward flow relationships as they affect the reporting of the law firm's performance. The differences between the inward flow (earned revenue) and the outward flow (expenses incurred in attempting to earn revenue) for a specific period will be equal to *net income* or *net loss*. Let's look more closely at these terms.

(A)	(B)	(C)	(D)

EARNED REVENUE — EXPENSES INCURRED = NET INCOME OR NET LOSS

If: (A) is greater than (B) = Net Income (C)

(A) is less than (B) = Net Loss (D)

(A) is equal to (B) = No Net Income

or

No Net Loss

**Purpose
of matching
principle**

The comparison between earned revenue and incurred expenses is known as the *matching principle*. Remember, our eventual goal is to measure how well the law practice is performing (net income or net loss) as well as provide an update on the firm's financial position.

Now let's analyze the September business transactions for the law firm.

SEPTEMBER 1–30: Provided legal services for $2,000 cash.

In the law firm's first month of operation a total of $2,000 in cash was received for legal services rendered (performed). In the diagram the asset cash is increased by $2,000. Revenue is also increased by $2,000.

Revenue causes owner's equity to increase.

Notice the addition of a revenue column to the basic accounting equation; this new column will help the accountant in preparing financial reports. Keep in mind that as revenue (legal fees) increases, assets increase (remember the inward flow), causing the owner's equity to increase. In this case the inward flow from the earned revenue is the asset cash.

RUSSELL SMITH
ATTORNEY AT LAW

	ASSETS		=	LIABILITIES	+	OWNER'S EQUITY	
	Cash	+ Equipment	= Accounts Payable	+ R. Smith Investment	+	Revenue
CARRY OVER BALANCE	$ 9,500	+ $600	= $100	+	$10,000	
INCREASE IN CASH (7)	+2,000 (7)					
INCREASE IN OWNER'S EQUITY (8)						+ $2,000 (8)
ENDING BALANCE	$11,500	+ $600	= $100	+	$10,000	+ $2,000

To be sure, let's see whether the basic accounting equation still holds true:

ASSETS	= LIABILITIES +	OWNER'S EQUITY
$12,100	= $100 +	$12,000

cash	$11,500
equipment	600

investment	$10,000
revenue	2,000

The total of the assets, $12,100, is equal to the combined total of the liabilities plus owner's equity, $12,100. Although the basic accounting equation has been expanded (the revenue column has been added to owner's equity), its overall result has not changed. Notice that the $2,000 of revenue was indeed added to owner's equity.

SEPTEMBER 1–30: Provided legal services on credit $1,000.

Accounts receivable results from earned revenue even when cash is not yet received.

Russell Smith's law practice performed legal work on credit in the amount of $1,000. The firm did not receive the cash for these *earned* legal fees; it accepted an unwritten promise from these clients that payment would be received in the future. The amount the clients owe the practice is called *accounts receivable*. This inward flow of accounts receivable, an asset, was the result of the earned revenue (legal fees).

Remember, revenue is earned whether or not payment is received at the time the legal service is performed. Here revenue is increased $1,000 (because it is earned), and an inflow of assets ($1,000) called accounts receivable results. Hopefully, some of the accounts receivable will be turned into cash at a later date. Please don't forget we will be using the term *legal fees* to represent *revenue* for the Russell Smith law practice.

RUSSELL SMITH
ATTORNEY AT LAW

	ASSETS			=	LIABILITIES	+	OWNER'S EQUITY	
Cash	+ Accounts Receivable	+ Equipment	=		Accounts Payable	+	R. Smith Investment	+ Revenue
CARRY OVER BALANCE	$11,500		+ $600	=	$100	+	$10,000	+ $2,000
ACCOUNTS RECEIVABLE INCREASING (9)		+ $1,000 (9)						
REVENUE INCREASING (10)								+ 1,000 (10)
ENDING BALANCE	$11,500 +	$1,000	+ $600	=	$100	+	$10,000	+ $3,000

Don't forget that as revenue increases, owner's equity increases. Let's check to see if the basic accounting equation holds true:

ASSETS	=	LIABILITIES	+	OWNER'S EQUITY
$13,100	=	$100	+	$13,000

cash	$11,500
accounts receivable	1,000
equipment	600

investment	$10,000
revenue	3,000

The total of all the assets, $13,100, is equal to the combined total of the liabilities plus owner's equity ($13,100). The total revenue of $3,000 is added to owner's equity.

One point to emphasize: in the *accrual basis of accounting,* (1) revenue (here, legal fees) is earned, whether or not cash payment is received at the time the service is performed, and (2) an expense may result if incurred even if unpaid. In the *cash basis of accounting,* on the other hand, (1) revenue is recognized as earned when cash is received and (2) expenses are recognized or recorded when paid. The cash basis does not try to match earned revenue to expenses as does the accrual basis of accounting. The accrual basis thus offers the advantage that the reports of the law firm are comparable from period to period. They would not be if the cash basis were utilized, since revenue would be recognized only when cash was received and expenses would be reported only when paid. The cash basis may be satisfactory for some small businesses, but not for Russell Smith's law firm. Although the cash basis could provide more simplicity and convenience, Smith's accountant is very concerned about providing a realistic picture of net income, and for this reason he uses the accrual basis of accounting.

SEPTEMBER 1–30: Received $500 cash from previous revenue rendered on credit.

During September some of Smith's clients who had received services and promised to pay in the future decided to reduce what they owed the practice. In the last transaction, charged revenue for the month was $1,000. Of the $1,000 of charged revenue (remember that accounts receivable and revenue were increased) customers paid $500.

*Revenue is recorded once—
when it is earned.*

In the diagram below notice that the law firm increased the asset cash by $500 and reduced another asset, accounts receivable, by $500. *The total of assets does not change.* Notice the right-hand side of the expanded accounting equation has not been touched. The revenue was recorded when it was *earned. Do not record the same revenue twice.* This transaction is analyzing the situation after the revenue has been previously earned and recorded. We are actually recording the portion customers have paid of past revenue. This transaction represents a *shifting* of the composition of the assets—more cash for less accounts receivable.

RUSSELL SMITH
ATTORNEY AT LAW

	ASSETS			= LIABILITIES +	OWNER'S EQUITY	
	Cash	+ Accounts Receivable +	Equipment =	Accounts Payable	R. Smith + Investment +	Revenue
CARRY OVER BALANCE	$11,500	+ $1,000 +	$600 =	$100	+ $10,000 +	$3,000
CASH INCREASE (11)	+500 (11)					
DECREASE IN ACCOUNTS RECEIVABLE (12)		− 500 (12)				
ENDING BALANCE	$12,000	+ $ 500 +	$600 =	$100	+ $10,000 +	$3,000

ASSETS	= LIABILITIES +	OWNER'S EQUITY
$13,100	= $100 +	$13,000

cash	$12,000
accounts receivable	500
equipment	600

| investment | $10,000 |
| revenue | 3,000 |

Next:

SEPTEMBER 1-30: Paid $600 of salary expenses

It costs money to run a business. Remember back to the matching principle, which weighs or matches earned revenue against the expenses incurred in attempting to earn it.

Expenses can result even if payment is not yet due or paid in the accrual basis of accounting.

An expense doesn't have to be recorded as an expense *only at time of payment.* Expenses can result even if payment is not made due, or even billed for. For example, in turning out a product, a company may use electricity in July but not receive a bill till August. The cost of electricity is an expense in July, since it helped create earned revenue. By showing the expense when it occurs, we will be able to get a true picture of net income or net loss for July. The expense may be paid in cash, or, if the firm wants to postpone payment, a liability can be created (promise to pay later). Whether an *expense* is paid in cash or owed, it represents a *sacrifice or cost in operating a business.*

In the month of September the law practice *paid* $600 cash for salary expenses. These salaries were incurred for the purpose or in the process of earning revenue for the practice. As revenue or legal fees increased, the owner's equity in Smith's law practice increased. Notice that as revenue increases and expenses increase, both affect owner's equity as follows:

Revenue ↑ Owner's Equity ↑

Expenses ↑ Owner's Equity ↓

Please think of expenses as *increasing.* Even when you pay bills, you may reduce your cash, but the total of your expenses has risen. As expenses increase, they actually are decreasing the owner's equity, as shown above. Note in the first table on the facing page the addition of the expenses column to the owner's equity section.

The *increased* expense of $600 for salaries, then, has resulted in a $600 reduction to owner's equity.

RUSSELL SMITH
ATTORNEY AT LAW

	ASSETS			= LIABILITIES +		OWNER'S EQUITY	
	Cash	+ Accounts Receivable	+ Equipment =	Accounts Payable	+ R. Smith Investment	+ Revenue	− Expenses
CARRY OVER BALANCE	$12,000	+ $500	+ $600 =	$100	+ $10,000	+ $3,000	
CASH PAID (13)	− 600 (13)						
EXPENSES↑ OWNER'S EQUITY↓ (14)	___	___	___	___	___	___	− $600 (14)
ENDING BALANCE	$11,400	+ $500	+ $600 =	$100	+ $10,000	+ $3,000	− $600

Expenses cause owner's equity to decrease.

This incurred expense of $600 reduces the asset cash by $600, as well as owner's equity by $600 (notice the minus sign at the top of the expense column).

Does the expanded accounting equation balance in the format of the basic accounting equation?

ASSETS	= LIABILITIES +	OWNER'S EQUITY
$12,500	= $100 +	$12,400

cash	$11,400
accounts receivable	500
equipment	600

investment	$10,000
revenue	3,000
less expenses	(600)

The expense of $600 for salaries has *increased* Smith's expenses, which actually decreases the owner's equity.

Please don't forget to think of expense as increasing. It is this increase that really decreases owner's equity.

SEPTEMBER 1-30: Paid rent expense for month $400

During September the practice incurred rent expenses of $400. This rent *was not paid in advance*. The rent came due and it was paid.

As shown in the diagram below, the payment of rent *reduces* the asset cash by $400 as well as *increases* the expenses of the firm, resulting in a decrease in owner's equity.

RUSSELL SMITH
ATTORNEY AT LAW

		ASSETS		= LIABILITIES +		OWNER'S EQUITY		
	Cash	+ Accounts Receivable +	Equipment =	Accounts Payable	+ R. Smith Investment	+ Revenue	− Expenses
CARRY OVER BALANCE	$11,400 +	$500 +	$600 =	$100	+ $10,000	+ $3,000	− $600
CASH PAID (15)	− 400 (15)						
EXPENSES↑ OWNER'S EQUITY↓ (16)							− 400 (16)
ENDING BALANCE	$11,000 +	$500 +	$600 =	$100	+ $10,000	+ $3,000	− $1,000

Now let's see if the basic accounting equation balances.

ASSETS	= LIABILITIES +	OWNER'S EQUITY
$12,100	= $100 +	$12,000

cash	$11,000		investment	$10,000
accounts receivable	500		revenue	3,000
equipment	600		less expenses	(1,000)

Before we leave this transaction, a definition of *prepaid rent* is in order. *Rent paid in advance (which is not the situation of transaction) is considered an asset. As it expires, it then becomes an expense.* If the above transaction stated "paid rent three months in advance," the result would have been to:

1. ↑ asset—prepaid rent.
2. ↓ asset—cash.

Much more will be said later in the text. For now, remember: (1) Rent paid in advance is an asset; it represents value that has not expired. (2) As the rent that was paid in advance expires, an expense will result.

In discussing Russell Smith's payment of rent of $400, we assumed *rent had expired* and, therefore, was an expense. *Rent was not paid in advance.*

SEPTEMBER 1–30: Paid supplies expense $100.

During September the law practice paid $100 for supplies that were used up or *consumed* in its operations. In the diagram below notice that supplies expense represents a decrease in the asset cash, as well as an increase in an expense and, therefore, a reduction in owner's equity.

**RUSSELL SMITH
ATTORNEY AT LAW**

	Cash	+	Accounts Receivable	+	Equipment	=	Accounts Payable	+	Smith Investment	+	Revenue	−	Expenses
			ASSETS				= LIABILITIES +				OWNER'S EQUITY		
CARRY OVER BALANCE	$11,000	+	$500	+	$600	=	$100	+	$10,000	+	$3,000	−	$1,000
CASH PAID (17)	− 100 (17)												
EXPENSES↑ OWNER'S EQUITY↓ (18)												−	100 (18)
ENDING BALANCE	$10,900	+	$500	+	$600	=	$100	+	$10,000	+	$3,000	−	$1,100

Notice that the basic accounting equation balances:

	ASSETS	= LIABILITIES +	OWNER'S EQUITY
	$12,000	= $100 +	$11,900

cash	$10,900	
accounts receivable	500	
equipment	600	

investment	$10,000
revenue	3,000
less expenses	(1,100)

The final point this unit makes is a general rule about supplies. *Supplies are assets when acquired but will eventually be consumed or used up and become an expense.* In the case of Russell Smith's law practice, the supplies were used up and thus shown as an expense immediately. Much more will be said about this in future chapters. Do not memorize this rule, but be prepared to return to this page.

Now to a review of the objectives of Unit 3. At this time, in your own words, you should be able to:

1. Define the matching principle.
2. Define and differentiate inward and outward flow of assets.
3. Define and differentiate between net income and net loss.
4. Explain and differentiate between the basic accounting equation and the expanded accounting equation.
5. Differentiate between accrual basis of accounting and cash basis of accounting.
6. Explain the effects of revenue and expense on owner's equity.
7. Record transactions in an expanded accounting equation and balance the basic accounting equation as a check device.

Now complete the unit interactor and check your answer with the solution that follows.

UNIT INTERACTOR 3

Record the following transactions into the expanded accounting equation.

1. Bob Baker invested $10,000 in a new hair salon business.
2. Paid office rent expenses $400 (not paid in advance).
3. Received cash revenue $550.
4. Rendered service on account $5,000 to customers.
5. Paid advertising expense $15.
6. Received $10 from customer for previous services rendered on account.
7. Bought additional equipment on account $3,000.

SOLUTION to Unit Interactor 3

BOB BAKER SALON

	Cash	+ Accounts Receivable	+ Equipment	= Accounts Payable	+ B. Baker Investment	+ Revenue	− Expenses
		ASSETS		= LIABILITIES +	OWNER'S EQUITY		
1.	$10,000				$10,000		
BALANCE	10,000			=	10,000		
2.	−400						− $400
BALANCE	9,600			=	10,000		− 400
3.	+550					+ $ 550	
BALANCE	10,150			=	10,000	+ 550	− 400

BOB BAKER SALON (cont.)

| | ASSETS | | | = LIABILITIES + | OWNER'S EQUITY | | |
	Cash	+ Accounts Receivable	+ Equipment =	Accounts Payable	+ B. Baker Investment	+ Revenue	− Expenses
4.		+ $5,000				+ 5,000	
BALANCE	$10,150 +	5,000	=		$10,000	+ 5,550	− $400
5.	− 15						− 15
BALANCE	10,135 +	5,000	=		10,000	+ 5,550	− 415
6.	+ 10	− 10					
BALANCE	10,145 +	4,990	=		10,000	+ 5,550	− 415
7.			+ $ 3,000	$ 3,000			
BALANCE	————	————			————	————	————
ENDING BALANCE	$10,145 +	$4,990 +	$ 3,000 =	$ 3,000 +	$10,000	+ $5,550	− $415
			$18,135 =	$18,135			

Please don't be upset if your equal signs, or pluses, or minuses, are not exact in each of the above columns. At this point the ending balances are most important. You may have chosen to place zeroes where my solution parts are left blank; either way is fine.

LEARNING UNIT 4

Preparation of the Income Statement and Balance Sheet

Examining the transactions of Smith's law practice, we shall now try to answer the following questions:

1. How well did the law firm perform or operate for the month of September?
2. What is the firm's financial picture or position as of September 30, 19XX?

In this unit the accountant prepares two specific statements for Smith: the income statement and balance sheet.

THE INCOME STATEMENT

Purpose of income statement   Earlier in the chapter much was said about earned revenue and the expenses incurred to earn it. We noted that if revenues were greater than expenses, a profit or net income would result. The accounting report that shows business results in these terms (revenue minus expenses) is called an *income statement*. The income statement is often referred to as an earnings statement.

**RUSSELL SMITH
ATTORNEY AT LAW**

**Income Statement
For Month Ended September 30, 19XX**

Revenue		
Legal Fees		$3,000
*Less Expenses**		
Salaries Expense	$600	
Rent Expense	400	
Supplies Expense	100	
Total Expenses		1,100
Net Income for the Month		$1,900

*The term operating expenses may be used.

Income statement prepared
for a specific period of time

The heading of Russell Smith's income statement answers three questions: (1) who we are talking about [Russell Smith, Attorney at I aw], (2) what type of statement we are talking about [Income Statement], (3) what period of time we are talking about [month of September]. An income statement could cover a month, three months, six months, twelve months, or some other period. In Smith's income statement, notice the form, the way the different accounts are lined up, and that the dollar signs are not repeated for every number. A double line is used to emphasize the total figure, which reflects the difference between the earned revenues and all the expenses incurred in producing it. (Remember: revenue in the accrual basis of accounting is earned whether or not payment is received at the time the legal service is provided.)

But how does the income statement differ from the balance sheet?

At the end of August, a balance sheet was prepared to show the financial position of the law firm.

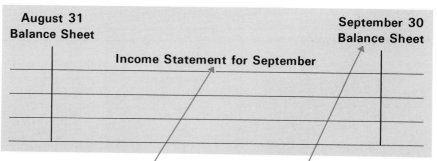

**August 31
Balance Sheet**

Income Statement for September

**September 30
Balance Sheet**

Balance sheet and
income statement compared

The income statement for September reports a summary of the operations for a *period of time* (September).

This information is needed to prepare a financial update of the status of the law firm as of a particular or *specific date* (September 30).

The net income* or net loss (revenue minus expense) in September will explain whether the owner's equity in the new balance sheet (September 30) will increase or decrease from the owner's equity shown in the balance sheet for August 31. The revenue and expense columns that were added to the basic accounting equation will now help summarize a figure for owner's equity.

BALANCE SHEET FOR SEPTEMBER 30

The following chart presents the ending balances we derived earlier for items in the expanded accounting equation of Russell Smith:

		ENDING BALANCES
1.	Cash	$10,900
2.	Accounts Receivable	500
3.	Equipment	600
4.	Accounts Payable	100
5.	Investment—Smith	10,000
6.	Revenue	3,000
7.	Expenses	(1,100)

Calculating ending owner's investment

The new balance sheet on September 30 is made up of assets, liabilities, and a *new figure for owner's equity.* This new figure for owner's equity is calculated as follows:

	BEGINNING OWNER'S INVESTMENT	$10,000
+	NET INCOME FOR SEPTEMBER FROM INCOME STATEMENT†	1,900
=	ENDING OWNER'S INVESTMENT	$11,900

†If a loss resulted, it would reduce owner's equity.

Balance sheet uses the ending figure for owner's investment.

Remember that the income statement is prepared first in order to calculate a figure for net income or net loss. The result will be used to *update* a new balance in the owner's equity section of the balance sheet.

*Some texts refer to net income as net earnings.

The following balance sheet was prepared by the accountant from the ending balances of the expanded accounting equation:

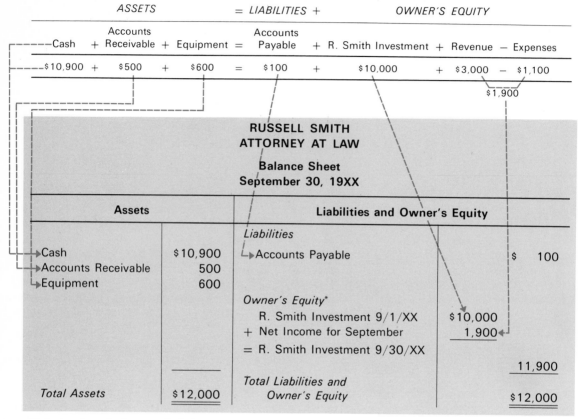

ASSETS			= LIABILITIES +		OWNER'S EQUITY		
Cash	+ Accounts Receivable	+ Equipment	= Accounts Payable	+ R. Smith Investment	+ Revenue	− Expenses
$10,900 +	$500 +	$600	= $100 +	$10,000	+ $3,000	− $1,100

$1,900

RUSSELL SMITH
ATTORNEY AT LAW

Balance Sheet
September 30, 19XX

Assets		Liabilities and Owner's Equity	
		Liabilities	
Cash	$10,900	Accounts Payable	$ 100
Accounts Receivable	500		
Equipment	600		
		Owner's Equity*	
		R. Smith Investment 9/1/XX	$10,000
		+ Net Income for September	1,900
		= R. Smith Investment 9/30/XX	
			11,900
		Total Liabilities and	
Total Assets	$12,000	Owner's Equity	$12,000

*Notice how the ending investment for R. Smith is calculated

BEGINNING INVESTMENT
+ NET INCOME (FROM INCOME STATEMENT)
= ENDING INVESTMENT

At this point you should be able to:

1. Define and state the purpose of an income statement.
2. Prepare an income statement in proper form.
3. Define and state the purpose of a balance sheet.
4. Compare and contrast the balance sheet and income statement.
5. Calculate a new or ending figure for owner's equity.
6. Prepare, in proper form, the balance sheet from the expanded accounting equation.

Now complete the unit interactor.

UNIT INTERACTOR **4**

JOE'S TAXI

Balance Sheet
February 28, 19XX

Assets		Liabilities and Owner's Equity	
		Liabilities	
Cash	$10,000	Accounts Payable	$ 1,000
Equipment	26,000		
		Owner's Equity	
		J. Wood Investment	
		2/28/XX	35,000
		Total Liabilities and	
Total Assets	$36,000	*Owner's Equity*	$36,000

Given the balance sheet as of February 28 for Joe's Taxi, your task is to prepare in proper form:

1. An updated income statement for March.
2. A balance sheet as of March 31, 19XX, based on the above and the following information:

JOE'S TAXI

ASSETS			=	LIABILITIES	+	OWNER'S EQUITY			
						J. Wood			
Cash	+	Equipment	=	Accounts Payable	+	Investment	+	Revenue	−	Expenses
$20,000	+	$30,000	=	$5,000	+	$35,000	+	$15,000	−	$5,000

Revenue is entitled Cab Fees Earned. Expenses are broken down as follows: Gas Expense $4,000; Repairs Expense $1,000.

JOE'S TAXI

Income Statement
For Month Ended March 31, 19XX

Revenue		
Cab Fees Earned		$15,000
*Less Expenses**		
Gas Expense	$4,000	
Repairs Expense	1,000	
Total Expenses		5,000
Net Income for Month		$10,000

*Or operating expenses.

JOE'S TAXI

Balance Sheet
March 31, 19XX

Assets		Liabilities and Owner's Equity		
		Liabilities		
Cash	$20,000	Accounts Payable		$ 5,000
Equipment	30,000			
		Owner's Equity		
		J. Wood Investment 3/1/XX	$35,000	
		+ Net Income for 3/XX	10,000	
		= J. Wood Investment 3/31/XX		45,000
		Total Liabilities and		
Total Assets	$50,000	*Owner's Equity*		$50,000

Notice the difference between owner's equity in the February Balance Sheet ($35,000) and in the March Balance Sheet ($45,000). This resulted from the net income of $10,000 in March, which increased owner's equity.

We have analyzed Russell Smith's business transactions and recorded them into the accounting equation. At each step we have checked that the total of assets was indeed equal to the combined total of liabilities plus owner's equity.

Once the information has been properly analyzed, recorded, classified, and summarized by means of the expanded accounting equation, appropriate reports can be prepared. We prepared an income statement, listing all the revenues and expenses; this report revealed how well the law firm performed for a *specific period of time*. Since we are using the accrual basis of accounting, the income statement of Russell Smith *matched* earned revenue against incurred expenses.

We also prepared another report—a balance sheet—which helped reveal the law firm's financial position as of a *particular date*. The balance sheet listed assets and liabilities and gave the ending figure for owner's equity, calculated by taking the beginning investment and adding net income to arrive at ending investment.

Chapter 1 has offered some insight into financial reports—their content, form, and how they are developed. Chapter 2 will show some steps we can take to streamline the accounting process and still achieve the desired end product.

Business transactions are recorded in the expanded accounting equation. The income statement matched earned revenue to incurred expenses to arrive at net income. When the balance sheet was prepared, net income was used to update owner's equity.

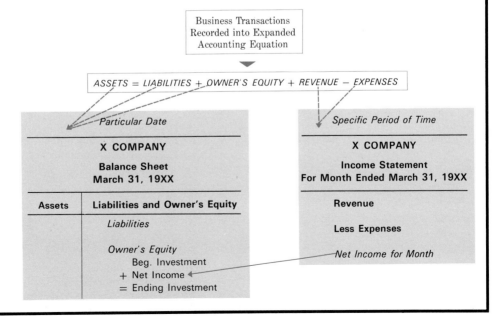

SUMMARY OF NEW ACCOUNTING LANGUAGE TERMS

Learning Unit 1

Accounts Payable: Amounts owed creditors that result from the purchase of goods or services on credit.

Assets: Properties (resources) of value owned by a business (cash, supplies, equipment, land).

Basic Accounting Equation: Assets = Liabilities + Owner's Equity.

Business Entity: In accounting it is assumed that a business is separate and distinct from the owners. Each unit or entity requires the accounting functions.

Cost Principle: All assets when purchased are recorded at cost and not at what you think they may be worth.

Equities: The interest or financial claim of creditors (liabilities) and owners (owner's equity) who supply the assets to a firm.

Liability: An obligation due in the future. Liabilities result in increasing the financial rights or claims of creditors to assets.

On Credit: Buy now, pay later; to charge; to create a liability.

Owner's Equity: Assets − Liabilities; the financial claims or interest of the owner to the assets of a business after subtracting the rights of the creditors from total assets.

Learning Unit 2

Account Form: Balance sheet listing assets on the left side and liabilities and owner's equity on the right side.

Accrual Basis of Accounting: An accounting system based on the matching principle. Revenues are recognized when they are earned whether cash is received or not. Expenses are recognized when they cause revenues to be earned. The receipt or payment of cash is not a determining factor in recognizing earned revenues and recognizing incurred expenses.

Balance Sheet: A report, as of a particular date, that shows a history or status of the amount of assets owned by a business as well as the amount of claims (liabilities and owner's equity) against these assets. This report is sometimes called a statement of financial position.

Cash Basis of Accounting: Opposite of accrual basis of accounting. In the cash basis revenue is recognized when cash is received, and expense results when a cash payment is made. The cash basis does not try to match earned revenue to incurred expenses for a specific period of time.

Expanded Accounting Equation: Assets = Liabilities + Owner's Equity + Revenue − Expenses.

Learning Unit 3

Accounts Receivable: An asset that indicates amounts owed by customers. This asset hopefully will turn into cash.

Expense: A sacrifice or cost incurred in running a business by consuming goods or services in producing revenue.

Matching Principle: Earned Revenue − Expenses Incurred = Net Income or Net Loss for a specific period of time.

Net Income: Amount by which earned revenue is greater than incurred expenses for a specific period of time.

Net Loss: Amount by which earned revenue is less than incurred expenses.

Prepaid Rent: Rent paid in advance. It represents an asset of value, which at a later date will expire and become an expense.

Rent Expense: Amount of rent that has expired.

Revenue: An inward flow of assets (cash/accounts receivable) that results from selling goods or providing a service.

Supplies: Assets acquired by a firm that have not been consumed or used up in its operation.

Supplies Expense: Amount of supplies that have been consumed or used up in the operation of a firm.

Ending Owner Investment: Beginning Owner Investment + Net Income = Ending Owner Investment.

Income Statement: An accounting report that shows the results or performance of a firm (revenues minus expenses) for a specific period of time. This report, which indicates net income or net loss, will help to update the balance sheet.

QUESTION INTERACTORS

1. What are the elements of the basic accounting equation?
2. What is the difference between assets and equities?
3. How is equity usually divided?
4. List four examples of assets.
5. The accounting equation doesn't always have to balance after each transaction. True or False? Why?
6. What three questions does the heading of a balance sheet answer?
7. Define an expense.
8. Define the accrual basis of accounting.
9. Define what is meant by "earned revenue."
10. The income statement shows the financial position of a business. True or false? Explain.
11. Explain the relationship between net income or net loss on the income statement and the owner's equity section of the balance sheet.
12. Explain the relationship between revenue and owner's equity.
13. Accounts receivable shows the amount of money we owe. Do you agree or disagree? Why?
14. Are the following statements true or false?
    a. Accounts payable is a liability.
    b. Cash is an asset.
    c. The inward flow of assets has no relationship at all to revenue.
    d. The income statement contains assets, liabilities, and owner's equity.
    e. The matching principle assumes revenue can be earned only when cash is received.
    f. The balance sheet is usually prepared before the income statement.
    g. A shift in assets causes the total of both sides of the accounting equation to be unchanged.
    h. As expenses increase, the result will be to increase owner's equity.
    i. The income statement shows the status of the firm as of a particular date.
    j. Liabilities indicate what customers owe us.
15. Classify each item in the following list. Possible classifications: assets, liabilities, owner's equity, revenue, expenses.
    a. Accounts payable
    b. Cash
    c. Land

d. Supplies expense
e. Rent expense
f. Legal fees
g. Accounts receivable
h. Equipment
i. Building
j. R. Mills investments

16. Assets = _____ + Owner's Equity.
17. Assets = _____ + Owner Investment + _____ − Expenses.
18. Define cost principle.
19. When revenue is earned, what types of assets could be affected?
20. The concept of business entity emphasizes that businesses are not separate or distinct from their owners. True or false? Explain.

PROBLEM INTERACTORS

1. Joe Francis decided to open up the J & F Car Wash. The following transactions resulted:

   1. Joe invested $5,000 cash from his personal bank account into the business.
   2. Purchased equipment for $2,000 in cash.
   3. Bought additional equipment on account $500.
   4. Paid $300 to partially reduce what was owed from transaction (3).

   Based on the above information, record these transactions into the basic accounting equation.

2. Enid Silberstein is the accountant for the Bleak Advertising Service. From the following information her task is to construct a balance sheet, as of September 30, 19XX, in proper form. Could you help her?

Cash	$5,000
Equipment	3,000
Building	6,000
Accounts Payable	9,000
Investment R. Jones	5,000

3. John Smith, owner of Smith's Plumbing Service, was anxious to see how well his firm performed for the month of October, 19XX. From the following information prepare, in proper form, an income statement for John Smith for the month of October.

Rental Expense	$ 3,000
Plumbing Service Revenue	11,000
Supplies Expenses	4,000
Utilities Expense	2,000

4. At the end of August, Ralph Bones decided to open his own dental practice. Analyze the following transactions by recording their effects on the expanded accounting equation.

   1. Ralph Bones invested $8,000 in his dental practice.
   2. Received $3,000 in cash for dental services rendered.
   3. Performed dental service for patients $1,000 on credit.
   4. Purchased new dental equipment $500 on account.
   5. Paid secretary's salary $300.
   6. Paid dental supplies expense for month $150.
   7. Paid rent expense for dental office $200.

*5. Jeff Jones, a retired army officer, proceeded to open Jones Cleaners. As his accountant, analyze the transactions listed below and present to Mr. Jones the following information in proper form.

   1. The analysis of the transactions by utilizing the expanded accounting equation.
   2. A balance sheet showing the position of the firm before opening as of October 31, 19XX.
   3. An income statement for the month of November.
   4. A balance sheet as of November 30, 19XX.

   OCT. 25: Jeff Jones invested $10,000 in the cleaning business from his own personal savings account.
   27: Purchased cleaning equipment $500 for cash from Ron Rose Co.
   28: Bought additional cleaning equipment on account $300 from Ron Rose Co.
   29: Paid $200 to Ron Rose Co. as partial payment of Oct. 28 transaction.

   (You should now prepare your balance sheet as of October 31, 19XX.)

   NOV. 1: Cleaned clothes for a customer and immediately collected $300 in cash.
   5: Paid salary of employees $150.
   8: Pressed suits for customers *on account* $100.
   10: Received $50 in partial payment of Nov. 8 transaction.
   15: Paid telephone bill $50.
   20: Completed cleaning service receiving $1,000 in cash.
   25: Bought additional cleaning equipment *on account* $50.
   30: Paid rent expense for month $100.
   30: Paid for cleaning supplies used $100 (an expense).

ADDITIONAL PROBLEM INTERACTORS

1-A. Paul Belle began a new business called the Quickie TV Repair Shop. The following transactions resulted:

   1. Paul invested $10,000 cash from his personal bank account into the TV repair shop.
   2. Bought equipment on account $600.

*Stars indicate *Chapter Overview Problems*, which summarize accounting concepts and procedures presented in the chapter.

3. Paid $400 in cash to reduce what was owed from transaction 2.

4. Purchased additional equipment for $3,000 in cash.

Based on the above information, record these transactions into the basic accounting equation.

2-A. Earl Miller is the legal counsel for Safe Realty. Earl has requested from the accountant a balance sheet as of November 30, 19XX, prepared in proper form. Could you act as Safe Realty's accountant and furnish Mr. Miller with a balance sheet as requested?

Investment of J. Safe	$10,000
Accounts Payable	25,000
Equipment	10,000
Building	15,000
Cash	10,000

3-A. Mike Fix, owner of the Mike's Fix-It Shop, was anxious to see how well his shop performed for the month of November, 19XX. From the following information prepare an income statement in proper form for Mike Fix for the month of November.

Rent Expense	$ 5,000
Telephone Expense	8,000
Repair Revenue	25,000
Repair Supplies Expense	5,000

4-A. Ron Smith at the end of March decided to open his own moving company. Analyze the following transactions by recording their effects on the expanded accounting equation.

1. Ron Smith invested $10,000 in the moving company.

2. Purchased new moving equipment $2,000 on account.

3. Received $5,000 in cash for moving a client from Boston to California.

4. Paid secretary's salary $150.

5. Moved a client from New York to Chicago on credit $3,000.

6. Paid rent expense for moving company $300.

7. Paid moving supplies expense for month $250.

5-A. Jeff Joy, a retired air force officer, opened the J. J. Aviation Flight School. As his accountant, analyze the transactions listed below and present to Mr. Joy the following information, in proper for ן:

1. The analysis of the transactions by utilizing the expanded accounting equation.

2. A balance sheet showing the financial position of the firm before opening as of November 30, 19XX.

3. An income statement for the month of December.
4. A balance sheet as of December 31, 19XX.

NOV. 25: Jeff Joy invested $200,000 in the J. J. Aviation School.
     28: Purchased aviation equipment $1,000 on account.
     28: Purchased aviation equipment for $2,000 in cash from IUT Corp.
  *29: Bought additional equipment from IUT Corp. for $3,000 on account.
DEC. 1: Provided flying lessons to business executives and immediately collected $4,000 in cash.
      5: Paid wages to flight instructors at aviation school $900.
      8: Provided flight instruction to students of North West Community College aviation program on account $18,000.
    12: Received from North West Community College $10,000 in cash as partial payment of December 8 transaction.
    14: Paid utilities bill $100.
    20: Gave parachute lessons, receiving $2,000 in cash.
    25: Bought additional aviation equipment on account $100.
    28: Paid rent expense for month on aviation hangar $4,000.
    30: Paid for aviation supplies used up (an expense) $300.

CHALLENGE PROBLEM INTERACTORS

1. On January 1, 198X, John Interesting invested $20,000 and began the Interesting Advertising Company. During 198X, the assets of the company had increased by $90,000, and the ending balance for owner's equity was $60,000.

   a. Determine the liabilities incurred during 198X.

   b. Determine the net income for 198X.

2. Each of the amounts shown below appeared on the December 31, 198X Balance Sheet and Income Statement of the Hole-in-One Driving Range:

Total expenses for 198X	$150,000
Beginning owner's equity	60,000
Ending owner's equity, 12/31/8X, assuming an additional investment of $40,000 by the owner during 198X	210,000
Total assets, 12/31/8X	290,000

   a. Determine the total liabilities as of 12/31/8X.

   b. Determine the net income for 198X.

   c. Determine the *total* revenue for 198X.

* You should now prepare the balance sheet as of November 30, 19XX.

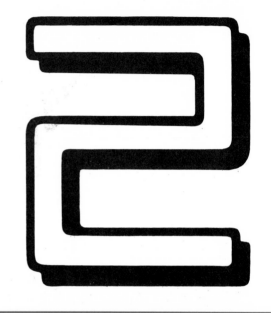

the systematic process of recording business transactions

In Chapter 1 we used the expanded accounting equation to analyze and record the business transactions of Russell Smith's law practice. Even though we dealt with only a few transactions, the cash column developed into a long list of pluses and minuses. There was no quick system of recording and summarizing increase and decrease of cash or other items. Imagine how *inefficient* this accounting equation would become, and how much space it would require, as hundreds and thousands of transactions occurred.

LEARNING UNIT 5

The Account

THE NEED FOR A SYSTEM

In this chapter we shall improve our system of recording accounting information so that we can handle numerous transactions in an efficient manner.

What was lacking in our approach in Chapter 1 was a system to record the increases and decreases in specific *individual items,* such as salary expense, supplies expense, rent expense. The device that allows us to do this is called an *account.*

Account				Account No.			
Date	Explanation	PR	Debit	Date	Explanation	PR	Credit

Purpose of a T-account

Shown above is a standard account, of which we will use a skeletal version, a *T-account*, so called because it looks like the letter T.

Each T-account will represent an individual item. This simplified version will make the explanations easier to follow. Notice below how we have added legal fees under Revenue and have put rent expense, supplies expense, and salary expense under Expenses.

$$ \textit{ASSETS} \quad = \textit{LIABILITIES} + \textit{OWNER'S EQUITY} + \textit{REVENUE} - \textit{EXPENSES} $$

THE T-ACCOUNT: ITS STRUCTURE AND CONTENT

Three parts of an account

Each T-account contains three basic parts:

---

*In Part Two of the text we will use other forms of the standard account. For now, the account will aid us in the classifying and recording functions of accounting.

All T-accounts have this structure. The left side of *any*-T-account is called the *debit* side.

Left side Dr.* (debit)	

Debit defined

Amounts of money entered on the left side of any account are said to be *debited* to an account. To repeat:

1. A debit is the left side of *any* account.
2. A number entered on the left side of any account is said to be debited to an account.

Credit defined

The right side of any T-account is called the credit side.

	Right side (credit) Cr.†

Amounts of money entered on the right side of an account are said to be *credited* to an account. To repeat:

1. A credit is the right side of *any* account.
2. A number entered on the right side of an account is said to be credited to an account.

In summation:

1. A debit is the left side of any account.
2. A credit is the right side of any account.
3. A number entered on the left side of any account is debited.
4. A number entered on the right side of any account is credited.

At this point DO NOT ASSOCIATE THE DEFINITION OF DEBIT AND CREDIT WITH THE WORDS *INCREASE* OR *DE-CREASE.* This would be a major error in accounting.

---

*The abbreviation for debit (Dr.) is from the Latin *debere.*
†The abbreviation for credit (Cr.) is from the Latin *credere.*

Below, we see a T-account with no heading. The heading is omitted to emphasize that, no matter which individual account is being balanced, the procedures will be the same.

Dr.		Cr.	
4/2	1,100	4/3	100
4/20	300	4/25	300
1,000	*1,400*		*400*

Notice that on the debit side (left side) the numbers debited (entered on left side) add up to $1,400. On the credit side (right side) the numbers credited (entered on the right side) add up to $400. The 4/2, 4/20, 4/3, 4/25 are the dates when the numbers were debited or credited.

The $1,400 and the $400 written in small numbers are called *footings*. These figures help us calculate the new balance of $1,000. Notice that the $1,000 is placed on the debit or left side, since the balance of the debit side is greater than that of the right side or credit side.

Remember, the ending balance of $1,000 doesn't tell us anything about increase or decrease. What it does tell us is that we have a debit balance of $1,000. The question of increases or decreases can only be decided by certain specific rules of debits and credits.

Before addressing this point, let's look at the objectives of this unit. You should be able to:

1. Define and state the purpose of an account.
2. State the purpose of a T-account.
3. Identify the three parts of an account.
4. Define a debit.
5. Define a credit.
6. Calculate the balance of an account.

UNIT INTERACTOR 5

Are the following statements true or false?

1. A standard account is a skeletal account used for demonstration purposes.
2. To calculate the balance on an account, the heading of the accounts must be part of the calculation.
3. A debit means increase.
4. A debit can be the left or right side of an account.

5. A credit is the left side of an account.

6.

Dr.	Cr.
1,000	400
200	300

The balance of the account is $500 Dr. balance.

SOLUTION to Unit Interactor **5**

1. False.   2. False.   3. False.   4. False.   5. False.   6. True.

LEARNING UNIT 6

Debits and Credits—Rules of the Game

THE RULES: A DOUBLE-ENTRY SYSTEM

Do you drive your car on the left-hand side of the road? Do you drive through red lights? In a baseball game does a runner rounding first base skip second base and run over the pitcher's mound to get to third? No—most of us don't do such things because we follow the rules; and usually we learn the rules first and reflect on the reasons for them afterward.

Instead of trying to understand first *how* the rules of debit and credit were developed in accounting, it will be easier to "play the game" first and then reflect back on the why's. This approach, though requiring some patience on the reader's part, will turn out in the end to be easiest.

Rules of debits and credits

EXAMPLES	CATEGORY	RULES OF DEBIT AND CREDIT*	
		INCREASE	*DECREASE*
CASH, ACCOUNTS RECEIVABLE, EQUIPMENT	Asset	Debit	Credit
ACCOUNTS PAYABLE	Liability	Credit	Debit
INVESTMENTS	Owner's Equity	Credit	Debit
LEGAL FEES EARNED	Revenue	Credit	Debit
RENT/SUPPLY EXPENSES	Expenses	Debit	Credit

*The definitions of debit and credit have not changed. The debit is the left side of any account. The credit is the right side of any account.

Our game now is to analyze Russell Smith's business transactions—the transactions we looked at in Chapter 1—using a system of accounts guided by the rules of debits and credits that will summarize increases and decreases of individual accounts. The goal will be to prepare the income statement and balance sheet for Russell Smith. Sound familiar? *If this game works, the rules of debits and credits and accounts will provide us with the same answers as in Chapter 1, but with greater ease and accuracy.*

Here we go:

THE MIND PROCESS: FIVE STEPS

There will be five steps to analyzing each business transaction of Russell Smith. We will use a mind-process chart to record these five steps. (Please keep in mind that the mind-process chart is a teaching device, not part of the formal accounting system.) The five steps will include:

Steps to analyze and record transactions

1. Which accounts are affected? Example: cash, accounts payable, rent expense.
2. Which category do the accounts fall into? You have five choices: assets, liabilities, owner's equity, revenue, and expenses. Example: cash is an asset.
3. Are the accounts increasing or decreasing? Example: receive cash—account is increasing (↑).
4. What is the rule? Go to rule chart.

CATEGORY	INCREASE	DECREASE
Asset ——————→	Debit*	Credit

*Increase in an asset is a debit.

5. Place amounts into accounts (in our case, T-accounts).

To answer the question in step 1 we need to know what the titles of the individual accounts are. To obtain these titles for Russell Smith's law practice the accountant developed what is called a *chart of accounts.*

Purpose of chart of accounts

This chart allows us to locate and identify accounts quickly. Let's look at a chart of accounts and analyze its contents.

ACCOUNT NUMBER	NAME OF ACCOUNT ITEM
100–299	ASSETS
110	Cash
141	Accounts Receivable
171	Equipment
300–499	LIABILITIES
310	Accounts Payable

(continued on next page)

ACCOUNT NUMBER	NAME OF ACCOUNT ITEM
500–699	*OWNER'S EQUITY*
510	R. Smith Investment
700–899	*REVENUE*
710	Legal Fees
900–1099	*EXPENSES*
910	Salary Expense
960	Rent Expense
980	Supplies Expense

Different companies will have different charts of accounts a
with different numbering systems.* As a company grows or as cha
occur, the chart of accounts may be expanded as needed.

Notice that all assets are numbered 100–299. Each item with
category of assets has a specific identity number. The gaps tha
been left, such as the spread of numbers between cash (110) and ac
receivable (141), allow other accounts to be added as needed v
disturbing the numbering system.

THE GAME: ANALYSIS OF TRANSACTIONS OF RUSSELL SMITH'S LAW PRACTICE

(A) AUGUST 28: Russell Smith invests $10,000 into busines

Mind-Process Chart for Analyzing Transactions

The mind-process chart is a teaching technique.

1 Accounts Affected	2 Category	3† Inc.↑ ↓Dec.	4 Rules	5 Appearanc T-Account
Cash	Assets	↑ Inc.	Dr.	Cash 1 (A) 10,000
R. Smith Investment	Owner's equity	↑ Inc.	Cr.	R. Sr Investm

†Increase ↑; decrease ↓.

*An example of a common numbering system would be:

100's Assets	200's Liabilities	300's O
400's Revenue	500's–700's Expenses	800's C
900's Other expenses		

Analysis of Chart

1. What does law firm receive?—cash. How does law firm receive cash?—by the investment of Smith. (Remember that the chart of accounts shows the individual numbers and titles of accounts.)
2. To date, the categories to choose from are assets, liabilities, owner's equity, revenue, or expense. Cash is an asset and Smith's investment is owner's equity.
3. The cash of the law firm, an *asset*, is *increasing*. The rights or claims of Smith are also increasing, since he invested money into the business.
4. The chart of Rules of Debit and Credit (p. 41) is reproduced below for your convenience in a slightly different form. Select whichever form of the chart you find easier to use. Both say the same thing. *Notice that the total amounts of debits are equal to the total amount of credits in columns 4 and 5 of the mind-process chart.* In this case the $10,000 debit to cash is indeed equal to the amount of the credit, $10,000 to Smith Investment.

Rules of debits and credits

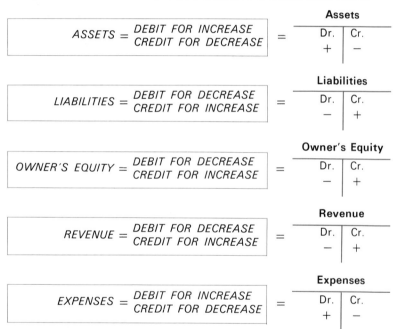

5. By the Rules of Debit and Credit an increase in an asset cash is a debit, so the $10,000 is debited—that is, it is entered on the left side of the cash account.

Cash 110

(A) 10,000	

An increase in the owner's claim or rights to the assets of a business is a credit of $10,000.

R. Smith Investment 510

	10,000 (A)

The rules of debit and credit
only tell us on which side
to place information.
Whether the debit or credit
represents ↑ or ↓ depends
on the accounts category—
asset, liability,
owner's equity, etc.

Let us now emphasize a major point: *Do not try to debit or credit an account in recording a business transaction until you have gone through the first three steps.* Here are the first three steps:

1. Which accounts are affected?
2. Which category are the accounts in?
3. Are the accounts increasing or decreasing?

Then: Go to the Rules of Debit and Credit before updating the individual accounts.

As we continue, the explanations will be brief, but don't forget to follow through the five steps in analyzing and recording each business transaction.

(B) AUGUST 29: Bought equipment for cash $500.

Mind Process for Analyzing and Recording Transactions	1 Accounts Affected	2 Category	3 ↑ ↓	4 Rules	5 T-Account Update
	Equipment	Asset	↑ Inc.	Dr.	**Equipment 171** (B)⊂500⊃ │
	Cash	Asset	↓ Dec.	Cr.	**Cash 110** (A) 10,000 │ ⊂500⊃(B)*

*The amounts involved in this specific transaction are circled to highlight the data. This is a teaching technique and is not part of the normal accounting process.

Analysis of Chart

1. What does law firm receive?—equipment. How did the firm get it?—paid cash.
2. Equipment is an asset. Cash is an asset.
3. The asset equipment is increasing. The asset cash is being reduced in order to buy the equipment.
4. An ↑ (inc.) in the equipment is debit; a ↓ (dec.) in the asset cash is a credit.
5.

Cash 110		**Equipment 171**	
(A) 10,000 │ ⊂500⊃(B)		(B)⊂500⊃ │	

Cash is credited for $500.   Equipment is debited for $500.

(C) AUGUST 30: Bought equipment on account $100.

1 Accounts Affected	2 Category	↑ 3 ↓	4 Rules	5 T-Account Update
Equipment	Asset	Inc. ↑	Dr.	**Equipment 171** (B) 500 (C) 100
Accounts Payable	Liability	Inc. ↑	Cr.	**Accounts Payable 310** 100 (C)

Analysis of Chart

1. The law firm receives equipment by promising to pay in the future. An obligation, accounts payable, is credited.
2. Equipment is an asset. Accounts payable is a liability.
3. The asset equipment is ↑ (inc.); the liability accounts payable is ↑ (inc.) because the law firm is increasing what it owes.
4. An increase in the asset equipment is a debit. An increase in the liability accounts payable is a credit.
5.

Equipment 171	
(B) 500	
(C) 100	

Equipment is debited for $100.

	Accounts Payable 310
	100 (C)

Accounts payable
is credited for $100.

(D) SEPTEMBER 1–30: Legal services for $2,000 cash.

1 Accounts Affected	2 Category	3 ↑ ↓	4 Rules	5 T-Account Update
Cash	Asset	Inc. ↑	Dr.	**Cash 110** (A)10,000 500 (B) (D) 2,000
Legal Fees	Revenue	Inc. ↑	Cr.	**Legal Fees 710** 2,000 (D)

46

Analysis of Chart

1. Firm has earned revenue from legal services and receives $2,000 in cash.
2. Legal fees is revenue. Cash is an asset.
3. Legal fees or revenue is increasing. Cash, an asset, is also increasing.
4. An increase in legal fees, a revenue, is credited. An increase in cash, an asset, is debited.

5.

Cash 110		Legal Fees 710	
(A) 10,000	500 (B)		2,000 (D)
(D) 2,000			

Cash is debited for $2,000.   Legal fees is credited for $2,000.

(E) SEPTEMBER 1-30: Legal fees completed on account $1,000.

1 Accounts Affected	2 Category	3 ↑ ↓	4 Rules	5 T-Account Update
Accounts Receivable	Asset	↑ Inc.	Dr.	**Accounts Receivable 141** (E) 1,000 |
Legal Fees	Revenue	↑ Inc.	Cr.	**Legal Fees 710** 2,000 (D) 1,000 (E)

Analysis of Chart

1. Law practice has earned revenue but has not received payment (cash). These clients are called *accounts receivable*. Revenue is earned whether payment is received or not at the time the legal services are provided; therefore, revenue from legal fees results for $1,000.
2. Accounts receivable is an asset. Legal fees is revenue.
3. Accounts receivable is ↑ (inc.) because the law practice has increased the amount owed to it for legal fees that have been earned, but not paid. Legal fees or revenue is ↑ (inc.).
4. An increase in the asset, accounts receivable, is a debit. An increase in revenue is a credit.

5.

Accounts Receivable 141		Legal Fees 710	
(E) 1,000			2,000 (D)
			1,000 (E)

Accounts receivable   Legal fees is
is debited $1,000.   credited for $1,000.

(F) SEPTEMBER 1–30: Collected $500 of the previously charged legal fees.

1 Accounts Affected	2 Category	3 ↑ ↓	4 Rules	5 T-Account Update
Cash	Asset	↑ Inc.	Dr.	**Cash 110** (A) 10,000 | 500 (B) (D) 2,000 (F) (500)
Accounts Receivable	Asset	↓ Dec.	Cr.	**Accounts Receivable 141** (E) 1,000 | (500) (F)

Analysis of Chart

1. The law firm collects $500 in cash from previous revenue. Since the revenue was recorded at the time it was earned, we need analyze only the *payment* part. Clients called accounts receivable will be paying their bills.
2. Cash is an asset. Accounts receivable is an asset.
3. Since clients are paying what is owed, cash (asset) is increasing and the amount owed, (accounts receivable) is decreasing. The total amount owed by clients to Smith is going down.
4. An increase in cash, an asset, is a debit. A decrease in accounts receivable, an asset, is a credit.
5.

Cash 110		Accounts Receivable 141	
(A) 10,000	500 (B)	(E) 1,000	(500) (F)
(D) 2,000			
(F) (500)			

Cash is debited for $500.

Accounts receivable is credited for $500.

(G) SEPTEMBER 1–30: Salary expense paid $600.

1 Accounts Affected	2 Category	3 ↑ ↓	4 Rules	5 T-Account Update
Salary expense	Expenses	↑ Inc.	Dr.	**Salary Expense 910** (G) (600) |

(continued on next page)

1 Accounts Affected	2 Category	3 ↑ ↓	4 Rules	5 T-Account Update
Cash	Asset	↓ Dec.	Cr.	**Cash 110** (A) 10,000 500 (B) (D) 2,000 ⟨600⟩ (G) (F) 500

Analysis of Chart

1. Law firm pays $600 worth of salary expense by cash.
2. Salary expense is an expense. Cash is an asset.
3. The salary expense of the law firm is ↑ (inc.), the result being a ↓ (dec.) to cash, which is paying for the expense.
4. An increase in salary expense, an expense, is a debit. A decrease in cash, an asset, is a credit.
5.

Salary Expense 910		**Cash 110**	
(G) ⟨600⟩		(A) 10,000	500 (B)
		(D) 2,000	⟨600⟩ (G)
		(F) 500	

Salary is debited for $600.   Cash is credited for $600.

(H) SEPTEMBER 1–30: Paid rent expense $400.

Mind Process for Analyzing and Recording Transactions

1 Accounts Affected	2 Category	3 ↑ ↓	4 Rules	5 T-Account Update
Rent Expense	Expenses	↑ Inc.	Dr.	**Rent Expense 960** (H) ⟨400⟩
Cash	Asset	↓ Dec.	Cr.	**Cash 110** (A) 10,000 500 (B) (D) 2,000 600 (G) (F) 500 ⟨400⟩ (H)

Analysis of Chart

1. The law firm expenses for rent are paid. Therefore, since rent was not prepaid, or paid in advance, the rent is treated as an expense. If the rent had been paid in advance, it would have been an asset; as the payment expired, it would have been an expense. To keep things simple (for at least a while), *the rent is due, has expired, and is an expense.* No rent was paid in advance.
2. Rent is an expense (since it was not paid in advance). Cash is an asset.
3. The rent is ↑ (inc.) our expenses, and the payment for the rent expense is ↓ (dec.) our cash, an asset.
4. An increase in rent expense, an expense, is a debit. A decrease in cash, an asset, is a credit.
5.

Rent Expense 960		Cash 110	
(H) 400		(A) 10,000	500 (B)
		(D) 2,000	600 (G)
		(F) 500	400 (H)

Rent expense is debited for $400.   Cash is credited for $400.

(I) SEPTEMBER 1–30: Paid supplies expense $100.

1 Accounts Affected	2 Category	3 ↑ ↓	4 Rules	5 T-Account Update
Supplies Expense	Expense	↑ Inc.	Dr.	**Supplies Expense 980** (I) 100
Cash	Asset	↓ Dec.	Cr.	**Cash 110** (A) 10,000 / 500 (B) (D) 2,000 / 600 (G) (F) 500 / 400 (H) 100 (I)

Analysis of Chart

1. The law firm pays for supplies expense by cash.
2. As a general rule, when supplies are purchased, they are an asset. When they are used up in the operation of the firm, they become an expense. In this transaction *we have assumed that the $100 of supplies has been used up in the operation of the firm; therefore, supplies used represents an expense.* Cash, of course, is an asset.
3. The expense of the supplies is ↑ (inc.), since they are being used up. Naturally, the payment of the supplies expense by cash is ↓ (dec.).

4. An increase in supplies expense, an expense, is a debit. A decrease in cash, an asset, is a credit.

5.

Cash 110	
(A) 10,000	500 (B)
(D) 2,000	600 (G)
(F) 500	400 (H)
	(100) (I)

Cash is credited for $100.

Supplies Expense 980	
(I) (100)	

Supplies expense is debited for $100.

THE LEDGER

Each page of ledger would contain one account.

The whole group of accounts that records data from business transactions of Russell Smith is called a *ledger*. This ledger may be in a bound book or a loose-leaf book. Where computers are used, the ledger could be part of a computer print-out. Usually one account is allocated or placed per page.* The ledger is reproduced below:

Cash 110	
(A) 10,000	500 (B)
(D) 2,000	600 (G)
(F) 500	400 (H)
	100 (I)

Accounts Payable 310	
	100 (C)

Salary Expense 910	
(G) 600	

Accounts Receivable 141	
(E) 1,000	500 (F)

R. Smith Investment 510	
	10,000 (A)

Rent Expense 960	
(H) 400	

Equipment 171	
(B) 500	
(C) 100	

Legal Fees 710	
	2,000 (D)
	1,000 (E)

Supplies Expense 980	
(I) 100	

Notice how this grouping of accounts gives us a much better organization than the expanded accounting equation. In each of the transactions we analyzed, did you notice that the total of all the debits was equal to the total of all the credits (columns 4 and 5 of the mind-process chart)? When Smith invested $10,000 in the business, the sum of the debit, $10,000, to cash was equal to the sum of the credit to Smith Investment. This double-entry analysis of transactions (where two or more accounts are affected, debits and credits) helps develop a mechanism of checking our recording of business transactions.

---

* The pages of a ledger are not numbered like a typical book but rather from the chart of accounts: 110, 141, 171, etc.

Looking back over what we have done so far, we can see that for every debit in a transaction, there resulted a credit of equal amount. In sum total, then, when all the transactions are recorded in accounts, the total of all the debits should be equal to the total of all the credits. This proving of the equality of debits and credits in the ledger is accomplished by the development of a *trial balance*. It is a list of account balances at a point in time.

Before moving on to the trial balance, though, let's review your knowledge of debits and credits. You should now be able to:

1. Define and list the five steps to analyzing and recording business transactions.
2. Define and explain the purpose of chart of accounts.
3. State the Rules of Debit and Credit.
4. Complete the mind-process chart for analyzing and recording transactions.
5. Define and state the purpose of a ledger.

UNIT INTERACTOR 6

Complete the mind-process charts based on the following transactions. From a chart of accounts the insurance company utilizes cash, accounts receivable, equipment, accounts payable, insurance fees, Mix investment, and rent expense. The account numbers are omitted for simplicity.

1. Paul Mix invests $2,000 into an insurance company.
2. Paid rent expense $200 for month (no payment was made in advance).
3. Purchased $700 of equipment on account.
4. Charged customer for insurance policies sold on account $1,000.

SOLUTION to Unit Interactor 6

Accounts Affected	Category	↑ ↓	Rules	T-Account Update
Cash	Asset	↑ Inc.	Dr.	**Cash** (1) 2,000
Mix Investment	Owner's equity	↑ Inc.	Cr.	**P. Mix Investment** 2,000 (1)

Accounts Affected	Category	↑ ↓	Rules	T-Account Update
Rent Expense	Expense	↑ Inc.	Dr.	**Rent Expense** (2) 200 |
Cash	Asset	↓ Dec.	Cr.	**Cash** (1) 2,000 | 200 (2)

Accounts Affected	Category	↑ ↓	Rules	T-Account Update
Equipment	Asset	↑ Inc.	Dr.	**Equipment** (3) 700 |
Accounts Payable	Liability	↑ Inc.	Cr.	**Accounts Payable** | 700 (3)

Accounts Affected	Category	↑ ↓	Rules	T-Account Update
Accounts Receivable	Asset	↑ Inc.	Dr.	**Accounts Receivable** (4) 1,000 |
Insurance Fees	Revenue	↑ Inc.	Cr.	**Insurance Fees** | 1,000 (4)

LEARNING UNIT 7

The Trial Balance and Preparation of the Financial Statements

PREPARATION OF TRIAL BALANCE

Reproduced for your convenience is the ledger of Russell Smith:

Cash 110		Accounts Payable 310		Salary Expense 910	
(A) 10,000	500 (B)		100 (C)	(G) 600	
(D) 2,000	600 (G)				
(F) 500	400 (H)				
12,500	100 (I)				
10,900	1,600				

Accounts Receivable 141		R. Smith Investment 510		Rent Expense 960	
(E) 1,000	500 (F)		10,000 (A)	(H) 400	
500					

Equipment 171		Legal Fees 710		Supplies Expense 980	
(B) 500			2,000 (D)	(I) 100	
(C) 100			1,000 (E)		
600			3,000		

Notice the footings that are used to balance each account. For example, the debit side of cash added to $12,500; the credit side, to $1,600. Since the debit side is larger, we subtract $1,600 from $12,500 to arrive at a new debit balance of $10,900. If an account has only one figure, the footing is not needed. When the accounts in the ledger are listed with their balances, a *trial balance* results.

The trial balance is not a formal report.

A trial balance of Russell Smith's accounts is listed on the facing page. Keep in mind that the trial balance is not a formal report. It is used as an aid in preparing the financial statement as well as in proving the accuracy of the recording of transactions into ledger accounts. Usually a trial balance lists assets, liabilities, owner's equity, revenue, and expenses in that order (which is the same order as that of the chart of accounts).

The next chapter will give a more detailed discussion of the trial balance. For now, notice the heading, how the accounts are listed, the debits in the left column, the credits in the right, and that the sum of debits is equal to the sum of credits. A trial balance may balance, but not be correct, if errors offset each other. More will be said later about errors.

**RUSSELL SMITH,
ATTORNEY AT LAW**

**Trial Balance
September 30, 19XX**

	Dr.	Cr.
Cash	10,900	
Accounts Receivable	500	
Equipment	600	
Accounts Payable		100
R. Smith Investment		10,000
Legal Fees		3,000
Salary Expense	600	
Rent Expense	400	
Supplies Expense	100	
	13,100	13,100

The double-entry bookkeeping system, which changed the balance of at least two accounts for each business transaction (columns 4 and 5 of the mind-process chart), always resulted in the total of debits being equal to the total of credits for each individual transaction. This trial balance is a way of checking the accuracy of the double-entry system of recording business transactions at the end of a period of time.

PREPARING FINANCIAL STATEMENTS

The diagram on page 56 shows how the income statement and balance sheet for the law practice can be prepared from a trial balance instead of from the expanded accounting equation. Before leaving this chart, take time to see how the figures are determined, especially for the new owner's equity of $11,900 on the balance sheet.

In Chapter 1

	ASSETS			= LIABILITIES +		OWNER'S EQUITY		
Cash	+ Accounts Receivable	+ Equipment	=	Accounts Payable	+ R. Smith Investment	+ Revenue	− Expenses
$10,900 +	$500	+ $600	=	$100	+	$10,000	+ $3,000	− $1100

In Chapter 1 we used this equation to prepare the income statement and balance sheet. But now in Chapter 2 the trial balance is used to prepare the statements.

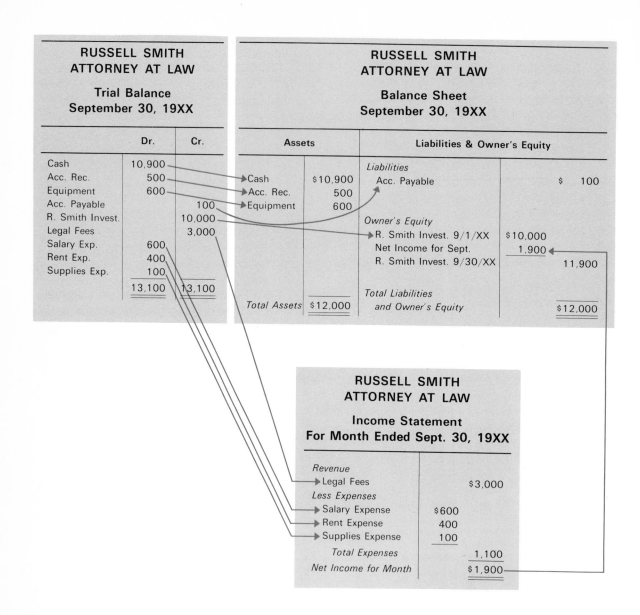

Notice how much easier it is to prepare the statement information from the trial balance instead of from the expanded accounting equation.

In conclusion, before moving on to Chapter 3 you should be able to:

1. Define and state the purpose of double-entry bookkeeping.
2. State and define the purpose of a trial balance.
3. Prepare a trial balance from a group of ledger accounts.
4. Differentiate among a trial balance, income statement, and balance sheet.
5. From a trial balance, prepare an income statement and balance sheet.

UNIT INTERACTOR 7

(1) Foot the following ledger accounts. Prepare (2) a trial balance for R. Jones Taxi, (3) the income statement for May, and (4) the balance sheet as of May 31, 19XX.

Cash 110		Accounts Payable 210	Rent Expense 510
1,000	10	100	10
25	20		
	100		

Accounts Receivable 120	R. Jones Investment 310	Gas Expense 520
50 | 25	1,000	20

Equipment 130	Fees Earned 410	Repair Expense 530
100	50	100

SOLUTION to Unit Interactor 7

Cash 110			Accounts Payable 210		Rent Expense 510	
1,000	10			100	10	
25	20					
895 1,025	100					
	130					

Accounts Receivable 120		R. Jones Investment 310		Gas Expense 520	
50	25		1,000	20	
25					

Equipment 130		Fees Earned 410		Repair Expense 530	
100			50	100	

R. JONES TAXI		
Trial Balance **May 31, 19XX**		
	Dr.	**Cr.**
Cash	895	
Accounts Receivable	25	
Equipment	100	
Accounts Payable		100
R. Jones Investment		1,000
Fees Earned		50
Rent Expense	10	
Gas Expense	20	
Repair Expense	100	
	1,150	1,150

R. JONES TAXI

Income Statement
For Month Ended May 31, 19XX

Revenues		
Fees Earned		$ 50
Expenses		
Rent Expense	$ 10	
Gas Expense	20	
Repairs Expense	100	
Total Expenses*		130
Net Loss for May		$ (80)

*Or total operating expenses.

R. JONES TAXI

Balance Sheet
May 31, 19XX

Assets		Liabilities and Owner's Equity		
		Liabilities		
Cash	$ 895	Accounts Payable		$ 100
Acc. Receivable	25			
Equipment	100			
		Owner's Equity		
		R. Jones Investment		
		5/1/XX	$1,000	
		Less: Net Loss	−80	
		R. Jones Investment		
		5/31/XX		920
		Total Liabilities and		
Total Assets	$1,020	*Owner's Equity*		$1,020

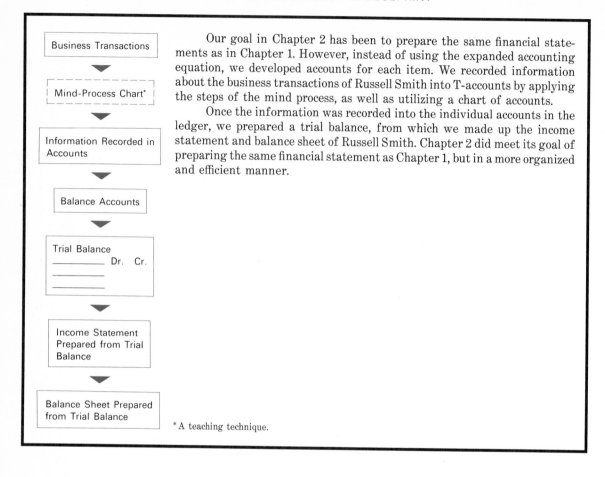

Our goal in Chapter 2 has been to prepare the same financial statements as in Chapter 1. However, instead of using the expanded accounting equation, we developed accounts for each item. We recorded information about the business transactions of Russell Smith into T-accounts by applying the steps of the mind process, as well as utilizing a chart of accounts.

Once the information was recorded into the individual accounts in the ledger, we prepared a trial balance, from which we made up the income statement and balance sheet of Russell Smith. Chapter 2 did meet its goal of preparing the same financial statement as Chapter 1, but in a more organized and efficient manner.

*A teaching technique.

SUMMARY OF NEW ACCOUNTING LANGUAGE TERMS

Learning Unit 5

Account: A device used in bookkeeping to record increases and decreases of business transactions relating to individual assets, liabilities, owner's equity, revenues, expenses, etc.

Credit: The right side of any account. A number entered on the right side of any account is said to be credited to an account.

Debit: The left side of any account. A number entered on the left side of any account is said to be debited to an account.

Standard Account: A formal account that includes columns for date, explanation, posting reference, debit, and credit.

T-Account: A skeleton version of a standard account, used for demonstration purposes.

Learning Unit 6

Chart of Accounts: A numbering system of accounts that lists the names and numbers of account titles to be used by a company.

Double-Entry System: An accounting concept, emphasizing that the recording of each business transaction affects two or more accounts, with the total of the debits being equal to the total of the credits.

Ledger: A group of accounts that records data from business transactions.

Mind Process: (1) What accounts are affected? (2) What category are the accounts in? (3) Are the accounts ↑ or ↓? (4) What are the specific rules of debits or credits affected by the first three steps of mind process?

Learning Unit 7

Trial Balance: A list of the ledger accounts showing each individual account with a debit or credit balance. The sum of debits should equal the sum of the credits.

QUESTION INTERACTORS

1. Define an account.
2. What is meant by "individual items or group of items" of assets? Give examples.
3. What is the difference between a T-account and a standard account?
4. What are the three basic parts of a T-account?
5. Define a debit.
6. Are the following statements true or false?
   a. A debit is the right side of any account.
   b. Debits and credits really mean increase and decrease.
   c. Footings are necessary to balance every account.
   d. Accounting has no real rules of debits and credits.
7. Supply the missing terms.
   a. An ↑ in an asset is a _____ .
   b. A ↓ in a liability is a _____ .
   c. An ↑ in revenue is a _____ .
8. What are the five steps of the mind process in analyzing business transactions?
9. Define the chart of accounts and explain how it helps in the mind process for analyzing business transactions.
10. When supplies are purchased, they are assets; when they are used up, they become expenses. Agree or disagree?
11. Define a ledger. In what physical form may it be found?
12. Give an example of footing and explain the procedures involved in footing.
13. Compare the financial statements prepared by the expanded accounting equation with those prepared from a trial balance.
14. Assets, liabilities, and owner's equity go on an income statement. Agree or disagree? Why?

15. A net loss increases owner's equity. Agree or disagree?
16. If the trial balance is in balance (Dr. = Cr.), does this assure complete accuracy in the recording of information in the ledger?

PROBLEM INTERACTORS

1. The following transactions occurred in the opening and operation of J. V. Glen TV Repair Shop:

    1. J. V. Glen opened a TV repair shop by investing $500 from his personal savings account.
    2. Purchased shop equipment on account $100.
    3. Paid rent expense for $50 (this was not paid in advance).
    4. Collected $100 for repairs performed in cash.
    5. Repaired a color TV *on credit* $100.

    Complete the mind-process chart in the Study Guide. The chart of accounts includes cash, accounts receivable, shop equipment, accounts payable, J. V. Glen investment, repair fees earned, and rent expense.

2. Robert Johnson opened a travel agency, and the following transactions resulted:

    1. Johnson invested $10,000 in the travel agency.
    2. Bought desk furniture on account $1,000.
    3. Agency received $5,000 in cash for travel arrangements completed for one of its clients.
    4. Paid advertising expense for the month $500.
    5. Paid rent expense for the month (not in advance) $300.
    6. Paid $400 in partial payment of what was owed in transaction (2).

    As Mr. Johnson's accountant, analyze and record the transactions in T-account form. The chart of accounts provides you with the possible individual account titles. Please set up a ledger of T-accounts and label each entry with the number of the transaction.

Chart of Accounts

ASSETS	REVENUE
Cash	Travel Fees Earned
Office Equipment	
LIABILITIES	**EXPENSES**
Accounts Payable	Advertising Expense
	Rent Expense
OWNER'S EQUITY	
R. Johnson Investment	

3. From the following T-accounts of the Jon Jones Talent Agency, foot the balance where appropriate and prepare a trial balance in proper form for May 31, 19XX.

Cash	
10,000 (A)	200 (D)
2,500 (G)	300 (E)
	500 (F)
	100 (H)

Accounts Payable	
200 (D)	400 (C)

Rent Expense	
500 (F)	

Accounts Receivable	
5,000 (B)	2,500 (G)

J. Jones Investment	
	10,000 (A)

Office Equipment	
400 (C)	
100 (H)	

Fees Earned	
	5,000 (B)

Utilities Expense	
300 (E)	

4. From the trial balance of Gordon Brown, Attorney at Law, listed below, prepare (1) an income statement for the month of May and (2) the balance sheet as of May 31, 19XX.

GORDON BROWN
ATTORNEY AT LAW

Trial Balance
May 31, 19XX

	Debit	Credit
Cash	700	
Office Equipment	500	
Accounts Payable		500
Wages Payable		125
Gordon Brown Investment		425
Revenue from Legal Fees		450
Utilities Expense	100	
Rent Expense	150	
Advertising Expense	50	
	1,500	1,500

*5. The chart of accounts for the Jones Trucking Co. is as follows (account numbers have been omitted for simplicity).

Chart of Accounts

ASSETS	REVENUE
Cash	Trucking Fees Earned
Accounts Receivable	
Office Equipment	
Trucks	

LIABILITIES	EXPENSES
Accounts Payable	Advertising Expense
	Gas Expense
	Salary Expense
	Telephone Expense

OWNER'S EQUITY
J. Jones Investment

The following transactions resulted for the Jones Trucking Company during the month of March:

1. Jones invested $15,000 into trucking business from his own personal savings.
2. Purchased trucks on account $20,000.
3. Bought office equipment for cash $1,000.
4. Paid advertising expense $400.
5. Collected, in cash, $2,000 for trucking services performed.
6. Paid the truck drivers $500 for salary.
7. Paid gas expense for trucks $250.
8. Performed trucking services for a customer on credit $3,000.
9. Paid telephone expense $19.
10. Received partial payment from Transaction (8) of $1,500.

Your task as the Jones' newly employed accountant is to:
a. Set up T-accounts in a ledger.
b. Record transactions in the T-accounts (place number of transaction next to entry).
c. Foot the T-accounts where appropriate.
d. Prepare a trial balance at the end of March.

e. Prepare from the trial balance, in proper form, an income statement for the month of March and a balance sheet as of March 31, 19XX.

ADDITIONAL PROBLEM INTERACTORS

1-A. Ralph Kline decided to open a shoe repair shop.

1. Ralph Kline opened his shoe repair shop by investing $1,000 into the business.
2. Repaired a pair of shoes on credit $50.
3. Purchased shoe repair equipment on account $200.
4. Paid advertising expense $50.
5. Received $200 in cash for repairing the football shoes of the local high school team.
6. Paid rent expense for month $50. (This was not paid in advance.)

Complete the mind-process chart in the Study Guide. The chart of accounts includes cash, accounts receivable, shop repair equipment, accounts payable, Ralph Kline investment, shoe repairs earned, rent expense, advertising expense.

2-A. Bob Fales opened up a new insurance agency. Record the following transactions in T-accounts (a simplified chart of accounts is provided below the transactions). (See Problem 3-A for the form of setting up the ledger.)

1. Bob Fales invested $5,000 into the insurance agency from his personal savings account.
2. Purchased office furniture on account $500.
3. Paid advertising expense $100.
4. Paid rent expense for month $50 (not paid in advance).
5. Insurance agency received $500 in cash for policies issued.
6. Paid $200 of what was owed from transaction 2.

ASSETS	REVENUE
Cash Office Furniture	Insurance Fees Earned
LIABILITIES	EXPENSES
Accounts Payable	Rent Expense Advertising Expense
OWNER'S EQUITY	
B. Fales Investment	

3-A. From the following T-accounts of Jim Rice Hair Salon: (a) foot balances where appropriate; (b) prepare a trial balance for April 30, 19XX.

Cash	
5,000 (A)	2,000 (C)
3,000 (F)	10 (D)
1,000 (G)	25 (E)

Accounts Receivable	
1,000 (G)	

Salon Equipment	
3,000 (B)	
2,000 (C)	

Accounts Payable	
	3,000 (B)

Jim Rice Investment	
	5,000 (A)

Salon Fees Earned	
	3,000 (F)
	2,000 (G)

Rent Expense	
10 (D)	

Utilities Expense	
25 (E)	

4-A. From the trial balance of John Sullivan, Dentist, prepare: (a) an income statement for the month of June and (b) a balance sheet as of June 30, 19XX.

JOHN SULLIVAN, DENTIST

Trial Balance
June 30, 19XX

	Debit	Credit
Cash	2,000	
Accounts Receivable	600	
Dental Equipment	600	
Accounts Payable		100
Wages Payable		100
John Sullivan Investment		1,000
Dental Fees Earned		2,200
Telephone Expense	25	
Rent Expense	75	
Supplies Expense	100	
	3,400	3,400

*5-A. Presented in a simplified form is the chart of accounts for the Ronald Tree Service.

Chart of Accounts

ASSETS	REVENUE
Cash	Tree Service Fees Earned
Accounts Receivable	
Tree Equipment	
Truck	

LIABILITIES	EXPENSES
Accounts Payable	Telephone Expense
	Rent Expense
	Supplies Expense
	Salary Expense

OWNER'S EQUITY
Jean Ronald Investment

The following transactions resulted for the month of July:

1. Jean Ronald invested $10,000 into the tree service business.
2. Purchased tree equipment on account $500.
3. Purchased a truck for cash $2,000.
4. Collected cash for tree pruning $3,000.
5. Performed cutting of tree limb on credit $8,000 for the city of Leaves.
6. Paid salary expense $300.
7. Received partial payment from the city of Leaves [transaction 5] $4,000.
8. Paid supplies expense $50; supplies were consumed in the operation of the business.
9. Paid telephone expense $30.
10. Paid rent expense for month (not paid in advance) $300.
11. Paid half of amount owed for tree equipment purchased in transaction 2.

Your task as the accountant is to:

a. Set up a ledger of T-accounts.
b. Record transactions in T-accounts. (Place number of transaction next to entry.)
c. Foot the T-accounts where appropriate.
d. Prepare a trial balance at the end of July.
e. Prepare from the trial balance, in proper form, an income statement for the month of July and a balance sheet as of July 31, 19XX.

1. Transactions for the first month of operation are recorded in the ledger of the Hi-Grade Repair Shop. Each transaction is lettered for identification.

Cash

a) 8,000	b) 600
f) 350	d) 1,000
m) 400	e) 100
o) 500	g) 200
	h) 500
	i) 200
	k) 500
	n) 200
	p) 50

Accounts Receivable

j) 700	o) 500
l) 300	

Repair Tools

b) 600	

Office Equipment

c) 1,000	

Repair Equipment

d) 3,000	

Accounts Payable

g) Office Eq. 200	c) 1,000
k) Repair Eq. 500	d) 2,000

Al Grade Investment

	a) 8,000

Repair Service Revenue

	f) 350
	j) 700
	l) 300
	m) 400

Advertising Expense

e) 100	

Rent Expense

h) 500	

Salary Expense

i) 200	
n) 200	

Utilities Expense

p) 50	

Using the information in the above ledger, determine the following:

a. What is the balance in the Cash account at the end of the month? _____

b. What is the total of Repair Service Revenue for the month? _____

c. How much is still owing on the Office Equipment at the end of the month? _____

How much is still owing on the Repair Equipment at the end of the month? _____

d. What is the total of ALL the assets at the end of the month? _____

e. What would be the amount of owner's equity at the end of the month, as it would appear on the Balance Sheet? _____

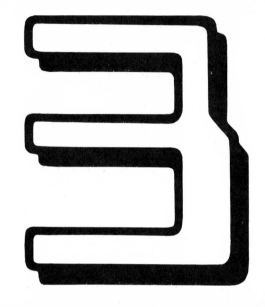

the accounting cycle: an overview

In Chapters 1 and 2 we have learned some accounting terminology, basic financial statements, and some of the rules of the game. In assembling these parts and pieces what is our goal? What are we trying to build? Let's develop what an architect would call a blueprint.

The accompanying accounting blueprint (cycle) will be repeated frequently in the next three chapters, reminding us of what step we are on in completing the procedures for each accounting period. (Please don't try to memorize the blueprint—simply use it as reference in the next three chapters.)

THE ACCOUNTING CYCLE—A BLUEPRINT OF PROCEDURES

	Steps	*Notes*
Steps of accounting cycle	1. Business transactions occur and generate source documents	Cash register tape, sales tickets, bills, checks, payroll cards
	2. Analyze and record business transactions into a journal	Called journalizing
	3. Post or transfer information from journal to ledger	Copying the debits and credits of the journal entries, placing them into the ledger accounts
	4. Prepare a trial balance	Summarizing each individual ledger account and listing these accounts and their balances to test for accuracy in recording transactions

Steps	Notes
5. Prepare a worksheet	A multi-column form that summarizes accounting information to complete the accounting cycle
6. Prepare financial statements	Income statement, balance sheet
7. Journalize and post adjusting entries	Refer to adjustment columns of worksheet
8. Journalize and post closing entries	Refer to income statement columns of worksheet
9. Prepare a post-closing trial balance	Proves the accuracy of the adjusting and closing process of the accounting cycle

This chapter, as it proceeds, will review some of the fundamentals to make sure that the reader has a strong understanding of concepts and procedures.

This chapter will present the first four steps of the accounting cycle in terms of transactions of the Katz Real Estate Agency. In the last two chapters we analyzed business transactions of Russell Smith's law

practice by the five steps of the mind process. The fifth step was the updating of the T-account balance. Although transactions can be recorded in the T-accounts, it would still be difficult to locate errors in the accounts, because a debit would be on one page of the ledger and a credit on another page. What is needed is a place where the entire transaction (Dr. and Cr.) can be found. This need to *link* the accounts together is accomplished by the recording of business transactions in a *journal*, a place where transactions are placed in chronological order (Jan. 1, 8, 15, etc.) before the ledger accounts are updated. Much more will be said about journals in this chapter.

Journal records transactions in chronological order.

Let's now analyze the business transactions of the Katz Real Estate Agency to see how to begin the accounting cycle.

LEARNING UNIT 8

Analyzing and Recording Business Transactions into a Journal—Steps 1 and 2 of the Accounting Cycle

THE GENERAL JOURNAL

The general journal, the simplest form of a journal, will be used to record the transactions of the Katz Real Estate Agency. Remember the journal provides a place where both parts of a transaction can be found, if needed, in locating errors.

When a transaction debit(s) + credit(s) is analyzed and recorded into a journal, it is called a *journal entry*. The process of recording the journal entry into the journal is called *journalizing*.

General Journal				Page 1
Date	Account Titles and Description	PR	Debit	Credit

The journal is called the *book of original entry*, since it will contain the first formal information about the business transactions. The ledger, a group of accounts, will be known as the *book of final entry*, since the information in the journal will be eventually copied to the ledger.

Relationship of journal to chart of accounts

Before the accountant can journalize the business transactions of Katz Real Estate, he needs the possible list of titles of accounts so as to title individual debits and credits. The chart of accounts of Katz Real

Estate is as follows. (Don't worry about accounts in the chart we haven't talked about or seen—you will learn about them by the end of the accounting cycle.)

Katz Real Estate Agency:
Chart of Accounts

ASSETS	OWNER'S EQUITY
110 Cash	340 S. Katz Investment
112 Accounts Receivable	342 S. Katz Withdrawal
114 Prepaid Rent	344 Income Summary
116 Office Supplies	
118 Automobile	
119 Accumulated Depreciation—Auto	
120 Office Equipment	
121 Accumulated Depreciation—Office Equipment	

	REVENUE
	450 Commission Fees Earned

LIABILITIES	EXPENSES
230 Accounts Payable	560 Office Salary Expense
232 Salaries Payable	562 Advertising Expense
	564 Telephone Expense
	566 Rent Expense
	568 Office Supplies Expense
	570 Depreciation Expense—Auto
	572 Depreciation Expense—Office Equipment

ANALYSIS AND RECORDING OF TRANSACTIONS

19XX JULY 1: Shelly Katz invests $30,000 cash and $3,300 worth of office equipment into Katz Real Estate Agency.

Analysis of Transaction

1 Accounts Affected*	2 Category	3 ↑ ↓	4 Rules
Cash	Asset	↑	Dr.
Office Equipment	Asset	↑	Dr.
S. Katz Investment	Owner's Equity	↑	Cr.

*Titles will come from the chart of accounts of Katz Real Estate Agency.

Katz Real Estate Agency received two assets, cash and equipment. Shelly Katz has the financial claim or right to the assets, since she supplied the cash and equipment to the real estate office.

Recording Transaction in Journal

General Journal					Page 1
Date	Account Titles and Description	PR	Debit*		Credit
19XX					
July 1	Cash		30,000 00		
	Office Equipment		3,300 00		
	S. Katz Investment				33,300 00
	Initial investment of cash and equipment by owner				

*For those who prefer to use dashes instead of zeros (for example, 30,000.00 or 30,000–) it is acceptable. Be sure to check with your instructor.

Structure of a journal entry

Notice that the above general journal entry contains the following information:

1. Year of journal entry — 19XX
2. Month of journal entry — July
3. Day of journal entry — 1
4. Name(s) of accounts debited — Cash/Office Equipment
5. Name(s) of accounts credited — Shelly Katz Investment
6. Description of transaction — Investment of cash and equipment
7. Amount of debit(s) — $33,300
8. Amount of credit(s) — $33,300

For now the PR (posting reference) column is blank; we will discuss it later.

Notice the following in the journal entry* above:

1. The location of the year, month, and day.
2. The accounts, cash and office equipment, are written on the first and second lines next to the date column in the account title and description section. The amounts of each account are entered in the debit columns. You will notice that the debit portion of the transaction is recorded in the journal first.
3. The account, S. Katz Investment, is written on the third line, indented one-half inch from the left side of the account titles and description. The credit portion of a transaction is placed after and below the debit portion.
4. The explanation of the journal entry follows immediately after the sequence of debit and credit account titles. The explanation is placed next to the date column. This allows for greater space to write explanations.

*A journal entry that requires three or more accounts is called a compound journal entry.

5. Following each transaction and explanation leave a space (some journals do not). This allows for clarity and less chance of mixing transactions.
6. The total amount of debits $33,300 is equal to the total amount of credits $33,300.

JULY 1: Paid rent for real estate office three months in advance $300.

Analysis of Transaction

1 Accounts Affected	2 Category	3 ↑ ↓	4 Rules
Prepaid Rent	Asset	↑	Dr.
Cash	Asset	↓	Cr.

To analyze this transaction, remember: when rent is paid in advance, it is considered an asset. As it expires over time, it becomes an expense.

The cash of Katz Real Estate has decreased in order to pay rent *in advance*. The company gains an asset, prepaid rent, but gives up cash, another asset, to get it. When the rent expires, it will become an expense, rent expense, thus reducing the asset prepaid rent. For now the total of the assets of Katz has not changed, but the composition has: less money more prepaid rent.

In light of the above, think back to Russell Smith's law practice. Prepaid rent was not involved there, because the firm never paid for *rent in advance*. The rent they paid for had already expired; therefore, it was an expense. Katz Real Estate does not show rent expense yet, because no rent has expired.

Recording Rent into Journal

1	Prepaid Rent			300 00	
	Cash				300 00
	Rent paid in advance				

Rent paid in advance is an asset of value.

Notice that only the day is entered in the date column. Since the year and month are entered at the top of the page from the investment transaction, there is not need to repeat the month title, until a new page is needed or the change of a month occurs.

Once again, as in all journal entries, the total amount of debits is equal to the total amount of credits.

JULY 3: Purchased an automobile from J. B. Mahoney on account to be specifically used for the real estate agency $3,000.

1 Accounts Affected	2 Category	3 ↑ ↓	4 Rules
Automobile	Asset	↑	Dr.
Accounts Payable	Liability	↑	Cr.

The agency adds a new asset, automobile. This account title, once again, came from chart of accounts. The firm also increases what it owes. This liability or obligation will hopefully be paid by cash in the future.

Recording of Transaction
in Journal

3	Automobile		300000	
	Accounts Payable			300000
	Purchase of auto on account			

JULY 8: Purchased office supplies $100, for cash.

Analysis of Transaction

1 Accounts Affected	2 Category	3 ↑ ↓	4 Rules
Office Supplies	Asset	↑	Dr.
Cash	Asset	↓	Cr.

Supplies become an expense when used up.

Remember the following guidelines:

1. When purchasing supplies they are an asset of value that has not been used up.
2. When the supplies are used up or consumed in the operation of the business, they are an expense.

In the situation above, we are dealing with item 1. When we analyzed Russell Smith, we were dealing with item 2. At some point when the supplies are consumed or used up, they will create an expense for Katz Real Estate.

8	Office Supplies		10000	
	Cash			10000
	Office supplies purchased for cash			

JULY 15: Collected in cash a commission from the sale of a home, $4,000.

Analysis of Transaction

	1 Accounts Affected	2 Category	3 ↑ ↓	4 Rules
	Cash	Asset	↑	Dr.
	Commission Fees Earned	Revenue	↑	Cr.

Received $4,000 in cash from a sale of a home. The revenue results in an inward flow of assets. This time the *inward flow* is in the form of cash.

Recording of Transaction in Journal

15	Cash		400000	
	Commission Fees Earned			400000
	Cash commission from sale of home			

JULY 16: Paid the office salaries for the first two weeks of July $600.

Analysis of Transaction

	1 Accounts Affected	2 Category	3 ↑ ↓	4 Rules
	Office Salary Expense	Expense	↑	Dr.
	Cash	Asset	↓	Cr.

Salaries represent an increase in the expenses of Katz Real Estate. The office reduces its cash to pay for this expense.

16	Office Salaries Expense	60000	
	Cash		60000
	Payment of office salaries		

JULY 21: Shelly Katz withdrew $500 for her own personal use from the business.

Analysis of Transaction*

	1	2	3	4
	Accounts Affected	Category	↑ ↓	Rules
	S. Katz Withdrawal	Withdrawal	↑	Dr.
	Cash	Asset	↓	Cr.

Withdrawals are shown on the balance sheet not on the income statement.

Withdrawal or drawings is defined as the money or assets Shelly Katz takes out of her business for her own personal satisfaction. *It is not a business expense.* This expense of $500 did not result from the operations of Katz Real Estate. In effect, withdrawals follow the same basic rules of debits and credits that apply to expenses. As withdrawal increases, it really reduces owner's equity.

Withdrawal

Dr.	Cr.
Increase	Decrease

The above debit to withdrawal indicates Shelly Katz has *increased* what she has taken out of the business. The credit to cash results because Shelly has taken some of the cash from the business.

Recording of Withdrawal
Transaction in Journal

21	S. Katz Withdrawal	50000	
	Cash		50000
	Cash withdrawal by Katz		

* Add these to the chart of rules of debits and credits:
  1. An increase in withdrawal is a debit.
  2. A decrease in withdrawal is a credit.

JULY 23: Sold a home; the commission earned $8,000 will not be paid to Katz Real Estate until August.

1 Accounts Affected	2 Category	3 ↑ ↓	4 Rules
Accounts Receivable	Asset	↑	Dr.
Commission Fees Earned	Revenue	↑	Cr.

In the accrual basis of accounting, revenue is recognized when it is earned, whether payment is received or not at the time the service was provided. Here, payment is not received, but revenue (commission fees) has been earned.

23	Accounts Receivable	8000 00	
	Commission Fees Earned		8000 00
	Fees earned but not collected from sale of home		

JULY 25: Paid the office salaries for the last two weeks of July $600.

1 Accounts Affected	2 Category	3 ↑ ↓	4 Rules
Office Salary Expense	Expense	↑	Dr.
Cash	Asset	↓	Cr.

Salaries represent an increase in the expense of the firm. The firm reduces its cash by $600 to pay increased expense.

25	Office Salaries Expense	600 00	
	Cash		600 00
	Payment of office salaries		

JULY 28: Paid J. B. Mahoney one-half of what was owed from July 3.

	1 Accounts Affected	2 Category	3 ↑ ↓	4 Rules
	Accounts Payable	Liability	↓	Dr.
	Cash	Asset	↓	Cr.

Katz Realty reduces cash to pay off part of obligation—accounts payable. The decrease in accounts payable is a debit.

General Journal					Page 2
Date	Account Titles and Description	PR	Debit	Credit	
19XX* July 28	Accounts Payable 　　Cash Reduced amount owed J. B. Mahoney		150000	150000	

*The year is optional. Check with your instructor.

Notice that since we are now on page 2 of the journal, the month is included along with the date and year.

JULY 29: Paid advertising expense $50.

	1 Accounts Affected	2 Category	3 ↑ ↓	4 Rules
	Advertising Expense	Expense	↑	Dr.
	Cash	Asset	↓	Cr.

The advertising was not paid in advance. This expense increased the expenses of the firm. Katz Real Estate decreased its cash to pay the increased expense.

29	Advertising Expense 　　Cash Paid advertising bill		5000	5000	

JULY 29: Paid telephone bill for the month $50.

Analysis of Transaction	1 Accounts Affected	2 Category	3 ↑ ↓	4 Rules
	Telephone Expense	Expense	↑	Dr.
	Cash	Asset	↓	Cr.

The use of the telephone represents an additional expense of $50 to Katz Real Estate. This increased expense was paid by decreasing the asset cash by $50.

Recording of Transaction in Journal

29	Telephone Expense			50 00	
	Cash				50 00
	Paid telephone bill				

That concludes the journal transactions of the Katz Real Estate Agency.

Before looking at the objectives of this unit, keep in mind that a general journal can be proved. This proving is accomplished by adding the debit column amounts on the page, and also adding the credit amounts. Hopefully the total of the debit column should be equal to the total of the credit column, although we will not be proving the general journal. (We will in future parts of text.) The footings of the total would normally be entered on the last line of each completed page or below the last entry of an incomplete page.

This completes Learning Unit 8 on "Analyzing and Recording Business Transactions in a Journal." In review, you should be able to:

1. Define and state the purpose of a journal.
2. Differentiate between a chart of accounts and a journal.
3. Analyze and record in proper form the transactions of a business into a general journal.

4. Define a compound journal entry.
5. Differentiate between a withdrawal and a business expense.
6. Compare and contrast a book of original entry to a book of final entry.

UNIT INTERACTOR 8

The following are the transactions of R. Lybel Insurance Agency. Please journalize the transactions in proper form. Of course, the solution is provided.

The chart of accounts for R. Lybel included Cash, Accounts Receivable, Prepaid Rent, Office Supplies, Office Equipment, Automobile, Accounts Payable, R. Lybel Investment, R. Lybel Withdrawal, Commission Fees Earned, Office Salaries Expense, Advertising Expense, Telephone Expense.

19XX JULY
1: R. Lybel invested $30,000 cash and $5,000 worth of equipment into R. Lybel Insurance Company.
1: Paid the insurance office rent for three months in advance $5,000.
3: Purchased on account an automobile from J. B. Safe. This vehicle will be used specifically for the insurance company $3,000.
8: Purchased office supplies $100 from Morse Co. for cash (consider this as a prepaid asset).
15: Collected in cash a commission from the sale of a policy $4,000.
16: Paid the office salaries for the first two weeks of July $600.
21: R. Lybel withdrew $1,000 from the business for her own personal use.
23: Sold a policy, however, the commission earned, $8,000, will not be paid to the insurance company until August.
25: Paid the office salaries for the last two weeks of July $600.
28: Paid J. B. Safe one-half of the amount that was owed from July 3.
29: Paid advertising bill $50.
29: Paid telephone bill for month, $50.

General Journal   **Page 1**
R. Lybel Insurance Co.

Date	Account Titles and Description	PR	Dr.	Cr.
19XX				
July 1	Cash		30,000 00	
	Office Equipment		5,000 00	
	R. Lybel Investment			35,000 00
	Initial investment of cash and equipment by owner			
1	Prepaid Rent		5,000 00	
	Cash			5,000 00
	Rent paid in advance			
3	Automobile		3,000 00	
	Accounts Payable			3,000 00
	Purchase of auto on account			
8	Office Supplies		100 00	
	Cash			100 00
	Office supplies purchased for cash			
15	Cash		4,000 00	
	Commission Fees Earned			4,000 00
	Cash commission from sale of policy			
16	Office Salaries Expense		600 00	
	Cash			600 00
	Payment of office salaries			
21	R. Lybel Withdrawal		1,000 00	
	Cash			1,000 00
	Cash withdrawal by R. Lybel			
23	Accounts Receivable		8,000 00	
	Commission Fees Earned			8,000 00
	Fees earned but not collected from sale of policy			
25	Office Salaries Expense		600 00	
	Cash			600 00
	Payment of office salaries			

General Journal   **Page 2**
R. Lybel Insurance Co.

Date	Account Titles and Description	PR	Dr.	Cr.
19XX July 28	Accounts Payable		1500 00	
	Cash			1500 00
	Reduced amount owed J. B. Safe			
29	Advertising Expense		50 00	
	Cash			50 00
	Paid advertising bill			
29	Telephone Expense		50 00	
	Cash			50 00
	Telephone bill			

LEARNING UNIT 9

Step 3 of the Accounting Cycle—
How to Post Journalized Transactions

REVIEW

In the last unit the business transactions of Katz Real Estate were journalized. The journal provided us with a central place for recording the debit and credit part(s) of a transaction. We were able to see the entire transaction. There was a definite *link* between the debit and credit.

Think back to how we made an income statement and balance sheet from T-accounts. The group of individual accounts was called a ledger. This ledger represented a record of the increases and decreases of each individual item or account.

So far we have completed two steps in the accounting cycle.

1. Business transactions occur.
2. Analyze and record business transactions into a journal.

This unit analyzes step 3 of the accounting cycle:

3. Post or transfer information from journal to ledger.

POSTING OF JOURNAL ENTRIES

How to post   The transferring, copying or recording of information from the journal to the ledger is known as *posting*. All journal entries (which are already in chronological order) are to be posted. The information from

85

the journals may be posted daily or at regular intervals. Let's look at the investment of S. Katz into Katz Real Estate to see how journal entries are posted.

General Journal
Katz Real Estate Agency — Page 1

Date	Account Titles and Description	PR	Dr.	Cr.
19XX				
July 1	Cash	110	30,000 00	
	Office Equipment	120	3,300 00	
	S. Katz Investment	340		33,300 00

Ledger

Account: Cash — Account No. 110

Date	Item	PR	Dr.	Date	Item	PR	Cr.
19XX							
July 1		GJ1	30,000 00				

Account: Office Equipment — Account No. 120

Date	Item	PR	Dr.	Date	Item	PR	Cr.
19XX							
July 1		GJ1	3,300 00				

Account: S. Katz Investment — Account No. 340

Date	Item	PR	Dr.	Date	Item	PR	Cr.
				19XX			
				July 1		GJ1	33,300 00

Referring to the previous transaction, notice that in transferring information from the journal to the ledger, *no new analysis is taking place in the ledger.* You are *copying* the information into the ledger.

CASH PART OF THE TRANSACTION

First let's look at the cash part of the transaction. Since cash is a debit of $30,000 in the journal, and since posting calls for copying the same information to the ledger, the following is posted to cash in the ledger on the debit side or left side.

Cash   110

19XX
July 1 GJ1 30,000

Posted to Ledger

1. Date	July 1, 19XX
2. Amount	$30,000
3. Page of journal from which the journal entry came is posted in PR (posting reference) column	GJ1

Information to Journal from Ledger

CROSS-REFERENCE. The account number of the cash account in the ledger (110) is placed in the PR column of the journal to indicate what account in the ledger, from the journal, has received the information. This part of the posting is then complete. This is called *cross-referencing.*

After Posting Cash

Purpose of posting

JOURNAL. In summary, if you opened up your journal and saw a debit for cash, you would see a 110 in the PR column that would tell you that the information about cash in the journal had been copied to the ledger in account no. 110.

LEDGER. If you looked at the cash account no. 110 in the ledger, you would see a debit of $30,000. By looking at the PR column you could tell that the information came from page 1 of the general journal.

JOURNAL/LEDGER. Notice that both the journal and the ledger contain exactly the same information.

OFFICE EQUIPMENT PART OF THE TRANSACTION

Since equipment is a debit of $3,300 in the journal and posting calls for the copying of same information to the ledger, the following is posted to office equipment in the ledger on the debit side (left side):

Office Equipment   120

19XX
July 1 GJ1 3,300

Posted to Ledger

1. Date	July 1, 19XX
2. Amount	$3,300
3. Page of journal from which the journal entry came is posted in PR column	GJ1

Information to Journal from Ledger

CROSS-REFERENCE. The account number of the office equipment account (120) in the ledger is placed in the PR column of the journal to indicate what account in the ledger has received the information. This part of posting is then complete.

After Posting Office Equipment

JOURNAL. In summary, if you opened up your journal and saw a debit to office equipment, you would see a 120 in the PR column. That would tell you that the same information about the office equipment had been copied from the journal to the ledger in account no. 120.

LEDGER. If you looked at the office equipment account no. 120 in the ledger, you would see a debit of $3,300. By looking at the PR column you could tell that the information came from page 1 of the general journal.

KATZ INVESTMENT PART OF THE TRANSACTION

Since Katz Investment is a credit of $33,300 in the journal and posting calls for copying the same information to the ledger, the following is posted to Katz Investment in the ledger on the credit side (right side):

S. Katz Investment		340
19XX		
July 1	GJ1	33,300

Posted to Ledger

1. Date   July 1, 19XX
2. Amount $33,300
3. Page of journal from which the journal entry is posted in PR column   GJ1

Information to Journal from Ledger

CROSS-REFERENCE. The account number of the Katz Investment account (340) in the ledger is placed in the PR column of the journal to indicate what account in the ledger had received the information and that this part of posting is complete.

After Posting Katz Investment

JOURNAL. In summary, if you opened up your journal and saw a credit to Katz Investment, you would see a 340 in the PR column. That would tell you that the same information about Katz Investment had been copied to the ledger in account no. 340.

LEDGER. If you looked at the Katz Investment account no. 340 in the ledger, you would see a credit of $33,300. By looking at the PR column you could tell that the information came from page 1 of the general journal.

This posting procedure is the same for all journal transactions. Before looking specifically at all the postings involved with Katz Real Estate, check your knowledge of posting in Unit Interactor 9A.

From the following journal and ledger accounts fill in the blanks:

General Journal					Page 13
Date	Account Titles and Description	PR	Dr.		Cr.
19XX Nov. 1	Cash	12	50000		
	Fees Earned	44			50000
	Cash revenue collected				

Ledger

Account: Cash　　　　　　　　　　　　　　　　　**Account No. 12**

Date	Item	PR	Dr.		Date	Item	PR	Cr.
19XX Nov. 1		GJ13	50000					

Account: Fees Earned　　　　　　　　　　　　　**Account No. 44**

Date	Item	PR	Dr.		Date	Item	PR	Cr.
					19XX Nov. 1		GJ13	50000

The transaction we are looking at is:

19XX Nov. 1: —Received cash revenue of $500 from clients.

1. Month of the journal entry _____
2. Day of the journal entry _____
3. Year of the journal entry _____
4. Credit amount _____
5. Name of account debited _____
6. Brief description of transaction _____
7. Number of account to which debit was posted _____
8. Name of account credited _____
9. Debit amount _____
10. Number of account to which credit was posted _____

Once again, notice that posting is the transferring of information from a journal to a ledger.

SOLUTION to Unit Interactor **9A**

1. November.
2. 1.
3. 19XX.
4. $500.
5. Cash.

6. Cash revenue collected.
7. 12.
8. Fees earned.
9. $500.
10. 44.

UNIT INTERACTOR 9B

Below are the journalized transactions of Katz Real Estate. Your task is (1) to post this information to the following ledger accounts: cash (account no. 110), accounts receivable (112), prepaid rent (114), office supplies (116), automobile (118), office equipment (120), accounts payable (230), S. Katz investment (340), S. Katz withdrawal (342), commissioned fees earned (450), office salary expense (560), advertising expense (562), telephone expense (564), and (2) to balance accounts where appropriate. Of course, the solution is provided.

General Journal   **Page 1**
Katz Real Estate Agency

Date	Account Titles and Description	PR	Dr.	Cr.
19XX				
July 1	Cash		30,000 00	
	Office Equipment		3,300 00	
	S. Katz Investment			33,300 00
	Initial investment of cash and equipment by owner			
1	Prepaid Rent		300 00	
	Cash			300 00
	Rent paid in advance			
3	Automobile		3,000 00	
	Accounts Payable			3,000 00
	Purchase of auto on account			
8	Office Supplies		100 00	
	Cash			100 00
	Office supplies purchased for cash			

				Dr.		Cr.	
15	Cash			4,000	00		
	Commission Fees Earned					4,000	00
	Cash commission from sale of home						
16	Office Salaries Expense			600	00		
	Cash					600	00
	Payment of office salaries						
21	S. Katz Withdrawal			500	00		
	Cash					500	00
	Cash withdrawal by Katz						
23	Accounts Receivable			8,000	00		
	Commission Fees Earned					8,000	00
	Fees earned but not collected from sale of home						
25	Office Salaries Expense			600	00		
	Cash					600	00
	Payment of office salaries						

General Journal   **Page 2**
Katz Real Estate Agency

Date	Account Titles and Description	PR	Dr.		Cr.	
19XX						
July 28	Accounts Payable		1500	00		
	Cash				1500	00
	Reduced amount owed J. B. Mahoney					
29	Advertising Expense		50	00		
	Cash				50	00
	Paid advertising bill					
29	Telephone Expense		50	00		
	Cash				50	00
	Telephone bill					

General Journal   **Page 1**
Katz Real Estate Agency

Date	Account Titles and Description	PR	Dr.	Cr.
19XX				
July 1	Cash	110	30,000 00	
	Office Equipment	120	3,300 00	
	S. Katz Investment	340		33,300 00
	Initial investment of cash and equipment by owner			
1	Prepaid Rent	114	300 00	
	Cash	110		300 00
	Rent paid in advance			
3	Automobile	118	3,000 00	
	Accounts Payable	230		3,000 00
	Purchase of auto on account			
8	Office Supplies	116	100 00	
	Cash	110		100 00
	Office supplies purchased for cash			
15	Cash	110	4,000 00	
	Commission Fees Earned	450		4,000 00
	Cash commission from sale of home			
16	Office Salaries Expense	560	600 00	
	Cash	110		600 00
	Payment of office salaries			
21	S. Katz Withdrawal	342	500 00	
	Cash	110		500 00
	Cash withdrawal by Katz			
23	Accounts Receivable	112	8,000 00	
	Commission Fees Earned	450		8,000 00
	Fees earned but not collected from sale of home			
25	Office Salaries Expense	560	600 00	
	Cash	110		600 00
	Payment of office salaries			

General Journal   **Page 2**
Katz Real Estate Agency

Date	Account Titles and Description	PR	Dr.	Cr.
19XX				
July 28	Accounts Payable	230	1500 00	
	Cash	110		1500 00
	Reduced amount owed J. B. Mahoney			
29	Advertising Expense	562	50 00	
	Cash	110		50 00
	Paid advertising bill			
29	Telephone Expense	564	50 00	
	Cash	110		50 00
	Telephone bill			

Account: Cash   **Account No. 110**

Date		Item	PR	Dr.	Date		Item	PR	Cr.
19XX					19XX				
July	1		GJ1	30,000 00	July	1		GJ1	300 00
	15		GJ1	4,000 00		8		GJ1	100 00
		30,300*		34,000 00		16		GJ1	600 00
						21		GJ1	500 00
						25		GJ1	600 00
						28		GJ2	1,500 00
						29		GJ2	50 00
						29		GJ2	50 00
									3,700 00

Account: Accounts Receivable   **Account No. 112**

Date		Item	PR	Dr.	Date	Item	PR	Cr.
19XX								
July	23		GJ1	8000 00				

*This figure represents the balance of cash after taking the difference between the individual debit column ($34,000) and credit column ($3,700).

93

Account: Prepaid Rent   **Account No. 114**

Date	Item	PR	Dr.	Date	Item	PR	Cr.
19XX July 1		GJ1	30000				

Account: Office Supplies   **Account No. 116**

Date	Item	PR	Dr.	Date	Item	PR	Cr.
19XX July 8		GJ1	10000				

Account: Automobile   **Account No. 118**

Date	Item	PR	Dr.	Date	Item	PR	Cr.
19XX July 3		GJ1	300000				

Account: Office Equipment   **Account No. 120**

Date	Item	PR	Dr.	Date	Item	PR	Cr.
19XX July 1		GJ1	330000				

Account: Accounts Payable   **Account No. 230**

Date	Item	PR	Dr.	Date	Item	PR	Cr.
19XX July 28		GJ2	150000	19XX July 3	*1500*	GJ1	300000

Account: S. Katz Investment   **Account No. 340**

Date	Item	PR	Dr.	Date	Item	PR	Cr.
				19XX July 1		GJ1	33,30000

Account: S. Katz Withdrawal   **Account No. 342**

Date	Item	PR	Dr.	Date	Item	PR	Cr.
19XX July 21		GJ1	500 00				

Account: Commission Fees Earned   **Account No. 450**

Date	Item	PR	Dr.	Date	Item	PR	Cr.
				19XX July 15		GJ1	4,000 00
				23		GJ1	8,000 00
							12,000 00

Account: Office Salary Expense   **Account No. 560**

Date	Item	PR	Dr.	Date	Item	PR	Cr.
19XX July 16		GJ1	600 00				
25		GJ1	600 00				
			1,200 00				

Account: Advertising Expense   **Account No. 562**

Date	Item	PR	Dr.	Date	Item	PR	Cr.
19XX July 29		GJ2	50 00				

Account: Telephone Expense   **Account No. 564**

Date	Item	PR	Dr.	Date	Item	PR	Cr.
19XX July 29		GJ2	50 00				

In review, you should be able to:

1. Define and state the purpose of posting.
2. Identify the elements to be posted.
3. From journalized transactions, post to the general ledger.
4. Calculate account balances after postings.

LEARNING UNIT 10

Preparing the Trial Balance—
Step 4 of the Accounting Cycle

TRIAL BALANCE OF KATZ REAL ESTATE

The list of the individual accounts with their balances taken from the ledger is called a *trial balance.*

The following trial balance was developed from the ledger accounts of Katz Real Estate that were just posted to and balanced in Unit Interactor 9B. If information was journalized or posted incorrectly, you can be sure your trial balance will not be correct.

Notice that each account has been balanced. Remember, the balance of an account is placed on the side of the account with the largest total. For example, after summarizing the debits and credits cash has a balance of $30,300 (Dr.).

The following is the trial balance for Katz Real Estate:

Trial balance lists the accounts in the same order as in the ledger.

KATZ REAL ESTATE AGENCY
TRIAL BALANCE
July 31, 19XX

	Dr.	Cr.
Cash	30,300	
Accounts Receivable	8,000	
Prepaid Rent	300	
Office Supplies	100	
Automobile	3,000	
Office Equipment	3,300	
Accounts Payable		1,500
Shelly Katz Investment		33,300
Shelly Katz Withdrawal	500	
Commission Fees Earned		12,000
Office Salary Expense	1,200	
Advertising Expense	50	
Telephone Expense	50	
	46,800	46,800

The trial balance of Katz Real Estate shows that the sum of debits is equal to the sum of credits. The trial balance could be in balance and never show (1) a transaction that may have been omitted in the journalizing process, or (2) a transaction incorrectly analyzed and recorded in

The totals of a trial balance
can balance
and be <u>in</u>correct.

the journal. Let's take a look at a brief example of how a trial balance could be in balance, debits equal credits, but not contain correct amounts in each ledger account. If a journal entry should have been debit to cash and credit to accounts payable, but was recorded as debit to cash and credit to salaries payable, all will balance, but the analysis of transaction is incorrect. Salaries payable is too high and accounts payable too low, but total liabilities are correct. Obviously, it is of crucial importance to be accurate in the journalizing and posting process.

MINI REVIEW: WHAT TO DO IF A TRIAL BALANCE DOESN'T BALANCE

This is a crucial review; please read it slowly.

Once transactions are journalized and posted to the ledger, the next step in the accounting cycle is the preparation of a trial balance. To prepare the ledger for the trial balance:

1. Balance each account in the ledger.
2. List in the order of the ledger (for those with balances) the accounts with debit balances in the left column and credit balance accounts in the right side. (Assets, Liabilities, Owner's Equity, Revenue, Expense.)
3. The total of the debits should equal the total of the credits.
4. If the total amounts of debits and credits are not equal, the following should be considered:
   a. If the difference is 10, 100, 1,000, etc., you probably have made a mathematical error in addition.
   b. If the difference is equal to one individual account balance in the ledger, see if you didn't omit one by error. Possibly the figure was not posted from the general journal.
   c. Divide the difference by 2; then check to see if a debit should have been a credit and vice versa in the ledger or trial balance. Example: $150 difference ÷ 2 = $75. This means you may have placed a $75 as a debit to an account instead of a credit or vice versa.
   d. (a) Divide the difference by 9. If the quotient comes out even, this may mean a decimal point is out of place: $995.00 ⟶ $99.50. This is called a *slide*.
   (b) Divide the difference by 9. If the quotient comes out odd, check to see if digits have been transposed. For example, if the quotient is 27 ÷ 9 = 3, the difference of *transposition* (difference between transposed numbers) is 3. 14.55 ⟶ 41.55, the difference of 3.
   e. Compare the balances in the trial balance to the ledger accounts to check for copying errors.
   f. Check postings to see if omissions occurred.
   g. Take a coffee break before beginning again.

Correcting the trial balance:
what to do
if your trial balance
doesn't balance

UNIT INTERACTOR 10

From the following ledger accounts, balance each account as needed and prepare a trial balance for R. Duck as of October 31, 19XX. The information in the ledger has been posted from the general journal.

Cash 110	
5,000	150
780	1,200
600	400
	800

Equipment 140	
800	
2,200	

R. Duck Withdrawal 320	
400	

Accounts Receivable 120	
1,270	

Accounts Payable 210	
1,200	2,200

Service Revenue 410	
	780
	1,870

Supplies 130	
150	

R. Duck Investment 310	
	5,800

Operating Expenses 510	
800	

SOLUTION to Unit Interactor 10

R. DUCK
Trial Balance
October 31, 19XX

	Dr.	Cr.
Cash	3,830	
Accounts Receivable	1,270	
Supplies	150	
Equipment	3,000	
Accounts Payable		1,000
R. Duck Investment		5,800
R. Duck Withdrawal	400	
Service Revenue		2,650
Operating Expenses	800	
	9,450	9,450

In summary, you should be able to:

1. Balance ledger accounts and prepare, in proper form, a trial balance.
2. Analyze and correct a trial balance that doesn't balance.

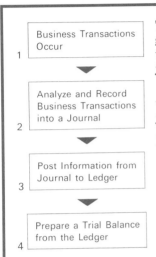

1 Business Transactions Occur

2 Analyze and Record Business Transactions into a Journal

3 Post Information from Journal to Ledger

4 Prepare a Trial Balance from the Ledger

The transactions of Katz Real Estate were analyzed and recorded in the general journal. This journal recorded the debit and credit portions of transactions. The titles that were used to record the information in the journal were obtained from the chart of accounts.

Once the transactions were journalized, the information in the journal was posted to the ledger. After the posting process was completed both the journal and ledger, contained the same information, but in different forms. Each account in the ledger of Katz was balanced. Then a list of the ledger was taken to arrive at a trial balance.

SUMMARY OF NEW ACCOUNTING LANGUAGE TERMS
Learning Unit 8

Accounting Cycle: For each accounting period, the process that begins with the recording of business transactions into a journal and ends with the completion of a post-closing trial balance.

Book of Final Entry: A place that receives information about business transactions from a book of original entry (a journal). Example: a ledger.

Book of Original Entry: A place that records the first formal information about business transactions. Example: a journal.

Compound Journal Entry: A journal entry that requires more than two accounts.

General Journal: The simplest form of a journal, which records information in chronological order. This journal links the debit and credit parts of transactions together.

Journal: A place where transactions are placed or recorded in chronological order before the ledger accounts are updated. The journal links the debit and credit parts of transactions together. The pages of a journal are in numerical order (p. 1, 2, 3, etc.) in contrast to a ledger that is set up based upon chart of accounts.

Journal Entry: The transaction (debits and credits) that is recorded into a journal once it is analyzed.

Journalizing: The process of recording a journal entry into the journal.

Trial Balance: An informal report that lists the ledger accounts and their balances in the ledger and that aids in proving the equality of debits and credits from the recording of transactions.

Withdrawal: A nonbusiness expense that results when an owner takes out money or other assets from a business for his own personal satisfaction.

Learning Unit 9

Cross-Reference: The process during posting of recording the account number of the ledger account in the PR column of the journal. The purpose of cross-referencing is to show which account the information on a specific line has been posted to.

Posting: The transferring, copying, or recording of information from a journal to a ledger.

Learning Unit 10

Slide: The error that results in adding or deleting zeros in the writing of a number. Example: 79200 $\longrightarrow$ 7920.

Transposition: The rearrangement of digits of a number by accident. Example: 152 $\longrightarrow$ 125.

QUESTION INTERACTORS

1. What steps of the accounting cycle were completed in Chapter 3?
2. Give four examples of source documents.
3. Why is a journal in chronological order?
4. What purpose(s) does a journal serve?
5. Define *journal entry, journalizing, book of original entry,* and *book of final entry.*
6. What is the relationship of the chart of accounts to the accounting cycle?
7. Give an example of a compound journal entry.
8. What is the difference between prepaid rent and rent expense?
9. Differentiate between a business expense and a withdrawal.
10. Define *posting.*
11. Posting is nothing more than copying the same information that was in a journal to the ledger. Agree or disagree?
12. What is meant by cross-reference?
13. How is an account balance calculated?
14. Give an example of a situation where a trial balance could balance but be incorrect.
15. Are the following statements true or false?
    a. A journal is the same as a ledger.
    b. Posting can only be completed monthly.
    c. Journal entries are entered in chronological order.
    d. In posting to a ledger the date, amount, and page number of journal are important.
    e. The posting reference (PR) column in the ledger tells the account number of the ledger account.
    f. In a journal, debits are to the left, closest to the date column, and credits are indented and listed below the debits.
    g. When supplies are purchased, they represent an asset; when they are used or consumed in the operations of a business, they become an expense.
    h. Rent paid in advance is an expense.
    i. The trial balance lists accounts in the same order as the ledger.

j. If an account has a zero balance, it still should always be listed in trial balance.

k. If the difference in the debit and credit total of a trial balance is divisible by two, a mathematical error may have been committed.

l. In the accrual basis of accounting revenue is earned, whether payment is received or not at the time the service is provided.

m. The trial balance is a formal report.

16. The trial balance is of more help in preparing financial statements than the expanded accounting equation. Please comment.

PROBLEM INTERACTORS

1. John Gibson decided to open up a Pet Care Center. This center would care for sick animals. The Pet Care Center opened for business on March 1, 19XX. The following transactions resulted:

MAR. 1: J. Gibson invested $15,000 in cash as well as $5,000 in equipment in the Pet Care Center.

1: Paid the Pet Care Center rent for two months *in advance* $500.

3: Purchased *on account* office equipment $2,000 from Phil Mahoney Stationery.

10: Purchased supplies $150 in cash from Ralph Suppliers.

12: Received $3,000 in cash from pet fees collected for the care of a rabbit.

18: Paid secretary salary $100.

20: John Gibson withdrew $200 for his personal use.

25: Paid cleaning expense $50.

28: Paid advertising expense $150.

29: Performed pet care work on a squirrel for $1,000; however, payment will not be received until April.

30: Paid Phil Mahoney Stationery one-half of amount owed from March 3 transaction.

Your task is to journalize the above transactions. The chart of accounts is as follows:

ASSETS	*REVENUE*
10 Cash	40 Earned Pet Fees
12 Accounts Receivable	
14 Prepaid Rent	
16 Office Supplies	
18 Office Equipment	

LIABILITIES	*EXPENSES*
20 Accounts Payable	50 Advertising Expense
	52 Salary Expense
	54 Cleaning Expense

OWNER'S EQUITY

30 J. Gibson Investment
32 J. Gibson Withdrawal

*2. Maureen DiAni, on May 1, 19XX, opened up the DiAni Beauty Salon. The following transactions occurred in May.

MAY 1: Maureen DiAni invested $10,000 into the beauty salon.
     1: Paid $200—May rent in advance.
     3: Purchased $500 of salon equipment from J. E. Moore on account.
     5: Received $500 cash for styling hair at a local convention.
     8: Purchased $250 of salon supplies for cash.
     9: Performed hair treatments for a local TV star $1,200, but will not receive payment until June.
    10: Paid salary of assistant $100.
    15: Maureen DiAni withdrew from the business $15 for her own personal use.
    28: Paid electrical expense $20.
    29: Paid telephone bill for May $15.

Your task is to:
a. Set up the ledger based upon the chart of accounts below.
b. Journalize the May transactions.
c. Post the journalized transactions to the ledger.
d. Foot and calculate the ledger account balance.
e. Prepare trial balance as of May 31, 19XX.
The chart of accounts of the DiAni Salon is as follows:

ASSETS	REVENUE
111 Cash	411 Salon Fees Earned
112 Accounts Receivable	
114 Prepaid Rent	
121 Beauty Supplies	
131 Salon Equipment	

LIABILITIES	EXPENSES
211 Accounts Payable	511 Electrical Expense
	521 Salary Expense
	531 Telephone Expense

OWNER'S EQUITY	
311 M. DiAni Investment	
321 M. DiAni Withdrawal	

*3. The following transactions occurred in June, 19XX, for the Dick Doherty Talent Agency.

JUNE 1: D. Doherty invested $500 cash into the talent agency.
1: Bought equipment on account $300.
3: Earned talent fees of $500, but payment from client will not be received until July.
5: Dick Doherty withdrew $50 for his own personal satisfaction.
7: Paid wage expense $100.
9: Placed a client on a local TV show, receiving in cash for talent fees $500.
15: Bought supplies for cash $100.
28: Paid telephone bill for June $25.
29: Paid advertising expense $200.
30: Paid wage expense $100.

The chart of accounts of the Dick Doherty Talent Agency is as follows:

ASSETS	OWNER'S EQUITY
110 Cash	310 D. Doherty Investment
120 Accounts Receivable	320 D. Doherty Withdrawal
130 Supplies	
140 Equipment	

LIABILITIES	REVENUE
210 Accounts Payable	410 Talent Fees Earned

	EXPENSES
	510 Wage Expense
	520 Telephone Expense
	530 Advertising Expense

Your task is to:
a. Set up the ledger based upon the chart of accounts.
b. Journalize the June transactions.
c. Post the journalized entries to the ledger.
d. Balance the ledger accounts.
e. Prepare a trial balance for June 30, 19XX.

ADDITIONAL PROBLEM INTERACTORS

1-A. Bob Flynn, who always wanted to open his own business, established the Flynn Roofing Company. The following transactions occurred in October, 19XX, the first month of operation.

OCT. 1: Bob Flynn invested $20,000 cash as well as $8,000 of roofing equipment in the business.
1: Paid the rent for three months in advance $300.
10: Purchased roofing supplies on account $200 from R. T. Suppliers (prepaid).
12: Purchased roofing equipment $1,000 in cash.

15: Received $5,000 in cash for completing a roofing contract.

18: Bob Flynn withdrew from the business $300 for his own personal use.

28: Paid advertising bill $300.

30: Completed roofing on new apartment complex $3,000. Payment will not be received until November.

30: Paid R. T. Suppliers one-half the amount owed from October 10 transaction.

Your task is to journalize the above transactions. The chart of accounts is as follows:

ASSETS	OWNER'S EQUITY
10 Cash	30 B. Flynn Investment
12 Accounts Receivable	32 B. Flynn Withdrawal
14 Prepaid Rent	
16 Roofing Supplies	
18 Roofing Equipment	

LIABILITIES	REVENUE
20 Accounts Payable	40 Earned Roofing Fees

	EXPENSES
	50 Advertising Expense

*2-A. Dave Adams carpentry shop is opened on August 1, 19XX. The chart of accounts for the carpentry shop is as follows:

ASSETS	REVENUE
110 Cash	410 Carpentry Fees Earned
112 Accounts Receivable	
115 Prepaid Rent	
120 Carpentry Supplies	
130 Carpentry Equipment	

LIABILITIES	EXPENSES
210 Accounts payable	510 Repair Expenses
	520 Utilities Expenses
	530 Advertising Expense

OWNER'S EQUITY	
310 D. Adams Investment	
320 D. Adams Withdrawal	

Your task is to:

a. Set up the ledger based on the chart of accounts.

b. Journalize the August transactions.

c. Post the journalized transactions to the ledger.

d. Foot and calculate the ledger account balances by footing.

e. Prepare the August 31, 19XX, trial balance.

AUG. 1: Dave Adams invested $5,000 in the carpentry shop.

1: Dave rented a garage for three months in advance $400.

3: Purchased $230 of carpentry supplies on account from J. B. Suppliers.

8: Purchased carpentry equipment for cash $800.

10: Received $50 cash from the refinishing of a kitchen table.

15: Dave Adams withdrew $50 from the business for his own personal use.

18: Completed the construction of a back porch for $500. Payment will not be received until September.

28: Paid repair expense for drill $15.

29: Paid utilities expense $20.

30: Paid advertising bill $55.

*3-A. The following is the chart of accounts for the Jim Corbett Plumbing Service.

ASSETS	OWNER'S EQUITY
110 Cash	310 J. Corbett Investment
115 Accounts Receivable	320 J. Corbett Withdrawals
130 Plumbing Supplies	
140 Plumbing Equipment	

LIABILITIES	REVENUE
210 Accounts Payable	410 Plumbing Fees Earned

	EXPENSES
	520 Advertising Expense
	530 Salary Expense
	540 Electrical Expense

The following transactions occurred in April:

19XX APR. 1: Jim Corbett invested $50 of plumbing equipment into the business.

5: Repaired a leaky faucet receiving $150 in cash.

8: Paid salary expense $50.

10: Bought plumbing supplies on account $15.

13: J. Corbett withdrew $10 from the business for his own personal use.

18: Paid electrical expense bill $55.

24: Repaired a kitchen sink on credit $40.

30: Paid advertising expense $15.

19XX APR. 30: Paid $5 as a down payment of amount owed from April 10 transaction.

Your task is to:

a. Set up a ledger based on the chart of accounts.
b. Journalize the April transactions.
c. Post the journal entries to the ledger.
d. Foot and calculate balances to the ledger accounts.
e. Prepare a trial balance as of April 30, 19XX.

CHALLENGE PROBLEM INTERACTOR

Below is a list of account balances of the Fender-Bender Auto Repair Shop for the year ended December 31, 19XX. (Accounts are in alphabetic order.)

a. Prepare a trial balance in proper *order* and form.
b. From the trial balance (in proper order) determine the following:
   1. Total assets as of 12-31-19XX.
   2. Ending owner's equity as of 12-31-19XX (as owner's equity would appear on the balance sheet.)

Accounts Payable	$ 9,300
Accounts Receivable	2,000
Advertising Expense	1,300
Andy Bender, Investment	26,000
Andy Bender, Withdrawals	5,000
Auto Repair Supplies	700
Building	25,000
Cash	1,500
Office Equipment	2,900
Prepaid Insurance	1,800
Property Tax Expense	2,300
Repair Equipment	3,400
Repair Service Revenue	16,700
Telephone Expense	500
Wages Expense	5,600

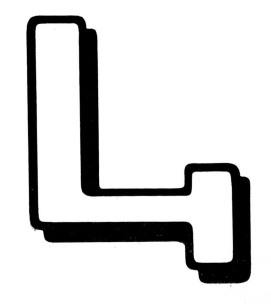

the
accounting cycle
continued

The last chapter presented steps 1 through 4 of the accounting cycle:

1. Business transactions occur
2. Analyze and record business transactions into a journal
3. Post or transfer information from journal to ledger
4. Prepare a trial balance

This chapter focuses on steps 5 and 6:

5. Prepare a worksheet
6. Prepare financial statements

Let's look at step 5, preparing a worksheet.

LEARNING UNIT 11

The Purpose of a Worksheet—
Step 5 of Cycle

The worksheet is not a formal report. The following columnar form is called a worksheet. Its purpose is to provide a "scratch pad" or "behind-the-scenes" device for aiding the accountant of Katz Real Estate in completing the accounting cycle.

KATZ REAL ESTATE AGENCY

Worksheet
For Month Ended July 31, 19XX

Account Titles	Trial Balance		Adjustments		Adjusted Trial Balance		Income Statement		Balance Sheet	
	Dr.	Cr.	Dr.	Cr.	Dr.	Cr.	Dr.	Cr.	Dr.	Cr.
Cash	3030000									
Accounts Receivable	800000									
Prepaid Rent	30000									
Office Supplies	10000									
Automobile	300000									
Office Equipment	330000									
Accounts Payable		150000								
S. Katz Investment		3330000								
S. Katz Withdrawal	50000									
Commission Fees Earned		1200000								
Office Salaries Expense	120000									
Advertising Expense	5000									
Telephone Expense	5000									
	4680000	4680000								

This worksheet *is not a formal report.* Compare it in your mind to the rough draft of a research paper. When the research paper is complete, in proper form (like a balance sheet), no one sees the "scrap paper" that made the final report possible. The worksheet helps the accountant find errors before financial statements are prepared.

COMPLETING THE WORKSHEET

THE HEADING. Notice in the worksheet for Katz Real Estate the heading:

Structure of a worksheet

Katz Real Estate Agency	(Name of company)
Worksheet	(Name of the working paper)
For Month Ended July 31, 19XX	(Date and the length of the accounting period represented by the worksheet)

THE TRIAL BALANCE COLUMNS. Since the accountant of Katz Real Estate does utilize a worksheet in completing the accounting cycle, he places the trial balance of Katz Real Estate directly on the worksheet and therefore there is no need to prepare a separate trial balance. Remember, the trial balance is also an informal report to check the recording accuracy of the ledger accounts. The accountant is careful in checking the trial balance, since an error at this stage of the worksheet will carry throughout.

Keep in mind that this trial balance is the same as we prepared in the last chapter.

THE ADJUSTMENTS COLUMN. In learning how to complete the adjustments column, let's first look at why Katz Real Estate would need each adjustment. Do not try to complete the adjustments column without knowing why. *WHY:* At the end of a period of time (a month, three months, a year)—in this case July 31 for Katz Real Estate—the accountant is concerned that some of the accounts making up the trial balance do not show up-to-date or proper amounts. The accounts of concern to the accountant are starred below.

The account balances that have to be brought up to date

Account Titles	Trial Balance	
	Dr.	Cr.
Cash	30,300	
Accounts Receivable	8,000	
*Prepaid Rent	300	
*Office Supplies	100	
*Automobile	3,000	
*Office Equipment	3,300	
Accounts Payable		1,500
Shelly Katz Investment		33,300
Shelly Katz Withdrawal	500	
Commission Fees Earned		12,000
*Office Salary Expense	1,200	
Advertising Expense	50	
Telephone Expense	50	
	46,800	46,800

Let's look at each account separately. After each one is analyzed, the worksheet will be reproduced to show how the adjustment column will help to update the trial balance.

Prepaid Rent

Back on July 1 the Katz Real Estate Agency paid three months rent in advance. The accountant realized that the rent expense would be $100 per month ($300 ÷ 3 months).

Remember, when the Katz Real Estate Agency paid in advance for the rent, it was considered to be an asset called prepaid rent. When the asset, prepaid rent, begins to expire or get used up, it becomes an expense. Now it is July 31, and one month's rent that was paid in advance has expired and thus becomes an expense.

The amount of rent expired is the adjustment figure used to update rent expense and prepaid rent.

Look at the above trial balance for prepaid rent. Should the account be $300, or is there really only $200 of prepaid rent left as of July 31? What will then be needed to bring prepaid rent to the "true" or up-to-date balance?

↑Rent Expense by $100.
↓Prepaid Rent by $100.

Let's summarize. If we *don't adjust* or bring our rent expense up to its proper amount:

1. Expenses for Katz Real Estate for July will be too low.
2. The asset prepaid rent will be too high.

The result is:

1. Income statement profit or net income will be too high.
2. Both sides of the balance sheet (assets and owner's equity) will be too high.

In terms of our mind-process chart, this adjustment would look as follows:

Accounts Affected	Category	↑ ↓	Rule
Rent Expense	Expense	↑	Dr.
Prepaid Rent	Asset	↓	Cr.

Let's see how we enter this adjustment on the worksheet.

Rent expense is listed below trial balance since it was not in original trial balance.

A. **1.** An increase in the expense Rent Expense of $100
2. A decrease in the asset Prepaid Rent of $100

KATZ REAL ESTATE AGENCY

Worksheet
For Month Ended July 31, 19XX

Account Titles	Trial Balance Dr.	Trial Balance Cr.	Adjustments Dr.	Adjustments Cr.	Adjusted Trial Balance Dr.	Adjusted Trial Balance Cr.
Cash	3030000					
Accounts Receivable	800000					
Prepaid Rent	30000			(A)10000		
Office Supplies	10000					
Automobile	300000					
Office Equipment	330000					
Accounts Payable		150000				
S. Katz Investment		3330000				
S. Katz Withdrawal	50000					
Commission Fees Earned		1200000				
Office Salaries Expense	120000					
Advertising Expense	5000					
Telephone Expense	5000					
	4680000	4680000				
Rent Expense			(A)10000			

In looking at the above worksheet trial balance, we see there is no account at present for rent expense. Therefore, below the account titles listed add the account rent expense. Place $100 in the debit side of the adjustment column on the same line as rent expense and place $100 in the credit side of the adjustment column on the same line as prepaid rent. Notice that the debit of $100 is equal to the credit of $100. Note the coding of each adjustment by a letter: (A) rent expense, (A) prepaid rent.

No matter how you slice the cake, unless the adjustment for prepaid rent takes place, both the income statement and balance sheet will be inaccurate. Our expenses on the income statement will be too low and our assets and owner's equity on the balance sheet will be too high. Keep in mind that there was no source document that stimulated the recording of a transaction for a prepaid rent expired—thus, the need for adjustment. Now let's look at another type of adjustment.

Office Supplies

At the end of July the accountant received information that of the $100 of office supplies purchased by Katz Real Estate on July 8 only $40 worth were left (or on hand) as of July 31.

Remember, when the supplies were purchased they were considered an asset. As the supplies get used up or consumed in the operation of the real estate firm, they become expenses. Let's look at office supplies:

The adjustment for supplies deals with the amount of supplies *used up*.

1. Office supplies $100
2. *Office supplies left $40* (July 31)—on hand
3. Office supplies used up or consumed $60 in the operation of the business for the month of July.

Therefore, the asset office supplies is really too high (it should be $40, not $100) on the trial balance. Meanwhile, if we don't show the additional expense of supplies used up, the net income of Katz Real Estate will be too high. Once again, no matter how you cut that cake, adjusting or bringing up to date the true amount of office supplies and office supplies expense is a must in showing accurate financial reports.

Let's summarize: If the adjustment to office supplies does not take place:

1. Expenses for July will be too low.
2. The asset office supplies will be too high.

The result is:

1. Income statement profit or net income will be too high.
2. Both sides of the balance sheet (assets and OE) will be too high.

Now let's look at the adjustment for office supplies in terms of the mind-process chart.

Accounts Affected	Category	↑ ↓	Rule
Office Supplies Expense	Expense	↑	Dr.
Office Supplies	Asset	↓	Cr.

Let's see how we enter this adjustment on the worksheet.

HOW TO ENTER ADJUSTMENT
FOR OFFICE SUPPLIES
ON WORKSHEET

B. **1.** An increase in office supplies expense $60
2. A decrease in office supplies of $60

The office supplies expense
indicates amount of supplies
used up.

Account Titles	Trial Balance Dr.	Trial Balance Cr.	Adjustments Dr.	Adjustments Cr.	Adjusted Trial Balance Dr.	Adjusted Trial Balance Cr.
		KATZ REAL ESTATE AGENCY				
		Worksheet				
		For Month Ended July 31, 19XX				
Cash	3030000					
Accounts Receivable	800000					
Prepaid Rent	30000			(A) 10000		
Office Supplies	10000			(B) 6000		
Automobile	300000					
Office Equipment	330000					
Accounts Payable		150000				
S. Katz Investment		3330000				
S. Katz Withdrawal	50000					
Commission Fees Earned		1200000				
Office Salary Expense	120000					
Advertising Expense	5000					
Telephone Expense	5000					
	4680000	4680000				
Rent Expense			(A) 10000			
Office Supplies Expense			(B) 6000			

Since the account office supplies expense is not listed in the account titles, we must list it below rent expense. Place $60 in debit side of the adjustment column on the same line as office supplies expense. Place $60 in the credit side of the adjustment column on the same line as office supplies. Notice that the total of the debit is equal to the total of the credit. Each adjustment is letter-coded.

Automobile

Historical cost will not change. In the beginning of July, Katz Real Estate bought an auto for $3,000. The automobile at the time of purchase was recorded in the journal as a debit of $3,000. This $3,000 represented the *historical* cost of this asset to the real estate agency. The historical cost is defined as the cost of the auto at the time when it is purchased by Katz Real Estate.

The car is expected to have a useful life of five years. The Katz accountant allocates (spreads) this cost of $3,000 over the limited life of the car's usefulness, so that the balance sheet will reflect a clearer picture of (1) the original cost (historical) of the equipment and (2) the amount of cost that has been allocated to an expense by the business.

There are many methods of calculating or estimating how much of the cost of the auto should be allocated or spread each day, month, year, etc. For our purpose, the cost of the auto will be allocated at the rate of $50 per month.

Notice how this is calculated:

$$\frac{\$3,000 \ (COST \ OF \ AUTO)}{5 \ YEARS \ (DURATION \ OF \ LIFE)} = \$600 \ PER \ YEAR$$
$$= \$600 \div 12 \ MONTHS = \$50 \ PER \ MONTH$$

Since a portion of the auto's usefulness expires each accounting period (as in the case of $50 per month), this cost represents an expense to Katz Real Estate. This spreading of the cost of the auto over its expected useful life is known as *depreciation*. Let's take a closer look at the concept of depreciation.

Remember, the auto helps create revenue for Katz Real Estate. Since we are trying to match earned revenue with incurred expenses, it is important to estimate on the income statement the *depreciation expense* that results from using or consuming part of the usefulness of the auto.

The double-entry system in accounting called for the sum of debits to equal the sum of credits. We have analyzed so far (1) a debit or increase to depreciation expense. But what about the credit? (2) When depreciation is recorded, Katz' accountant is crediting an account called *accumulated depreciation.** This account will accumulate, build up, or summarize the amount of depreciation that has been taken on the auto. Let's look at a mini section of a balance sheet.

ASSETS

1. Historical cost of auto is not changed	Auto	$3,000 (1)
	Less accumulated	
2. Amount of depreciation	depreciation	50 (2)
3. Unused amount of auto on Katz' books after first		$2,950 (3)

3. Unused amount of auto on Katz' books after first month's depreciation. This figure doesn't tell us what the resale of the car would bring. It shows the unused amount of the auto that will be depreciated in future years for future periods of time. Cost of the asset less its accumulated depreciation is often termed *book value,* sometimes called *carrying value.*

Accumulated depreciation is called a *contra asset.* It has the opposite balance of an asset. As accumulated depreciation ↑ (inc.) (credit), it will reflect the expired amount or amount of depreciation taken on the auto on Katz' accounting book.

Students often ask, "Why not debit depreciation expense and credit the auto?" "Why do you need accumulated depreciation?" The accumulated depreciation account allows us to answer the following questions:

1. What is the historical cost of the auto? ($3,000)
2. As of July 31, how much depreciation has been taken on the auto? ($50)

If the accumulated depreciation auto were not used and the auto account were credited, neither question 1 nor 2 could be answered. Let's see why.

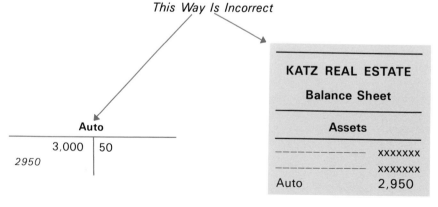

This Way Is Incorrect

The incorrect way shows
historical cost would be lost.

Auto

3,000	50
2950	

KATZ REAL ESTATE

Balance Sheet

Assets

———————	xxxxxxx
———————	xxxxxxx
Auto	2,950

* May be referred to as a *negative asset account.*

Notice that historical cost is the amount of the cost of auto at the time of purchase. If you look at the mini sections of the balance sheet, the cost of the auto would be $2,950. The users of the balance sheet *could not see* actual cost (historical cost) of the auto. They would see $2,950, not $3,000.

Now let's look at question 2. If you look at that mini balance sheet section, the only information it gives is that the auto unexpired amount of depreciation is $2,950 in Katz' accounting books. There is no place to see how much the auto has depreciated. *We need an accumulated depreciation account to see the relationship of the original or historical cost of the auto and the amount of depreciation that has been taken or accumulated over a period of time.*

In summary, the accumulated depreciation auto account deducts the amount of depreciation that has occurred or resulted from the original cost of equipment. The auto is an asset. The accumulated depreciation auto is a contra asset. An ↑ (inc.) asset (auto) is a debit. An ↑ (inc.) contra asset (accumulated depreciation—auto) is a credit. As accumulated depreciation auto increases, it really represents a ↓ (dec.) in the amount of the auto's usefulness remaining on the books of Katz Real Estate. Notice that cash is not involved in this or any adjustment. The way that depreciation indirectly affects cash is that:

Depreciation expense goes on the income statement, which results in

1. ↑ (inc.) total expenses,
2. less profit,
3. therefore, less to be paid in taxes.

Keep in mind:

1. COST OF AUTO	
− 2. ACCUMULATED DEPRECIATION—AUTO	
= 3. UNUSED AMOUNT OF AUTO ON ACCOUNTING BOOKS	

Before placing the adjustment for depreciation on the worksheet, let's see how the mind-process chart would appear.

Accounts Affected	Category	↑ ↓	Rule
Depreciation Expense—Auto	Expense	↑	Dr.
Accumulated Depreciation—Auto	Contra-Asset	↑	Cr.

Notice the historical cost
of the auto on the worksheet
has not been changed
($3,000).

C **1.** An increase in depreciation expense—auto
2. An increase in accumulated depreciation—auto

KATZ REAL ESTATE AGENCY

Worksheet
For Month Ended July 31, 19X

Account Titles	Trial Balance Dr.	Trial Balance Cr.	Adjustments Dr.	Adjustments Cr.	Adjus Ba Dr.
Cash	3030000				
Accounts Receivable	800000				
Prepaid Rent	30000			(A) 10000	
Office Supplies	10000			(B) 6000	
Automobile	300000				
Office Equipment	330000				
Accounts Payable		150000			
S. Katz Investment		3330000			
S. Katz Withdrawal	50000				
Commission Fees Earned		1200000			
Office Salary Expense	120000				
Advertising Expense	5000				
Telephone Expense	5000				
	4680000	4680000			
Rent Expense			(A) 10000		
Office Supplies Expense			(B) 6000		
Depreciation Expense—Auto			(C) 5000		
Acc. Dep.—Auto				(C) 5000	

Since both accounts depreciation expense—auto and accumulated depreciation—auto are not listed in the account titles, it is necessary to list both accounts below office supplies expense in the account titles column.

In the worksheet place $50 in the debit side of the adjustment column on the same line as depreciation expense—auto. Place $50 in the credit side of the adjustment column on the same line as accumulated depreciation—auto. Notice that the total of the debit is equal to the total of the credit.

Office Equipment

The cost of the office equipment is $3,300 on the books of Katz Real Estate. The accountant estimated the usefulness or limited life of the equipment to be five years. The cost of the office equipment would be allocated or spread as follows:

or

$$\frac{\$3{,}300 \ (COST \ OF \ OFFICE \ EQUIPMENT)}{5 \ YEARS} = \$660 \ PER \ YEAR$$

$$\frac{\$660 \ PER \ YEAR}{12 \ MONTHS} = \$55 \ PER \ MONTH.$$

Since the explanation of office equipment is quite similar to that for the auto, we can keep it brief.

As with the auto, when depreciation is taken, two things happen for the month of July:

1. $55 (inc.)↑ depreciation expense—office equipment
2. $55 (inc.)↑ accumulated depreciation—office equipment

The entry for depreciation *does not* directly affect cash. It will help reduce amount of taxes owed.

Notice that the auto and the office equipment have separate depreciation expense accounts as well as accumulated depreciation.

Auto	*Office Equipment*
Depreciation Expense—Auto	*Depreciation Expense—Office Equipment*
Accumulated Depreciation—Auto	*Accumulated Depreciation—Office Equipment*

Why? To identify specific information such as historical cost and accumulated depreciation for each item.

D. **1.** An increase in depreciation expense—office equipment
   2. An increase in accumulated depreciation—office equipment

Before placing the adjustment for depreciation on the worksheet, let's look at how the mind-process chart would appear.

Accounts Affected	Category	↑ ↓	Rule
Depreciation Expense—Office Equipment	Expense	↑	Dr.
Accumulated Depreciation—Office Equipment	Contra-Asset	↑	Cr.

Notice the historical cost of the office equipment has not been changed ($3,300).

KATZ REAL ESTATE AGENCY

Worksheet

For Month Ended July 31, 19XX

Account Titles	Trial Balance Dr.	Trial Balance Cr.	Adjustments Dr.	Adjustments Cr.	Adjusted T Balance Dr.
Cash	3030000				
Accounts Receivable	800000				
Prepaid Rent	30000			(A) 10000	
Office Supplies	10000			(B) 6000	
Automobile	300000				
Office Equipment	330000				
Accounts Payable		150000			
S. Katz Investment		3330000			
S. Katz Withdrawal	50000				
Commission Fees Earned		1200000			
Office Salary Expense	120000				
Advertising Expense	5000				
Telephone Expense	5000				
	4680000	4680000			
Rent Expense			(A) 10000		
Office Supplies Expense			(B) 6000		
Dep. Exp.—Auto			(C) 5000		
Acc. Dep.—Auto				(C) 5000	
Dep. Exp.—Office Equipment			(D) 5500		
Acc. Dep.—Office Equipment				(D) 5500	

Since both accounts depreciation expense—office equipment and accumulated depreciation—office equipment are not listed in the account titles, it is necessary to list both accounts below accumulated depreciation—auto in the account titles column. In the above worksheet, place $55 in the debit side of the adjustment column on the same line as depreciation expense—office equipment. Place $55 in the credit side of the adjustment column on the same line as accumulated depreciation—office equipment. Notice that the total of the debit is equal to the total of the credit.

Now let's look at the last adjustment for Katz Real Estate.

Salaries

The Katz Real Estate Agency in July paid $1,200 in office salary expenses (see trial balance of any previous worksheet in chapter).

On July 25 the last salary checks were paid. Since we are concerned with information as of July 31, our goal is to update the office salary expense. What is the true office salary expense for July? Is it $1,200?

During the days of July 28, 29, 30, 31, John Murray worked for the real estate office, but his next payment or paycheck is not due until August. For these four days he earned $180. The question is whether this $180 is an expense to the real estate firm in July before the salary expense is paid. Should the expense for office salary for John Murray be shown as an expense to Katz Real Estate in August when it is due and paid?

Remember back to the matching principle. We continuously try to match earned revenue with expenses that resulted in earning those revenues. In this case, by working those four days, John Murray was able to create some real estate revenues in July. Although John will not be paid until August, it is important to show his office salary expense in July, when the revenue was earned. The results are:

1. ↑ office salaries expense $180
2. ↑ salaries payable $180

In effect, we have shown the true expense for salaries $1,380 instead of $1,200.

Office Salaries Expense

| 1,200 | |
| 180 | |

An expense can be incurred without being paid in the accrual basis of accounting as long as it has helped in creating earned revenue for a period of time.

Katz Real Estate has increased a liability called salaries payable, indicating that the firm owes money for salaries.

Next month when the firm pays John Murray, it will reduce its liability, salaries payable, as well as decrease its cash.

Remember, although Katz Real Estate does not pay cash for this expense until August (the next payroll), it is an expense in the month that it resulted in the earning of real estate revenue. Remember back to the accrual basis: an expense may result even if unpaid or not yet due.

E. **1.** An increase in office salaries expense $180
    2. An increase in salaries payable $180

    In terms of the mind-process chart, the following could be constructed:

Accounts Affected	Category	↑ ↓	Rule
Office Salaries Expense	Expense	↑	Dr.
Salaries Payable	Liability	↑	Cr.

KATZ REAL ESTATE AGENCY

Worksheet
For Month Ended July 31, 19XX

Account Titles	Trial Balance Dr.	Trial Balance Cr.	Adjustments Dr.	Adjustments Cr.	Adjusted Balance Dr.
Cash	30 300 00				
Accounts Receivable	8 000 00				
Prepaid Rent	300 00			(A) 100 00	
Office Supplies	100 00			(B) 60 00	
Automobile	3 000 00				
Office Equipment	3 300 00				
Accounts Payable		1 500 00			
S. Katz Investment		33 300 00			
S. Katz Withdrawal	500 00				
Commission Fees Earned		12 000 00			
Office Salary Expense	1 200 00		(E) 180 00		
Advertising Expense	50 00				
Telephone Expense	50 00				
	46 800 00	46 800 00			
Rent Expense			(A) 100 00		
Office Supplies Expense			(B) 60 00		
Dep. Exp.—Auto			(C) 50 00		
Acc. Dep.—Auto				(C) 50 00	
Dep. Exp.—Office Equipment			(D) 55 00		
Acc. Dep.—Office Equipment				(D) 55 00	
Salaries Payable				(E) 180 00	

Since the account office salaries expense is already listed in the account titles, place $180 on the debit side of the adjustment column on the same line as office salaries expense. Since salaries payable is not listed in the account titles, add the account title salaries payable below accumulated depreciation—office equipment. Place $180 in the credit side of the adjustment column on the same line as salaries payable. Remember, salaries payable is a liability. Notice below that adding the debit column of the adjustment column (445) and the credit column (445) helps prove the accuracy of your math. Remember, if the analysis is incorrect, the adjustment column totals could be correct, but the answer incorrect.

After completing each two columns of a worksheet, be sure to total the columns.

KATZ REAL ESTATE AGENCY

Worksheet

For Month Ended July 31, 19XX

Account Titles	Trial Balance Dr.	Trial Balance Cr.	Adjustments Dr.	Adjustments Cr.	Adjusted Balance Dr.
Cash	3030000				
Accounts Receivable	800000				
Prepaid Rent	30000			(A) 10000	
Office Supplies	10000			(B) 6000	
Automobile	300000				
Office Equipment	330000				
Accounts Payable		150000			
S. Katz Investment		3330000			
S. Katz Withdrawal	50000				
Commission Fees Earned		1200000			
Office Salaries Expense	120000		(E) 18000		
Advertising Expense	5000				
Telephone Expense	5000				
	4680000	4680000			
Rent Expense			(A) 10000		
Office Supplies Expense			(B) 6000		
Dep. Exp.—Auto			(C) 5000		
Acc. Dep.—Auto				(C) 5000	
Dep. Exp.—Office Equipment			(D) 5500		
Acc. Dep.—Office Equipment				(D) 5500	
Salaries Payable				(E) 18000	
			44500	44500	

THE ADJUSTED TRIAL BALANCE COLUMN. Completing the adjusted trial balance columns represents the process of summarizing the information that has been placed in the trial balance as well as the adjustment columns.

The following chart is a tool for you to use to see how the balance of each account is carried over to the adjusted trial balance on the worksheet. This chart is strictly a teaching tool and is not part of the formal accounting process.

Account Titles	(1) Account Balance on Trial Balance	Balance Dr. Cr.	(2) Change Adjustment Column Inc. ↑/Dec. ↓ No Change	Balance of Account on Adjusted Trial Balance (1) + (2) = (3)* Dr.	Cr.
Cash	30,300	Dr.		30,300	
Accounts Receivable	8,000	Dr.		8,000	
Prepaid Rent	300	Dr.	↓100 Cr.	200	
Office Supplies	100	Dr.	↓ 60 Cr.	40	
Automobile	3,000	Dr.		3,000	
Office Equipment	3,300	Dr.		3,300	
Accounts Payable	1,500	Cr.			1,500
S. Katz Investment	33,300	Cr.			33,300
S. Katz Withdrawal	500	Dr.		500	
Commission Fees Earned	12,000	Cr.			12,000
Office Salary Expense	1,200	Dr.	↑180 Dr.	1,380	
Advertising Expense	50	Dr.		50	
Telephone Expense	50	Dr.		50	
Rent Expense			↑100 Dr.	100	
Office Supplies Expense			↑ 60 Dr.	60	
Dep. Exp.—Auto			↑ 50 Dr.	50	
Acc. Dep.—Auto			↑ 50 Cr.		50
Dep. Exp.—Office Equipment			↑ 55 Dr.	55	
Acc. Dep.—Office Equipment			↑ 55 Cr.		55
Salaries Payable			↑180 Cr.		180

*Two debits are added together; two credits are added together; for a debit and a credit—the difference is taken.

The information on the chart, when carried over to the worksheet, looks as follows:

KATZ REAL ESTATE AGENCY

Worksheet

For Month Ended July 31, 19XX

Account Titles	Trial Balance Dr.	Trial Balance Cr.	Adjustments Dr.	Adjustments Cr.	Adjusted Trial Balance Dr.	Adjusted Trial Balance Cr.	Income Dr.
Cash	3030000				3030000		
Accounts Receivable	800000				800000		
Prepaid Rent	30000			(A) 10000	20000		
Office Supplies	10000			(B) 6000	4000		
Automobile	300000				300000		
Office Equipment	330000				330000		
Accounts Payable		150000				150000	
S. Katz Investment		3330000				3330000	
S. Katz Withdrawal	50000				50000		
Commission Fees Earned		1200000				1200000	
Office Salary Expense	120000		(E) 18000		138000		
Advertising Expense	5000				5000		
Telephone Expense	5000				5000		
	4680000	4680000					
Rent Expense			(A) 10000		10000		
Office Supplies Expense			(B) 6000		6000		
Dep. Exp.—Auto			(C) 5000		5000		
Acc. Dep.—Auto				(C) 5000		5000	
Dep. Exp.—Office Equipment			(D) 5500		5500		
Acc. Dep.—Office Equipment				(D) 5500		5500	
Salaries Payable				(E) 18000		18000	
			44500	44500	4708500	4708500	

When the columns are added, notice that the sum of debits is equal to the sum of credits ($47,085).

THE INCOME STATEMENTS AND BALANCE SHEET COLUMNS.
Before we attempt to fill out the last four columns of the worksheet, it
is important to review (1) what accounts are listed in an income statement, (2) what accounts are listed in a balance sheet, and (3) how a new
figure is calculated for owner's equity. *Remember, the new figure for OE
will be used when the balance sheet statement is prepared.*

To answer the first two points, the following table is constructed
for your convenience:

Do not try to memorize
this chart.
Use it as a reference.

Account Titles	Category	Usual* Balance	Income Statement Dr.	Income Statement Cr.	Balance Sheet Dr.	Balance Sheet Cr.
Cash	Asset	Dr.			X	
Accounts Receivable	Asset	Dr.			X	
Prepaid Rent	Asset	Dr.			X	
Office Supplies	Asset	Dr.			X	
Automobile	Asset	Dr.			X	
Office Equipment	Asset	Dr.			X	
Accounts Payable	Liability	Cr.				X
S. Katz Investment	Owner's Equity	Cr.				X
S. Katz Withdrawal	Withdraw (OE)	Dr.			X	
Commission Fees Earned	Revenue	Cr.		X		
Office Salary Expense	Expense	Dr.	X			
Advertising Expense	Expense	Dr.	X			
Telephone Expense	Expense	Dr.	X			
Rent Expense	Expense	Dr.	X			
Office Supplies Expense	Expense	Dr.	X			
Depreciation Expense—Auto	Expense	Dr.	X			
Accumulated Depreciation—Auto	Contra-Asset	Cr.				X
Depreciation Expense—Office Equipment	Expense	Dr.	X			
Accumulated Depreciation—Office Equipment	Contra-Asset	Cr.				X
Salaries Payable	Liability	Cr.				X

*For example, the difference between the debits and credits of cash *usually* results in a debit balance.

As for the third point, keep in mind the following:

Owner's Equity
BEGINNING OWNER'S INVESTMENT
+ NET INCOME   (REVENUES − EXPENSES)
− WITHDRAWALS
= ENDING OWNER'S INVESTMENT

Now let's look at the income statement columns.

KATZ REAL ESTATE AGENCY

Worksheet
For Month Ended July 31, 19XX

Account Titles	Adjusted Trial Balance Dr.	Cr.	Income Statement Dr.	Cr.	Balanc Dr.
Cash	3030000				
Accounts Receivable	800000				
Prepaid Rent	20000				
Office Supplies	4000				
Automobile	300000				
Office Equipment	330000				
Accounts Payable		150000			
S. Katz Investment		3330000			
S. Katz Withdrawal	50000				
Commission Fees Earned		1200000		1200000	
Office Salary Expense	138000		138000		
Advertising Expense	5000		5000		
Telephone Expense	5000		5000		
Rent Expense	10000		10000		
Office Supplies Expense	6000		6000		
Dep. Exp.—Auto	5000		5000		
Acc. Dep.—Auto		5000			
Dep. Exp.—Office Expense*	5500		5500		
Acc. Dep.—Office Expense*		5500			
Salaries Payable		18000			
	4708500	4708500	174500	1200000	
Net Income			1025500		
			1200000	1200000	

*Notice that accumulated depreciation and salaries payable do not go on the income statement. Accumulated depreciation is a contra-asset found on the balance sheet. Salaries payable is a liability found on the balance sheet.

Notice that the revenue of $12,000 and all the individual expenses are listed in the income statement columns. The revenue, since it has a credit balance, is placed in the credit column of the income statement columns and the expenses, debit balances, are placed in the debit side of the income statement columns. Once the debits and credits are placed in the columns, you should:

1. Total the debits and credits.
2. Show the balance between the debit and credit columns.
3. Total the columns.

	Dr.		Cr.	
Total Expenses	1,745.00	12,000.00	Total Revenue
Net Income	10,255.00		
	12,000.00	12,000.00	

The difference between $12,000 Cr. and $1,745 Dr. indicates a net income of $10,255. Record the $10,255 on the debit column, so as to balance the debit and credit columns. Notice in the above worksheet* that the label net income is added in the account title column on the same line as the $10,255. Net income $10,255 is placed in the debit column of the income statement column of the worksheet. The $12,000 total indicates that the two columns are in balance.

Now let's conclude the preparation of the worksheet by filling out the balance sheet columns. Keep in mind how new owner's investment results

(A)	BEGINNING OWNER'S INVESTMENT
(B)	+ NET INCOME
(C)	− WITHDRAWALS
(D)	= NEW OR ENDING OWNER'S INVESTMENT†

Notice in the following part of the worksheet how the accounts are carried to the balance sheet columns from the adjusted trial balance columns. Notice that the figure of $10,255 was carried over from the income statement columns.

* When there is a net income, it will be placed in the debit columns of the income statement section of the worksheet. If you had a net loss, it would be placed in the credit side.
† Notice that item D is not found on the worksheet.

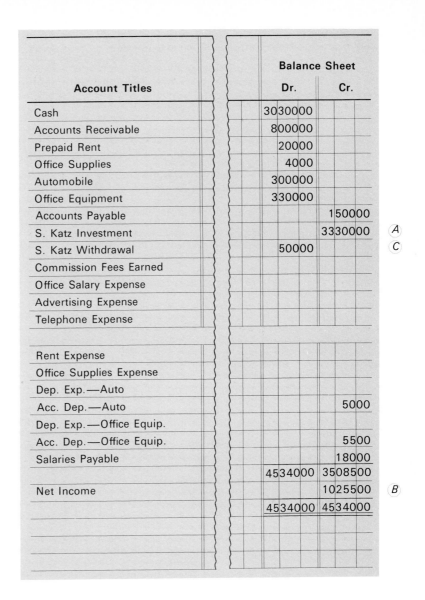

Account Titles	Balance Sheet Dr.	Balance Sheet Cr.	
Cash	3030000		
Accounts Receivable	800000		
Prepaid Rent	20000		
Office Supplies	4000		
Automobile	300000		
Office Equipment	330000		
Accounts Payable		150000	
S. Katz Investment		3330000	A
S. Katz Withdrawal	50000		C
Commission Fees Earned			
Office Salary Expense			
Advertising Expense			
Telephone Expense			
Rent Expense			
Office Supplies Expense			
Dep. Exp.—Auto			
Acc. Dep.—Auto		5000	
Dep. Exp.—Office Equip.			
Acc. Dep.—Office Equip.		5500	
Salaries Payable		18000	
	4534000	3508500	
Net Income		1025500	B
	4534000	4534000	

On the balance sheet column of the worksheet notice:

The one figure $43,055 for ending investment is not found on the worksheet.

Credit Column	(A)	BEGINNING OWNER'S INVESTMENT		$33,300
Credit Column	(B)	+ NET INCOME (CARRIED OVER FROM STATEMENT COLUMNS)		10,255
				43,555
Debit Column	(C)	− WITHDRAWAL		500
	(D)	= ENDING OWNER'S INVESTMENT		$43,055

This worksheet doesn't contain the ending figure for owner's investment; therefore, notice how the accountant is able to pull the information from the worksheet. Remember, the worksheet is a tool for gathering information to complete the accounting cycle. It is not a formal report.

Look carefully at S. Katz Investment $33,300, S. Katz Withdrawal $500, and Net Income of $10,255. Do you understand how ending investment will be calculated?

THE COMPLETED WORKSHEET

In summary, the following is the completed worksheet of the Katz Real Estate Agency.

KATZ REAL ESTATE AGENCY
Worksheet
For Month Ended July 31, 19XX

Account Titles	Trial Balance Dr.	Trial Balance Cr.	Adjustments Dr.	Adjustments Cr.	Adjusted Trial Balance Dr.	Adjusted Trial Balance Cr.	Income Statement Dr.	Income Statement Cr.	Balance Sheet Dr.	Balance Sheet Cr.
Cash	3030000				3030000				3030000	
Accounts Receivable	800000				800000				800000	
Prepaid Rent	30000			(A)10000	20000				20000	
Office Supplies	10000			(B) 6000	4000				4000	
Automobile	300000				300000				300000	
Office Equipment	330000				330000				330000	
Accounts Payable		150000				150000				150000
S. Katz Investment		3330000				3330000				3330000
S. Katz Withdrawal	50000				50000				50000	
Commission Fees Earned		1200000				1200000		1200000		
Office Salary Expense	120000		(E)18000		138000		138000			
Advertising Expense	5000				5000		5000			
Telephone Expense	5000				5000		5000			
	4680000	4680000								
Rent Expense			(A)10000		10000		10000			
Office Supplies Expense			(B) 6000		6000		6000			
Dep. Exp.—Auto			(C) 5000		5000		5000			
Acc. Dep.—Auto				(C) 5000		5000				5000
Dep. Exp.—Office Equipment			(D) 5500		5500		5500			
Acc. Dep.—Office Equipment				(D) 5500		5500				5500
Salaries Payable				(E)18000		18000				18000
			44500	44500	4708500	4708500	174500	1200000	4534000	3508500
Net Income							1025500			1025500
							1200000	1200000	4534000	4534000

Remember, this worksheet aids the accountant in recording, classifying, and accumulating information about each account. Now, before preparing the financial statements from the worksheet, let's review. At this point you should be able to:

1. Define and state the purpose of a worksheet.
2. Differentiate between a formal report and a worksheet.
3. Prepare a worksheet from (1) accounts in the ledger and (2) adjustment data received.

UNIT INTERACTOR 11

Here is a trial balance. Fill out the worksheet, assuming the needed adjustments are:

1. Depreciation expense—store equipment	$1.00
2. Insurance expired	1.00
3. Supplies used up	3.00
4. Wages owed, but not paid for	2.00
(they are an expense in the old year)	

Remember, take your time. This interactor tests your ability to handle each account individually. If you have been memorizing, go back to the learning unit you have just completed to analyze the whys of handling each account. This interactor uses small numbers to simplify calculations.

J. ROFF

Trial Balance
December 31, 19XX

	Dr.	Cr.
Cash	10	
Accounts Receivable	2	
Prepaid Insurance	3	
Store Supplies	4	
Store Equipment	7	
Acc. Dep.—Store Equipment		4
Accounts Payable		1
J. Roff Investment		15
J. Roff Withdrawal	2	
Revenue from Clients		18
Rent Expense	2	
Wage Expense	8	
Total	38	38

SOLUTION to Unit Interactor **11**

J. ROFF
Worksheet
For Month Ended December 31, 19XX

Account Titles	Trial Balance Dr.	Trial Balance Cr.	Adjustments Dr.	Adjustments Cr.	Adjusted Trial Balance Dr.	Adjusted Trial Balance Cr.	Income Statement Dr.	Income Statement Cr.	Balance Sheet Dr.	Balance Sheet Cr.
Cash	1000				1000				1000	
Accounts Receivable	200				200				200	
Prepaid Insurance	300			(B)100	200				200	
Store Supplies	400			(C)300	100				100	
Store Equipment	700				700				700	
Acc. Dep.—Store Equipment		400		(A)100		500				500
Accounts Payable		100				100				100
J. Roff Investment		1500				1500				1500
J. Roff Withdrawal	200				200				200	
Revenue from Clients		1800				1800		1800		
Rent Expense	200				200		200			
Wage Expense	800		(D)200		1000		1000			
	3800	3800								
Dep. Exp.—Equipment			(A)100		100		100			
Insurance Expense			(B)100		100		100			
Supplies Expense			(C)300		300		300			
Wages Payable				(D)200		200				200
			700	700	4100	4100	1700	1800	2400	2300
Net Income							100			100
							1800	1800	2400	2400

132

Preparation of the Financial Statements from the Worksheet— Step 6 of Cycle

THE INCOME STATEMENT

KATZ REAL ESTATE AGENCY

Worksheet

For Month Ended July 31, 19XX

Account Titles	Trial Balance Dr.	Trial Balance Cr.	Adjustments Dr.	Adjustments Cr.	Adjusted Trial Balance Dr.	Adjusted Trial Balance Cr.	Income Statement Dr.	Income Statement Cr.	Balance Sheet Dr.	Balance Sheet Cr.
Commission Fees Earned		1200000				1200000		1200000		
Office Salaries Expense	120000		(E) 18000		138000		138000			
Advertising Expense	5000				5000		5000			
Telephone Expense	5000				5000		5000			
	4680000	4680000								
Rent Expense			(A) 10000		10000		10000			
Office Supplies Expense			(B) 6000		6000		6000			
Dep. Exp.—Auto			(C) 5000		5000		5000			
Acc. Dep.—Auto				(C) 5000		5000				5000
Dep. Exp.—Office Equipment			(D) 5500		5500		5500			
Acc. Dep.—Office Equipment				(D) 5500		5500				5500
Salaries Payable				(E) 18000		18000				18000
			44500	44500	4708500	4708500	174500	1200000	4534000	3508500
Net Income							1025500			1025500
							1200000	1200000	4534000	4534000

The information above has been taken from the Katz worksheet. The reason the top portion of the worksheet is being omitted is that we are concerned first with preparing the income statement, and so our attention focuses on the income statement columns of the worksheet. The following income statement was prepared by the Katz Real Estate accountant.

The income statement
columns of a worksheet
contain the information
to prepare
an income statement.

KATZ REAL ESTATE AGENCY

Income Statement

For Month Ended July 31, 19XX

Revenue:		
Commission Fees Earned		$12,000
Less Expenses:		
Office Salaries Expense	$1,380	
Advertising Expense	50	
Telephone Expense	50	
Rent Expense	100	
Office Supplies Expense	60	
Depreciation Expense—Auto	50	
Depreciation Expense—Office Equipment	55	
Total Expenses		1,745
Net Income		$10,255

Remember, all the information was obtained from the income statement columns of the worksheet. The net income figure of $10,255 is also found at the bottom of the income statement column of the worksheet. The worksheet provided the needed information to construct the income statement.

THE BALANCE SHEET

Account Titles	Adjusted Trial Balance Dr.	Cr.	Income Statement Dr.	Cr.	Balance Sheet Dr.	Cr.
Cash	3030000				3030000	
Accounts Receivable	800000				800000	
Prepaid Rent	20000				20000	
Office Supplies	4000				4000	
Automobile	300000				300000	
Office Equipment	330000				330000	
Accounts Payable		150000				150000
S. Katz Investment		3330000				3330000
S. Katz Withdrawal	50000				50000	
Commission Fees Earned		1200000		1200000		
Office Salary Expense	138000		138000			
Advertising Expense	5000		5000			
Telephone Expense	5000		5000			
Rent Expense	10000		10000			
Office Supplies Expense	6000		6000			
Depreciation Expense—Auto	5000		5000			
Acc. Dep.—Auto		5000				5000
Dep. Exp.—Office Equipment	5500		550C			
Acc. Dep.—Office Equipment		5500				5500
Salaries Payable		18000				18000
	4708500	4708500	174500	1200000	4534000	3508500
Net Income			1025500			1025500
			1200000	1200000	4534000	4534000

The following balance sheet was prepared from the worksheet. Notice above how the net income will be used (brought over on the worksheet) to increase owner's investment.

KATZ REAL ESTATE AGENCY

Balance Sheet
July 31, 19XX

Assets			Liabilities and Owner's Equity		
Cash		$30,300	Liabilities		
Accounts Receivable		8,000	Accounts Payable	$1,500	
Prepaid Rent		200	Salaries Payable	180	
Office Supplies		40	Total Liabilities		$ 1,680
Auto (at cost)	$3,000				
Less Accumulated			Owner's Equity		
Depreciation	50	2,950	S. Katz Investment		
Office Equipment			7/1/XX	$33,300	
(at cost)	3,300		Net Income		
Less Accumulated			for July	10,255	
Depreciation	55	3,245	Less S. Katz		
			Withdrawal	(500)	
			S. Katz Investment		
			7/31/XX		43,055
			Total Liabilities and		
Total Assets		$44,735	Owner's Equity		$44,735

The figure for total assets $44,735 is <u>not</u> found on the worksheet.

Remember, all the above information comes from the balance sheet column of the worksheet except the total $44,735.* Notice how accumulated depreciation is kept separate for auto and office equipment. This balance sheet reflects the financial status of Katz Real Estate as of July 31 (or a particular date).

At this point you should be able to:

1. Prepare an income statement from a worksheet.
2. Prepare a balance sheet from a worksheet.

---

* The $44,735 is not on the worksheet because of the balance sheet statement that: (1) Accumulated depreciation is being placed with $2,950 auto, $3,245 office equipment. One figure summarizes the unexpired portions of auto and equipment. (2) Withdrawals is being placed as part of owner's equity.

Some students feel that if the total for the assets on the balance sheet is different from that on the worksheet, there is an error. This is not true. The worksheet supplies the needed figures. The accountant then utilizes these figures to prepare the statement.

Now see whether you can prepare, in proper form, an income statement and balance sheet from the information below.

HOWARD'S DELI

Worksheet

For Month Ended December 31, 19XX

Account Titles	Trial Balance Dr.	Trial Balance Cr.	Adjustments Dr.	Adjustments Cr.	Adj. Trial Balance Dr.	Adj. Trial Balance Cr.	Income Statement Dr.	Income Statement Cr.	Balance Sheet Dr.	Balance Sheet Cr.
Cash	260000								260000	
Supplies	425000			(A) 225000					200000	
Prepaid Insurance	52000			(B) 4000					48000	
Equipment	1200000								1200000	
Acc. Dep.—Equipment		380000		(C) 9500						389500
H. Wells Investment		1064000								1064000
H. Wells Withdrawal	60000								60000	
Deli Fees		1335000						1335000		
Wages Expense	612000		(D) 36000				648000			
Miscellaneous Expense	170000						170000			
	2779000	2779000								
Supplies Expense			(A) 225000				225000			
Insurance Expense			(B) 4000				4000			
Dep. Exp.—Equipment			(C) 9500				9500			
Wages Payable				(D) 36000						36000
			274500	274500			1056500	1335000	1768000	1489500
Net Income							278500			278500
							1335000	1335000	1768000	1768000

SOLUTION to Unit Interactor **12**

HOWARD'S DELI

Income Statement

For Month Ended December 31, 19XX

Revenue:		
Deli Fees		$13,350
Less Expenses:		
Wages Expense	$6,480	
Supplies Expense	2,250	
Depreciation Expense—Equipment	95	
Insurance Expense	40	
Miscellaneous Expense	1,700	
Total Expenses		10,565
Net Income		$ 2,785

HOWARD'S DELI

Balance Sheet
December 31, 19XX

Assets			Liabilities and Owner's Equity		
			Liabilities		
Cash		$ 2,600	Wages Payable		$ 360
Supplies		2,000			
Prepaid Insurance		480			
Equipment	$12,000		Owner's Equity*		
Less Accumulated			H. Wells		
Depreciation	3,895	8,105	Investment		
			12/1/XX	$10,640	
			Net Income $2,785		
			Less		
			Withdrawals (600)	2,185	
			H. Wells		
			Investment		
			12/31/XX		12,825
			Total Liabilities and		
Total Assets		$13,185	Owner's Equity		$13,185

*The use of three columns in owner's equity is *another* way of lining up the figures. (On page 135 we used only two columns. The end result will not change.)

THE ACCOUNTING CYCLE CONTINUED—A BLUEPRINT

5 — Prepare a Worksheet

6 — Prepare Financial Statements

In an attempt to complete the accounting cycle in an efficient manner, we constructed a worksheet for Katz Real Estate. This worksheet was prepared two columns at a time. After each two columns were completed, they were totaled to make sure they balanced. Once adjustments were entered on the worksheet, both the debit and credit columns were added. The original trial balance columns, updated by the adjustments column, gave us the needed data to complete the adjusted trial balance columns.

The last four columns of the worksheet saw data being placed in the income statement and or balance sheet columns. The revenue and expenses were in the income statement columns, and assets, liabilities, withdrawals, and beginning owner investment were listed in the balance sheet columns.

The income statement was prepared from the income statement columns of the worksheet. The net income found on the worksheet will also be the same on the formal income statement.

In the preparation of the balance sheet, the worksheet did not provide the one ending figure for owner's equity; therefore, from the worksheet the beginning owner's equity, net income, and withdrawals were calculated to show on the balance sheet the ending investment.

The worksheet did contain all the needed information to prepare financial statements, although the information for the balance sheet required a working knowledge of where and how to place figures on the balance sheet.

SUMMARY OF NEW ACCOUNTING LANGUAGE TERMS

Learning Unit 11

Accrued Salaries: Salaries that are unpaid and unrecorded and will not come due for payment till next accounting period. An adjustment is needed in the accrual basis of accounting to reflect proper amounts at the end of the accounting period in salaries expense and salaries payable.

Accumulated Depreciation: A contra-asset that summarizes or accumulates the amount of depreciation that has been taken on an asset (auto equipment). The historical cost of the asset minus accumulated depreciation reveals the amount of depreciation that has not been taken, which reflects the unused (unexpired) amount of the asset's usefulness on the books of the company. An asset could be fully depreciated but worth a great deal—example, an antique car.

Adjusting: The process of bringing accounts up or down to their correct balances at the end of an accounting period.

Book Value: Cost of equipment less accumulated depreciation.

Depreciation: The allocation (spreading) of the cost of an asset (auto, equipment) over its expected useful life.

Historical Cost: The actual cost of an asset at time of purchase.

Worksheet: A columnar form device used by accountants to aid them in completing the accounting cycle. It is not a formal report.

QUESTION INTERACTORS

1. How can a worksheet be compared to the rough draft of a term paper?
2. The worksheet is a formal report. Agree or disagree? Why?
3. A trial balance is never entered directly on the worksheet. Agree or disagree? Why?
4. Explain the purpose of adjustments.
5. When does prepaid rent become an expense?
6. If supplies are consumed in the operation of a business, they are considered to be assets. Agree or disagree? Why?
7. Define historical cost.
8. Why are the new accounts listed on the worksheet below the trial balance?
9. Explain what is meant by limited life.
10. Define accumulated depreciation.
11. Depreciation is an estimate in spreading the cost of an asset (car, equipment) over its expected useful life. True or false?
12. Accumulated depreciation is found on the income statement. Agree or disagree? Why?
13. Define a contra-account. Give an example.
14. Relate the matching principle as refers to salaries owed but not paid.
15. Define the matching principle.
16. Withdrawals is found on what column of the worksheet?
17. Which statement should be prepared first, the balance sheet or the income statement? Why?
18. What accounts make up an income statement?
19. What accounts are needed to calculate the new figure for owner's investment?

PROBLEM INTERACTORS

1. Below is the trial balance of Abby Ellen Cleaners before adjustment.

ABBY ELLEN CLEANERS

Trial Balance
December 31, 19XX

	Dr.	Cr.
Cash	100	
Accounts Receivable	200	
Supplies	300	
Equipment	400	
Accumulated Depreciation—Equipment		100
A. Ellen Investment		1,000
A. Ellen Withdrawal	200	
Cleaning Revenue		100
Total	1,200	1,200

Adjustment data on December 31:

1. Supplies on hand $200
2. Depreciation taken on equipment $100

Your task is to complete a partial worksheet up to the adjusted trial balance for December 31, 19XX, for Abby Ellen Cleaners.

2. Below is the trial balance for Jay's Auto Repair for December 31, 19XX.

JAY'S AUTO REPAIR

Trial Balance
December 31, 19XX

	Dr.	Cr.
Cash	340	
Accounts Receivable	360	
Prepaid Rent	360	
Auto Supplies	425	
Auto Equipment	3,000	
Acc. Dep.—Auto Equipment		900
Accounts Payable		115
J. Jones Investment		1,000
Auto Revenue		11,200
Heat Expense	3,580	
Advertising Expense	2,000	
Wage Expense	3,150	
Total	13,215	13,215

Adjustment data to update the trial balance:

1. Rent expired $100
2. Auto supplies on hand (left) $150
3. Depreciation—auto equipment $100
4. Wages earned by workers but not paid or due until January $50

Your task is to prepare a worksheet for Jay's Auto Repair for the month of December.

*3. The following is the trial balance for Tim's Air Conditioning Service.

TIM'S AIR CONDITIONING SERVICE
Trial Balance
November 30, 19XX

	Dr.	Cr.
Cash	1,235	
Prepaid Insurance	48	
Repair Supplies	285	
Repair Equipment	1,443	
Acc. Dep.—Repair Equipment		210
Accounts Payable		52
Tim Clean Investment		907
Revenue from Air Conditioning Repairs		3,027
Wages Expense	952	
Rent Expense	180	
Advertising Expense	53	
Total	4,196	4,196

Adjustment data to update trial balance:

1. Expired insurance $37
2. Repair supplies left on hand $62
3. Depreciation on repair equipment $145
4. Wages earned but unpaid $16

Your task is to:
a. Complete a worksheet for Tim's Air Conditioning Service for the month of November.
b. Prepare an income statement for November and balance sheet as of November 30, 19XX.

*4. The following is the trial balance for the Joe Green Gymnasium.

JOE GREEN GYMNASIUM

Trial Balance
October 31, 19XX

	Dr.	Cr.
Cash	101,244	
Prepaid Advertising	480	
Prepaid Rent	600	
Gym Equipment	13,200	
Acc. Dep.—Gym Equipment		660
Accounts Payable		20,000
J. Green Investment		92,000
J. Green Withdrawal	400	
Gym Revenue		12,560
Printing Expense	400	
Utilities Expense	3,600	
Repair and Maintenance Expense	5,120	
Miscellaneous Expense	176	
Total	125,220	125,220

Adjustment data:

1. Advertising expired $200
2. Rent expired $300
3. Depreciation—gym equipment $300

Your task is to:
a. Prepare the worksheet for Joe at the end of October.
b. Prepare the income statement for October and balance sheet as of October 31, 19XX.

ADDITIONAL PROBLEM INTERACTORS

1-A. The following is the trial balance of the Russell Advertising Agency.

RUSSELL ADVERTISING AGENCY

Trial Balance
December 31, 19XX

	Dr.	Cr.
Cash	500	
Accounts Receivable	1,000	
Office Supplies	1,500	
Office Equipment	2,000	
Acc. Dep.—Office Equipment		500
J. Russell Investment		5,000
J. Russell Withdrawal	1,000	
Advertising Revenue		500
Total	6,000	6,000

Adjustment data on December 31:

1. Supplies used up $500
2. Depreciation taken on office equipment $200

Your task is to complete a worksheet up to the adjusted trial balance for December 31, 19XX, for the Russell Advertising Agency.

2-A. Below is the trial balance for Mike's Window Washing Service for December 31, 19XX.

MIKE'S WINDOW WASHING Trial Balance December 31, 19XX		
	Dr.	**Cr.**
Cash	68	
Accounts Receivable	72	
Prepaid Rent	72	
Window Supplies	85	
Window Equipment	600	
Acc. Dep.—Window Equipment		180
Accounts Payable		23
M. Jon Investment		200
Window Revenue		2,240
Utilities Expense	716	
Advertising Expense	400	
Salary Expense	630	
Total	2,643	2,643

Adjustment data to update trial balance:

1. Rent expired $20
2. Window supplies used up $30
3. Depreciation—window equipment $20
4. Salaries earned by workers of Mike's Window but not paid or due until January $10

Your task is to prepare a worksheet for Mike's Window Washing Service for December.

3-A. The following is the trial balance for the Fast Moving Service.

FAST MOVING SERVICE

Trial Balance
October 31, 19XX

	Dr.	Cr.
Cash	585	
Prepaid Insurance	144	
Moving Supplies	855	
Moving Truck	4,329	
Acc. Dep.—Moving Truck		630
Accounts Payable		156
J. Fast Investment		2,721
J. Fast Withdrawal	3,120	
Revenue from Moving		9,081
Wages Expense	2,856	
Rent Expense	540	
Advertising Expense	159	
Total	12,588	12,588

Adjustment data to update trial balance:

1. Expired insurance $20
2. Moving supplies used up $250
3. Depreciation on moving truck $50
4. Wages earned but unpaid $65

Your task is to:

a. Complete a worksheet for the Fast Moving Service for October.
b. Prepare an income statement for October and balance sheet as of October 31, 19XX.

*4-A. The following is the trial balance for J. Beep Taxi for July 31, 19XX.

J. BEEP TAXI

Trial Balance
July 31, 19XX

	Dr.	Cr.
Cash	3,600	
Prepaid Advertising	3,000	
Prepaid Rent	1,200	
Taxi	4,400	
Accounts Payable		2,400
J. Beep Investment		6,000
J. Beep Withdrawal	19,000	
Taxi Fees Earned		35,000
Electrical Expense	3,000	
Utilities Expense	8,800	
Repair and Maintenance Expense	300	
Miscellaneous Expense	100	
Total	43,400	43,400

Adjustment data:

1. Advertising expense $1,000
2. Rent expired $500
3. Depreciation on taxi $500

Your task is to:
a. Prepare the worksheet for J. Beep for the month of July.
b. Prepare the income statement for July and balance sheet as of July 31, 19XX.

CHALLENGE PROBLEM INTERACTORS

A partial trial balance for the Spongy Car Washing Company as of December 31, 1982 is shown below:

Accounts Receivable	3,300	
Prepaid Insurance	1,600	
Prepaid Rent	3,600	
Car Washing Supplies	820	
Car Washing Equipment	25,000	
Accumulated Depreciation—		15,000
Car Washing Equipment		
Car Washing Revenue		32,000
Salaries Expense	13,800	
Utilities Expense	1,500	

In good general journal form, journalize the following adjusting entries using the related information in the partial trial balance above.

1. On January 1, 1979, the car washing equipment was purchased. The equipment has an expected life of 5 years and no salvage value (trade-in).
2. The Prepaid Insurance account represents the *balance* of a 3-year fire insurance policy which started on January 1, 1981.
3. The Prepaid Rent account represents rent paid in advance for 2 years on January 1, 1982.
4. A count of the car washing supplies on hand as of December 31, 1982, shows an inventory of $120.
5. The Salaries Expense account represents 11½ months of salaries paid. The last half of December is adjusted on December 31, 1982.

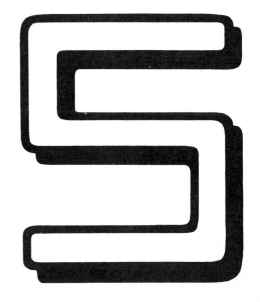

the completion of the accounting cycle

In the last two chapters we completed the following steps of the accounting cycle:

1. Business transaction occurred.
2. Business transactions were analyzed and recorded into a journal.
3. Information was posted or transferred from journal to ledger.
4. A trial balance was prepared.
5. A worksheet was completed.
6. Financial statements were prepared.

This chapter completes the accounting cycle for Katz Real Estate for the month of July by the following steps:

7. Journalize and post adjusting entries.
8. Journalize and post closing entries.
9. Prepare a post-closing trial balance.

LEARNING UNIT 13

Journalize and Post Adjusting Entries

RECORDING JOURNAL ENTRIES FROM THE WORKSHEET

Purpose of adjusting entries

Many students have asked the purpose of journalizing adjusting entries. They claim that the information is already on the worksheet—

why do it again? They forget that the worksheet is an informal report. The information concerning the adjustments has not been (a) *placed into the journal*, nor (b) *posted to the ledger accounts*.

Therefore, the process is quite simple to bring certain amounts up-to-date in the ledger. All the information needed for steps (a) and (b) is found in the adjustment columns of the worksheet.

Account Titles	Trial Balance Dr.	Trial Balance Cr.	Adjustments Dr.	Adjustments Cr.
Cash	3030000			
Accounts Receivable	800000			
Prepaid Rent	30000			(A)10000
Office Supplies	10000			(B)6000
Automobile	300000			
Office Equipment	330000			
Accounts Payable		150000		
S. Katz Investment		3330000		
S. Katz Withdrawal	50000			
Commission Fees Earned		1200000		
Office Salary Expense	120000		(E)18000	
Advertising Expense	5000			
Telephone Expense	5000			
	4680000	4680000		
Rent Expense			(A)10000	
Office Supplies Expense			(B)6000	
Dep. Exp.—Auto			(C)5000	
Acc. Dep.—Auto				(C)5000
Dep. Exp.—Office Equipment			(D)5500	
Acc. Dep.—Office Equipment				(D)5500
Salaries Payable				(E)18000
			44500	44500

Journalizing adjusting entries   The following journalized entries for the Katz Real Estate Agency were taken from the adjustments columns in the above worksheet:

Date	Account Titles and Description	PR	Dr.	Cr.
	Adjusting entries			
31	Rent Expense	566	100 00	
	Prepaid Rent	114		100 00
31	Office Supplies Expense	568	60 00	
	Office Supplies	116		60 00
31	Depreciation Expense—Auto	570	50 00	
	Accumulated Depreciation—Auto	119		50 00
31	Depreciation Expense—Office Equipment	572	55 00	
	Accumulated Depreciation—Office Equipment	121		55 00
31	Office Salaries Expense	560	180 00	
	Salaries Payable	232		180 00

Once these journalized adjusting entries are posted to the ledger, the accounts making up the financial statements that were prepared from the worksheet will equal the updated ledger.

T-ACCOUNT UPDATE

Posting adjusting entries to ledger

Look at the specific adjusted accounts in the ledger of Katz Real Estate. T-accounts are shown before and after the posting of entries.

Accounts Before Adjustments Posted | Accounts After Adjustments Posted

(A)
Prepaid Rent 114: 300
Rent Expense 566:

Prepaid Rent 114: 300 | 100
Rent Expense 566: 100

(B)
Office Supplies 116: 100
Office Supplies Expense 568:

Office Supplies 116: 100 | 60
Office Supplies Expense 568: 60

(C)
Depreciation Expense—Auto 570:
Accumulated Depreciation—Auto 119:

Depreciation Expense—Auto 570: 50
Accumulated Depreciation—Auto 119: 50

(D)
Depreciation Expense—Office Equipment 572:
Accumulated Depreciation—Office Equipment 121:

Depreciation Expense—Office Equipment 572: 55
Accumulated Depreciation—Office Equipment 121: 55

(E)
Office Salary Expense 560: 600, 600
Salaries Payable 232:

Office Salary Expense 560: 600, 600, 180
Salaries Payable 232: 180

Now you should be able to:

1. Define and state the purpose of adjusting entries.
2. Journalize adjusting entries from worksheet.
3. Post journalized adjusting entries to the ledger.
4. Compare specific ledger accounts before and after posting of the journalized adjusting entries.

UNIT INTERACTOR 13

From the following worksheet: (1) journalize and post the adjusting entries and (2) compare the adjusted ledger accounts before and after the adjustments are posted. T-accounts are provided.

HOWARD'S ᴅ ᴉ

Workshee

For Month Ended Decem r 31, 19XX

Account Titles	Trial Balance Dr.	Trial Balance Cr.	Adjustments Dr.	Adjustments Cr.	Income Statement Dr.	Income Statement Cr.	Balance Sheet Dr.	Balance Sheet Cr.
Cash	260000						260000	
Supplies	425000			(A) 225000			200000	
Prepaid Insurance	52000			(B) 4000			48000	
Equipment	1200000						1200000	
Acc. Dep.—Equipment		380000		(C) 9500				389500
H. Wells Investment		1064000						1064000
H. Wells Withdrawal	60000						60000	
Deli Fees		1335000				1335000		
Wage Expense	612000		(D) 36000		648000			
Miscellaneous Expense	170000				170000			
	2779000	2779000						
Supplies Expense			(A) 225000		225000			
Insurance Expense			(B) 4000		4000			
Dep. Exp.—Equipment			(C) 9500		9500			
Wages Payable				(D) 36000				36000
			274500	274500	1056500	1335000	1768000	1489500
Net Income					278500			278500
					1335000	1335000	1768000	1768000

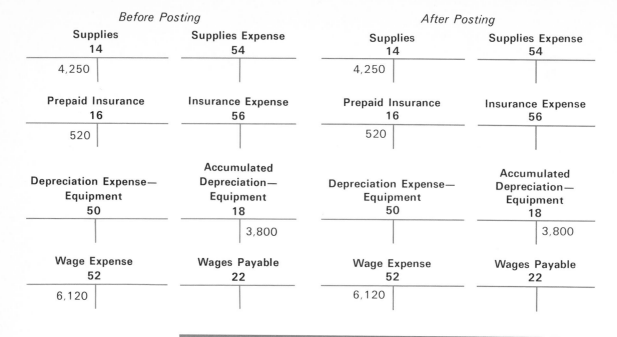

Before Posting

Supplies 14	Supplies Expense 54
4,250	

Prepaid Insurance 16	Insurance Expense 56
520	

Depreciation Expense— Equipment 50	Accumulated Depreciation— Equipment 18
	3,800

Wage Expense 52	Wages Payable 22
6,120	

After Posting

Supplies 14	Supplies Expense 54
4,250	

Prepaid Insurance 16	Insurance Expense 56
520	

Depreciation Expense— Equipment 50	Accumulated Depreciation— Equipment 18
	3,800

Wage Expense 52	Wages Payable 22
6,120	

SOLUTION to Unit Interactor 13

		Adjustments			
31	Supplies Expense		54	2250 00	
	Supplies		14		2250 00
31	Insurance Expense		56	40 00	
	Prepaid Insurance		16		40 00
31	Depreciation Expense—Equipment		50	95 00	
	Accumulated Depreciation—Equipment		18		95 00
31	Wage Expense		52	360 00	
	Wages Payable		22		360 00

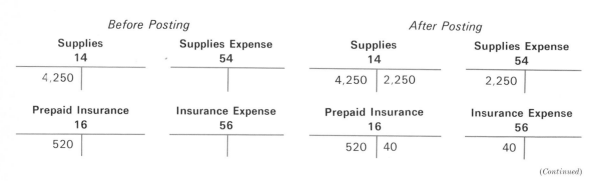

Before Posting

Supplies 14	Supplies Expense 54
4,250	

Prepaid Insurance 16	Insurance Expense 56
520	

After Posting

Supplies 14	Supplies Expense 54
4,250	2,250
	2,250

Prepaid Insurance 16	Insurance Expense 56
520	40
	40

(Continued)

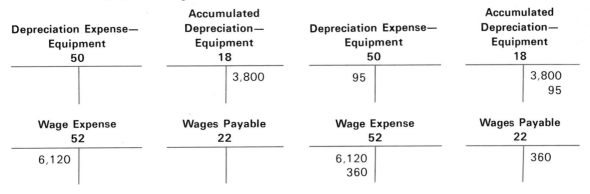

Before Posting				After Posting			
Depreciation Expense—Equipment		Accumulated Depreciation—Equipment		Depreciation Expense—Equipment		Accumulated Depreciation—Equipment	
50		18		50		18	
			3,800	95			3,800
							95
Wage Expense		Wages Payable		Wage Expense		Wages Payable	
52		22		52		22	
6,120				6,120			360
				360			

LEARNING UNIT 14

Journalize and Post Closing Entries

TEMPORARY AND PERMANENT ACCOUNTS

Almost everyone has a kitchen, but few of us take an accountant's view of it. At our house we categorize the pots, dishes, forks, etc., which we use day in and day out, as permanent parts of our kitchen. The milk, juice, meats, and vegetables are considered to be temporary kitchen accounts; these temporary items will not last very long. The refrigerator, sometimes full, is carried on the kitchen books from month to month.

At the end of each month we try to summarize the amount of food left, as well as the amount of expenses that resulted in the operation of the kitchen. We are interested in the kitchen's financial position.

Our household policy is to (1) summarize the effects of the temporary accounts on our investment into the kitchen; (2) clear up, or summarize the effects of the temporary accounts, so as to prepare for the recording of new kitchen transactions in the future. You can do the same in your kitchen, if you like, when you master the techniques of this unit.

Remember the expanded equation:

$$ASSETS = LIABILITIES + OWNER'S\ EQUITY + REVENUE - EXPENSES$$

Since we have dealt with withdrawals, the expanded accounting equation can be updated to:

$$
\begin{array}{ccc}
1 & 2 & 3 \\
ASSETS = LIABILITIES & + & OWNER'S\ EQUITY
\end{array}
$$
$$
\begin{array}{ccc}
4 & 5 & 6 \\
+\ REVENUE & -\ EXPENSES & -\ WITHDRAWALS
\end{array}
$$

As withdrawals increase ↑ Owner's Equity ↓ decreases.

Now, let's begin our discussion by looking at assets, liabilities, and owner's equity which are called *permanent accounts*.

$$
\begin{array}{ccc}
1 & 2 & 3 \\
ASSETS = LIABILITIES & + & OWNER'S\ EQUITY
\end{array}
$$

Why? The balances in cash, supplies, accounts payable, etc. and the new figure for owner's equity are carried over from one accounting period (here one month) to another. Remember, an accounting period could be one month, three months, or one year. These accounts whose balances are carried over to the next period are known as permanent accounts.

What about revenues, expenses, and withdrawals?

$$
\begin{array}{ccc}
4 & 5 & 6 \\
REVENUES = EXPENSES & - & WITHDRAWALS
\end{array}
$$

At the end of each accounting period (one month, three months, one year), revenues, expenses, and withdrawals are *temporary* accounts and are summarized to arrive at the ending figure for owner's equity. Remember, the term temporary accounts means that the balances in certain accounts *will not* be carried over to the next period of time.

$$
\begin{array}{l}
BEGINNING\ OWNER'S\ EQUITY \\
+\ NET\ INCOME \\
\overline{-\ WITHDRAWALS} \\
=\ ENDING\ OWNER'S\ EQUITY
\end{array}
$$

Therefore, the process of (1) summarizing the effects of revenue, expenses, and withdrawals on owner's equity; and (2) preparing or clearing these revenues, expenses, and withdrawal accounts in the ledger (to a zero balance) for the next accounting period is called *closing*.

In essence, when the closing process is complete the accounting equation will be reduced to

$$
ASSETS = LIABILITIES + ENDING\ OWNER'S\ EQUITY
$$

Permanent
_____
Assets
Liabilities
Owner's Investment

Temporary
_____
Revenue
Expense(s)
Withdrawal

instead of

$$ASSETS = LIABILITIES + OWNER'S \; EQUITY \\ + \; REVENUE - EXPENSES - WITHDRAWAL$$

GOALS OF CLOSING

Purpose of closing entries

All revenue, expenses, and withdrawals will have a zero balance at the end of the closing process, which summarizes their effects on owner's equity, eventually calculating the *new* or ending figure for *owner's equity* at the end of the accounting period, as well as clearing each temporary account to zero. Then we can gather new information about revenue, expenses, and withdrawal transactions in the new period.

After closing entries are journalized and posted to ledger, all temporary accounts will have a zero balance in the ledger.

If the closing process is completed correctly at the end of each accounting period, only assets, liabilities, and an ending figure for owner's equity will be carried over to the next accounting period. Let's look now at the steps needed to complete the closing process.

HOW TO JOURNALIZE CLOSING ENTRIES

In the last unit, which covered adjusting entries, all the information for the journalizing of the transactions came from the adjustment columns of the worksheet.

For our present purpose, the information needed to complete closing entries will be found in the income statement columns of the worksheet.

There are four steps to be performed in journalizing closing entries:

1. Clear the revenue balance and transfer it to income summary (a temporary account in the ledger needed for closing).

$$REVENUE \longrightarrow INCOME \; SUMMARY$$

2. Clear the individual expense balances and transfer it to income summary.

$$EXPENSES \longrightarrow INCOME \; SUMMARY$$

Steps to close temporary accounts to owner's equity

3. Clear the balance in income summary to owner's equity.

$$INCOME \; SUMMARY \longrightarrow OWNER'S \; EQUITY$$

4. Clear the balance in withdrawals to owner's equity.

$$WITHDRAWALS \longrightarrow OWNER'S \; EQUITY$$

In pictorial form this would be:

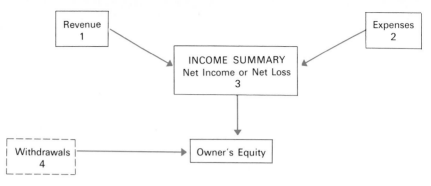

Income Summary

Income Summary	
Expenses	Revenue

Keep in mind that this information must be first journalized and then copied or posted to the appropriate ledger accounts. When we use the term owner's equity we are referring to owner's investment.

KATZ REAL ESTATE AGENCY

Worksheet

For Month Ended July 31, 19XX

Account Titles	Adjusted Trial Balance Dr.	Cr.	Income Statement Dr.	Cr.	Balance Sheet Dr.	Cr.
Cash	3030000				3030000	
Accounts Receivable	800000				800000	
Prepaid Rent	20000				20000	
Office Supplies	4000				4000	
Auto	300000				300000	
Office Equipment	330000				330000	
Accounts Payable		150000				150000
S. Katz Investment		3330000				3330000
S. Katz Withdrawal	50000				50000	
Commission Fees Earned		1200000		1200000		
Office Salary Expense	138000		138000			
Advertising Expense	5000		5000			
Telephone Expense	5000		5000			
Rent Expense	10000		10000			
Office Supplies Expense	6000		6000			
Dep. Exp.—Auto	5000		5000			
Acc. Dep.—Auto		5000				5000
Dep. Exp.—Office Equipment	5500		5500			
Acc. Dep.—Office Equipment		5500				5500
Salaries Payable		18000				18000
	4708500	4708500	174500	1200000	4534000	3508500
Net Income			1025500			1025500
			1200000	1200000	4534000	4534000

Now, using the above worksheet, let's take our time, step by step, to journalize the closing entries. Keep in mind that all the upcoming figures can be found in the worksheet.

Goal after closing:

In order to reach our goal, what must be done with the following? Before closing:

By debiting commission fees earned and crediting income summary we will be able to:

1. Bring the temporary account commission fees earned to a zero balance.
2. Transfer the information from commission fees earned to income summary.

The following is the journalized closing entry for step 1:

July 31	Commission Fees Earned	450	12,000 00	
	Income Summary	344		12,000 00

Notice by looking at the income statement columns in the worksheet that the commission fees earned had a credit balance. To close or clear it to zero, a debit was in order. What the worksheet doesn't tell us is where to carry the balance in commission fees earned in the closing process (which we now know is income summary). Please remember that income summary is a temporary account in the ledger that will help summarize information in the closing process. By the end of the closing process income summary will have a zero balance.

Goal after closing:

**Office Salary Expense
560**

1,380	1,380

**Advertising Expense
562**

50	50

**Telephone Expense
564**

50	50

**Rent Expense
566**

100	100

**Office Supplies Expense
568**

60	60

**Depreciation Expense Auto
570**

50	50

**Depreciation Expense Office Equipment
572**

55	55

**Income Summary
344**

1,745	12,000
	(Step 1)

In order to reach the above goal, what must be done with the following expenses before closing?

What we start with
Here is what is in ledger
for each expense
before step 2 of closing
entries is journalized
and posted.

Office Salary Expense 560	Advertising Expense 562	Telephone Expense 564
1,380	50	50

Rent Expense 566	Office Supplies Expense 568	Depreciation Expense Auto 570
100	60	50

Depreciation Expense Office Equipment 572
55

How to reach end product
This compound journal entry
when posted does reach
our goal of closing out
each individual expense
to a zero balance
and bringing the total
of the expenses
to income summary.

By crediting each individual expense and debiting income summary for the total of all the expenses we will be able to:

1. Bring all expenses to a zero balance.
2. Transfer the information about the expenses to income summary.

The following is the journalized closing entry for step 2:

31	Income Summary		344	1745 00	
	Office Salary Expense		560		1380 00
	Advertising Expense		562		50 00
	Telephone Expense		564		50 00
	Rent Expense		566		100 00
	Office Supplies Expense		568		60 00
	Depreciation Expense—Auto		570		50 00
	Depreciation Expense—Office Equipment		572		55 00

In the income statement columns of the worksheet all the expenses were listed as debits. If we want to reduce each expense to zero and they are all debits, we will have to credit each one.

The worksheet, once again, doesn't tell you where the expenses are to be brought in order to summarize them in the closing process, but it does give you the amount of $1,745. Remember, the worksheet is a tool. The accountant realizes that the information about the expenses will be transferred to income summary.

Goal after closing:

End product

After step 3, in ledger,
income summary should
have a zero balance,
and this information
(net income, $10,255)
should be transferred to
S. Katz investment.

Income Summary 344		S. Katz Investment 340
1,745	12,000	33,300
10,255	*10,255*	10,255

In order to transfer the balance of $10,255 from income summary (check the bottom debit column of the income statement column on worksheet) to owner's equity it will be necessary to debit the income summary for $10,255 (the difference between the revenues and expenses) and credit or increase owner's equity of S. Katz investment. The results will be to:

1. Clear income summary a temporary account to zero.
2. Summarize the effects on owner's equity of revenue and expenses, which have been accumulated in income summary from steps 1 and 2 of the closing process.

In this case there is a profit of $10,255. Once again, the worksheet has this information. As a matter of fact, notice how the $10,255 on the income statement column of the worksheet was brought over to the credit side of the balance sheet column of the worksheet. The journalized closing entry for step 3 is:

How to reach end product

Since the balance
in income summary
was $10,255 credit,
we debit to clear balance
to zero and update
S. Katz investment
by a credit.

31	Income Summary	344	10,255 00		
	S. Katz Investment	340		10,255 00	

Remember, the worksheet does not update ledger accounts. To this point the three closing journal entries when posted will have (1) cleared all revenue and expense accounts to arrive at a zero balance, and (2) summarized the effect of the revenue and expense accounts on owner's equity. Keep in mind that income summary now has a zero balance as well.

Now let's look at withdrawal.

*STEP 4: Withdrawal Balance Cleared
to Owner's Equity*

Goal after closing:

S. Katz Withdrawal 342		S. Katz Investment 340	
500	500	500	33,300
			10,255

In order to reach the goal of bringing the withdrawal account to a zero balance, as well as summarizing its effect on owner's equity, the following must be done:

1. Credit withdrawal.
2. Debit owner's equity.

The closing entry would be journalized as follows:

31	S. Katz Investment	340	500 00	
	S. Katz Withdrawal	342		500 00

Keep in mind:

> BEGINNING OWNER'S EQUITY
> + NET INCOME
> ── WITHDRAWAL
> = ENDING OWNER'S EQUITY

Withdrawal is a nonbusiness expense and thus is not closed to income summary. In order to differentiate a withdrawal from an expense it is closed separately.

This temporary account withdrawal will then balance to zero to begin the next accounting period. This will be helpful to keep track of withdrawals each accounting period. Remember, as withdrawals Inc.↑, owner's equity Dec.↓.

SUMMARY

The closing journal entries, when posted, (1) reduce all revenues, expenses, and withdrawal accounts to a zero balance (this will allow a clear picture of revenue, expense, and withdrawals for the recording of transactions for the next accounting period); (2) summarize the effects of revenue, expense, and withdrawals on owner's equity.

The general ledger of Katz Real Estate, after adjusting and closing entries have been posted, will be presented after the section on balancing and ruling. Please notice that the accounts have been balanced and ruled. The purpose of ruling is to separate amounts from the past accounting period. The following brief section will help you gain some insight into the balancing and ruling process (which is quite mechanical).

The mechanical process of closing entries when (1) journalized and (2) posted leaves only permanent accounts in ledger with balances to be brought forward to next period of time.

HOW TO BALANCE AND RULE

Before starting the next accounting period, we balance and rule the permanent accounts in the ledger. This allows the balances in each account to be carried over to the next accounting period. Remember, all the temporary accounts have been closed to the owner's equity.

Let's look at an account to see how it is balanced and ruled.

Account: Accounts Payable   **Account No. 13**

Date		Item	PR	Dr.	Date		Item	PR	Cr.
19XX Dec.	27		GJ1	2,000 00	19XX Dec.	25	*9,000*	GJ1	11,000 00
	31	Balancing	√	9,000 00					
				11,000 00					
				11,000 00					11,000 00
					Jan.	1	Balance Brought Forward	√	9,000 00

Steps

1. Balance the account as you did in the past: $9,000.
2. This balance of $9,000 is brought to the left side (smaller total) of accounts payable so as to "balance both sides to equal $11,000." Notice the single line. This provides a check to see if both column totals are in balance before the balance is brought forward.
3. Double lines are drawn to indicate as of end of December that totals have been ruled.
4. The balance of $9,000 (step 1) is brought forward below the double lines on the side on which the balance of the account exists. The check mark (√) indicates that this entry did not come from the journal.

Keep in mind that the above account is a permanent account. All temporary accounts (revenue, expense, withdrawals) will not have balances brought forward, since the closing process will make their balances zero. Also, if a permanent account has only one figure, it is not necessary to balance and bring forward the balance. This process of balancing and ruling has many variations, as we shall see later.

KATZ REAL ESTATE AGENCY: LEDGER

Account: Cash   **Account No. 110**

Date		Item	PR	Dr.	Date		Item	PR	Cr.
19XX					19XX				
Jul.	1		GJ1	30,000 00	Jul.	1		GJ1	300 00
	15		GJ1	4,000 00		8		GJ1	100 00
		30,300		*34,000 00*		16		GJ1	600 00
						21		GJ1	500 00
						25		GJ1	600 00
						28		GJ2	1,500 00
						29		GJ2	50 00
						29		GJ2	50 00
									3,700 00
						31	Balancing	✓	30,300 00
									34,000 00
				34,000 00					34,000 00
Aug.	1	Balance Brought Forward	✓	30,300 00					

Account: Accounts Receivable   **Account No. 112**

Date		Item	PR	Dr.	Date	Item	PR	Cr.
19XX								
Jul.	23		GJ1	8000 00				

Account: Prepaid Rent   **Account No. 114**

Date		Item	PR	Dr.	Date		Item	PR	Cr.
19XX					19XX				
Jul.	1	*200*	GJ1	300 00	Jul.	31	Adjustment	GJ2	100 00
						31	Balancing	✓	200 00
									300 00
				300 00					300 00
Aug.	1	Balance Brought Forward	✓	200 00					

Notice how word "adjustment" is entered *into item column*

Account: Office Supplies   Account No. 116

Date		Item	PR	Dr.	Date		Item	PR	Cr.
19XX					19XX				
Jul.	18	*40*	GJ1	100 00	Jul	31	Adjustment	GJ2	60 00
						31	Balancing	√	40 00
				100 00					*100 00*
									100 00
Aug.	1	Balance Brought Forward	√	40 00					

Account: Auto   Account No. 118

Date		Item	PR	Dr.	Date	Item	PR	Cr.
19XX								
Jul.	3		GJ1	3000 00				

Account: Accumulated Depreciation—Auto   Account No. 119

Date	Item	PR	Dr.	Date		Item	PR	Cr.
				19XX				
				Jul.	31	Adjustment	GJ2	50 00

Account: Office Equipment   Account No. 120

Date		Item	PR	Dr.	Date	Item	PR	Cr.
19XX								
Jul.	1		GJ1	3300 00				

Account: Accumulated Depreciation—Office Equipment Account No. 121

Date	Item	PR	Dr.	Date		Item	PR	Cr.
				19XX Jul.	31	Adjustment	GJ2	55 00

Account: Accounts Payable Account No. 230

Date		Item	PR	Dr.	Date		Item	PR	Cr.
19XX Jul.	28		GJ2	1500 00	19XX Jul.	3	*1500*	GJ1	3000 00
	31	Balancing	√	1500 00					
				3000 00					
				3000 00					3000 00
					Aug.	1	Balance Brought Forward	√	1500 00

Account: Salaries Payable Account No. 232

Date	Item	PR	Dr.	Date		Item	PR	Cr.
				19XX Jul.	31	Adjustment	GJ2	180 00

Account: S. Katz Investment Account No. 340

Date		Item	PR	Dr.	Date		Item	PR	Cr.
19XX Jul.	31	Closing	GJ2	500 00	19XX Jul.	1		GJ1	33,300 00
	31	Balancing	√	43,055 00		31	Closing	GJ2	10,255 00
							43,055		
				43,555 00					*43,555 00*
				43,555 00					43,555 00
					Aug.	1	Balance Brought Forward	√	43,055 00

Account: S. Katz Withdrawal — Account No. 342

Date		Item	PR	Dr.	Date		Item	PR	Cr.
19XX					19XX				
Jul.	31		GJ1	500 00	Jul.	31	Closing	GJ2	500 00

Account: Income Summary — Account No. 344

Date		Item	PR	Dr.	Date		Item	PR	Cr.
19XX					19XX				
Jul.	31	Closing	GJ2	1,745 00	Jul.	31	Closing	GJ2	12,000 00
	31	Closing	GJ2	10,255 00					
				12,000 00					
				12,000 00					12,000 00

Account: Commission Fees Earned — Account No. 450

Date		Item	PR	Dr.	Date		Item	PR	Cr.
19XX					19XX				
Jul.	31	Closing	GJ2	12,000 00	Jul.	15		GJ1	4,000 00
						23		GJ1	8,000 00
				12,000 00					*12,000 00*
									12,000 00

Account: Office Salary Expense — Account No. 560

Date		Item	PR	Dr.	Date		Item	PR	Cr.
19XX					19XX				
Jul.	16		GJ1	600 00	Jul.	31	Closing	GJ2	1380 00
	25		GJ2	600 00					
	31	Adjustment	GJ2	180 00					
				1380 00					
				1380 00					1380 00

Account: Advertising Expense
Account No. 562

Date		Item	PR	Dr.	Date		Item	PR	Cr.
19XX					19XX				
Jul.	29		GJ2	50 00	Jul.	31	Closing	GJ2	50 00

Account: Telephone Expense
Account No. 564

Date		Item	PR	Dr.	Date		Item	PR	Cr.
19XX					19XX				
Jul.	29		GJ2	50 00	Jul.	31	Closing	GJ2	50 00

Account: Rent Expense
Account No. 566

Date		Item	PR	Dr.	Date		Item	PR	Cr.
19XX					19XX				
Jul.	31	Adjustment	GJ2	100 00	Jul.	31	Closing	GJ2	100 00

Account: Office Supplies Expense
Account No. 568

Date		Item	PR	Dr.	Date		Item	PR	Cr.
19XX					19XX				
Jul.	31	Adjustment	GJ2	60 00	Jul.	31	Closing	GJ2	60 00

Account: Depreciation Expense—Auto   Account No. 570

Date		Item	PR	Dr.	Date		Item	PR	Cr.
19XX					19XX				
Jul.	31	Adjustment	GJ2	50|00	Jul.	31	Closing	GJ2	50|00

Account: Depreciation Expense—Office Equipment   Account No. 572

Date		Item	PR	Dr.	Date		Item	PR	Cr.
19XX					19XX				
Jul.	31	Adjustment	GJ2	55|00	Jul.	31	Closing	GJ2	55|00

At this point you should be able to:

1. Differentiate between a permanent and a temporary account.
2. Given beginning owner's equity, net income, and withdrawals, calculate a figure for ending owner's equity.
3. State the purpose of closing entries.
4. Differentiate between the process of adjusting vs. closing.
5. List the four steps for journalizing closing entries.
6. Balance and rule accounts.
7. Explain the role of the worksheet in completing the four steps of journalizing closing entries.

UNIT INTERACTOR 14

From the following worksheet your task is to:

1. Journalize closing entries.
2. Draw a diagram summarizing the closing steps of Howard Deli, which is owned by Howard Wells.
3. Calculate the new figure for H. Wells investment by posting the closing entries to T-accounts.

HOWARD'S DELI

Worksheet

For Month Ended December , 19XX

Account Titles	Trial Balance Dr.	Trial Balance Cr.	Adjustments Dr.	Adjustments Cr.	Adjusted Trial Balance Dr.	Adjusted Trial Balance Cr.	Income Statement Dr.	Income Statement Cr.	Balance Sheet Dr.	Balance Sheet Cr.
Cash	260000								260000	
Supplies	425000			(A)225000					200000	
Prepaid Insurance	52000			(B)4000					48000	
Equipment	1200000								1200000	
Acc. Dep.—Equipment		380000		(C)9500						389500
H. Wells Investment		1064000								1064000
H. Wells Withdrawal	60000								60000	
Deli Fees		1335000						1335000		
Wage Expense	612000		(D)36000				648000			
Miscellaneous Expense	170000						170000			
	2779000	2779000								
Supplies Expense			(A)225000				225000			
Insurance Expense			(B)4000				4000			
Dep. Exp.—Equipment			(C)9500				9500			
Wages Payable				(D)36000						36000
			274500	274500			1056500	1335000	1768000	1489500
Net Income							278500			278500
							1335000	1335000	1768000	1768000

Steps in completing the closing:

1. Close revenues.
2. Close expenses.
3. Close balance of income summary to H. Wells investment.
4. Close withdrawal to owner's equity.

SOLUTION to Unit Interactor 14

(1)	*Deli Fees*	13,350	
	Income Summary		13,350
(2)	*Income Summary*	10,565	
	Wage Expense		6,480
	Miscellaneous Expense		1,700
	Supplies Expense		2,250
	Insurance Expense		40
	Depreciation Expense		95
(3)	*Income Summary*	2,785	
	H. Wells Investment		2,785
(4)	*H. Wells Investment*	600	
	H. Wells Withdrawal		600

| Wage Expense |
| Miscellaneous Expense |
| Supplies Expense |
| Insurance Expense |
| Depreciation Expense |
| $10,565 |

| Deli Fees |
| $13,350 |

Income Summary

| 10,565 | 13,350 |

| H. Wells Withdrawals | H. Wells Investment |
| $600 | $2,785* |

*This will be added to H. Wells beginning investment.

What the ledger looks like after closing entries have been journalized and posted to the ledger:

H. Wells Investment

| 600 | 10,640 |
| | 2,785 |

Deli Fees

| 13,350 | 13,350 |

Insurance Expense

| 40 | 40 |

H. Wells Withdrawal

| 600 | 600 |

Wage Expense

| 6,480 | 6,480 |

Depreciation Expense Equipment

| 95 | 95 |

Income Summary

| 10,565 | 13,350 |
| 2,785 | |

Miscellaneous Expense

| 1,700 | 1,700 |

Supplies Expense

| 2,250 | 2,250 |

H. WELLS

BEGINNING OWNER'S EQUITY	$10,640
+ NET INCOME	2,785
− WITHDRAWALS	(600)
	12,825
= ENDING OWNER'S EQUITY	$12,825

The Post-Closing Trial Balance

PREPARING A POST-CLOSING TRIAL BALANCE

The last step in the accounting cycle is the preparation of a post-closing trial balance.

This post-closing trial balance aids in checking whether the ledger is in balance and the individual accounts are correct for the beginning of the next accounting period. It helps prove the accuracy of the adjusting and closing process. The procedure for taking a post-closing trial balance is the same as for a trial balance, except that, since closing entries has summarized all temporary accounts, the post-closing trial balance will contain only permanent accounts (balance sheet). Keep in mind that adjustments have occurred.

UNIT INTERACTOR 15

From the ledger accounts of Katz Real Estate could you prepare the post-closing trial balance? The ledger can be found at the end of the last unit, beginning on page 161.

SOLUTION to Unit Interactor 15

KATZ REAL ESTATE

Post-Closing Trial Balance
July 31, 19XX

Cash	30,300	
Accounts Receivable	8,000	
Prepaid Rent	200	
Office Supplies	40	
Automobile	3,000	
Accumulated Depreciation—Automobile		50
Office Equipment	3,300	
Accumulated Depreciation—Office Equipment		55
Accounts Payable		1,500
Salaries Payable		180
S. Katz Investment		43,055
	44,840	44,840

THE ACCOUNTING CYCLE REVIEWED

The following is the list of the steps we completed in the accounting cycle for Katz Real Estate for the month of July:

STEPS	EXPLANATION
1. Business transactions occur and generate source documents	Cash register tape, sales tickets, bills, checks, payroll cards
2. Analyze and record business transactions into a journal	Called journalizing
3. Post or transfer information from journal to ledger	Copying the debits and credits of the journal entries into the ledger accounts
4. Prepare a trial balance	Summarizing each individual ledger account and listing those accounts to test for accuracy in recording transactions
5. Prepare a worksheet	A multicolumn form that summarizes accounting information to complete the accounting cycle
6. Prepare financial statements	Income statement and balance sheet
7. Journalize and post adjusting entries	Refer to adjustment columns of worksheet
8. Journalize and post closing entries	Refer to income statement columns of worksheet
9. Prepare a post-closing trial balance	Proves the accuracy of the adjusting and closing process of the accounting cycle

We have analyzed the accounting cycle for a period of one month in order to simplify transactions and clarify accounting theory and procedures without introducing repetitive detail. In actual practice, some businesses may close their books every three or six months, but the majority actually operate on a one-year accounting cycle.

If the accounting cycle is yearly and it starts on January 1, it is operating in *a calendar year*. A company not operating on a calendar-year basis, but having an accounting period of twelve consecutive months is operating in what is called a *fiscal year*. A fiscal year may also coincide with a calendar year.

THE ACCOUNTING CYCLE COMPLETED—A BLUEPRINT

7

Journalize and Post Adjusting Entries

8

Journalize and Post Closing Entries

9

Prepare a Post-Closing Trial Balance

In the previous chapter the financial statements were prepared from the worksheet. However, much of the information on the worksheet has not been posted to the ledger.

In an attempt to bring the ledger up-to-date, as related to adjustments, the information in the adjustments column of the worksheet is journalized and posted to the ledger. Now *ledger* accounts, such as rent expense, accumulated depreciation, salaries payable, are at up-to-date balances.

Our ledger still does not show the *ending balance* of owner's investment. We have not yet summarized the effects of the temporary account on the owner's investment. At this point the ledger contains balances in revenues, expenses, withdrawals, etc. Our aims are to:

1. Update the ledger to reflect the ending investment balance.
2. Clear all temporary accounts to prepare for next accounting period.

For these purposes we prepare journal entries to clear all information regarding revenues and expenses to a temporary account called income summary. The income summary account can then used to help arrive at a new figure for owner's investment. (Please don't forget we transferred withdrawals directly to owner's investment.)

When the closing journal entries are posted, owner's investment in the ledger now has its ending balance. All temporary accounts have a zero balance and are ready to start all over for the next period. The only accounts in the ledger are permanent accounts, which will have their balances brought or carried forward to the next fiscal period.

From the ending balance of the permanent accounts a post-closing trial balance is prepared, containing assets, liabilities, and one ending figure for owner's equity. The process of journalizing and posting adjusting and closing entries has cleared all temporary accounts and updated the ledger accounts, owner's investment, to an updated ending balance.

SUMMARY OF NEW ACCOUNTING LANGUAGE TERMS

Learning Unit 13

Adjusting Journal Entries: Journal entries that are needed to eventually update specific ledger account balances to reflect correct balances at the end of an accounting period. Remember, the worksheet was only an informal device for accountants.

Closing Journal Entries: Journal entries that are prepared to (a) reduce or clear all temporary accounts to a zero balance, (b) update owner's equity to a new balance. This process involves: (1) clearing revenue balance and transferring it to income summary, (2) clearing the individual expense balances and transferring them to income summary, (3) clearing the balance in income summary to owner's equity, (4) clearing the balance in withdrawals to owner's equity.

Permanent Accounts: Accounts whose balances are carried over to the next accounting period. Example: Assets = Liabilities and a new figure for owner's equity.

Temporary Accounts: Accounts at the end of an accounting period whose balances are not carried over to the next period of time. These accounts—revenue, expenses, withdrawals—help summarize a new or ending figure for owner's equity to begin the next accounting period. Keep in mind that income summary is also a temporary account.

Learning Unit 15

Post-Closing Trial Balance: The final step in the accounting cycle that lists the accounts in the ledger and their balances after adjusting the closing entries have been posted. This trial balance is made up of assets, liabilities, and a new figure for ending owner's equity. Only permanent accounts appear on the post-closing trial balance. The accounts in the post-closing trial balance are the same that will be found on the balance sheet.

1. Explain the purpose of journalizing adjusting entries.
2. The worksheet eliminates the need to journalize and post adjusting entries. Comment.
3. Adjustments are complete when the trial balance is prepared. Agree or disagree? Why?
4. What is meant by a temporary account?
5. Give three examples of a permanent account.
6. Define what is meant by the accounting period. Give examples.
7. List the accounts that usually update owner's equity.
8. Define closing entries.
9. What are the purposes of closing entries?
10. What is the purpose of having temporary accounts that have a zero balance at the end of an accounting period?
11. What is the difference between an expense and a withdrawal?
12. Which type of accounts are carried over to the next accounting period?
13. List the four steps to journalize closing entries.
14. The data needed to journalize adjusting and closing entries can be found in the worksheet. Agree or disagree?
15. Define income summary.
16. Income summary is not found in the general ledger. True or false? Discuss.
17. Define post-closing trial balance.
18. The post-closing trial balance is made up of assets, liabilities, and revenue. Agree or disagree? Discuss.
19. An accounting period is always a calendar year. Agree or disagree? Why?
20. The calendar year is also called the fiscal year. True or false? Explain.

PROBLEM INTERACTORS

1. From the worksheet:
   a. Journalize the adjusting entries.
   b. Journalize the closing entries.
   c. Prepare a post-closing trial balance.

B. BON REPAIRS
Worksheet
For Month Ending December 31, 19XX

Account Titles	Trial Balance Dr.	Cr.	Adjustments Dr.	Cr.	Adjusted Trial Balance Dr.	Cr.	Income Statement Dr.	Cr.	Balance Sheet Dr.	Cr.
Cash	15200				15200				15200	
Supplies	7000			(A) 2000	5000				5000	
Prepaid Rent	6000			(C) 1000	5000				5000	
Auto	136000				136000				136000	
Acc. Dep.—Auto		48000		(B) 10000		58000				58000
Accounts Payable		6200				6200				6200
B. Bon Investment		77000				77000				77000
B. Bon Withdrawal	48000				48000				48000	
Insurance Fees		184000				184000		184000		
Salaries Expense	72000		(D) 8000		80000		80000			
Telephone Expense	23200				23200		23200			
Advertising Expense	4800				4800		4800			
Gas Expense	3000				3000		3000			
	315200	315200								
Supplies Expense			(A) 2000		2000		2000			
Depreciation Expense—Auto			(B) 10000		10000		10000			
Rent Expense			(C) 1000		1000		1000			
Salaries Payable				(D) 8000		8000				8000
			21000	21000	333200	333200	124000	184000	209200	149200
Net Income							60000			60000
							184000	184000	209200	209200

2. Given the following data for B. Bon Repairs:

B. BON REPAIRS
Trial Balance
June 30, 19XX

	Dr.	Cr.
Cash	7,575	
Accounts Receivable	2,000	
Prepaid Insurance	75	
Repair Supplies	25	
Repair Equipment	750	
Truck	825	
Accounts Payable		375
B. Bon Investment		8,325
B. Bon Withdrawal	125	
Repair Fees		3,000
Salaries Expense	300	
Telephone Expense	15	
Advertising Expense	10	
Total	11,700	11,700

Adjustment data:

1. $50 of insurance expired.
2. $10 of repair supplies on hand.
3. Depreciation of repair equipment $50.
4. Depreciation on truck $100.
5. Salaries earned by employees of B. Bon but not yet due $20.

Your task is to:
a. Prepare a worksheet.
b. Journalize adjusting entries.
c. Journalize closing entries.
d. Calculate B. Bon ending investment.

3.** Given the following data for Bob's Fix It Shop:

MAR. 1: Bob Fast invested $20,000 cash and $7,200 worth of fix-it equipment into the Fix It Shop.
1: Paid rent for three months in advance $900.
3: Purchased a delivery truck for use in the business $3,600.
8: Purchased fix-it supplies from John Swift Co. for $200 on account.
16: Collected fix-it fees from customers $10,000.
18: Paid salaries expense for first two weeks of March $400.
22: Bob Fast withdrew $300 from the business for his own personal use.
24: Fixed an antique car; however, the fees earned $12,000 will not be paid to Bob's Fix It Shop until June.
30: Paid salary expense for next two weeks in March $400.
30: Paid John Swift Co. one-half of what was owed from March 8 transaction.
30: Paid advertising expense $40.
30: Paid telephone bill for month $45.

Adjustment data:

1. Rent expired $300.
2. $100 of supplies on hand at end of month.
3. Depreciation on delivery truck $100 ($3,600/3 years = $1,200 per year or $100 per month).
4. Depreciation on fix-it equipment ($7,200/6 years = $1,200 per year or $100 per month).
5. Salaries earned but not paid $20 for month of March.

** Double-starred problems summarize parts of the text. This problem summarizes Chapter 1 through 5.

Chart of accounts:

ASSETS	LIABILITIES
112 Cash	230 Accounts Payable
114 Accounts Receivable	232 Salaries Payable
116 Prepaid Rent	
118 Fix-It Supplies	
120 Delivery Truck	
0120 Accumulated Depreciation— Truck	
122 Fix-It Equipment	
0122 Accumulated Depreciation— Equipment	

REVENUE	OWNER'S EQUITY
450 Fix-It Fees	340 B. Fast Investment
	0340 B. Fast Withdrawal
	342 Income Summary

EXPENSES
560 Salaries Expense
562 Advertising Expense
564 Telephone Expense
566 Rent Expense
568 Fix-It Supplies Expense
570 Depreciation Expense—Truck
572 Depreciation Expense—Equipment

Your task is to:

a. Open accounts in the ledger from the chart of accounts.
b. Journalize March transactions (explanations can be eliminated to save space).
c. Post to the ledger.
d. Foot and balance accounts.
e. Prepare a worksheet.
f. Prepare the financial statements.
g. Journalize and post adjusting and closing entries.
h. Foot and rule the ledger. Be sure to carry balances appropriately forward.
i. Prepare a post-closing trial balance.

1-A. From the worksheet:
   a. Journalize the adjusting entries.
   b. Journalize the closing entries.
   c. Prepare a post-closing trial balance.

MIX BOWLING LANES
Worksheet
For the Month Ended December 31, 19XX

Account Titles	Trial Balance Dr.	Trial Balance Cr.	Adjustments Dr.	Adjustments Cr.	Adjusted Trial Balance Dr.	Adjusted Trial Balance Cr.	Income Statement Dr.	Income Statement Cr.	Balance Sheet Dr.	Balance Sheet Cr.
Cash	7600				7600				7600	
Bowling Supplies	3500			(A) 1500	2000				2000	
Prepaid Insurance	3000			(B) 1000	2000				2000	
Office Equipment	68000				68000				68000	
Acc. Dep.—Office Equipment		24000		(C) 6000		30000				30000
Accounts Payable		3100				3100				3100
R. Mix Investment		38500				38500				38500
R. Mix Withdrawal	24000				24000				24000	
Bowling Fees		92000				92000		92000		
Salary Expense	36000		(D) 4000		40000		40000			
Utilities Expense	11600				11600		11600			
Advertising Expense	2400				2400		2400			
Cleaning Expense	1500				1500		1500			
	157600	157600								
Bowling Supplies Expense			(A) 1500		1500		1500			
Insurance Expense			(B) 1000		1000		1000			
Dep. Exp.—Office Equipment			(C) 6000		6000		6000			
Salaries Payable				(D) 4000		4000				4000
			12500	12500	167600	167600	64000	92000	103600	75600
Net Income							28000			28000
							92000	92000	103600	103600

2-A. Given the following data for J. Ray Co.:

J. RAY CO.

Trial Balance
June 30, 19XX

	Dr.	Cr.
Cash	15,150	
Accounts Receivable	4,000	
Prepaid Rent	150	
Plumbing Supplies	50	
Plumbing Equipment	1,500	
Truck	1,650	
Accounts Payable		750
J. Ray Investment		16,650
J. Ray Withdrawal	250	
Plumbing Fees		6,000
Salaries Expense	600	
Advertising Expense	30	
Telephone Expense	20	
Total	23,400	23,400

Adjustment data:

1. $100 of rent expired.
2. $20 of plumbing supplies on hand (not used up).
3. Depreciation on plumbing equipment $100.
4. Depreciation on truck $300.
5. Salaries earned by employees of J. Ray but not yet due $50.

Your task is to:

a. Prepare a worksheet.
b. Journalize closing entries.
c. Calculate J. Ray ending investment.

3-A. Given the following data for Ron's Plowing Service:

JAN. 1: Ron invested $10,000 in cash and $2,400 worth of snow equipment into the plowing company.

1: Paid rent for two months in advance for garage space $500.

4: Purchased snow plow $6,000 on account from J. P. Worth.

6: Purchased snow supplies for $500 cash.

8: Collected $15,000 from plowing a local shopping center.

JAN. 12: Ron Morin withdrew $600 from the business for his own personal use.
20: Plowed school parking lots, payment not to be received until August $6,000.
26: Paid wages to employees $4,000.
28: Paid J. P. Worth one-half of amount owed for snow plow.
30: Paid advertising expense $540.
30: Paid telephone expense $40.

Adjustment data:

1. Rent expired $250.
2. Snow supplies used up for month $200.
3. Depreciation on snow plow $100 ($6,000/5 years = $1,200 per year or $100 per month).
4. Depreciation on snow equipment $50 ($2,400/4 years = $600 per year or $50 per month).
5. Salaries earned but not paid $100 per month of January.

Chart of accounts:

ASSETS	*REVENUE*
110 Cash	410 Plowing Fees
115 Accounts Receivable	
120 Prepaid Rent	
125 Snow Supplies	
130 Snow Plow	
0130 Accumulated Depreciation— Snow Plow	
135 Snow Equipment	
0135 Accumulated Depreciation— Snow Equipment	

LIABILITIES	*EXPENSES*
210 Accounts Payable	510 Salaries Expense
215 Salaries Payable	515 Advertising Expense
	520 Telephone Expense
	525 Rent Expense
	530 Snow Supplies Expense
	535 Depreciation Expense— Snow Plow
	540 Depreciation Expense— Snow Equipment

OWNER'S EQUITY

310 Ron Morin Investment
0310 Ron Morin Withdrawal
315 Income Summary

Your task is to:

a. Open accounts in the ledger from the chart of accounts.
b. Journalize January transactions.
c. Post to the ledger.
d. Foot and balance accounts.
e. Prepare a worksheet.
f. Prepare the financial statements.
g. Journalize and post adjusting and closing entries.
h. Foot and rule the ledger. Be sure to carry appropriate balance forward.
i. Prepare a post-closing trial balance.

CHALLENGE PROBLEM INTERACTOR

The assets of the Tap-Tap Dance Studio on December 31, 1981 amounted to $80,000; liabilities, $45,000.

The assets of the Tap-Tap Dance Studio on December 31, 1982 amounted to $120,000; liabilities, $70,000.

During 1982, the owner, Henry Tap, invested an additional $20,000 and withdrew $22,000 for his personal use.

Determine the net income for 1982.

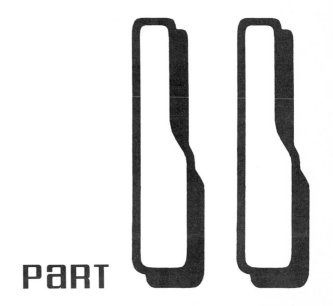

PART **11**

Special Journals for a Merchandise Company

sales journal

Ralph Jones, a former real estate broker with the Katz Real Estate Agency, decided to open up a wholesale sporting goods shop. In Part One of this text we analyzed the Russell Smith Law Office as well as Katz Real Estate; both firms represented *service* companies. The lawyer provided legal services and the real estate firm provided customers the service of finding homes or home buyers; neither had physical goods to resell to customers. When you ride in a taxi or get your hair styled, these businesses, too, are providing services. If you shop in your local supermarket, however, you are physically taking home goods called *merchandise*. A supermarket would be classified as a merchandise company, since it stocks merchandise for resale to customers; it is the selling of merchandise that creates sales or revenue. From this point on, the term sales refers to the revenue for a merchandise company.

The sporting goods store we will now analyze is classified as a wholesale merchandise company. It will sell items to retail companies (who in turn will sell them to the public). Its merchandise might include bowling balls, ski equipment, ski jackets, and tennis equipment. Many businesses combine the providing of services and the selling of merchandise. For example, if a hair stylist decided to carry a line of hair sprays to sell to his customers, his shop would be both providing a service (cutting hair) and selling merchandise.

INTRODUCTION TO SPECIAL JOURNALS

The Katz Real Estate accountant offered to handle the accounting books of Ralph's new sporting goods shop. The following is a summary of conversation between Ralph and the accountant:

Purpose of special journals

A. The general journal used by Katz Real Estate would not be efficient for recording business transactions of the new sporting goods shop. The accountant pointed out that the sporting goods store would have many sales on account to record. It would be inefficient to keep writing the words *accounts receivable* and *sales* in the general journal. This would put quite a burden on a bookkeeper, whose time was limited. What is needed are journals that save repetitive work in journalizing and posting transactions.

B. To handle the detail needed to journalize and eventually post many transactions, a set of special journals will be developed, each of which will record certain types of transactions of the sporting goods store. These journals will simplify the journalizing process, as well as reduce the number of postings the bookkeeper will have to complete.

C. Special journals will allow a division of labor. More than one person can record transactions at once, so that each can become a specialist in one area of the recording and posting process.

D. In an attempt to develop a sound, flexible, and efficient means of journalizing and posting transactions, the following special journals will be designed, keeping in mind the particular needs of the sporting goods company. (Please do not try to memorize the types of journals.) We will be spending one chapter on each of them and by the end of Part Two we will have analyzed them all. This chapter will concern only the sales journal. Any transaction that doesn't fit into these special journals will be recorded in the general journal.

Sales journal	Sale of merchandise on account
Cash receipts journal	Receiving cash from any source
Purchase journal	Buying of merchandise or other items on account
Cash payments journal (Cash disbursement journal)	Paying of cash for any purpose

E. In designing the journals listed above, we will adapt them—their form, column headings, etc.—specifically for the sporting goods shop. If at some time these special journals are not effective, or not needed, possibly owing to decreased number of business transactions, other types of journals can be designed and utilized.

For now, let's study the projections of a high-volume sporting goods store, from which we can begin to understand the purposes and procedures in utilizing special journals.

LEARNING UNIT 16

The Sales Journal: Structure and Purpose

STRUCTURE OF THE SALES JOURNAL

Purpose of a sales journal

At the end of the first month in operation, the sales journal of Ralph's Sporting Goods recorded only *sales made on account*. Whenever a sale was *earned* by selling merchandise, but payment was not received (these customers are called accounts receivable), the transactions involving accounts receivable and sales were entered into a sales journal.

What about a cash sale? Cash sales are recorded in the cash receipts journal, which we will look into after we examine the structure of the sales journal.

Sales journal records only sales *on* account.

The sales journal designed by the accountant for Ralph's Sporting Goods is as follows:

Sales Journal

Date	Invoice No.	Description of Accounts Receivable	Terms	PR	Amount of: Dr.—Accounts Receivable Cr.—Sales

Each company may have different columns reflecting its individual needs. The journal for Ralph's Sporting Goods, for example, has no sales tax column. If the store collected sales tax, a column for the tax might be advisable. The journal for the recording of sales tax would probably look as follows:

Sales Journal						
Date	Invoice No.	Description of Accounts Receivable	PR	Accounts Receivable Dr.	Sales Tax Payable Cr.	Sales Cr.

For example, if on July 1 customer A purchased some merchandise on account for $100, invoice no. 10, plus a 3% sales tax, the sales journal would look as follows:

Sales Journal						
Date	Invoice No.	Description of Accounts Receivable	PR	Accounts Receivable Dr.	Sales Tax Payable Cr.	Sales Cr.
19XX July 1	10	Customer A		103	3	100

That is, $100 sales + $3 sales tax = amount owed $103.*

We are, however, assuming that no sales tax need be collected by the sporting goods shop since it is a wholesale company.

Later on further references will be made to the sales tax, and this brief section should be used for reference when end-of-chapter problems are tried; however, let's look specifically at Ralph's sales journal, which doesn't utilize sales tax.

PURPOSE OF THE SALES JOURNAL

On January 3 Bob Baker Corporation purchased merchandise from Ralph's Sporting Goods, on account, for $3,500, invoice no. 1. Based on the mind-process chart:

---

* If a customer returns merchandise, the sales tax payable account will be reduced by a debit to sales tax payable.

1	2	3		4	Special Journal
		↑	↓		
Accounts Affected	Category	Inc.	Dec.	Rule	Sales Journal
Accounts Receivable	Asset	↑Inc.		Dr.	Why? Sale on account
Sales	Revenue	↑Inc.		Cr.	

The effects of the sale of merchandise would result in an increase to accounts receivable, as well as an increase to sales. Remember, when a sale is earned, the inflow of assets from the sale is usually in the form of cash and/or accounts receivable. In this case, the asset accounts receivable is increasing. The transaction recorded in the sales journal is:

Sales Journal

Date	Invoice No.	Description of Accounts Receivable	Terms	PR*	Amount of Accounts Receivable—Dr. Sales—Cr.
19XX Jan. 3	1	B. Baker	2/10, n/30		3,500

*This column will be explained later.

Where is the above information obtained? Below is the invoice or bill, which includes:

1. the date of the sale on account,
2. the invoice number,
3. the name and address of the customer,
4. credit terms of sale (we'll get to this in a moment),
5. the amount of sale.

2/10, *n*/30: 2% discount if paid within 10 days, or total bill due within 30 days.

RALPH JONES SPORTING GOODS
26 Sable Road
Salem, MA 01970
Telephone: 745-1174

Invoice No. 1
Date: 1/3/XX

Terms: 2/10, n/30

SOLD TO: Bob Baker Corporation
3 Esson Street
Boston, MA 01930

Quantity	Description of Merchandise	Model	Unit Price	Total
10 prs.	Ski Boots	4A	$50/per pr.	$ 500
300	Ski Jackets	775	$10/per jacket	3,000
				$3,500

Notice the terms of credit, 2/10, n/30. This means that if Bob Baker Corporation is able to pay its bill within ten days, it receives a 2% cash discount (2% × $3,500 = $70), or the full amount of $3,500 is due within thirty days. The invoice number 1 that is placed in the above journal is taken directly from the invoice.

SAVING JOURNAL TIME

In looking at the sales journal, notice that this sale on account to Baker is recorded on one line. Think back to the general journal and how it would have looked: the debit on one line, the credit on the next, and a third line for the explanation. *One line in the sales journal now summarizes three lines in the general journal.*

The heading of the sales journal explains that each line that is entered in it will:

↑ Accounts Receivable
↑ Sales

There is no need to keep writing the words accounts receivable and sales for the transaction. The heading description of accounts receivable indicates to whom the sale on account has been made.

CONTROLLING ACCOUNTS AND SUBSIDIARY LEDGER

Purpose of subsidiary ledger

To this point, all information about accounts receivable has been posted in the ledger account entitled accounts receivable. What would happen if Bob Baker Corp. called the sporting goods shop to ask for an update on the amount owed? Would Ralph's Sporting Goods have to search through all the invoices to find the balance owed by Baker?

Can the general ledger accounts receivable provide this specific information about an individual customer? The answer is no. To date we have not developed individual accounts receivables for each credit customer.

It is possible to replace accounts receivable in the ledger with a separate accounts receivable account for each individual customer of Ralph's Sporting Goods. Can you imagine how large the ledger would be if this were done? The preparation of the trial balance, as well as the balance sheet, would be quite time-consuming. It would also increase the chances of posting errors.

In an attempt to overcome this problem, a book or file is developed that contains, in alphabetical order, the specifics or the individual records of the amounts various credit customers owe Ralph. This separate ledger of individual credit customers is called the *accounts receivable subsidiary ledger*.

Purpose of controlling accounts

If Ralph's Sporting Goods adds up what each charge customer owes from the subsidiary ledger, it should equal the summarizing figure in accounts receivable in the general ledger (principal ledger) at the end of the month.

The accounts receivable account in the principal or general ledger is called the *controlling account,* since it summarizes or controls the accounts receivable subsidiary ledger. Remember, the sum of the individual customers in the accounts receivable subsidiary ledger will be equal to the one figure in the controlling account in the general or principal ledger after postings at the end of the month. Let's now look at how to post the sales journal in relation to (1) the general ledger (principal ledger) and (2) the accounts receivable subsidiary ledger.

POSTING THE SALES JOURNAL

Keep in mind that the general ledger is organized by the numbering of the chart of accounts. The accounts receivable subsidiary ledger is arranged alphabetically, which makes it easier to add new credit customers or delete inactive customers. The following is the complete sales journal for January for Ralph's Sporting Goods. Notice the ($\sqrt{}$) in the posting reference column and the 112/410 at the bottom of the posting reference column. These will now be explained.

Sales Journal					Page 1
Date	Invoice No.	Description of Accounts Receivable	Terms	PR	Amount of: Dr.—Accounts Receivable Cr.—Sales
19XX					
Jan. 3	1	B. Baker Corp.	2/10, n/30	$\sqrt{}$	3,500
6	2	D. Adams Corp.	2/10, n/30	$\sqrt{}$	2,500
9	3	B. Baker Corp.	2/10, n/30	$\sqrt{}$	1,500
16	4	A. Sling Co.	2/10, n/30	$\sqrt{}$	1,600
22	5	B. Baker Corp.	2/10, n/30	$\sqrt{}$	2,000
24	6	A. Sling Co.	1/10, n/30	$\sqrt{}$	2,000
30	7	J. Keen Co.	2/10, n/30	$\sqrt{}$	5,000
31		Total		112/410*	18,100

*Some texts prefer to place the parenthesized account numbers (112) and (410) below the $18,100.

Up to now we have been using T-accounts or standard accounts to show balance in the ledger. In reality, a more practical account form that is used in the real world looks as follows. This type of account will give a more up-to-date balance after information is entered.

Date	Item	PR	Dr.	Cr.	Balance

This three-column account will also be used to record ledger information about subsidiary ledgers. We will now see the use of the three-column balance account in the posting of the sales journal (as well as other journals in the future) to general and subsidiary ledgers.

POSTING TO THE ACCOUNTS RECEIVABLE SUBSIDIARY LEDGER

A check (√) is placed in the PR column of the sales journal as soon as possible (daily) after each sale on account has been posted to the accounts receivable subsidiary ledger. This immediate updating to the individual accounts of credit customers in the accounts receivable subsidiary ledger will provide Ralph with up-to-date balances of the amounts owed for a specific credit customer.

For example, let's now reproduce the sales journal showing how the amounts of the sales on account are posted to the accounts receivable subsidiary ledger. Remember, a check (√) is placed in the PR column only after the specific amount of the sale on account has been transferred from the journal to the customer's account in the subsidiary ledger. (See the top footnote on the facing page.)

Sales Journal					Page 1
Date	Invoice No.	Description of Accounts Receivable	Terms	PR	Amount of: Dr.—Accounts Receivable Cr.—Sales
19XX					
Jan. 3	1	B. Baker Corp.	2/10, n/30	√	3,500
6	2	D. Adams Corp.	2/10, n/30	√	2,500
9	3	B. Baker Corp.	2/10, n/30	√	1,500
16	4	A. Sling Co.	2/10, n/30	√	1,600
22	5	B. Baker Corp.	2/10, n/30	√	2,000
24	6	A. Sling Co.	1/10, n/30	√	2,000
30	7	J. Keen Co.	2/10, n/30	√	5,000
				112	
31		Total		410	18,100

DAILY POSTINGS TO SUBSIDIARY LEDGERS:

Accounts Receivable Subsidiary Ledger

D. Adams Corporation

Date	PR	Dr.	Cr.	Bal.
19XX Jan. 6	SJ1	2,500		2,500

As soon as B. Baker Corp. is entered into sales journal (Jan. 3), it is immediately posted to accounts receivable subsidiary ledger. When the posting is complete a (√) is placed in PR of sales journal. The (√) in the journal will always indicate subsidiary ledger has been updated.

B. Baker Corporation*

Date		PR	Dr.	Cr.	Bal.
19XX					
Jan.	3	SJ1	3,500		3,500
	9	SJ1	1,500		5,000
	22	SJ1	2,000		7,000

J. Keen Company

Date		PR	Dr.	Cr.	Bal.
19XX					
Jan.	30	SJ1	5,000		5,000

A. Sling Company

Date		PR	Dr.	Cr.	Bal.
19XX					
Jan.	16	SJ1	1,600		1,600
	24	SJ1	2,000		3,600

For example, if B. Baker Corp. calls on January 23 and asks for an update on its balance as of January 22, the bookkeeper of Ralph's Sporting Goods can turn to the accounts receivable subsidiary ledger and look up B. Baker Corp., which is in alphabetical order, and immediately find the balance of $7,000 ($3,500 + $1,500 + $2,000).[†]

What would have happened if the individual accounts in the subsidiary accounts receivable ledger had not been updated daily? If the January 22 sales to Baker on account had not been posted (√) to the subsidiary ledger, the bookkeeper would not have had the latest or up-to-date balance for Baker. He or she could possibly check the sales journal or thumb through recent invoices not posted as well as check the last balance in the subsidiary ledger.

Now let's look at how the information from the sales journal is posted to the general ledger.

---

[*] In the subsidiary ledger the card for each customer will include his business address, invoice no., etc. For simplicity this has been omitted. The balance in the T-account represents a *debit* balance the same as in a controlling account.

[†] Notice how the three-column account allows a running balance to be kept. Two debits will be added; two credits added. If there is one debit figure and a credit figure, the difference will be taken. If an unusual balance results, often brackets or the Dr. or Cr. abbreviation will be entered in the balance column next to the ending balance.

Sales Journal — Page 1

Date	Invoice No.	Description of Accounts Receivable	Terms	PR	Amount of: Dr.—Accounts Receivable Cr.—Sales
19XX					
Jan. 3	1	B. Baker Corp.	2/10, n/30	✓	3,500
6	2	D. Adams Corp.	2/10, n/30	✓	2,500
9	3	B. Baker Corp.	2/10, n/30	✓	1,500
16	4	A. Sling Co.	2/10, n/30	✓	1,600
22	5	B. Baker Corp.	2/10, n/30	✓	2,000
24	6	A. Sling Co.	1/10, n/30	✓	2,000
30	7	J. Keen Co.	2/10, n/30	✓	5,000
				112	
31		Total		410*	18,100

*The 112 and 410 *could have been* recorded under the 18,100 when the totals were posted to accounts receivable and sales.

POSTED AT END OF MONTH:
TOTAL OF Dr.—ACCOUNTS RECEIVABLE Cr.—SALES

The total of $18,100 is posted at the end of the month to accounts receivable and sales in the general ledger. Notice the (✓) in the journal indicates the accounts receivable subsidiary ledger has been updated *during* the month.

Accounts Receivable — 112

Date	PR	Dr.	Cr.	Bal.
19XX				
Jan. 31	SJ1	18,100		18,100

Sales — 410

Date	PR	Dr.	Cr.	Bal.
19XX				
Jan. 31	SJ1		18,100	18,100

When the total of the sales journal of $18,100 is posted to the general ledger accounts receivable no. 112 as a debit and to sales no. 410

as a credit, these account numbers are placed in the post reference column (PR) of the sales journal on the same line as the total. Notice that:

*Accounts Receivable
Subsidiary Ledger*

General Ledger

The sum of the accounts receivable subsidiary ledger, $18,100, does indeed equal the balance in accounts receivable, $18,100, in the general ledger at the end of the month.

Adams	$ 2,500
Baker	7,000
Keen	5,000
Sling	3,600
	$18,100

=

Accounts Receivable 112

Date	PR	Dr.	Cr.	Bal.
19XX				
Jan. 31	SJ1	18,100		18,100

At this point you should be able to:

1. Differentiate between a service company and a merchandise firm.
2. Define and state the purpose of a special journal.
3. State the purpose of the sales journal.
4. Define what is meant by an invoice.
5. Define 2/10, n/60.
6. Define and state the purpose of a controlling account.
7. Define and state the purpose of a subsidiary ledger.
8. Record sales on account into a sales journal.
9. Post from a sales journal to (a) the accounts receivable subsidiary ledger, (b) the general ledger.

UNIT INTERACTOR 16

Record the following sales on account in the sales journal, total the journal, and post as appropriate.

SEPT.   1: Invoice no. 109 to Miller and Co. $100.
      29: Sold merchandise on account to Mitchell and Mark, Inc., invoice no. 633, for $2,000.

SOLUTION to Unit Interactor 16

Sales Journal				Page 1
Date	**Invoice No.**	**Accounts Debited**	**PR (folio)**	**Accounts Receivable—Dr. Sales—Cr.**
19XX				
Sept. 1	109	Miller and Co.	$\checkmark$	100
29	633	Mitchell and Mark	$\checkmark$	2,000
30		Totals	10/50*	2,100

*The 10/50 could have been placed under the 2,100:

2,100
———
(10)(50)

Posting Rules:

1. During the month (daily) post to each individual account (Miller and Co., Mitchell and Mark) in the accounts receivable subsidiary ledger. A check ($\checkmark$) is placed in the posting reference column.

2. At the end of the month the total of $2,100 is posted to the general ledger as a debit to accounts receivable and credit to sales. These account numbers in the ledger are then placed in the posting reference column (10/50) after postings are complete.

Accounts Receivable Subsidiary Ledger

Miller and Company

Date	PR	Dr.	Cr.	Bal.
19XX				
Sept. 1	SJ1	100		100

Mitchell and Mark

Date	PR	Dr.	Cr.	Bal.
19XX				
Sept. 29	SJ1	2,000		2,000

General Ledger

Accounts Receivable   10

Date	PR	Dr.	Cr.	Bal.
19XX				
Sept. 30	SJ1	2,100		2,100

Sales   50

Date	PR	Dr.	Cr.	Bal.
19XX				
Sept. 30	SJ1		2,100	2,100

LEARNING UNIT 17

Sales Returns and Allowances

Sales Returns and Allowances

Dr.	Cr.
+	−

An account (a contra-account) that shows price reductions caused by customers returning merchandise or keeping merchandise with price reductions caused by defective merchandise or customer dissatisfaction

It is anticipated by Ralph Jones that very little merchandise will be returned by customers (sales returns). Ralph also believes that since his products are of high quality, few sales allowances will have to be made for defects or performance. With this in mind, the accountant decided *not* to set up a special journal for sales returns and allowances. All sales returns and allowances would be recorded into a general journal.

CREDIT MEMORANDUM

On January 10, merchandise that was purchased by D. Adams Corp. was returned because of defects found. Ralph's Sporting Goods issued the following *credit memorandum* to D. Adams Corp.

	Credit Memo No. 1
RALPH'S SPORTING GOODS 26 Sable Road Salem, MA 01970 Telephone: 745-1174	
CREDIT TO: D. Adams Corp. 5 View Avenue Chelsea, MA. 01115	
We credit your account for: 100 Bowling Balls Returned	$500

The issuing of this credit memorandum will (1) reduce the sales of Ralph's Sporting Goods and (2) reduce the amount owed by D. Adams Corp. (since this was a charged sale) to Ralph's Sporting Goods.

Purpose of sales returns and allowances

Although sales returns and allowances are expected to be few, Ralph Jones wants to know *exactly* their amount. Therefore instead of directly reducing sales (by a debit), a new account entitled *sales returns and allowances* will be debited. This will allow the sales account to reflect total sales before any sales returns or allowances result. Sales returns and allowances is really a contra-account that will reduce total sales.

SALES	*Cr.*
LESS: SALES RETURNS AND ALLOWANCES	*Dr.*
= ACTUAL SALES	

In terms of the mind-process chart, issuing a credit memorandum on the books of Ralph would result in:

Accounts Affected	Category	↑ ↓	Rule
Sales Returns and Allowances	↓ to Sales (contra-account)	↑	Dr.
Accounts Receivable—D. Adams	Asset	↓	Cr.

JOURNALIZING SALES RETURNS

The above credit memorandum is recorded in the general journal of Ralph's Sporting Goods as follows:

General Journal				
Date	Account Titles and Descriptions	PR	Dr.	Cr.
19XX Jan. 10	Sales Returns and Allowances* Accounts Receivable—D. Adams Corp.		500	500

* If sales tax were involved, the entry would have:

Seller doesn't owe as much sales tax, since customer has returned merchandise ▷

Sales Returns and Allowances
Sales Tax Payable
   Accounts Receivable – XX

◁ Sales returns and allowances are increasing

◁ Customer doesn't owe as much (don't forget to update subsidiary as well)

Remember a special journal is assumed not to be needed. If the accountant at some time chose to develop a special journal for sales returns and allowances it would look as follows:

Sales Returns and Allowances Journal				
Date	Credit Memo No.	Account Credited	PR	Sales Ret. and Allowances—Dr. Accounts Receivable—Cr.
19XX Jan. 10	1	D. Adams Corp.		500

POSTING TO SUBSIDIARY AND GENERAL LEDGERS

Now let's look at the general journal to see how to post (1) to the accounts receivable subsidiary ledger to the account of D. Adams and (2) from the sales returns and allowances and accounts receivable accounts in the general journal to the general ledger.

Since few journal entries will be recorded in the general journal, Ralph's accountant has decided to post *all* information as soon as it is entered.

After posting:

Date	Account Titles and Descriptions	PR	Dr.	Cr.
19XX Jan. 10	Sales Returns and Allowances	412	500	
	Accounts Receivable—D. Adams	112 √		500

Three postings:*

412 A debit of $500 is recorded in sales returns and allowances, account no. 412, in the general ledger. When this is done, the account number is placed in the PR column of the journal.

√ The check indicates that $500 has been posted as a credit to the account of D. Adams Corp. in the accounts receivable subsidiary ledger.

112 The credit of $500 is also posted to accounts receivable in the controlling account in the general ledger. When this is done the account number (112) is placed in the PR column of the journal.

Notice that the diagonal in the PR column allows for the (√) and account number. The three postings are needed to keep the controlling account, as well as the subsidiary ledger, up to date.

In summary, as transactions were entered into a sales journal, they were posted immediately to the individual customer's account and a (√) was placed in the PR column of the sales journal. The total of the sales journal was posted at the end of the month to the general ledger accounts, sales and accounts receivable. If a credit memo was issued and entered into a general journal, all postings to the subsidiary ledger and general ledger were done when the entry was journalized.

At this point you should be able to:

1. Define and state the purpose of sales returns and allowances.
2. Define what is meant by credit memorandum.
3. Journalize and post transactions resulting from a credit memorandum.

---

*Some companies may choose to post the general ledger accounts at the end of the month. The text assumes these journal entries will be few, and thus all parts are posted immediately.

Bob Smith issued to Mitchell and Mark a credit memorandum for merchandise returned on January 9, credit memorandum no. 45, $500. The account number for accounts receivable is 112 and for sales returns and allowances is 412.

Your task is to journalize and post the credit memorandum for Bob Smith.

Accounts Receivable Subsidiary Ledger

Mitchell and Mark

Date		PR	Dr.	Cr.	Bal.
19XX Jan.	2	SJ1	1,000		1,000

SOLUTION to Unit Interactor **17**

General Journal					Page 1
Date	**Account Titles and Descriptions**	**PR**	**Dr.**	**Cr.**	
19XX Jan. 9	Sales Returns and Allowances	412	500		
	Accounts Receivable—Mitchell and Mark	112 √		500	

Post:

1. A debit of $500 to sales returns and allowances in the general ledger. When this is done, the account number (412) is put in the posting reference column.
2. To accounts receivable as a credit on the general ledger. When this is done, the account number (112) is put in the post reference column.
3. To Mitchell and Mark in our accounts receivable subsidiary ledger to show they don't owe us as much money (because they returned some goods or services to us). When this is posted a check (√) is placed in the post reference column.

Mitchell and Mark

Date		PR	Dr.	Cr.	Bal.
19XX					
Jan.	2	SJ1	1,000		1,000
	9	GJ1		500	500

Accounts Receivable   **112**

Date		PR	Dr.	Cr.	Bal.
19XX					
Jan.	9	GJ1		500	500 Cr.*

*or <500>

Sales Returns and Allowances   **412**

Date		PR	Dr.	Cr.	Bal.
19XX					
Jan.	9	GJ1	500		500

RECORDING SALES ON ACCOUNT WITHOUT A SALES JOURNAL

Before we go on to our next special journal, let's look at what a business could do if it chose not to use a sales journal to record sales on account.

The business could keep carbons of the sales invoice and post from it directly to the subsidiary ledger. The invoices would be kept together for the month and then totaled on an adding machine; the total for sales and accounts receivable could be placed in a general journal by debiting accounts receivable and crediting sales.

If the sales journal is eliminated, the bookkeeper is relieved of the burden of entering information in a journal and then posting it. However, many businesses utilize a sales journal to ensure accuracy. Once again, the journals developed for each business depend on its needs.

As you will see in the problems that follow, the sales journal takes many forms. Some companies not only want a figure for total sales, but want it broken down by products. For example, if a drug store wanted to keep track of sales of ice cream and medicine, it could have two columns in its sales journal to record sales—one for medicines and one for ice cream. Keep in mind that in this chapter the owner of Ralph's Sporting Goods was concerned with the total sales of the company. He did not ask the accountant to break down sales into, say, sportswear, baseball equipment, bowling equipment, etc.

As the accountant, please complete the problems at the end of the chapter. Notice that some of the problems have different headings than does the sales journal in the chapter. Two businesses seldom have exactly the same needs, and accounting journals should provide for this flexibility.

THE SALES JOURNAL—A BLUEPRINT

Part Two takes a closer look at the recording of transactions into special journals, rather than solely into general journals. Special journals will save recording and posting time. This chapter centers on the sales journal, which records only sales on account.

As a transaction is entered into the sales journal, it is immediately posted to the accounts receivable subsidiary ledger; then a check is placed in the post reference column. At the end of the month the totals of the columns of the journal are posted to the general ledger accounts. It is important to remember that the general ledger contains one account for accounts receivable. This is called the controlling account, since at the end of the month the sum of the amounts that the individual customers owe should be equal to the balance in the controlling accounts receivable account in the general ledger.

If a sales journal records sales tax, the sum of the sales plus the sales tax should equal the amount owed by the customer. Sales tax represents a liability that the seller must pay to proper authorities. When this happens, sales tax payable will be debited and cash will be credited.

When a company issues a credit memorandum, the end result on the books shows that sales returns and allowances has increased and that the customer does not owe as much money. Therefore, it will be important to post this information about the customer to the accounts receivable subsidiary ledger and the controlling account.

Keep in mind that some companies prefer to use the sales invoices in the sales journal.

Summary of How to Post

Situation 1—Sale on account:

Sales Journal				END OF MONTH	DURING THE MONTH
DATE	Description	PR	Accounts Receivable: Dr. Sales: Cr.	Total of column is posted to general ledger accounts, accounts receivable, and sales.	Accounts receivable subsidiary ledger is updated as soon as transaction is entered in sales journal. A (√) indicates posting is complete to the subsidiary ledger customer account.
		√ √ √ √ √			
		( ) ( )			

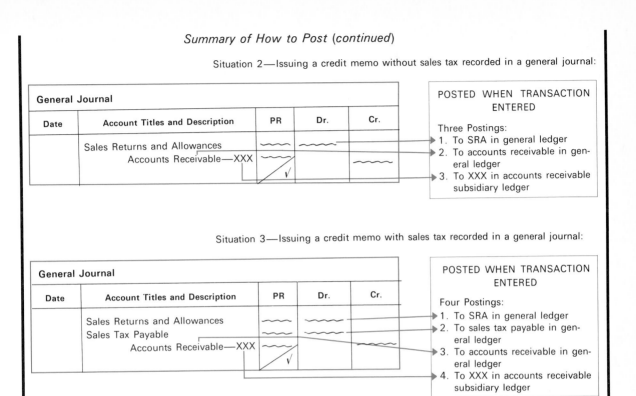

Situation 2—Issuing a credit memo without sales tax recorded in a general journal:

General Journal				
Date	Account Titles and Description	PR	Dr.	Cr.
	Sales Returns and Allowances			
	Accounts Receivable—XXX	√		

POSTED WHEN TRANSACTION ENTERED

Three Postings:
1. To SRA in general ledger
2. To accounts receivable in general ledger
3. To XXX in accounts receivable subsidiary ledger

Situation 3—Issuing a credit memo with sales tax recorded in a general journal:

General Journal				
Date	Account Titles and Description	PR	Dr.	Cr.
	Sales Returns and Allowances			
	Sales Tax Payable			
	Accounts Receivable—XXX	√		

POSTED WHEN TRANSACTION ENTERED

Four Postings:
1. To SRA in general ledger
2. To sales tax payable in general ledger
3. To accounts receivable in general ledger
4. To XXX in accounts receivable subsidiary ledger

SUMMARY OF NEW ACCOUNTING LANGUAGE TERMS

Learning Unit 16

Accounts Receivable Subsidiary Ledger: A book or file that contains in alphabetical order the *individual* records of amounts owed by various credit customers. During the month this subsidiary ledger is continually updated to reflect current balances.

Controlling Account—Accounts Receivable: The accounts receivable account in the general ledger, after postings are complete, shows a firm the total amount of money owed to it. This figure, broken down in the accounts receivable subsidiary ledger, indicates specifically who owes the money. If the accounts receivable subsidiary ledger is added up at the end of a month, it should equal the balance found in the controlling account—accounts receivable.

Invoice: A bill reflecting a sale on credit.

Merchandise Company: A firm that resells merchandise (goods) to its customers.

Principal Ledger: General ledger.

Sales: When merchandise is sold, it represents a sale (revenue) for the firm.

Sales Journal: A special journal used to record *only* sales made on account.

Service Company: A firm that does not sell goods (merchandise) to its customers but rather performs a service to earn its revenue.

Special Journal: A journal used to record similar groups of transactions. Example: the sales journal records all sales on account.

Credit Memorandum: A piece of paper sent by the seller to a customer who has returned merchandise previously purchased on credit. The credit memorandum indicates to the customer that the seller is reducing the amount owed by the customer, owing to the sales returns and allowances.

Sales Returns and Allowances: An account in the ledger of the seller that records merchandise that is being returned by the customer for defects, inadequate performance, etc.

QUESTION INTERACTORS

1. Explain why a sales journal is needed for recording large numbers of sales on account.
2. How can a sales journal save posting labor?
3. Once a journal is designed, it can never be changed. Agree or disagree? Why?
4. Differentiate between a service company and a merchandise firm.
5. Explain what is meant by a controlling account.
6. The subsidiary ledger is really the general ledger. Agree or disagree? Why?
7. If the sales journal has recorded 200 transactions for the month, how many times will sales have to be posted to the general ledger?
8. What does 2/15, n/60 mean?
9. a. An ↑ in sales is a _____ .
   b. A ↓ in sales is a _____ .
   c. An ↑ in sales returns and allowances is a _____ .
   d. A ↓ in sales returns and allowances is a _____ .
10. Define what a credit memorandum is and give an example where one may be used.
11. Accounts receivable subsidiary has to be posted monthly. Agree or disagree? Why?
12. What are the three postings needed to record the issuing of a credit memo to B. P. Ralph for $500 of merchandise returned?
13. Explain how the sales invoices could possibly replace the sales journal.
14. The accounts receivable subsidiary ledger is used for cash customers only. Please comment.
15. Explain why the balance of each customer is not found in the general ledger.
16. Explain why each entry in the sales journal is not recorded in the accounts receivable controlling account.
17. When merchandise is returned, why not just debit sales instead of debiting sales returns and allowances? You're the manager—your comment would be appreciated.
18. When should a firm design and use a sales returns and allowances journal instead of a general journal?
19. What is meant by a principal ledger?
20. Sales tax should never be recorded in a sales journal. Please comment.

PROBLEM INTERACTORS

1. On September 1 Ron Smith opened up a wholesale creative crafts store. Terms of all sales on account are 2/10, n/30.

   19XX, SEPT. 15: Sold merchandise on account to Sloan Corp. $600. Invoice no. 1.

   21: Sold merchandise on account to Apples Corp. $300. Invoice no. 2.

   23: Issued a credit memorandum no. 1 to Sloan Corp. for $200 of merchandise returned due to poor workmanship.

   25: Sold merchandise on account to Ryan Company $500. Invoice no. 3.

   29: Issued a credit memorandum no. 2 to Apples Corp. for $100 of merchandise returned due to cracks.

   Your task is to:

   a. Set up a partial general ledger made up of accounts receivable 112, sales 410, and sales returns and allowances 411.

   b. Set up an accounts receivable subsidiary ledger for Sloan Corp., Apples Corp., and Ryan Company.

   c. Record the above transactions in the sales journal (page 1) and general journal (page 2) as appropriate.

   d. Post to the subsidiary accounts receivable ledger and general ledger as appropriate.

   e. List the amount and name of each customer owing money to Ron Smith's shop at the end of the month.

   f. Show how the controlling account is equal to the sum total of the accounts receivable subsidiary ledger.

*2. On December 1, 19XX, the accounts receivable subsidiary ledger had the following balances for Smith's Electrical Supplies.

J. Rose Company

Date	PR	Dr.	Cr.	Bal.
19XX 12/1	Bal.*			500

B. Blum Company

Date	PR	Dr.	Cr.	Bal.
19XX 12/1	Bal.			200

Ginny Creations

Date	PR	Dr.	Cr.	Bal.
19XX 12/1	Bal.			100

* The word "Bal." is written to indicate J. Rose has a balance of $500. In your study guide a (√) is placed to indicate it is a balance, and the word "Bal." is written into the item column.

The general ledger (partial) had balances of:

	Account No.	
(1) Accounts receivable	110	$800
(2) Sales tax payable	210	100
(3) Electrical sales	410	0
(4) Sales returns & allowances	420	0

Your task is to:

a. Record the December transactions in the sales journal (page 4) and or general journal (page 2) as appropriate.

b. Post to the accounts receivable subsidiary ledger and general ledger when appropriate.

c. Calculate the total amount of sales tax payable due at the end of December.

d. List the accounts and the balance of individual customers owed to Smith at the end of December. Does it balance with accounts receivable in the general ledger? The heading of the sales journal is provided as follows:

Sales Journal						Page 4
Date	Invoice No.	Customer's Name Accounts Receivable	PR	Accounts Receivable Dr.	Sales Tax Payable Cr.	Electrical Sales Cr.

19XX, DEC.

1: Sold electrical merchandise to J. Rose $600, invoice no. 50 plus 5% sales tax.

5: Sold electrical merchandise to B. Blum $300, invoice no. 51 plus 5% sales tax.

8: Sold electrical merchandise to Ginny Creations $5,000, invoice no. 52 plus a 5% sales tax.

10: Issued a credit memorandum no. 10 to J. Rose for $300 for defective electrical merchandise returned from Dec. 1 transaction. (Be careful to record the reduction in sales tax payable as well.)

12: Sold electrical merchandise to B. Blum $200, invoice no. 53 plus 5% sales tax.

*3. Mom Katz opened up The Pizza Pad. Here are the sales journal headings for The Pizza Pad.

Sales Journal						Page 1
Date	Sales Slip Number	Customer's Name	PR	Accounts Receivable Dr.	Pizza Sales Cr.	Grocery Sales Cr.

Your task is to:

a. Open up the following accounts in the general ledger:

Account No.	Account Name
110	Accounts Receivable
410	Pizza Sales
420	Grocery Sales
430	Sales Returns and Allowances—Grocery

b. Open up the following accounts in the accounts receivable subsidiary ledger:

Russell David
Abby Ellen
Ann Katz

c. Record the transactions of The Pizza Pad (all journals are page 1).

d. Post to the accounts receivable subsidiary ledger and/or general ledger where appropriate.

e. Verify that the amount of the individual balances in the accounts receivable subsidiary ledger is equal to the amount in the controlling account.

19XX, NOV. 1: Sold on account to Russell David grocery merchandise $100. Sales slip no. 1.

4: Sold on account to Abby Ellen Pizza merchandise $50. Sales slip no. 2.

8: Sold $150 of grocery merchandise to Ann Katz on account. Sales slip no. 3.

10: Issued a credit memorandum no. 1 to Russell David for $20 of grocery merchandise returned due to spoilage.

15: Sold on account pizza merchandise to Abby Ellen $15. Sales slip no. 4.

19: Sold grocery merchandise on account to Ann Katz $300. Sales slip no. 5.

25: Sold on account pizza merchandise to Russell David $350. Sales slip no. 6.

ADDITIONAL PROBLEM INTERACTORS

1-A. On August 1, Jim Corbett Co. opened up a mail order watch company. All sales on account have credit terms of 1/10, n/30.

19XX, AUG. 15: Sold merchandise on account to D. Doherty Corp. $500. Invoice no. 1.

20: Sold merchandise on account to Doran Corp. $5,000. Invoice no. 2.

19XX, AUG. 22: Issued a credit memorandum no. 1 to Doran Corp. for $1,000 of merchandise returned due to defective workmanship.

25: Sold merchandise on account to Roland Corp. $750. Invoice no. 3.

28: Issued a credit memorandum no. 2 to D. Doherty Corp. $100 for merchandise returned for defective performance.

Your task is to:

a. Set up a partial general ledger made up of accounts receivable 110, sales 410, and sales returns and allowances 411.

b. Set up an accounts receivable subsidiary ledger for Doherty Corp., Doran Corp., and Roland Corp.

c. Record the above transactions in the sales journal (page 1) and or general journal (page 1) and post to the subsidiary accounts receivable ledger and general ledger as appropriate.

d. List the amount and name of each customer owing money to Jim Corbett mail order at the end of the month.

e. Show how the controlling accounts is equal to the sum total of the accounts receivable subsidiary ledger.

*2-A. On December 1, 19XX, the accounts receivable subsidiary ledger had the following balances for John's Grocery.

Brenner Corporation

Date	PR	Dr.	Cr.	Bal.
19XX 12/1	Bal.			600

Kate Corporation

Date	PR	Dr.	Cr.	Bal.
19XX 12/1	Bal.			250

Mick Corporation

Date	PR	Dr.	Cr.	Bal.
19XX 12/1	Bal.			200

Karen Corporation

Date	PR	Dr.	Cr.	Bal.
19XX 12/1	Bal.			150

The general ledger (partial) has balances of:

Acct. No.	Acct. Name	Balance
110	Accounts Receivable	$1,200
210	Sales Tax Payable	200
310	Grocery Sales	0
312	Sales Returns and Allowances	0

Your task is to:

a. Record the December transactions in the sales journal (page 5) or general journal (page 4).

b. Post to the accounts ledger when appropriate.

c. Calculate total amount of sales tax payable due at the end of December.

d. List the individual customer accounts and the balance owed to John's Grocery at end of December. Does it balance with accounts receivable in the general ledger? The heading of the sales journal is as follows:

Sales Journal						**Page 5**
Date	Invoice No.	Customer's Name	PR	Accounts Receivable Dr.	Sales Tax Payable Cr.	Grocery Sales Cr.

19XX, DEC. 1: Sold merchandise to Brenner Corp. $800, invoice no. 55, plus a 5% sales tax.

8: Sold merchandise to Mick Corp. $500, invoice no. 56, plus a 5% sales tax.

9: Sold merchandise to Kate Corp. $3,000, invoice no. 57, plus a 5% sales tax.

10: Issued credit memorandum no. 15 to Brenner Corp. for $400 for stale merchandise sold on account. (Be careful to record the reduction to sales tax payable as well.)

12: Sold merchandise to Karen Corp. $300, invoice no. 58, plus a 5% sales tax.

* 3-A. Ron Seller opened up an ice cream parlor. The shop sold ice cream and candy. The following is the sales journal heading for the ice cream shop (all journals are page 1).

Date	Sales Slip No.	Customer's Name	PR	Accounts Receivable Dr.	Ice Cream Sales Cr.	Candy Sales Cr.

Your task is to:

a. Open up the following accounts in the general ledger:

Accounts Receivable	110
Ice Cream Sales	310
Candy Sales	312
Sales Returns and Allowances—Candy	314

b. Open up the following accounts in the accounts receivable subsidiary ledger:

Philip Deen
Sherri Lapatin
Donna Rose
Peter Selznick

c. Record the transactions of the ice cream parlor.

d. Post to the subsidiary ledger and general ledger when appropriate.

e. Verify that the amount of the individual balances in the accounts receivable subsidiary ledger is equal to the amount in the controlling account.

19XX, DEC.　1: Sold on account to Donna Rose candy $15. Sales slip no. 1.

3: Sold on account to Philip Deen ice cream $50. Sales slip no. 2.

7: Sold $100 of candy to Sherri Lapatin on account. Sales slip no. 3.

8: Issued a credit memorandum no. 1 to Sherri Lapatin for $10 for candy returned due to spoilage.

19: Sold on account ice cream to Peter Selznick $100. Sales slip no. 4.

24: Sold candy on account to Donna Rose $150. Sales slip no. 5.

28: Sold on account to Philip Deen $50 of ice cream. Sales slip no. 6.

CHALLENGE PROBLEM INTERACTOR

The accounts receivable control account debit balance at the end of an accounting period does not agree with the total of the balances of the customer's accounts in the accounts receivable subsidiary ledger. Indicate whether each of the following situations would cause this difference. Each statement is an independent assumption.

	Yes	No
1. A cash sale to J. L. Stingy, a customer, was recorded in the sales journal as a sale on account.	_____	_____
2. A sale on account that was recorded in the sales journal was posted as a credit to the customer's subsidiary ledger account.	_____	_____
3. A return of a credit sale was journalized in the general journal and posted to the accounts receivable control account and the subsidiary ledger, but the posting to the sales return and allowance account was omitted.	_____	_____
4. A charge sale to H. L. Homer was recorded in the sales journal and incorrectly posted as a debit to H. L. Homer's individual subsidiary account.	_____	_____
5. The total of the amount column in the sales journal had been posted as a transposed number to the accounts receivable control account.	_____	_____

Explain each answer, *Yes* or *No,* in detail.

7

cash receipts
journal

In the last chapter the sales journal of Ralph's Sporting Goods was analyzed. Recall that the sales journal recorded only sales made *on account*. Now let's turn our attention to the special journal of Ralph's Sporting Goods that records all transactions involving the *receipt of cash from any source*. (Checks are considered to be cash.)

LEARNING UNIT 18

The Cash Receipts Journal: Structure and Purpose

Keep in mind that the cash receipts journal will provide many of the same features of the other special journals:

1. Save journalizing time and labor.
2. Allow division of labor in recording transactions.
3. Help update the accounts receivable subsidiary ledger.

Based upon what Ralph told him, the accountant designed the cash receipts journal as follows:

Cash Receipts Journal							Page 1
Date	Accounts	PR	Sundry Account Cr.	Sales Cr.	Accounts Receivable Cr.	Sales Discount Dr.	Cash Dr.

CASH (Dr.). This column records the receipt of cash (or check) from any source. The debit indicates cash will be increasing. Remember that the special journal is receiving an *inward* flow of cash. The other columns in the journal explain why the inward flow of cash occurs.

SALES DISCOUNT (Dr.). The customers of Ralph's Sporting Goods have a chance to pay early and receive a sales discount. This column collects the amount of sales discounts. Notice that it is a debit. In effect, the sales discounts (Dr.) will eventually reduce total sales (Cr.).

Sales discount is a contra-revenue (sales) account increased by a Dr. (Remember, revenue is increased by a Cr.)

SALES	*Cr.*
LESS: SALES DISCOUNT	*Dr.*
= AMOUNT OF ACTUAL SALES AFTER DISCOUNTS ARE TAKEN BY CUSTOMERS	

ACCOUNTS RECEIVABLE (Cr.). This column reduces the amount customers owed Ralph's Sporting Goods. Remember that, in the sales journal, sales on account are recorded as a debit to accounts receivable and a credit to sales. Now the cash receipts journal is receiving payment from customers, thereby reducing accounts receivable and increasing cash.

SALES (Cr.). Remember that the cash receipts journal is used to record transactions involving the receipt of cash. This column records the *cash sales* made; keep in mind that the cash column records the actual cash received. All sales made on account will *not* be recorded in this column. This column is designed by the accountant to record only cash sales.

SUNDRY ACCOUNT (Cr.). This column is often called *miscellaneous sources*. It is used when receipt of cash does not come from cash sales or payment of charge sales by customers. The column provides flexibility for recording infrequent transactions that result in an inflow of cash. If a transaction occurs frequently, it may call for the adding of another special column in the journal.

RECORDING TRANSACTIONS INTO THE CASH RECEIPTS JOURNAL

In January the following transactions are recorded in the cash receipts journal of Ralph's Sporting Goods. Let us look first at the mind-process charts.

JANUARY 2: Ralph invested $20,000 cash into the business.

Accounts Affected	Category	↑ ↓	Rule
Cash	Asset	↑	Dr.
Jones Investment	Owner's Equity	↑	Cr.

JANUARY 13: Sold merchandise for $3,500 cash.

Accounts Affected	Category	↑ ↓	Rule
Cash	Asset	↑	Dr.
Sales	Revenue	↑	Cr.

JANUARY 15: Sold merchandise for $1,500 cash.

Accounts Affected	Category	↑ ↓	Rule
Cash	Asset	↑	Dr.
Sales	Revenue	↑	Cr.

JANUARY 16: Received payment from D. Adams Corp. for invoice no. 2, $2,000, less discount.

Accounts Affected	Category	↑ ↓	Rule
Cash	Asset	↑	Dr.
Sales Discount	↓ to Revenue	↑*	Dr.
Accounts Receivable	Asset	↓	Cr.

*The total of sales discounts taken by customers is increasing. Remember, sales discount is a contra-revenue account.

JANUARY 16: B. Baker Corp. paid invoice no. 1, dated January 3, $3,500, no discount.

Accounts Affected	Category	↑ ↓	Rule
Cash	Asset	↑	Dr.
Accounts Receivable	Asset	↓	Cr.

JANUARY 28: B. Baker Corp. paid invoice no. 5, dated January 22, $2,000, less discount.

Accounts Affected	Category	↑ ↓	Rule
Cash	Asset	↑	Dr.
Sales Discount	↓ to Revenue	↑	Dr.
Accounts Receivable	Asset	↓	Cr.

JANUARY 28: A. Sling Co. paid invoice no. 4, dated January 16, $1,600, no discount.

Accounts Affected	Category	↑ ↓	Rule
Cash	Asset	↑	Dr.
Accounts Receivable	Asset	↓	Cr.

JANUARY 29: Borrowed $10,000 from the bank. Interest is not due for five years.

Accounts Affected	Category	↑ ↓	Rule
Cash	Asset	↑	Dr.
Notes Payable*	Liability	↑	Cr.

*Notes Payable means Ralph's Sporting Goods made a definite written promise to pay $10,000 in the future. We will not concern ourselves with interest until the note is paid back.

RECORDING TRANSACTIONS INTO CASH RECEIPTS JOURNAL

The need for a special journal for cash

Notice how many times the words *cash, sales, sales discount,* and *accounts receivable* showed up in the above charts. If a general journal were used, imagine the amount of time that would be needed by a bookkeeper to write these words. Then, of course, each journal entry would have to be posted.

In order to avoid this repetitive work and process information rapidly, as well as reduce labor costs, the above transactions involving the receiving of cash were entered in the cash receipts journal of Ralph's Sporting Goods as follows (we will deal with posting soon):

Cash Receipts Journal							**Page 1**
Date	Account Credited	PR	Sundry Cr.	Sales Cr.	Accounts Receivable Cr.	Sales Discount Dr.	Cash Dr.
19XX							
Jan. 2	R. Jones Investment	310	20,000				20,000
13	Cash Sales	X		3,500			3,500
15	Cash Sales	X		1,500			1,500
16	D. Adams Corp.	✓			2,000	40	1,960
16	B. Baker Corp.	✓			3,500		3,500
28	B. Baker Corp.	✓			2,000	40	1,960
28	A. Sling Co.	✓			1,600		1,600
29	Notes Payable	212	10,000				10,000
31	Totals		30,000	5,000	9,100	80	44,020
			(X)	(410)	(112)	(414)	(110)

Notice that the total of the debit column(s) is equal to the total of the credit column(s).

DEBIT COLUMNS		=	CREDIT COLUMNS			
Cash	+ Sales Discount	=	Accounts Receivable +		Sales	+ Sundry
$44,020 +	$80	=	$9,100	+	$5,000	+ $30,000
	$44,100				$44,100	

This process of checking that the total debits are equal to the total credits of the cash receipts journal is called *cross-footing*. This is done before the totals are posted. Cross-footing aids in verifying that the journalizing process has been completed accurately. Also, if a bookkeeper were using more than one page for cash receipts journal, the balances on the bottom of one page would be brought forward to the next page. This verifying of totals would result in less "work" when trying to find journalizing or posting errors at a later date.

POSTING THE CASH RECEIPTS JOURNAL:
A COLUMN-BY-COLUMN ANALYSIS

CASH (Dr.). The total of the column, $44,020, is posted as a debit to cash (account no. 110) in the general ledger at the end of the month. No individual entries are posted during the month. When the total is posted to cash (110), the account number is placed below the total of the cash column in the cash receipts journal. This shows that the posting of cash is complete.

Cash Receipts Journal	Page 1
	Cash Dr.
	20,000
	3,500
	1,500
	1,960
	3,500
	1,960
	1,600
	10,000
	44,020
	(110)

Total of cash posted to cash
in general ledger,
end of month.

SALES DISCOUNT (Dr.). The total of the column is posted as a debit of $80 to sales discount in the general ledger (account no. 414) at the end of the month. No individual entries are posted during the month. When the total is posted to sales discount (account no. 414), the account number is placed below the total of the sales discount column in the cash receipts journal. This indicates that the posting is complete.

Total of sales discount posted to sales discount in general ledger, end of month

Cash Receipts Journal		Page 1
	Sales Discount Dr.	
	40	
	40	
	80	
	(414)	

ACCOUNTS RECEIVABLE (Cr.)

Cash Receipts Journal				Page 1
	Accounts Credited	PR	Accounts Receivable Cr.	
	D. Adams Corp.	√	2,000	
	B. Baker Corp.	√	3,500	
	B. Baker Corp.	√	2,000	
	A. Sling Co.	√	1,600	
			9,100	
			(112)	

Total is posted to accounts receivable in the general ledger at end of month. Account no. 112

Individual credits to accounts receivable customer posted daily. A (√) is placed in PR when posted. See next page.

Accounts Receivable					112
Date		PR	Dr.	Cr.	Bal.
19XX					
Jan.	10	GJ1		500	500 Cr.*
	31	SJ1	18,100		17,600
	31	CRJ1		9,100	8,500

* ⟨500⟩. Some bookkeepers prefer to add regular brackets ⟨   ⟩ instead of writing Dr. or Cr. to indicate an unusual balance.

Notice the accounts receivable subsidiary ledger is not found in the general ledger and is updated daily *during* the month.

D. Adams Corp.

Date		PR	Dr.	Cr.	Bal.
19XX					
Jan.	6	SJ1	2,500		2,500
	10	GJ1		500	2,000
	16	CRJ1		2,000	–0–

B. Baker Corp.

Date		PR	Dr.	Cr.	Bal.
19XX					
Jan.	3	SJ1	3,500		3,500
	9	SJ1	1,500		5,000
	16	CRJ1		3,500	1,500
	22	SJ1	2,000		3,500
	28	CRJ1		2,000	1,500

J. Keen Corp.

Date		PR	Dr.	Cr,	Bal.
19XX					
Jan.	30	SJ1	5,000		5,000

A. Sling Co.

Date		PR	Dr.	Cr.	Bal.
19XX					
Jan.	16	SJ1	1,600		1,600
	24	SJ1	2,000		3,600
	28	CRJ1		1,600	2,000

SALES (Cr.). The total of the column $5,000 is posted to sales account no. 410 as a credit in the general ledger at the end of the month. No individual entries are posted during the month. An (X) in the PR column shows that no posting is done during the month.

Total of sales is posted to sales in general ledger, end of month.

Cash Receipts Journal				Page 1
	PR		Sales Cr.	
	X		3,500	
	X		1,500	
			5,000	
			(410)	

SUNDRY (Cr.). The total of $30,000 is not posted. Place an (X) to show *not* to post the total. The $30,000 is not made up of one item; it is made up of R. Jones investment as well as notes payable. Therefore, R. Jones investment is posted to the general ledger account R. Jones investment (310) daily. When this is done, the account number, 310, is placed in the PR column to show posting is complete.

Notes payable is posted to the general ledger, account no. 212, daily. When this is done, the number of the account, 212, is placed in the PR column to show that posting is complete.*

Cash Receipts Journal			Page 1
Accounts Credited	PR	Sundry Cr.	
R. Jones Investment	310	20,000	

Notes Payable	212	10,000	
Totals		30,000	
		(X)	

The total of the sundry column is not posted. The (X) indicates no posting necessary.

General Ledger

Jones Investment   **310**

Date	PR	Dr.	Cr.	Bal.
19XX				
Jan. 2	CRJ1		20,000	20,000

Notes Payable   **212**

Date	PR	Dr.	Cr.	Bal
19XX				
Jan. 29	CRJ1		10,000	10,000

*Some companies may choose to post the individual items in the Sundry column monthly.

Now let's summarize the cash receipts journal and its posting rules:

Cash Receipts Journal   **Page 1**

Date	Accounts Credited	PR	Sundry Cr.	Sales Cr.	Accounts Receivable Cr.	Sales Discount Dr.	Cash Dr.
19XX							
Jan. 2	R. Jones Investment	310	20,000				20,000
13	Cash Sales	X		3,500			3,500
15	Cash Sales	X		1,500			1,500
16	D. Adams Corp.	✓			2,000	40	1,960
16	B. Baker Corp.	✓			3,500		3,500
28	B. Baker Corp.	✓			2,000	40	1,960
28	A. Sling Co.	✓			1,600		1,600
29	Notes Payable	212	10,000				10,000
31	Totals		30,000	5,000	9,100	80	44,020
			(X)	(410)	(112)	(414)	(110)

Not posted	Totals posted to general ledger at end of month*

Accounts Receivable Subsidiary Ledger

D. Adams Co.

Date	PR	Dr.	Cr.	Bal.
19XX				
Jan. 6	SJ1	2,500		2,500
10	GJ1		500	2,000
16	CRJ1		2,000	–0–

R. Baker

Date	PR	Dr.	Cr.	Bal.
19XX				
Jan. 3	SJ1	3,500		3,500
9	SJ1	1,500		5,000
16	CRJ1		3,500	1,500
22	SJ1	2,000		3,500
28	CRJ1		2,000	1,500

General Ledger

Cash   **110**

Date	PR	Dr.	Cr.	Bal.
19XX				
Jan. 31	CRJ1	44,020		44,020

Accounts Receivable   **112**

Date	PR	Dr.	Cr.	Bal.
19XX				
Jan. 10	GJ1		500	500 Cr.
31	SJ1	18,100		17,600
31	CRJ1		9,100	8,500

*Also includes Jones Investment and Notes Payable which was posted daily from the Sundry column.

(continued on next page)

Accounts Receivable Subsidiary Ledger

J. Keen

Date		PR	Dr.	Cr.	Bal.
19XX Jan.	30	SJ1	5,000		5,000

A. Sling

Date		PR	Dr.	Cr.	Bal.
19XX Jan.	16	SJ1	1,600		1,600
	24	SJ1	2,000		3,600
	28	CRJ1		1,600	2,000

General Ledger

Notes Payable   212

Date		PR	Dr.	Cr.	Bal.
19XX Jan.	29	CRJ1		10,000	10,000

Jones Investment   310

Date		PR	Dr.	Cr.	Bal.
19XX Jan.	2	CRJ1		20,000	20,000

Sales   410

Date		PR	Dr.	Cr.	Bal.
19XX Jan.	31	CRJ1		5,000	5,000

Sales Discount   414

Date		PR	Dr.	Cr.	Bal.
19XX Jan.	31	CRJ1	80		80

In review, at this time you should be able to:

1. Define and state the purpose of the cash receipts journal.
2. Explain how the cash receipts journal can save journalizing time and posting labor.
3. Differentiate between posting to the accounts receivable subsidiary ledger and posting to the general ledger.
4. Explain the difference between a sale and a sales discount.
5. Define and explain the purpose of cross-footing the cash receipts journal.
6. Explain the purpose of the Sundry column in the cash receipts journal.

Journalize, and post when appropriate, the following transactions into the cash receipts journal.

19XX, DEC. 1: Jim Smith paid partially what he owed us ($100, less a 2% discount or $98).
2: Made a sale to Paul Silas for cash of $200.
4: Borrowed $2,000 cash from a bank.

Cash Receipts Journal							Page 1
Date	Account Name	Folio (PR)	Sundry Account Cr.	Sales Cr.	Accounts Receivable Cr.	Sales Discount Dr.	Cash Dr.

Accounts Receivable Subsidiary Ledger

P. Silas

Date		PR	Dr.	Cr.	Bal.
19XX Dec.	1	Bal.			350

J. Smith

Date		PR	Dr.	Cr.	Bal.
19XX Dec.	1	Bal.			300

Partial General Ledger

Cash   110

Date	PR	Dr.	Cr.	Bal.

Accounts Receivable   120

Date		PR	Dr.	Cr.	Bal.
19XX Dec.	1	Bal.			650

Notes Payable   310

Date	PR	Dr.	Cr.	Bal.

Sales   410

Date		PR	Dr.	Cr.	Bal.
19XX Dec.	1	Bal.			650

Sales Discount   420

Date	PR	Dr.	Cr.	Bal.

Cash Receipts Journal							Page 1
Date	Account Name	Folio* (PR)	Sundry Account Cr.	Sales Cr.	Accounts Receivable Cr.	Sales Discount Dr.	Cash Dr.
19XX							
Dec. 1	Jim Smith	✓			100	2	98
2	Cash Sale	X		200			200
4	Notes Payable	310	2,000				2,000
31	Totals		2,000	200	100	2	2,298
			(X)	(410)	(120)	(420)	(110)

*Folio is another term used for *posting reference* (PR).

POSTING RULES

Sundry (Cr.)

Total of $2,000 is not posted! Place an (X) to show not to post total. Notes payable is posted to general ledger at any time during the month. When this is done, the account number, 310, is put into the folio* column.

Sales (Cr.)

Total of column ($200) is posted to sales (account no. 410) as a credit in the general ledger at the end of the month. No individual entries are posted during the month. An (X) is put in the folio column to show not to post each amount.

Accounts Receivable (Cr.)

The total of the column ($100) is posted as a credit to accounts receivable in general ledger (account no. 120) at the end of the month. During the month each individual entry (Jim Smith, etc.) is posted daily as a credit to the account in the accounts receivable subsidiary ledger. When this is done, a check (✓) is put in the folio column to show that the posting has been done.

Sales Discount (Dr.)

Total of column ($2) is posted as a debit to sales discount in the general ledger (account no. 420) at the end of the month. No individual entries are posted during the month.

Cash (Dr.)

Total of column ($2,298) is posted as a debit to cash (account no. 110) in the general ledger at the end of the month. No individual entries are posted during the month.

Accounts Receivable Ledger (Subsidiary)   General Ledger

P. Silas

Date		PR	Dr.	Cr.	Bal.
19XX					
Dec.	1	Bal.			350

J. Smith

Date		PR	Dr.	Cr.	Bal.
19XX					
Dec.	1	Bal.			300
	1	CRJ1		100	200

Cash   110

Date		PR	Dr.	Cr.	Bal.
19XX					
Dec.	31	CRJ1	2,298		2,298

Accounts Receivable   120

Date		PR	Dr.	Cr.	Bal.
19XX					
Dec.	1	Bal.			650
	31	CRJ1		100	550

Notes Payable   310

Date		PR	Dr.	Cr.	Bal.
19XX					
Dec.	4	CRJ1		2,000	2,000

Sales   410

Date		PR	Dr.	Cr.	Bal.
19XX					
Dec.	1	Bal.			650
	31	CRJ1		200	850

Sales Discount   420

Date		PR	Dr.	Cr.	Bal.
19XX					
Dec.	31	CRJ1	2		2

No posting was made to Paul Silas since it was a cash sale.

LEARNING UNIT 19

How to Prove the Accounts Receivable Subsidiary Ledger

PREPARING THE SCHEDULE OF ACCOUNTS RECEIVABLE

Let's look now at the accounts receivable subsidiary ledger of Ralph's Sporting Goods after all posting has been completed from the sales, cash receipts, and general journal. Notice that the posting reference column shows from what page of the journal the information was posted.

D. Adams Corp.

Date		Description*	PR	Dr.	Cr.	Bal.
19XX						
Jan.	6	Invoice No. 2	SJ1	2500 00		2500 00
	10	Merchandise Returned—Invoice No. 2	GJ1		500 00	2000 00
	16	Payment of Invoice No. 2	CRJ1		2000 00	. . .

Bob Baker Corp.

Date		Description*	PR	Dr.	Cr.	Bal.
19XX						
Jan.	3	Invoice No. 1	SJ1	3500 00		3500 00
	9	Invoice No. 3	SJ1	1500 00		5000 00
	16	Payment of Invoice No. 1	CRJ1		3500 00	1500 00
	22	Invoice No. 5	SJ1	2000 00		3500 00
	28	Payment of Invoice No. 5	CRJ1		2000 00	1500 00

*Depending on the needs of individual companies this column may contain detailed information such as invoice numbers, terms, etc. For our purpose in the text, the only pertinent information you may want to enter would be invoice number. Check with your instructor for specific class requirements.

J. Keen Co.

Date		Description	PR	Dr.	Cr.	Bal.
19XX						
Jan.	30	Invoice No. 7	SJ1	5000 00		5000 00

A. Sling Co.

Date		Description	PR	Dr.	Cr.	Bal.
19XX						
Jan.	16	Invoice No. 4	SJ1	1600 00		1600 00
	24	Invoice No. 6	SJ1	2000 00		3600 00
	28	Payment of Invoice No. 4	CRJ1		1600 00	2000 00

By listing the customer accounts that have balances, we obtain a schedule of accounts receivable:

RALPH'S SPORTING GOODS
Schedule of Accounts Receivable
January 31, 19XX

B. Baker Corp.	$1,500
J. Keen Co.	5,000
A. Sling Co.	2,000
Total Accounts Receivable	$8,500

Does the sum of the accounts receivable subsidiary ledger equal the accounts receivable, the controlling account at the end of January?

Taken from Ralph's Sporting Goods is accounts receivable, the controlling account in the general ledger, after postings:

Accounts Receivable					Account No. 112
Date	Item	PR	Dr.	Cr.	Bal.
19XX					
Jan. 10		GJ1		500 00	500 00 Cr.
31		SJ1	18,100 00		17,600 00
31		CRJ1		9,100 00	8,500 00

Purpose of schedule of accounts receivable

Notice that the debit balance of $8,500 is equal to the sum of all the individual balances of customers owing Ralph's Sporting Goods store money from previously earned sales on account. The balance of the controlling account, accounts receivable $8,500, in the general ledger does indeed equal the sum of the individual customer balances in the accounts receivable subsidiary ledger. The schedule of accounts receivable can help forecast potential cash inflows as well as possible credit and collection decisions.

At this point you should be able to:

1. Explain the advantages of using the three-column account in the subsidiary accounts receivable ledger.
2. Define and state the purpose of a schedule of accounts receivable.
3. Prepare a schedule of accounts receivable.
4. Show the relationship of the accounts receivable controlling account to the subsidiary accounts receivable ledger.

UNIT INTERACTOR 19

From the accounts receivable subsidiary ledger, prepare a schedule of accounts receivable for Jim's Plumbing.

Audio Co.					
Date	Item	PR	Dr.	Cr.	Bal.
19XX					
Oct. 3	. . .	SJ35	11,604 00		11,604 00
13	. . .	CRJ14		11,604 00	
27	. . .	SJ35	11,908 00		11,908 00

Freeman Products

Date	Item	PR	Dr.	Cr.	Bal.
19XX Oct. 26	. . .	SJ35	36000		36000

Wells Co.

Date	Item	PR	Dr.	Cr.	Bal.
19XX Aug. 24	. . .	SJ35	11,38500		11,38500
Oct. 24	. . .	CRJ14		1,20000	10,18500

SOLUTION to Unit Interactor **19**

JIM'S PLUMBING

Schedule of Accounts Receivable
October 31, 19XX

Audio Products	$11,908.00
Freeman Co.	360.00
Wells Co.	10,185.00
Total Accounts Receivable	$22,453.00

THE QUESTION OF SALES TAX

The total of sales tax payable would be posted to sales tax payable in general ledger at end of month.

Many states require the collection of a sales tax. For the Ralph's Sporting Goods operation assume we have no sales tax; however, if there were one, the following type of journal might have been designed.

Date	Accounts Credited	PR	Sundry Cr.	Sales Tax Payable Cr.	Sales Cr.	Accounts Receivable Cr.	Sales Discount Dr.	Cash Dr.

The total of the sales tax would be posted to sales tax payable in the general ledger at the end of the month. It represents a liability of the merchant to forward the tax to the city, state, etc.

The problems at the end of the chapter show a variety of headings for cash receipts journals of particular companies. Although the headings may change, the theory remains the same.

The cash receipts journal records all inflow of cash from any source. Like other special journals, it lessens the time required for recording and posting functions.

The two most difficult columns of the cash receipts journal involve sundry and accounts receivable. The total of the sundry column is never posted. Individual items in the accounts receivable column require immediate posting to the specific customer in the accounts receivable subsidiary ledger to indicate that payment was received and that the customer doesn't owe as much.

Keep in mind that only sales on account would be recorded on the sales journal. All cash sales would be recorded on the cash receipts journal. Once information is updated in the accounts receivable subsidiary ledger from the sales journal, cash receipts journal, and general journal, a schedule of accounts receivable can be prepared that lists out the customers' names and the amount each presently owes.

Here is a summary of how to post:

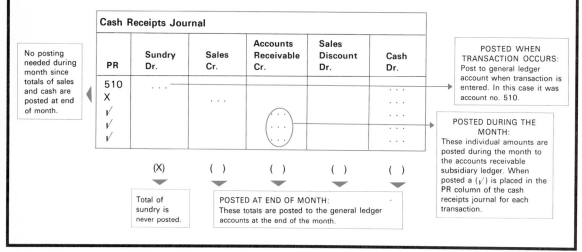

SUMMARY OF NEW ACCOUNTING LANGUAGE TERMS

Learning Unit 18

Cash Receipts Journal: A special journal that records all transactions involving the receipt of cash from any source.

Cross-Footing: The process of proving the total debit columns of a special journal are equal to the total credit columns of a special journal.

Notes Payable: Amounts owed to creditors that involve an unconditional written promise to pay to the order to someone at some date in the future a certain sum of money. Notes payable represent a liability found on the balance sheet.

Sales Discount: An account that records the amount of discounts customers receive for early payment. Sales discount is a contra-revenue account that causes sales to decrease. Sales are increased by credits; thus, this contra-revenue account (sales discount) is increased by debits. Sales discount has a debit balance that will be shown on an income statement as a reduction of revenue.

Sundry: Miscellaneous accounts column(s) in a special journal, which records parts of transactions that do not occur too often. If transactions occur frequently, additional column headings for the journal may be appropriate.

Learning Unit 19

Schedule of Accounts Receivable: A list of the customers, in alphabetical order, from the accounts receivable subsidiary ledger that have an outstanding balance. This total should be equal to the balance of accounts receivable controlling account at the end of the month.

Three-Column Account: A type of account that allows the balance to be immediately shown after an entry is recorded. It is an expanded form of a standard account.

QUESTION INTERACTORS

1. What is the purpose of the cash receipts journal?
2. How does the cash receipts journal save posting labor?
3. What is the usual balance of sales discount?
4. What function does the sundry column in the cash receipts journal serve?
5. Explain the difference between accounts payable and notes payable.
6. If cash is received from 300 individual transactions for one month, how many postings will be needed in the cash receipts journal?
7. The total of the sundry column is never posted. Why?
8. Cash sales should be recorded in the sales journal. Explain.
9. What purpose does cross-footing serve?
10. What effect does sales discount have on sales?
11. Explain why the controlling account, accounts receivable, is not found in the subsidiary accounts receivable ledger.
12. What is the difference between a sales slip and an invoice?
13. Explain why a schedule of accounts receivable is prepared.
14. What is the relationship of the controlling account, accounts receivable, to the schedule of accounts receivable and sales?
15. Explain why some cash receipts journals need a column for sales tax.
16. The cash receipts journal is never redesigned once the headings are started. Explain.
17. What is the relationship between the sales journal and cash receipts journal as relates to accounts receivable and sales?
18. The general journal records only sales for cash. Explain.
19. Will a schedule of accounts receivable be accurate if the postings of the sales journal are not complete? Explain.
20. Explain the division of labor in relationship to the cash receipts journal.

1. Record the following in the cash receipts journal of Martha's Pad. Be sure to post when appropriate to the accounts receivable subsidiary ledger and general ledger. All sales have credit terms of 2/10, n/60. Please prepare a schedule of accounts receivable.

19X7, JAN. 1: Borrowed $5,000 cash from the Victory Bank, signing a written note promising to pay back the full amount plus 5% interest on Dec. 1, 19X7.
3: Cash sales collected $400.
7: Received $1,000 cash from Smith & Lowes for the balance due on its account. No discount.
18: Received cash from John Block in payment of Jan. 12 invoice. Less discount.
25: Received cash from Ralph Ford in payment of Jan. 20 invoice. Less discount.
27: Cash sales collected $1,000.

Accounts Receivable Subsidiary Ledger

John Block

Date		PR	Dr.	Cr.	Bal.
19X7					
Jan.	12	SJ1	1,800		1,800
	18	SJ1	2,000		3,800

Ralph Ford

Date		PR	Dr.	Cr.	Bal.
19X7					
Jan.	20	SJ1	2,000		2,000
	25	SJ1	500		2,500

Smith & Lowes

Date		PR	Dr.	Cr.	Bal.
19X6					
Dec.	15	SJ1	1,000		1,000

General Partial Ledger

Cash   110

Date	PR	Dr.	Cr.	Bal.

Accounts Receivable   112

Date		PR	Dr.	Cr.	Bal.
19X7					
Jan.	1	Bal.	1,000		1,000
	31	SJ1	6,300		7,300

Notes Payable   210

Date	PR	Dr.	Cr.	Bal.

Sales   410

Date		PR	Dr.	Cr.	Bal.
19X7					
Jan.	1	Bal.		1,000	1,000
	31	SJ1		6,300	7,300

Sales Discount   412

Date	PR	Dr.	Cr.	Bal.

Cash Receipts Journal Heading							Page 1
Date	Account Name	PR	Sundry Cr.	Sales Cr.	Accounts Receivable Cr.	Sales Discount Dr.	Cash Dr.

*2. John Allson operates a retail shoe store.

a. Record the following transactions in the sales journal (page 5), cash receipts journal (page 2), and general journal (page 1) for the month of May (a continuation of the months of April).

19XX, MAY
1: John Allson invested an additional $11,000 in the shoe store.

3: Sold $500 of merchandise on account to C. Paul, sales ticket no. 50, terms 1/10, n/30.

4: Sold $300 of merchandise on account to Phil Mahoney, sales ticket no. 51, terms 1/10, n/30.

9: Sold $200 of merchandise on account to Gordon Brown, sales ticket no. 52, terms 1/10, n/30.

10: Received cash from C. Paul in payment of May 3, sales ticket no. 50, less discount.

20: Sold $1,000 of merchandise on account to Maureen DiAnni, sales ticket no. 53, terms 1/10, n/30.

22: Received cash payment from Phil Mahoney in payment of May 4 transaction, sales ticket no. 51.

23: Collected cash sales for $3,000.

24: Issued credit memorandum no. 10 to Maureen DiAnni for $500 of merchandise returned from May 20 sales on account.

26: Received cash from Maureen DiAnni in payment of May 20 sales ticket no. 53. (Don't forget about the credit memo and discount.)

28: Collected cash sales for $2,000.

30: Sold shoe rack equipment for $500 cash. (Beware.)

30: Sold merchandise $2,000 on account to Phil Mahoney, sales ticket no. 54, terms 1/10, n/30.

31: Issued credit memorandum no. 11 to Phil Mahoney for $200 of merchandise returned from May 30, sales ticket no. 54.

b. Post from the three journals to the accounts receivable ledger and general ledger as needed.

c. Prepare a schedule of accounts receivable. Verify the controlling account to the accounts receivable subsidiary ledger.

The following information is given:

ALLSON SHOES

Schedule of Accounts Receivable
April 30, 19XX

G. Brown	$200
M. DiAnni	400
P. Mahoney	300
C. Paul	200
Total	$1,100

Partial General Ledger

Cash   **10**

Date		PR	Dr.	Cr.	Bal.
19XX May	1	Bal.			19,500

Accounts Receivable   **12**

Date		PR	Dr.	Cr.	Bal.
19XX May	1	Bal.			1,100

Shoe Rack   **14**

Date		PR	Dr.	Cr.	Bal.
19XX May	1	Bal.			500

J. Allson Investment   **30**

Date		PR	Dr.	Cr.	Bal.
19XX May	1	Bal.			20,000

Sales   **40**

Date		PR	Dr.	Cr.	Bal.
19XX May	1	Bal.			1,100

Sales Discount   **42**

Date	PR	Dr.	Cr.	Bal.

Sales Returns and Allowances   **44**

Date	PR	Dr.	Cr.	Bal.

Sales Journal Page 5

Date	Invoice No.	Terms	Account Debited	PR	Accounts Receivable—Dr. Sales—Cr.

Cash Receipts Journal Page 2

Date	Customer Account Credited	PR	Sundry Cr.	Sales Cr.	Accounts Receivable Cr.	Sales Discount Dr.	Cash Dr.

*3. Ron's Market opened up for business on April 1. There is a 5% sales tax on all sales. The following are the headings of Ron's sales journal and cash receipts journal. Notice that Ron is interested in keeping sales of groceries separate from liquor sales. Ron offers no sales discounts.

Sales Journal Page 1

Date	Customer	Sales Ticket	PR	Accounts Receivable Dr.	Sales Tax Payable Cr.	Grocery Sales Cr.	Liquor Sales Cr.

Cash Receipts Journal Page 1

Date	Description of Receipt	PR	Sundry Cr.	Accounts Receivable Cr.	Sales Tax Payable Cr.	Grocery Sales Cr.	Liquor Sales Cr.	Cash Dr.

The following transactions resulted in April:

19XX, APR. 1: Ron Jones invested $8,000 into the market from his own personal savings account.

5: From the cash register tapes, cash grocery sales were $3,000 plus sales tax collected $150.

5: From the cash register tapes, cash liquor sales were $2,000 plus sales tax collected $100.

8: Sold groceries on account to Jeff Kline, sales ticket no. 1, $200 plus sales tax.

9: Sold liquor to Howard Seligman on account $300, sales ticket no. 2, plus sales tax.

19XX, APR. 15: Issued a credit memorandum no. 1 to Jeff Kline for $100 for groceries returned. (Be sure to reduce sales tax payable for Ron.)

19: Howard Seligman paid half of amount owed from sales ticket no. 2, date April 9.

21: Sold groceries to Ken Sorkin $100 on account plus sales tax, sales ticket no. 3.

24: Sold liquor on account to Ed Newburgh $400 plus sales tax, sales ticket no. 4.

25: Issued a credit memorandum no. 2 to Ken Sorkin for $50 for groceries returned from sales ticket no. 3 dated April 21.

29: Cash sales taken from the cash register tape showed:
(1) Groceries—$1,000 + $50 sales tax collected.
(2) Liquor—$2,000 + $100 sales tax collected.

29: Sold groceries to Howard Seligman on account $200, sales ticket no. 5 (plus sales tax).

30: Received payment from Howard Seligman of sales ticket no. 5 dated April 29.

a. Record the above in the sales journal, cash receipts journal, or general journal.

b. Cross-foot or total columns of journals.

c. Post to subsidiary ledger and general ledger when appropriate.

d. Prepare a schedule of accounts receivable for the end of April. Verify it to the controlling account.

Account numbers are as follows: cash (10), accounts receivable (12), sales tax payable (20), Ron Jones Investment (30), grocery sales (40), sales returns and allowances (42), liquor sales (44).

ADDITIONAL PROBLEM INTERACTORS

1-A. Record the following in the cash receipts journal. Be sure to post when appropriate to the accounts receivable subsidiary ledger and general ledger. All sales have credit terms of 2/10, n/60.

19XX, APR. 1: Borrowed $10,000 from Slink Bank, signing a note promissory to pay back the full amount plus 5%. Interest due on Nov. 1, 19XX.

7: Received $3,000 cash from Rang Corp. for the balance due on its account. No discount.

8: Collected cash sales $500.

8: Received payment from Butler Corp. in payment of March 30 invoice. (Please don't forget discount.)

24: Received payment from Molly Corp. in payment of April 20 invoice. (Please don't forget discount.)

30: Collected cash sales $2,000.

The following information is given:

Accounts Receivable Subsidiary Ledger

Rang Corporation

Date		PR	Dr.	Cr.	Bal.
19XX					
Mar.	10	SJ1	3,000		3,000

Butler Corporation

Date		PR	Dr.	Cr.	Bal.
19XX					
Mar.	30	SJ1	1,000		1,000

Molly Corporation

Date		PR	Dr.	Cr.	Bal.
19XX					
Apr.	20	SJ1	500		500

General Ledger

Cash   110

Date	PR	Dr.	Cr.	Bal.

Accounts Receivable   120

Date		PR	Dr.	Cr.	Bal.
19XX					
April	1	Bal.			4,000
	30	SJ1	500		4,500

Notes Payable   210

Date	PR	Dr.	Cr.	Bal.

Sales   310

Date		PR	Dr.	Cr.	Bal.
19XX					
April	1	Bal.			4,000
	30	SJ1		500	4,500

Sales Discount   312

Date	PR	Dr.	Cr.	Bal.

Cash Receipts Journal							Page 1
Date	Account Name	PR	Sundry Cr.	Sales Cr.	Accounts Receivable Cr.	Sales Discount Dr.	Cash Dr.

*2-A. Mike Rang operates a retail toy store.

a. Record the following transactions in the sales journal, cash receipts journal, and general journal (all page 10) for the month of June (a continuation of the month of May).

19XX, JUNE

1: Mike Rang invested an additional $5,000 into the toy store.

2: Sold $150 of merchandise on account to Pat Bond, sales ticket no. 55, terms 2/10, n/30.

3: Sold $400 of merchandise on account to Rich Venner, sales ticket no. 56, terms 1/10, n/30.

9: Sold $100 of merchandise on account to Mike Raff, sales ticket no. 57, terms 1/10, n/30.

11: Received cash from Pat Bond in payment of June 2 sales ticket no. 55 less discount.

20: Sold $2,000 of merchandise on account to Joe Smooth, sales ticket no. 58, terms 1/10, n/30.

22: Received cash payment from Rich Venner in payment of June 3 transaction, sales ticket no. 56.

23: Collected $5,000 from cash sales.

24: Issued credit memorandum no. 110 to Joe Smooth for $1,000 of merchandise returned from June 20 sale on account.

26 Received cash from Joe Smooth in payment of June 20 sales ticket no. 58. (Don't forget about credit memo and discount.)

28: Collected cash sales $1,000.

29: Sold shelving equipment for $200 cash. (This is not a sale.)

29: Sold merchandise on account $1,000 to Joe Smooth, sales ticket no. 59, terms 1/10, n/30.

30: Issued credit memorandum no. 111 to Joe Smooth for $500 of merchandise refund for June 29 sales ticket no. 59.

b. Post from the three journals (all page 10) to the accounts receivable subsidiary ledger as needed.

c. Prepare a schedule of accounts receivable. Verify the controlling account to the accounts receivable subsidiary ledger.

The following information is given:

MIKE'S TOY STORE

Schedule of Accounts Receivable
May 31, 19XX

P. Bond	$100
M. Raff	200
J. Smooth	300
R. Venner	200
Total	$800

Cash				110
Date	PR	Dr.	Cr.	Bal.

Accounts Receivable				112
Date	PR	Dr.	Cr.	Bal.
19XX June 1	Bal.			800

Shelving Equipment				114
Date	PR	Dr.	Cr.	Bal.
19XX June 1	Bal.			200

M. Rang Investment				310
Date	PR	Dr.	Cr.	Bal.

Sales				410
Date	PR	Dr.	Cr.	Bal.
19XX June 1	Bal.			800

Sales Discount				412
Date	PR	Dr.	Cr.	Bal.

Sales Returns and Allowances				414
Date	PR	Dr.	Cr.	Bal.

Headings of cash receipts and sales journals:

Sales Journal					Page 10
Date	Invoice No.	Account Debited	PR	Terms	Accounts Receivable—Dr. Sales—Cr.

Cash Receipts Journal							Page 10
Date	Customer Account Credited	PR	Sundry Cr.	Sales Cr.	Accounts Receivable Cr.	Sales Discount Dr.	Cash Dr.

* 3-A. Kelly Martin opened up a new delicatessen on June 1. The state requires tax of 5%. The following are the headings of the sales journal and cash receipts journal of Kelly's Deli. Notice that Kelly wants to keep take-out and restaurant sales separate.

Sales Journal							Page 1
Date	Customer	Sales Slip	PR	Accounts Receivable Dr.	Tax Payable Cr.	Restaurant Sales Cr.	Take-out Sales Cr.

Cash Receipts Journal								Page 1
Date	Description of Receipt	PR	Sun-dry Cr.	Accounts Receivable Cr.	Tax Payable Cr.	Restaurant Sales Cr.	Take-out Sales Cr.	Cash Dr.

19XX, JUNE
1: Kelly Martin invested $5,000 into the deli from his own personal savings account.

6: From the cash register tapes take-out sales were $2,000 plus tax collected $100.

6: From the cash register tapes restaurant sales were $4,000 plus tax of $200.

8: Sold 5 lb. of salami to go on account to Bill Flynn $100, sales ticket no. 1, plus tax.

9: Hosted a luncheon meeting for Ed Bell $400 on account, sales ticket no. 2, plus tax.

14: Issued a credit memorandum no. 1 to Bill Flynn for $50 for 2½ lb. of salami returned. (Be sure to reduce tax payable for Kelly.)

18: Ed Bell paid one-fourth of amount owed from sales ticket no. 2 dated June 9.

21: Sold bagels and cream cheese to go to Sue Fields on account for $200 plus tax, sales ticket no. 3.

23: Provided a sit-down lunch for Joe Black on account $60 plus tax, sales ticket no. 4.

25: Issued credit memorandum no. 2 to Sue Field for $100 for bagels that were returned from sales ticket no. 3 dated June 21. (Don't forget to reduce tax payable.)

26: Cash sales taken from register tape:
(1) Take-out: $2,000 + $100 tax.
(2) Restaurant sales: $1,000 + $50 tax.

29: Sold deli to go to Ed Bell on account $100, sales ticket no. 5, plus tax.

19XX, JUNE 30: Received payment from Ed Bell of sales ticket no. 5 dated June 29.

a. Record the above in the sales journal, cash receipts journal, or general journal.
b. Cross-foot or total columns of the journal.
c. Post to the subsidiary ledger and general ledger when appropriate.
d. Prepare a schedule of accounts receivable at the end of June. Verify it to the controlling account.

Account numbers are as follows: cash (110), accounts receivable (120), tax payable (220), K. Martin investment (330), restaurant sales (440), take-out sales (442), sales returns and allowances (446).

CHALLENGE PROBLEM INTERACTOR

Below are the necessary columns of a general journal, sales journal, and cash receipts journal. Post these journals to the proper ledger accounts.

Open the following accounts in the ledger:

Cash no. 10
Accounts receivable no. 15
Notes payable no. 20
G. Whiz investment no. 30
Sales no. 40
Sales discounts no. 42
Sales returns and allowances no. 44
Subsidiary ledger accounts:
 Happy Co.
 Indifferent Co.
 Sad Co.

General Journal				Page 1
Date	Accounts	PR	Debit	Credit
	Sales Returns & Allowances		600	
	Acc. Rec.—Sad Co.			600

Sales Journal			Page 1
Date	Accounts	PR	Amount
	Happy Co.		3,000
	Sad Co.		2,000
	Indifferent Co.		4,000
	Total		9,000

Cash Receipts Journal							Page 1
Date	Accounts	PR	Sundry Account	Cash Sales	Accounts Receivable	Sales Discount	Cash
	G. Whiz Investment		10,000				10,000
	Happy Co.				3,000	60	2,940
	Notes Payable		2,000				2,000
	Cash Sales			1,500			1,500
	Sad Co.				1,400	28	1,372
	Cash Sales			1,800			1,800
	Totals		12,000	3,300	4,400	88	19,612

purchase
journal

The purchase journal for Ralph's Sporting Goods is designed for buying merchandise or items on account.

The Purchase Journal: Structure and Purpose

Here is the journal heading:

Purchase Journal							Page 1
			Accounts Payable	Purchases	Sundry Account Dr.		
Date	Accounts Credited	PR	Cr.	Dr.	Account	PR	Amount

The column for purchases will record the cost of merchandise for resale.*

For Ralph's Sporting Goods the following transactions occurred that affect the purchase journal:

19XX, JAN. 2: Purchased merchandise from Pete Regan Company on account $5,000, terms 2/10, n/30.

*For the time being, when we develop mind-process charts, the account purchases will fall in the category of "cost of merchandise for resale."

19XX, JAN. 9: Purchased merchandise from Pete Regan Company on account $4,000, terms 2/10, n/30.

11: Purchased merchandise from Russell Slater on account $5,000, terms 1/15, n/60.

21: Purchased delivery truck $3,600 on account from Mike's Garage.

27: Purchased merchandise from King Company on account $6,000, terms 2/10, n/30.

29: Purchased merchandise from Pete Regan Company on account $6,000, terms 2/10, n/30.

ANALYSIS OF TRANSACTIONS THAT ARE RECORDED IN PURCHASE JOURNAL

Let's analyze each transaction through the mind-process charts.

JAN. 2: Purchased merchandise from Pete Regan Company on account $5,000, 2/10, n/30.

Accounts Affected	Category	↑ ↓	Rule
Purchases	Cost of merchandise for resale	↑	Dr.
Accounts Payable	Liability	↑	Cr.

Purchases are merchandise for resale.

Notice that purchases is defined as merchandise for resale. For example, when you go to a supermarket and buy a can of soup, it represents merchandise or purchases to the supermarket (from a wholesaler) that is now being resold to you, the customer.

The purchases account for Ralph doesn't tell us at what price the merchandise is sold to the customer. We do know that these purchases have increased the amount Ralph owes to Pete Regan Company.

Let's look at the actual purchase invoice that Pete Regan Company sends to Ralph's Sporting Goods.

PETE REGAN COMPANY 18 Fifth Avenue Roland, Maryland Telephone: 111-22184 Shipping:* Northern Trucking Co. SOLD TO: Ralph Jones Sporting Goods 26 Sable Rd. Salem, Mass 01970	Customer Order Date: 1/2/XX **Invoice No. 81** Date Shipped 1/8/XX Terms 2/10, n/30

Quantity	Description	Unit Price	Amount
100	Army Tents	$50	$5,000 $5,000

*We have not yet discussed shipping terms. They involve who shall pay the cost of shipping—the seller or the buyer. This cost of bringing the goods into the store does not represent the "selling price." Purchases are the cost to Ralph to bring the merchandise into the store; what he sells it for will surely be higher than his cost to bring the merchandise into the store.

Since the credit terms are 2/10, n/30, Ralph's Sporting Goods has ten days to pay the bill in order to take advantage of a 2% cash discount. Otherwise the bill for the full amount of the purchases is due within thirty days.

JAN. 9: Purchased from Regan Company merchandise on account, $4,000, terms 2/10, n/30.

Accounts Affected	Category	↑ ↓	Rule
Purchases	Cost of merchandise for resale	↑	Dr.
Accounts Payable	Liability	↑	Cr.

Once again, the merchandise Ralph's is bringing into the store will hopefully be resold to customers, and the cost is recorded in the purchases journal. Ralph's has increased what it owes Regan. Remember, at this point we do not know the price which the goods will be sold to customers.

JAN. 11: Purchased merchandise from Russell Slater on account $5,000, terms 1/15, n/60.

Accounts Affected	Category	↑ ↓	Rule
Purchases	Cost of merchandise for resale	↑	Dr.
Accounts Payable	Liability	↑	Cr.

Ralph buys merchandise for resale to his customers for a cost of $5,000. What he will sell it for, we don't know. We do know Ralph now owes $5,000 for the merchandise, or $4,950 if he pays the bill within fifteen days and receives the 1% discount.

JAN. 21: Purchased delivery truck $3,600 on account from Mike's Garage.

Accounts Affected	Category	↑ ↓	Rule
Delivery Truck	Asset	↑	Dr.
Accounts Payable	Liability	↑	Cr.

Delivery truck is not considered a purchase (merchandise for resale) since it is used in running Ralph's operations.

Please notice: In the first three transactions merchandise was bought by Ralph for resale to Ralph's customers. *The delivery truck is not meant for resale to Ralph's customers.* The delivery truck will be used in the operation of the sporting goods store. It is an asset that is being used to produce sales for Ralph. If Ralph were in the business of selling delivery trucks, then the truck would be considered purchases, or merchandise for resale to customers. This is *not* the case.

In summary:

1. If an asset is purchased for use in the operations of a business, do not record it in the purchase account. Record it as, for example, truck, supplies, or whatever.
2. If merchandise is for resale to customers, record it in the purchase account. Remember, the purchase account only tells us the cost (to Ralph) of the merchandise that is for resale. The purchase account does not tell the price that Ralph is charging to his customers.

Let's analyze the remaining transactions affecting the purchases journal.

JAN. 27: Purchased merchandise from King Company on account $6,000, terms 2/10, n/30.

Accounts Affected	Category	↑ ↓	Rule
Purchases	Cost of merchandise for resale	↑	Dr.
Accounts Payable	Liability	↑	Cr.

JAN. 29: Purchased merchandise from Pete Regan Company on account $6,000, terms 2/10, n/30.

Accounts Affected	Category	↑ ↓	Rule
Purchases	Cost of merchandise for resale	↑	Dr.
Accounts Payable	Liability	↑	Cr.

If your task were to journalize each of these transactions into a general journal, imagine how many times you would have to:

1. Write the word purchases.
2. Write the word accounts payable.
3. Write explanations for each journal entry.

If you had to post you would have to:

1. Post many times to the purchase account in the general ledger.
2. Post many times to the accounts payable account in the general ledger.

STRUCTURE OF PURCHASE JOURNAL

The special journal developed for purchases, when journalized and posted, would look as follows for Ralph's Sporting Goods:

Purchase Journal					Page 1		
Date	Accounts Credited	PR	Accounts Payable Cr.	Purchases Dr.	Sundry Account Dr.		
					Account	PR	Amount
19XX							
Jan. 2	Pete Regan Co.	✓	5,000	5,000			
9	Pete Regan Co.	✓	4,000	4,000			
11	Russell Slater	✓	5,000	5,000			
21	Mike's Garage	✓	3,600		Delivery Truck	116	3,600
27	King Corp.	✓	6,000	6,000			
29	Pete Regan Co.	✓	6,000	6,000			
31	Total		29,600	26,000			3,600
			(210)	(510)			(X)

Before explaining the purchase journal and its postings column by column, let's take a look at the controlling account and the subsidiary ledger for accounts payable.

CONTROLLING ACCOUNT AND SUBSIDIARY LEDGER

If Ralph comes into the bookkeeping office and asks how much the company owes Pete Regan as of January 11, will the accounts payable in the general ledger provide the answer to the question? No! The bookkeeper will have to search the purchase journal or purchase invoices. This can be very time-consuming and is not very cost effective.

Accounts payable subsidiary ledger defined

In the chapters on the sales and cash receipts journal, we developed an accounts receivable subsidiary ledger. Now, instead of looking at individual customers that owe Ralph money, we want to develop a system of keeping track of the amount Ralph owes to companies for merchandise, supplies, equipment, etc., that were bought on account.

The accounts receivable subsidiary ledger represented a potential inflow of cash, while the accounts payable subsidiary ledger represents a potential outflow of cash. Of course, it is possible to replace accounts payable in the general ledger with a separate accounts payable account for each company from which Ralph buys merchandise, supplies, equipment, etc. on account. The size of the account (general ledger) would be cumbersome if such transactions were numerous. Also, the preparation of the trial balance as well as the income statement and balance sheet would be quite complex, and many more postings would be needed if the general ledger contained many individual accounts.

Relationship of subsidiary ledger to general ledger

To overcome these problems, we develop a book or file, arranged alphabetically, that lists the companies Ralph owes money to from purchases on account. This separate ledger is called the *accounts payable subsidiary ledger.*

If Ralph's Sporting Goods adds up what it owes each company from purchases on account, it should equal the summarizing figure for accounts payable found in the general ledger (principal ledger) at the end of the month.

The accounts payable account in the principal or general ledger is called the *controlling account*, since it summarizes or controls the accounts payable subsidiary ledger.

POSTING THE PURCHASE JOURNAL

ACCOUNTS PAYABLE (Cr.). Each time an entry is made in the accounts payable (Cr.) column of the purchase journal, the accounts payable subsidiary ledger should be updated daily. Each time an entry is posted to the individual subsidiary ledger account, a (✓) is placed in the purchase journal PR column. At the end of the month the total of $29,600 is posted as a credit to accounts payable (210) in the general ledger. When this is done, the account number, 210, is placed below the total of the column.

The accounts payable subsidiary is not updated at the end of the month. The total of this column is posted at the end of the month to accounts payable in general ledger.

Purchase Journal			Page 1
Date	Accounts Credited	PR	Accounts Payable Cr.
19XX			
Jan. 2	Pete Regan Co.	✓*	5,000
9	Pete Regan Co.	✓	4,000
11	Russell Slater	✓	5,000
21	Mike's Garage	✓	3.600
27	King Corp.	✓	6,000
29	Pete Regan Co.	✓	6,000
31	Total		29,600
			(210)

*Daily postings to the accounts payable subsidiary ledger.

King Corp

Date	PR	Dr.	Cr.	Bal.
19XX				
Jan. 27	PJ1		6,000	6,000

Mike's Garage

Date	PR	Dr.	Cr.	Bal.
19XX				
Jan. 21	PJ1		3,600	3,600

Pete Regan Co.

Date	PR	Dr.	Cr.	Bal.
19XX				
Jan. 2	PJ1		5,000	5,000
9	PJ1		4,000	9,000
29	PJ1		6,000	15,000

Russell Slater

Date	PR	Dr.	Cr.	Bal.
19XX				
Jan. 11	PJ1		5,000	5,000

Accounts Payable   210

Date	PR	Dr.	Cr.	Bal.
19XX				
Jan. 31	PJ1		29,600	29,600

PURCHASES COLUMN (Dr.). The total of the purchases column is posted at the end of the month to the purchase account, no. 510, in the general ledger. No postings are necessary during the month.

Total of purchases is posted to purchases in general ledger at end of the month.

Purchase Journal		Page 1
	Purchases	
. . .	**Dr.**	. . .
	5,000	
	4,000	
	5,000	
	6,000	
	6,000	
	26,000	
	(510)	

General Ledger

Purchases				510
Date	PR	Dr.	Cr.	Bal.
19XX				
Jan. 31	PJ1	26,000		26,000

Do not post total of sundry.

SUNDRY (Dr.). The total of the sundry column is never posted. Place an (X) to indicate not to post the total. A debit to delivery truck is posted as soon as it is entered in the sundry column to delivery truck in the general ledger.

Purchase Journal			Page 1
	Sundry Account—Dr.		
	Account	PR	Amount
. . .	Delivery Truck	116	3,600
			3,600
			(X)

General Ledger

Delivery Truck				116
Date	PR	Dr.	Cr.	Bal.
19XX				
Jan. 21	PJ1	3,600		3,600

In summary, the purchase journal and posting rules are as follows:

			Accounts Payable Cr.	Purchases Dr.	Sundry Account Dr.		
Date	Accounts Credited	PR			Account	PR	Amount
19XX							
Jan. 2	Pete Regan Co.	√	5,000	5,000			
9	Pete Regan Co.	√	4,000	4,000			
11	Russell Slater	√	5,000	5,000			
21	Mike's Garage	√	3,600		Delivery Truck	116	3,600
27	King Corp.	√	6,000	6,000			
29	Pete Regan Co.	√	6,000	6,000			
31	Total		29,600	26,000			3,600
			(210)	(510)			(X)

Purchase Journal — Page 1

King Corp.

Date		PR	Dr.	Cr.	Bal.
19XX					
Jan.	27	PJ1		6,000	6,000

Delivery Truck 116

Date		PR	Dr.	Cr.	Bal.
19XX					
Jan.	21	PJ1	3,600		3,600

Mike's Garage

Date		PR	Dr.	Cr.	Bal.
19XX					
Jan.	21	PJ1		3,600	3,600

Accounts Payable 210

Date		PR	Dr.	Cr.	Bal.
19XX					
Jan.	31	PJ1		29,600	29,600

Pete Regan Co.

Date		PR	Dr.	Cr.	Bal.
19XX					
Jan.	2	PJ1		5,000	5,000
	9	PJ1		4,000	9,000
	29	PJ1		6,000	15,000

Purchases 510

Date		PR	Dr.	Cr.	Bal.
19XX					
Jan.	31	PJ1	26,000		26,000

Russell Slater

Date		PR	Dr.	Cr.	Bal.
19XX					
Jan.	11	PJ1		5,000	5,000

Ralph's Sporting Goods now sets up a system to check the merchandise, supplies, equipment, etc. for quality and prompt delivery and to check the amounts being charged for correctness. As the goods are received, the accounting department gets a copy of the receiving report, indicating receipt of goods is in order and payment should begin.

At this point you should be able to:

1. Differentiate between purchases and equipment.
2. Define and state the purpose of the purchase journal.
3. Define the accounts payable subsidiary ledger.
4. Explain the relationship between the accounts payable controlling account and the accounts payable subsidiary ledger.
5. Record purchases of merchandise, equipment, supplies, etc. on account in a purchase journal.
6. Post, as appropriate, from a purchase journal to the accounts payable subsidiary ledger and the general ledger.

1. Journalize into the purchase journal the following transactions. Notice that the headings are changed slightly from those in the chapter. Remember, each journal is designed to meet the needs of a particular firm.

Purchase Journal								Page 1
Date	Accounts Credited	PR	Accounts Payable Cr.	Purchases Dr.	Store Supplies Dr.	Sundry Dr.		
						Account	PR	Amount

19XX, DEC. 3: Bought merchandise on account from J. P. Shoes $3,000.
        5: Bought store supplies on account from U.S. Supplies $200.
        8: Bought car on account from T. T. Used Cars $5,000.

2. Post when appropriate to the accounts payable subsidiary ledger as well as accounts payable and other general ledger accounts. Account numbers are as follows: store supplies (215), equipment (281), accounts payable (311), purchases (510).
3. Verify that the accounts payable subsidiary ledger equals the controlling account accounts payable in the general ledger at the end of the month.

SOLUTION to Unit Interactor **20**

Purchase Journal								Page 1
Date	Accounts Credited	PR	Account Payable Cr.	Purchases Dr.	Store Supplies Dr.	Sundry Dr.		
						Account	PR	Amount
19XX Dec. 3	J. P. Shoes	√	3,000	3,000				
5	U. S. Supplies	√	200		200			
8	T. T. Used Cars	√	5,000			Equipment	281	5,000
31	Totals		8,200	3,000	200			5,000
			(311)	(510)	(215)			(X)

(311) *ACCOUNTS PAYABLE:* During the month post to J. P. Shoes, U.S. Supplies, and T. T. Used Cars in the accounts payable subsidiary ledger as credits. When this is done, checks (✓) are placed in the posting reference column. The total ($8,200) is posted, too, as a credit to accounts payable account no. 311 in the general ledger at the end of the month.

(510) *PURCHASES:* The total of the column is posted at the end of the month to purchases account no. 510 in the general ledger.

(215) *STORE SUPPLIES:* The total of this column is posted at the end of the month to store supplies account no. 215 in the general ledger.

SUNDRY: The total of this column is never posted. An (X) is placed to show this. A debit to equipment (281) is posted to the general ledger as soon as it is entered.

Accounts Payable Subsidiary Ledger

J. P. Shoes

Date		PR	Dr.	Cr.	Bal.
19XX					
Dec.	3	PJ1		3,000	3,000

T. T. Used Cars

Date		PR	Dr.	Cr.	Bal.
19XX					
Dec.	8	PJ1		5,000	5,000

U. S. Supplies

Date		PR	Dr.	Cr.	Bal.
19XX					
Dec.	5	PJ1		200	200

General Ledger

Store Supplies   215

Date		PR	Dr.	Cr.	Bal.
19XX					
Dec.	31	PJ1	200		200

Equipment   281

Date		PR	Dr.	Cr.	Bal.
19XX					
Dec.	8	PJ1	5,000		5,000

Accounts Payable   311

Date		PR	Dr.	Cr.	Bal.
19XX					
Dec.	31	PJ1		8,200	8,200

Purchases   510

Date		PR	Dr.	Cr.	Bal.
19XX					
Dec.	31	PJ1	3,000		3,000

Purchase Returns and Allowances

THE DEBIT MEMORANDUM

On January 11, as seen in the purchase journal, Ralph's Sporting Goods purchased $5,000 of merchandise on account from Russell Slater. This order was specifically for 200 baseball gloves at $25 each. When the shipment arrived on January 14, the receiving department of Ralph's found 40 gloves were defective. Ralph issued the following debit memorandum to Russell Slater:

The debit memo indicates Ralph does not owe as much money as was indicated in his purchase journal.

	Debit Memorandum 1
RALPH'S SPORTING GOODS	
26 Sable Road	
Salem, MA 01970	DATE: January 14, 19XX
TO: Russell Slater Corp.	
11114 Rodway Street	
Lincoln, Iowa 51160	

We debit your account

40 gloves at $25.00 per glove returned via parcel post order #11111
$1,000

At some point in the future Russell Slater will issue Ralph a credit memorandum, which will reduce Russell Slater's sales and decrease their accounts receivable. But right now we are concerned with the books of Ralph's Sporting Goods. What accounts will be affected by issuing this debit memo or receiving a credit memorandum from Russell Slater? Let's first set up a mind-process chart.

Accounts Affected	Category	↑ ↓	Rule
Accounts Payable	Liability	↓	Dr.
Purchase Returns and Allowances	Decrease to the cost of merchandise for resale	↑	Cr.

By returning the merchandise:

Result of debit memo

1. Ralph owes less to Russell Slater.
2. The cost of merchandise for resale has decreased—we returned these items, thereby reducing our cost, since we are not buying them.

Since Ralph's Sporting Goods has no special journal for purchase returns and allowances, the issuing of a debit memo to Russell or the receiving of the credit memo from Russell will be recorded in the general journal.

Ralph is concerned about the number of purchases that are returned in a year. Why? Returns are time-consuming, a burden on the accountant and the receiving and shipping departments, and displeasing to customers who are awaiting sporting goods.

Purchase returns and allowances, a credit balance, causes decrease to the cost of merchandise for resale.

By keeping a special account called purchase returns and allowances, separate from purchases, Ralph will be able to keep an eye on the amount of difficulties he is having with purchases that have to be returned or on the amount of reduction he is allowed on the price he pays for defective items that can possibly still be sold to customers at a reduced price.

> (Dr.) PURCHASES
> LESS (Cr.) PURCHASE RETURNS AND ALLOWANCES
> ---
> = COST OR AMOUNT OF PURCHASES AFTER RETURNS
> OR ADJUSTMENTS

This purchase return is recorded in the journal as follows:

General Journal					Page 1
Date	Account Titles and Description	PR	Dr.		Cr.
19XX Jan. 14	Accounts Payable—R. Slater		1,000		
	Purchase Returns and Allowances				1,000
	Debit Memo #1				

HOW TO POST PURCHASE RETURNS

In order to post needed information to (1) the accounts payable subsidiary ledger—Russell Slater and (2) the purchase returns and allowances and accounts payable in the general ledger, the following postings are needed:

General Journal*					Page 1
Date	Account Titles and Description	PR	Dr.		Cr.
19XX Jan. 14	Accounts Payable—R. Slater	210 √	1,000		
	Purchase Returns and Allowances	512			1,000
	Debit Memo #1				

*Issuing a debit memo or receiving a credit memo results in this general journal entry.

The three postings are:

1. 512—Post to purchase return and allowance as a credit in the general ledger (account no. 512). When this is done, place the account number 512 in the posting reference column of the journal on the same line as purchase returns and allowances.
2. $\checkmark$—Post to Russell Slater in the accounts payable subsidiary ledger to show we don't owe Russell as much money. When this is done, place a ($\checkmark$) in the journal in the PR column below the diagonal line in the same line as accounts payable.
3. 210—Post to accounts payable as a debit in the general ledger account no. 210. When this is done, place in the PR column the account number 210, above the diagonal on the same line as accounts payable.

At this point you should be able to:

1. Define and state the purpose of purchase returns and allowances.
2. Define what is meant by "issuing a debit memorandum."
3. Compare and contrast a debit memorandum issued with a credit memorandum received.
4. Journalize and post a debit memorandum issued or a credit memorandum received.

UNIT INTERACTOR 21

John Rollins Co. issued a debit memorandum on September 4 for defective merchandise, $200, debit memorandum no. 10, to R. Brothers. Your task is to journalize and post the debit memorandum.

Accounts Payable Subsidiary Ledger

R. Brothers

Date		PR	Dr.	Cr.	Bal.
19XX					
Sept.	1	Bal.			500

General Ledger

Accounts Payable   210

Date		PR	Dr.	Cr.	Bal.
19XX					
Sept.	1	Bal.			500

Purchases   510

Date		PR	Dr.	Cr.	Bal.
19XX					
Sept.	1	Bal.			500

Purchase Returns and Allowances   512

Date	PR	Dr.	Cr.	Bal.

SOLUTION to Unit Interactor 21

General Journal*					Page 1
Date		**FOLIO (PR)**	**Dr.**	**Cr.**	
19XX Sept. 4	Accounts Payable—R. Brothers	210 / ✓	200		
	Purchase Returns and Allowances	512		200	

*This journal entry could have resulted from receiving a credit memo.

Post:

1. To accounts payable (as a debit) in the general ledger. When this is done the account number 210 is put in the PR column.
2. To R. Brothers in our accounts payable subsidiary ledger to show we don't owe R. Brothers as much money (because we returned some purchases). When this is done, a (✓) is put in the PR column below the diagonal line.
3. A credit of $200 to purchase returns and allowances in the general ledger. When this is done, the account number, 512, is put in the PR column.

Accounts Payable Subsidiary Ledger

R. Brothers

Date		PR	Dr.	Cr.	Bal.
19XX Sept.	1	Bal.			500
	4	GJ1	200		300

General Ledger

Accounts Payable   210

Date		PR	Dr.	Cr.	Bal.
19XX Sept.	1	Bal.			500
	4	GJ1	200		300

Purchases   510

Date		PR	Dr.	Cr.	Bal.
19XX Sept.	1	Bal.			500

Purchase Returns and Allowances   512

Date		PR	Dr.	Cr.	Bal.
19XX Sept.	4	GJ1		200	200

Before you go on to the problems at the end of the chapter, recall (from our discussion of the sales journal) that many businesses use the actual sales invoices to replace the sales journal. The same holds true for a purchase journal. The original invoices are used to post information to the accounts payable subsidiary ledger as well as general ledger accounts.

Once again, keep in mind that each business has different needs, different manpower and financial resources, all of which will affect how the special journals will be set up, if at all.

THE PURCHASE JOURNAL—
A BLUEPRINT

This chapter is concerned with recording information about the *buyer*. Previous discussions have centered upon special journals involving recording transactions of the seller. Keep in mind that sooner or later a seller of goods becomes a buyer of other goods. The relationship is continually changing.

This special purchase journal records all types of purchases or items on account. Cash purchases *will not* be recorded in the purchase journal. Careful distinction should be made between a purchase (merchandise) and other items bought on account. A purchase represents merchandise for resale, whereas other items in a store may help create sales but not be intended to be resold to customers.

Instead of looking at an accounts receivable subsidiary ledger, we are interested in what amounts we owe to individual suppliers. Therefore, we establish an accounts payable subsidiary ledger along with a controlling account, accounts payable, in the general ledger.

As transactions are recorded into the purchases journal, the accounts payable subsidiary ledger is immediately updated to indicate current balances of accounts owed specific suppliers. The total should be equal to the balance in the controlling account, accounts payable, in the general ledger at the end of the month.

If a company buys some merchandise that is unsatisfactory, it may decide to issue a debit memorandum to the supplier. This memo, issued by the buyer, indicates to the supplier that the buyer is reducing the amount owed (accounts payable) and that merchandise is being returned.

Upon receiving this debit memo, the seller usually issues a credit memo. Whether the buyer issues a debit memo or receives a credit memo, *the end result will be to reduce accounts payable and show that a purchase return and allowance has resulted on the books of the buyer.*

Here is a summary of how to post. Situation 1: Purchase of merchandise or other items on account.

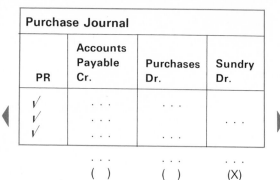

POSTED DURING THE MONTH:
These individual accounts are posted during the month to the accounts payable subsidiary ledger. When posted a ($\sqrt{}$) is placed in the PR column of the purchase journal for each transaction.

Purchase Journal

PR	Accounts Payable Cr.	Purchases Dr.	Sundry Dr.
$\sqrt{}$	. . .	. . .	
$\sqrt{}$	. . .	. . .	. . .
$\sqrt{}$	. . .	. . .	
	. . .	. . .	. . .
	( )	( )	(X)

POSTED WHEN TRANSACTION ENTERED:
Post to general ledger account when transaction is entered.

POSTED AT THE END OF MONTH:
These totals are posted to the general ledger accounts at the end of the month. Examples: accounts payable, purchases.

Total of sundry is never posted.

Situation 2: Issuing a debit memo or receiving a credit memo.

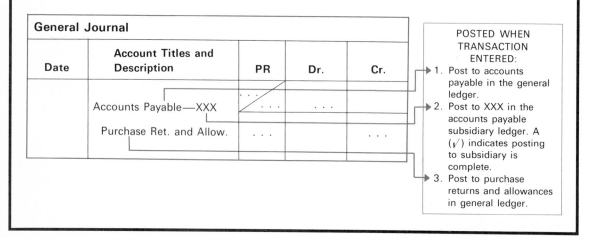

General Journal

Date	Account Titles and Description	PR	Dr.	Cr.
	Accounts Payable—XXX	. . .	. . .	
	Purchase Ret. and Allow.	. . .		. . .

POSTED WHEN TRANSACTION ENTERED:
1. Post to accounts payable in the general ledger.
2. Post to XXX in the accounts payable subsidiary ledger. A ($\sqrt{}$) indicates posting to subsidiary is complete.
3. Post to purchase returns and allowances in general ledger.

SUMMARY OF NEW ACCOUNTING LANGUAGE TERMS

Learning Unit 20

Accounts Payable Subsidiary Ledger: A book or file that contains in alphabetical order the specific amount owed companies from purchases on account. During the month this subsidiary ledger is continually updated to reflect current balances.

Cash Discount: Discounts that result from early payment.

Controlling Account—Accounts Payable: The accounts payable account in the general ledger, after postings are complete, showing a firm the total amount owed from purchases and other items on account. This figure is broken down in the accounts payable subsidiary ledger, indicating specifically individuals or companies owed the money. If one adds up the accounts payable subsidiary ledger at the end of a month, it should be equal to the balance in the controlling account—accounts payable.

Purchase Invoice: A form used to purchase goods or merchandise.

Purchase Journal: A special journal that records the buying of merchandise or items on account.

Purchases: Merchandise for resale.

Terms—2/10, n/30: If payment is received within 10 days, a 2% discount is available; if not, the bill is due within 30 days with no discount.

Learning Unit 21

Debit Memorandum: A piece of paper issued by a customer to a seller, indicating some purchase returns and allowances have resulted and therefore the customer now owes less from previous purchases on account. Eventually the seller will issue a credit memo to confirm the sales returns and allowances as well as to decrease accounts receivable.

Purchase Returns and Allowances: An account in the ledger that records the amount of defective or unacceptable merchandise returned to suppliers and/or price reductions given for defective items that could possibly still be sold to customers, but at a reduced price.

QUESTION INTERACTORS

1. All purchase journals have at least three column headings. Discuss.
2. Define the purpose of a purchase journal.
3. What is the difference between merchandise for resale versus equipment and supplies of a firm?
4. What is the normal balance of the purchase account?
5. The purchases account tells the amount charged customers for the sale of merchandise. Agree or disagree?
6. What is the difference between a purchase invoice and a sales invoice?
7. Explain the difference between the accounts payable subsidiary ledger and the accounts receivable subsidiary ledger.
8. Explain why there is only one controlling accounts payable account in the general ledger instead of individual accounts payable for each supplier of merchandise, supplies, equipment, etc. on account.

9. What is the normal balance of the controlling account, accounts payable? Why?

10. The accounts payable subsidiary ledger is updated monthly. Please comment.

11. The purchases account is found in the subsidiary ledger. Please comment.

12. The total of the sundry column is usually posted at the end of the month. Agree or disagree?

13. When is the sundry account of the purchase journal posted?

14. Explain the difference between a debit memorandum and a credit memorandum. Please give an example.

15. What is the relationship between purchases and purchase returns and allowances?

16. If a credit memorandum is received and recorded in the general journal, how many postings will be needed? Explain.

17. All companies utilize a purchase journal. Please comment.

18. What is the relationship of the sales journal to the purchase journal?

19. Do all credit memos get recorded in the general journal? Comment.

20. How can purchase invoices replace a purchase journal?

PROBLEM INTERACTORS

1. Record the following transactions in the purchase journal of Rong Stationery Company. Post information as appropriate. Account numbers are as follows: shelving equipment (15), cash register (17), accounts payable (21), purchases (50).

Purchase Journal					Sundry Dr.		Page 1
Date	Accounts Credited	PR	Accounts Payable Cr.	Purchases Dr.	Account	PR	Amount

19XX, JAN.   5: Purchased merchandise on account from Bo Peep Corporation $100.

7: Bought racks on account for the stationery store from Jones Company $500.

15: Purchased $300 of merchandise on account from Ron Company.

23: Bought a cash register on account for use in business from N.C.P. Corporation $100.

2. The Mahoney Book Store uses a purchase journal or a general journal to record the following transactions (continued from March).

19XX, APR.   5: Purchased merchandise on account from Jim Smith Co. $100.

19XX, APR. 5: Purchased merchandise on account from Burton Company $500.

10: Purchased supplies on account from AMU Corporation $20.

12: Received credit memorandum no. 12 from Jim Smith Co. for defective merchandise $50 that was previously purchased.

14: Purchased office equipment on account from Jones Company $100.

15: Purchased merchandise on account from Jim Smith Co. $500.

24: Received credit memorandum no. 15 from AMU Corp. for supplies returned $5 that was previously purchased.

25: Received credit memorandum no. 18 from Burton Co. for damaged merchandise $100 that was previously purchased.

28: Purchased supplies on account from AMU Corp. $20.

The journal headings are shown below. Notice that the book store keeps a separate column for purchases of supplies that will be used in the operations of business. Your task is to (a) journalize the transactions, (b) post as appropriate, and (c) find the sum balance in the accounts payable subsidiary ledger. Does it match the controlling account?

General Journal				Page 10
Date	Account Titles and Description	PR	Dr.	Cr.

Purchase Journal							Page 10
Date	Accounts Credited	PR	Accounts Payable Cr.	Purchases Dr.	Supplies Dr.	Sundry Dr.	
						Account	PR	Amount

Accounts Payable Subsidiary Ledger

General Ledger

AMU Corp.

Date	PR	Dr.	Cr.	Bal.
19XX Apr. 1	Bal.			100

Store Supplies   110

Date	PR	Dr.	Cr.	Bal.

(continued on next page)

Burton Company

Date	PR	Dr.	Cr.	Bal.
19XX Apr. 1	Bal.			400

Jones Company

Date	PR	Dr.	Cr.	Bal.
19XX Apr. 1	Bal.			450

J. Smith Co.

Date	PR	Dr.	Cr.	Bal.
19XX Apr. 1	Bal.			250

Office Equipment   **120**

Date	PR	Dr.	Cr.	Bal.

Accounts Payable   **210**

Date	PR	Dr.	Cr.	Bal.
19XX Apr. 1	Bal.			1200

Purchases   **510**

Date	PR	Dr.	Cr.	Bal.
19XX Apr. 1	Bal.			10,000

Purchase Returns and Allowances   **512**

Date	PR	Dr.	Cr.	Bal.

*3. J. V. Small opened up a grocery store. He told his accountant that a great deal of advertising would take place on T V and radio and in local newspapers. All advertising would be purchased on account. Based upon the needs J. V. expressed, his accountant designed the following purchase journal.

Purchase Journal								Page 1
Date	Purchased From	PR	Accounts Payable Cr.	Purchases Dr.	Grocery Advertising Expense Dr.	Sundry Dr.		
						Account	PR	Amount

As the bookkeeper of J. V.'s Grocery Store, please journalize and post where appropriate the following transactions. The account numbers are as follows: delivery truck (15), parking lot (18), trash equipment (19), accounts payable (20), purchases (50), grocery advertising expense (61).

19XX, JAN. 2: Received a $300 invoice from J. Advertising Co. for brochures purchased to inform customers of opening of grocery store.

5: Purchased merchandise on account from Joy Sling Co. $150.

8: Received a bill from J. Watson Co. for the delivery of a new trash disposal $100.

15: Received bill from local television station for spot television advertisements $150.

18: Purchased merchandise on account from Jim's wholesale $300.

20: Received a bill from J. Printing Co. for the preparation of window advertisements in local stores $150.

25: Purchased merchandise on account from M. Ross Dairy $1,000.

26: Purchased a delivery truck on account $5,000 from John's Auto.

30: Purchased a parking lot across the street from the grocery store on account from J. Regan $10,000.

ADDITIONAL PROBLEM INTERACTORS

1-A. The following are the headings of the purchase journal used by John's Shoe Store.

Purchase Journal						Page 1		
						Sundry Dr.		
Date	Accounts Credited	PR	Accounts Payable Cr.	Purchases Dr.		Account	PR	Amount

Your task is to journalize and post the following transactions of John's Shoe Store that relate to the purchase journal. Account numbers are as follows: office supplies (10), shoe racks (12), accounts payable (20), purchases (50).

19XX, APR. 2: Bought on account shoe racks for displaying merchandise from Apples Corp. $300.

9: Purchased merchandise from J. B. Rubber Co. $250 on account.

15: Purchased $450 of merchandise on account from Howard Slater Corp.

23: Purchased on account office supplies $100 from Ron Stationery.

2-A. Jim Ploss' Restaurant uses a purchase journal to record the following transactions (you will notice this is *not* the first month of operation).

19XX, DEC. 3: Received a credit memorandum $50 from A. Zero Corp. for defective merchandise that was previously purchased.

5: Purchased merchandise on account from A. Zero Corp. $100.

10: Purchased merchandise on account from C. Reed Corp. $300.

12: Purchased merchandise on account from B. Zoll Corp. $200.

14: Purchased restaurant equipment on account from E. Valley Corp. $500.

16: Purchased merchandise on account from A. Zero Corp. $100.

25: Received a credit memorandum from B. Zoll Corp. for defective merchandise $100.

26: Issued a debit memo to C. Reed Corp. for defective merchandise $100.

28: Purchased restaurant supplies $25 on account from C. Reed Corp.

Your task is to:

a. Journalize the transactions.

b. Post as appropriate.

c. Find the sum balance in the accounts payable subsidiary ledger at the end of December. Does it match the controlling account?

Jim's Restaurant Purchase Journal								Page 10
Date	Accounts Credited	PR	Accounts Payable Cr.	Purchases Dr.	Restaurant Supplies Dr.	Sundry Dr.		
						Account	PR	Amount

Notice that the restaurant keeps a separate column for purchases of restaurant supplies that will be used in the operations of the business.

Accounts Payable Subsidiary Ledger

C. Reed Corp.

Date	PR	Dr.	Cr.	Bal.
19XX Dec. 1	Bal.			60

B. Zoll Corp.

Date	PR	Dr.	Cr.	Bal.
19XX Dec. 1	Bal.			100

General Ledger

Restaurant Supplies 110

Date	PR	Dr.	Cr.	Bal.

Restaurant Equipment 112

Date	PR	Dr.	Cr.	Bal.

E. Valley Corp.

Date	PR	Dr.	Cr.	Bal.
19XX Dec. 1	Bal.			40

A. Zero Corp.

Date	PR	Dr.	Cr.	Bal.
19XX Dec. 1	Bal.			300

Accounts Payable   **200**

Date	PR	Dr.	Cr.	Bal.
19XX Dec. 1	Bal.			500

Purchases   **500**

Date	PR	Dr.	Cr.	Bal.
19XX Dec. 1	Bal.			25,000

Purchase Returns and Allowances   **510**

Date	PR	Dr.	Cr.	Bal.

* 3-A. Mark Neen recently opened up a shoe store. Based upon the needs he expressed to his accountant, the following purchase journal was designed.

Purchase Journal   **Page 1**

Date	Purchased From	PR	Accounts Payable Cr.	Purchases Dr.	Maintenance Dr.	Sundry Dr. Account	Sundry Dr. PR	Sundry Dr. Amount

As the bookkeeper of the shoe store, please journalize and post (when appropriate) the following transactions. Account numbers are as follows: store supplies (15), store equipment (18), accounts payable (20), purchases (50), maintenance expense (52).

19XX, JUL. 3: Purchased merchandise on account from J. Ron Co. $1,500.

4: Received a $500 invoice from Ron Ling Cleaning Service for window washing that was performed on account.

6: Received a bill from B. Blum Co. for the cleaning of rugs for the shoe store $250.

16: Purchased store supplies on account from Z. Kool $300.

18: Purchased merchandise on account from P. Ansel Co. $400.

20: Received a bill from D. Clark for floor washing $200.

24: Purchased merchandise on account from B. Moore Co. $400.

28: Purchased a desk on account from B. Merry Stationery $350.

30: Purchased merchandise on account from D. Beattie Co. $5,000.

CHALLENGE PROBLEM INTERACTOR

The accounts payable control account credit balance at the end of an accounting period does not agree with the total of the balances of the creditor's accounts in the accounts payable subsidiary ledger. Indicate whether each of the following situations would cause this difference. Each statement is an independent assumption. Explain each answer in detail.

	Yes	*No*
1. A purchase of $25 was recorded correctly in the purchase journal, but it was posted to the individual creditor's account as $52.		
2. A purchase from M. A. Winder Co. was recorded in the purchase journal and posted as a credit to the individual account of M. A. Binder, a *customer*.		
3. Recorded the general journal entry for a purchase return. The entry was posted to the general ledger accounts only.		
4. A purchase of office supplies on account was recorded in the debit column for store supplies in the purchase journal.		
5. A purchase on account from A. R. Rother Co. was recorded in the purchase journal and posted as a debit to the individual account of A. R. Rather Co.		

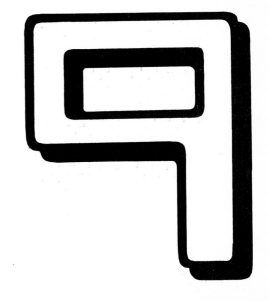

the
cash payments
journal

In analyzing the journals of Ralph's Sporting Goods, we have considered (1) the sales journal (sales made on account), (2) the cash receipts journal (receipt of money from any source), (3) the purchase journal (purchase of merchandise, supplies, equipment, etc. on account), and (4) the general journal (sales returns and allowances, purchase returns and allowances, etc.).

LEARNING UNIT 22

The Cash Payments Journal: Structure and Purpose

STRUCTURE OF CASH PAYMENTS JOURNAL

Purpose of cash payments journal

No mention has been made yet of how to record transactions that involve the payment of cash. Our attention will now be focused on the cash payments (cash disbursements) journal. This special journal records all transactions that involve the *paying of cash*, be it the buying of assets, or the payment of cash to operate other phases of Ralph's Sporting Goods.

Like the other special journals, the cash payments journal will contain special columns to allow Ralph's Sporting Goods to record repetitive transactions that involve the payment of cash. This special journal will save posting labor by utilizing the totals of the columns. The cash payments journal also allows division of labor for its bookkeeper as well as providing a system of updating the accounts payable subsidiary ledger.

Based on Ralph's needs, the following cash payments journal is designed.

Date	Check No.	Accounts Debited	PR	Sundry Account Dr.	Accounts Payable Dr.	Purchase Discount Cr.	Cash Cr.

EXPLANATION OF COLUMNS

CASH (Cr.). This column records the paying of cash (by means of checks) for (1) decreasing accounts payable, (2) buying assets, (3) meeting costs or expenses involved in business operations.

The credit to the column indicates cash will be reduced. In reality, this column shows an *outward flow of cash.* The other columns in the journal will show why the outward flow occurs. Notice that there is a column to record the check numbers that are used to make payment.

As purchase discounts increase, the actual cost of purchases decreases.

PURCHASE DISCOUNT (Cr.). When merchandise is purchased on account, some suppliers offer discounts on the purchase price. For example, if John Rang bought $400 worth of merchandise on account on terms of 2/10, n/30, he would have the opportunity to receive a 2% discount (or $8) if the purchase were paid within ten days. If not, the full purchase price would be due within 30 days.

> *PURCHASES (Dr.)*
> *LESS: PURCHASE DISCOUNTS (Cr.)*
> *= COST OF PURCHASES AFTER PAYMENT IS MADE WITHIN DISCOUNT PERIOD*

If a purchase discount is missed, this may represent a sizable loss of money for a business.

ACCOUNTS PAYABLE (Dr.). This column shows the amount by which Ralph's Sporting Goods reduces what it owes suppliers of merchandise, supplies, equipment, etc. that were purchased on account. Keep in mind that in the purchase journal the credit to accounts payable increased what was owed suppliers for merchandise, supplies, and equipment bought on account. Now some of the obligations are being reduced by a debit to accounts payable. Of course, the other half of the transaction would involve cash (Cr.) and possibly purchase discounts (Cr.) if offered by the supplier.

SUNDRY ACCOUNT (Dr.). This column is sometimes called miscellaneous or other accounts. It was developed to record transactions that would not occur too often. In the case of Ralph's Sporting Goods, this column records the buying of assets, as well as the paying for expenses in cash. If either of these occurs frequently, other columns may be developed.

Now, before looking at how Ralph's transactions will be recorded in the cash payments journal, let's analyze, by the mind process, the following transactions, which are to be recorded for January in the cash payments journal of Ralph's Sporting Goods.

JAN. 2: Paid three months rent in advance, $300, check no. 1.

Accounts Affected	Category	↑ ↓	Rule
Prepaid Rent	Asset	↑	Dr.
Cash	Asset	↓	Cr.

JAN. 9: Paid cleaning service $150, check no. 2.

Accounts Affected	Category	↑ ↓	Rule
Cleaning Expense	Expense	↑	Dr.
Cash	Asset	↓	Cr.

JAN. 12: Paid Pete Regan Co. $4,900, invoice dated January 2, check no. 3 ($5,000 less a 2% discount).

Accounts Affected	Category	↑ ↓	Rule
Accounts Payable	Liability	↓	Dr.
Cash	Asset	↓	Cr.
Purchase Discount	↓Cost of merchandise for resale	↑	Cr.

Remember that an increase in purchases was a debit. Now Ralph's Sporting Goods is increasing the amount of purchase discounts taken by a credit.

Notice that as purchase discount ↑, it will reduce the cost of purchases. This can be compared to sales discount (Dr.), which reduces the total amount of sales (Cr.).

Purchase discounts cause the cost of merchandise for resale to decrease.

JAN. 13: Paid salaries, $1,200, check no. 4.

Accounts Affected	Category	↑ ↓	Rule
Salary Expense	Expense	↑	Dr.
Cash	Asset	↓	Cr.

JAN. 23: Paid Russell Slater amount owed, $4,000 less 1% discount, check no. 5.

Accounts Affected	Category	↑ ↓	Rule
Accounts Payable	Liability	↓	Dr.
Cash	Asset	↓	Cr.
Purchase Discount	↓Cost of merchandise for resale	↑	Cr.

Once again, as Ralph's Sporting Goods increases the amount of purchase discounts it takes, the total cost of purchases is reduced.

> PURCHASES
> LESS: PURCHASE DISCOUNTS
> ---
> = AMOUNT OF COST OF PURCHASES AFTER PURCHASE DISCOUNTS ARE TAKEN

JAN. 25: Purchased merchandise *for cash*, $750, check no. 6.

Accounts Affected	Category	↑ ↓	Rule
Purchases	Cost of merchandise for resale	↑	Dr.
Cash	Asset	↓	Cr.

This purchase goes into the cash payments journal rather than the purchase journal, since it was not made on account, but paid for in cash.

JAN. 30: Paid Pete Regan Co. for merchandise purchased on account on January 29, $6,000 less 2% discount, check no. 7.

Accounts Affected	Category	↑ ↓	Rule
Accounts Payable	Liability	↓	Dr.
Cash	Asset	↓	Cr.
Purchase Discount	↓Cost of merchandise for resale	↑	Cr.

Notice how many times the words cash, purchase discount, and accounts payable are involved in the above transactions. If you were the bookkeeper of Ralph's Sporting Goods and were using only a two-column general journal, you would be faced with a time-consuming task of journalizing each transaction. Think how many times you would have to rewrite the same words. Then, of course, instead of just posting one figure for cash from a special journal, you would have to post many items to the cash account in the general ledger. The analysis of postings would be the same for purchase discount and accounts payable.

SAVING OF POSTING TIME AND LABOR

In order to avoid this repetitive work, to process information rapidly, and to reduce labor costs, transactions involving the payment of cash for any purpose are entered in the cash payments journal of Ralph's Sporting Goods as follows:

Cash Payments Journal   Page 1

Date	Check No.	Accounts Debited	PR	Sundry Accounts Dr.	Accounts Payable Dr.	Purchase Discount Cr.	Cash Cr.
19XX							
Jan. 2	1	Prepaid Rent	114	300			300
9	2	Cleaning Expense	612	150			150
12	3	Pete Regan Co.	✓		5,000	100	4,900
13	4	Salaries	610	1,200			1,200
23	5	Russell Slater	✓		4,000	40	3,960
25	6	Purchases	510	750			750
30	7	Pete Regan Co.	✓		6,000	120	5,880
31		Total		2,400	15,000	260	17,140
				(X)	(210)	(514)	(110)

Note that the total of the debit columns is equal to the total of the credit columns.

TOTAL OF DEBIT COLUMNS	=	TOTAL OF CREDIT COLUMNS
Sundry + Accounts Payable	=	Purchase Discounts + Cash
$2,400 + $15,000	=	$260 + $17,140
$17,400		$17,400

As in other special journals, this checking that the total debits are equal to the total credits of the columns of the cash payments journal is called *cross-footing.* Cross-footing should be done before the totals are posted.

POSTING OF THE CASH PAYMENTS JOURNAL:
A COLUMN-BY-COLUMN ANALYSIS

CASH (Cr.). The total of the column $17,140 is posted as a credit to cash (account no. 110) in the general ledger at the end of the month. No individual entries are posted to the cash account during the month. The account number, 110, is placed below the total of the cash column in the cash payments journal to show that the posting of the total of cash is complete. What a pleasure it is to post only once instead of seven times.

Total of cash posted to cash in general ledger at end of month

Cash Payments Journal		Page 1
	Cash	
	300	
	150	
	4,900	
	1,200	
	3,960	
	750	
	5,880	
	17,140	
	(110)	

PURCHASE DISCOUNT (*Cr.*).   The total of the purchase discount is posted as a credit of $260 to purchase discount in the general ledger (account no. 514) at the end of the month. No individual entries are posted during the month. The account number, 514, is placed below the total of the purchase discount column in the cash payments journal. Here, instead of posting three times, we post once.

Total of purchase discount posted to purchase discount in general ledger at end of month

Cash Payments Journal		Page 1
	Purchase Discount (Cr.)	
. . .	. . .	. . .
	100	
. . .	. . .	. . .
	40	
. . .	. . .	. . .
	120	
	260	
	(514)	

Accounts Payable (Dr.)

Cash Payments Journal				Page 1
	Accounts Debited	PR	Accounts Payable Dr.	
. . .	Pete Regan Co.	✓	5,000	. . .
	. . .	. . .	. . .	
. . .	Russell Slater	✓	4,000	. . .
	. . .	. . .	. . .	
	Pete Regan Co.	✓	6,000	
	Total		15,000	
			(210)	

▼ ▼

Individual debits to accounts payable are posted daily; (✓) is placed in PR when posted.	Total posted to accounts payable in the general ledger at end of month.

Relationship of subsidiary ledger to general ledger

Partial Accounts Payable Subsidiary Ledger

Partial General Ledger

Pete Regan Co.

Date		PR	Dr.	Cr.	Bal.
19XX					
Jan.	2	PJ1		5,000	5,000
	9	PJ1		4,000	9,000
	12	CPJ1	5,000		4,000
	29	PJ1		6,000	10,000
	30	CPJ1	6,000		4,000

Russell Slater

Date		PR	Dr.	Cr.	Bal.
19XX					
Jan.	11	PJ1		5,000	5,000
	14	GJ1	1,000		4,000
	23	CPJ1	4,000		0

Accounts Payable   210

Date		PR	Dr.	Cr.	Bal.
19XX					
Jan.	14	GJ1	1,000		1,000 Dr.
	31	PJ1		29,600	28,600
	31	CPJ1	15,000		13,600

SUNDRY (Dr.). The total of $2,400 is not posted. Place an (X) to show not to post the column total. The $2,400 represents rent, cleaning, salary, and cash purchases, the specific amounts of which must be posted separately to be meaningful.

Cash Payments Journal
Page 1

Date	Check No.	Accounts Debited	PR	Sundry Accounts Dr.	. . .
19XX					
Jan. 2	1	Prepaid Rent	114	300	. . .
9	2	Cleaning Expense	612	150	. . .
. . .	. . .	. . . .	. . .	. . . .	. . .
13	4	Salaries	610	1,200	. . .
. . .	. . .	. . . .	. . .	. . . .	. . .
25	6	Purchases	510	750	. . .
				. . . .	. . .
31		Total		2,400	. . .
				(X)	

PREPAID RENT (Dr.).   Prepaid rent of $300 is posted daily to the general ledger account, prepaid rent account no. 114. When this is done, the account number, 114, is placed in the PR column next to prepaid rent in the cash payments journal. This indicates that the posting of prepaid rent from the sundry column to the general ledger has been completed.

Prepaid Rent   11

Date	PR	Dr.	Cr.	Bal.
19XX				
Jan. 2	CPJ1	300		300

CLEANING EXPENSE (Dr.).   Cleaning expense of $150 is posted daily to the general ledger account, cleaning expense account no. 612. When this is done, the account number, 612, is placed in the PR column next to cleaning expense in the cash payments journal. This indicates that the posting from the sundry column has been completed.

Cleaning Expense   612

Date	PR	Dr.	Cr.	Bal.
19XX				
Jan. 9	CPJ1	150		150

SALARIES EXPENSE (Dr.).   Salaries expense of $1,200 is posted daily to the general ledger account salaries expense account no. 610. When this is done, the account number, 610, is placed in the PR column next to salaries expense in the cash payment journal. This indicates that posting from the sundry column has been completed.

Salaries Expense   **610**

Date		PR	Dr.	Cr.	Bal.
19XX					
Jan.	13	CPJ1	1,200		1,200

PURCHASES (*Dr.*).   Cash purchases of $750 is posted daily to the general ledger account purchases, account no. 510. When this is done, the account number, 510, is placed in the PR column next to purchases in the cash payments journal. This indicates the information about purchases in the sundry column has been posted.

Purchases   **510**

Date		PR	Dr.	Cr.	Bal.
19XX					
Jan.	25	CPJ1	750		750
	31	PJ1	26,000		26,750

Please keep in mind that if an account results from recurring transactions a new column can be developed.

Now let's summarize the cash payments journal and its postings:

Cash Payments Journal   Page 1

Date	Check No.	Accounts Debited	PR	Sundry Dr.	Accounts Payable Dr.	Purchase Discount Cr.	Cash Cr.
19XX							
Jan. 2	1	Prepaid Rent	114	300			300
9	2	Cleaning Expense	612	150			150
12	3	Pete Regan Co.	√		5,000	100	4,900
13	4	Salaries	610	1,200			1,200
23	5	Russell Slater	√		4,000	40	3,960
25	6	Purchases	510	750			750
30	7	Pete Regan Co.	√		6,000	120	5,880
31		Total		2,400	15,000	260	17,140
				(X)	(210)	(514)	(110)

King Company

Date		PR	Dr.	Cr.	Bal.
19XX					
Jan.	27	PJ1		6,000	6,000

Mike's Garage

Date		PR	Dr.	Cr.	Bal.
19XX					
Jan.	21	PJ1		3,600	3,600

Pete Regan Co.

Date		PR	Dr.	Cr.	Bal.
19XX					
Jan.	2	PJ1		5,000	5,000
	9	PJ1		4,000	9,000
	12	CPJ1	5,000		4,000
	29	PJ1		6,000	10,000
	30	CPJ1	6,000		4,000

Russell Slater

Date		PR	Dr.	Cr.	Bal.
19XX					
Jan.	11	PJ1		5,000	5,000
	14	GJ1	1,000		4,000
	23	CPJ1	4,000		0

Cash   110

Date		PR	Dr.	Cr.	Bal.
19XX					
Jan.	31	CRJ1	44,020		44,020
	31	CPJ1		17,140	26,880

Prepaid Rent   114

Date		PR	Dr.	Cr.	Bal.
19XX					
Jan.	2	CPJ1	300		300

Accounts Payable   210

Date		PR	Dr.	Cr.	Bal.
19XX					
Jan.	14	GJ1	1,000		1,000 Dr.
	31	PJ1		29,600	28,600
	31	CPJ1	15,000		13,600

Purchases   510

Date		PR	Dr.	Cr.	Bal.
19XX					
Jan.	25	CPJ1	750		750
	31	PJ1	26,000		26,750

Purchase Discounts   514

Date		PR	Dr.	Cr.	Bal.
19XX					
Jan.	31	CPJ1		260	260

Salary Expense   610

Date		PR	Dr.	Cr.	Bal.
19XX					
Jan.	13	CPJ1	1,200		1,200

Cleaning Expense   612

Date		PR	Dr.	Cr.	Bal.
19XX					
Jan.	9	CPJ1	150		150

In review, at this time you should be able to:

1. Define and state the purpose of the cash payments journal.
2. Explain how the cash payments journal can save journalizing time and posting labor.
3. Differentiate between posting to the accounts payable subsidiary ledger and posting to the general ledger.
4. Explain the difference between a purchase and a purchase discount.
5. Define and explain the purpose of cross-footing the cash payments journal.
6. Explain the purpose of the sundry column in the cash payments journal.

UNIT INTERACTOR 22

Journalize, when appropriate, the following transactions in the cash payments journal. Be sure to post as appropriate.

19XX, SEPT. 5: Paid Jim's Supply Co. what was owed him ($600) less a 20% discount (purchase discount), check no. 2.
6: Paid Pete's Wholesale Co. $200 owed them, no purchase discount, check no. 3.
7: Paid $200 freight to ship some goods, check no. 4.

Cash Payments Journal   Page 1

Date	Check No.	Accounts Debited	PR	Sundry Dr.	Accounts Payable Dr.	Purchase Discount Cr.	Cash Cr.

Accounts Payable Subsidiary Ledger

Jim's Supply

Date		PR	Dr.	Cr.	Bal.
19XX Sept.	1	Bal.			600

Pete's Wholesale

Date		PR	Dr.	Cr.	Bal.
19XX Sept.	1	Bal.			200

General Ledger

Cash   110

Date		PR	Dr.	Cr.	Bal.
19XX Sept.	1	Bal.			10,000

Accounts Payable   250

Date		PR	Dr.	Cr.	Bal.
19XX Sept.	1	Bal.			800

General Ledger (Cont.)

Purchase Discount   **512**

Date	PR	Dr.	Cr.	Bal.

Freight   **615**

Date	PR	Dr.	Cr.	Bal.

SOLUTION to Unit Interactor 22

Cash Payments Journal   **Page 1**

Date	Check No.	Accounts Debited	PR	Sundry Dr.	Accounts Payable Dr.	Purchase Discount Cr.	Cash Cr.
19XX							
Sept. 5	2	Jim's Supply	✓		600	120	480
6	3	Pete's Wholesale	✓		200		200
7	4	Freight	615	200			200
30		Totals		200	800	120	880
				(X)	(250)	(512)	(110)

SUNDRY. Total of $200 is not posted. Place an (X) to show not to post the total. The freight is posted to the general ledger daily. When this is done the number, 615, is put into the PR column.

ACCOUNTS PAYABLE. The total $800 is posted as a debit to accounts payable account no. 250 in the general ledger at the end of the month. During the month each individual entry (to Jim's Supply and Pete's Wholesale) is posted as a debit to each account in the accounts payable subsidiary ledger. When this is done, a (✓) is put in the PR column.

PURCHASES DISCOUNT. Total of column $120 is posted as a credit to purchases discount account no. 512 in the general ledger at end of month. No individual entries are posted during the month.

CASH. Total of column $880 is posted as a credit to cash account no. 110 in the general ledger at end of month. No individual entries are posted during the month.

Accounts Payable Subsidiary Ledger   General Ledger

Jim's Supply

Date		PR	Dr.	Cr.	Bal.
19XX					
Sept.	1	Bal.			600
	5	CPJ1	600		0

Cash   **110**

Date		PR	Dr.	Cr	Bal.
19XX					
Sept.	1	Bal.			10,000
	30	CPJ1		880	9,120

Pete's Wholesale

Date		PR	Dr.	Cr.	Bal.
19XX					
Sept.	1	Bal.		200	200
	6	CPJ1	200		0

Accounts Payable   **250**

Date		PR	Dr.	Cr.	Bal.
19XX					
Sept.	1	Bal.			800
	30	CPJ1	800		0

Purchase Discount   **512**

Date		PR	Dr.	Cr.	Bal.
19XX					
Sept.	30	CPJ1		120	120

Freight   **615**

Date		PR	Dr.	Cr.	Bal.
19XX					
Sept.	7	CPJ1	200		200

LEARNING UNIT 23

How to Prepare the Accounts Payable Subsidiary Ledger

PREPARING SCHEDULE OF ACCOUNTS PAYABLE

After the postings of the purchase, cash payments, and general journal are complete, the list of the accounts payable subsidiary ledger accounts with balances is as follows:

King Company

Date		Description	PR	Dr.	Cr.	Bal.
19XX						
Jan.	27	Merchandise	PJ1		600000	600000

Mike's Garage

Date		Description	PR	Dr.	Cr.	Bal.
19XX						
Jan.	21	Delivery Truck	PJ1		360000	360000

Pete Regan Co.

Date		Description	PR	Dr.	Cr.	Bal.
19XX						
Jan.	2	Merchandise	PJ1		5,000 00	5,000 00
	9	Merchandise	PJ1		4,000 00	9,000 00
	12	Payment Merchandise	CPJ1	5,000 00		4,000 00
	29	Merchandise	PJ1		6,000 00	10,000 00
	30	Payment Merchandise	CPJ1	6,000 00		4,000 00

Russell Slater

Date		Description	PR	Dr.	Cr.	Bal.
19XX						
Jan.	11	Merchandise	PJ1		5000 00	5000 00
	14	Debit Memo	GJ1	1000 00		4000 00
	23	Payment Merchandise	CPJ1	4000 00		

RALPH'S SPORTING GOODS

Schedule of Accounts Payable
January 31, 19XX

King Company	$6,000
Mike's Garage	3,600
P. Regan Co.	4,000
Total Accounts Payable	$13,600

COMPARING SCHEDULE OF ACCOUNTS PAYABLE
TO THE CONTROLLING ACCOUNT

Does the sum of the accounts payable subsidiary ledger equal the balance in the accounts payable controlling account at the end of January?

Taken from Ralph's Sporting Goods general ledger is the following, after postings:

Accounts Payable   **Account No. 210**

Date		Item	PR	Dr.	Cr.	Bal.
19XX						
Jan.	14	Debit Memo—Slater	GJ1	1,000 00		1,000 00 Dr.
	31	Purchases on Account	PJ1		29,600 00	28,600 00
	31	Cash Payments	CPJ1	15,000 00		13,600 00

Notice that the credit balance of $13,600 is equal to the sum of all the individual balances of suppliers that Ralph owes money to from purchases on account.

The balance of the controlling account, accounts payable $13,600, in the general ledger does indeed equal the sum of the balances of the individual suppliers of purchases on account to Ralph in the subsidiary accounts payable ledger. The above schedule of accounts payable can help Ralph in forecasting his outflow of cash to pay liabilities as well as in seeing specifically to whom amounts are owed.

At this point you should be able to:

1. Explain the advantages of using the three-column account in the accounts payable subsidiary ledger.
2. Define and state the purpose of a schedule of accounts payable.
3. Prepare a schedule of accounts payable.
4. Show the relationship of the accounts payable controlling account to the accounts payable subsidiary ledger.

UNIT INTERACTOR 23

From the accounts payable subsidiary ledger, prepare a schedule of accounts payable for Peter's Appliance Company as of October 31, 19XX.

A.T. Corporation

Date		Item	PR	Dr.	Cr.	Bal.
19XX						
Oct.	3		PJ19		1406 00	1406 00
	9		PJ19		1208 00	2614 00
	12		CPJ16	1406 00		1208 00
	18		CPJ16	1208 00		— —

B.V. Corporation

Date		Item	PR	Dr.	Cr.	Bal.
19XX						
Sept.	26		PJ18		12,300 00	12,300 00
Oct.	19		PJ19		11,000 00	23,300 00
	24		CPJ16	22,300 00		1,000 00

Y. B. Corporation

Date		Item	PR	Dr.	Cr.	Bal.
19XX						
Sept.	25		PJ18		11,600 00	11,600 00
Oct.	2		PJ19		1,724 00	13,324 00
	23		CPJ16	12,600 00		724 00

PETER'S APPLIANCE COMPANY

Schedule of Accounts Payable
October 31, 19XX

B.V. Corp.	$1,000.00
Y.B. Corp.	724.00
Total Accounts Payable	$1,724.00

SALES TAX REVISITED

We saw earlier that the collecting of sales tax from sales in those states that have a sales tax created a liability called sales tax payable. When the business pays its sales tax with cash (by check), it will be entered in the cash payments journal. If the sales tax is paid frequently, a separate column may be developed. If not, the debit to sales tax payable may be placed in the sundry column. Remember, sales tax payable is found as a liability in the general ledger.

Keep in mind that if at some point customers return merchandise from previous sales, the business will adjust its sales tax payable to show it does not owe as much, since some sales were actually not earned, because sales return allowances resulted. We shall see this in a problem later on.

LEARNING UNIT 24

The Journal and Subsidiary Ledgers Summarized and Compared

Before we go on to other areas of concern involving the paying and controlling of cash by Ralph's Sporting Goods, this unit will review the purpose of each journal, subsidiary ledger, and general journal and see how they interrelate.

SUMMARY OF TRANSACTIONS—RALPH'S SPORTING GOODS

The brief discussion that follows, is based on the accompanying summary chart.

SUMMARY CHART—RALPH'S SPORTING GOODS

Transactions as a Seller	Transactions as a Buyer
Sales journal	Purchase journal
Cash receipts journal	Cash payments journal
Sales invoice	Purchase invoice
Sales	Purchases
Sales returns and allowances	Purchase returns and allowances
Sales discount	Purchase discount
Issue a credit memo	Receive a credit memo
Receive a debit memo	Issue a debit memo
General journal	General journal
Accounts receivable controlling account	Accounts payable controlling account
Accounts receivable subsidiary ledger	Accounts payable subsidiary ledger
Schedule of accounts receivable	Schedule of accounts payable

As we have seen, Ralph's Sporting Goods has acted as both a buyer of goods and a seller of merchandise.

Ralph used a sales journal to record sales made on account and a purchase journal to record purchases of merchandise, supplies, and equipment on account.

As a seller of sporting goods, Ralph's offered sales discounts as well as sales returns and allowances on defective merchandise from dissatisfied customers. As a purchaser, Ralph's received purchase discounts for prompt payments if goods were defective or not up to standards, having the opportunity to return the purchase or receive an allowance.

As a seller Ralph's issued credit memos that reduced its sales and decreased accounts receivable or cash. When Ralph's was a purchaser of merchandise on account and found defective goods, it issued a debit memo to the seller indicating it did not owe as much money, since some goods were being returned. Often, if appropriate, upon receiving a debit memo, the seller will issue the customer a credit memo.

If a customer calls to check on the amount he owes, Ralph's bookkeeper turns to the accounts receivable subsidiary ledger to find the individual balance of individual amounts owed. The bookkeeper provides Ralph with a list of the balance of individual customers owing money; this list is called a schedule of accounts receivable.

Ralph, being very concerned about paying bills on time, is interested in knowing the amount owed to individual suppliers from purchases of merchandise, supplies, or equipment on account. The bookkeeper is able to obtain this information from the accounts payable subsidiary ledger. Ralph is quite anxious to see the schedule of accounts payable, or the list of individual balances of suppliers Ralph owes money to.

At this point you should be able to:

Define and state the purpose of: Sales journal
Cash receipts
Sales invoice
Sales returns and allowances
Issuing a credit memo
Accounts receivable controlling
  account
Accounts receivable subsidiary
  ledger
Schedule of accounts receivable

in addition to: Purchase journal
Cash payments journal
Purchases
Purchases returns and allowances
Purchase discount
Issuing a debit memo
Accounts payable—controlling
  account
Accounts payable—subsidiary
  ledger
Schedule of accounts payable

UNIT INTERACTOR 24

Fill in the blanks of the following charts (both sides of the top line are filled out as an example).

Schedule of accounts receivable	Schedule of accounts payable
Sales discount	(1)
(2)	Purchase return and allowances
(3)	Purchases
Cash receipts journal	(4)
Sales invoice	(5)

SOLUTION to Unit Interactor 24

(1) Purchase discounts, (2) Sales returns and allowances, (3) Sales, (4) Cash payments, (5) Purchase invoice.

All payments of cash (by check) are recorded in the cash payments journal. The cash payments journal records specifically why the outward flow of cash is occurring.

The total of the sundry column of the journal is not posted; rather, the items in the sundry column are posted to general ledger accounts. If some transaction is recorded in the accounts payable (debit) column, information will have to be posted immediately to the individual supplier in the accounts payable subsidiary ledger.

The special journals, *in summary*, were separate books developed to record sales on account (sales journal), receiving of cash (cash receipts), purchases of items on account (purchases journal), and payment of cash (cash payments). Entries that did not fit into these journals were recorded in the general journal.

A company would usually have an accounts receivable subsidiary ledger and an accounts payable subsidiary ledger. Be sure to look at the relationship between the buyer and seller. This chart reviews the main ideas of Chapters 6, 7, 8, and 9; it is a summary of how to post.

Situation 1: Sale on Account

Sales Journal

Date	Description	PR	Accounts Receivable; Dr. Sales; Cr.
		✓	. . .
		✓	. . .
		✓	. . .
		✓	. . .
		✓	. . .
			. . .
			( ) ( )

DURING THE MONTH:	END OF MONTH:
Accounts receivable subsidiary ledger is updated as soon as transaction is entered in sales journal. A (✓) indicates posting is complete to the subsidiary customer account.	Total of column is posted to general ledger accounts, accounts receivable, and sales.

Situation 2: Issuing a Credit Memo Without Sales Tax
Recorded in a General Journal

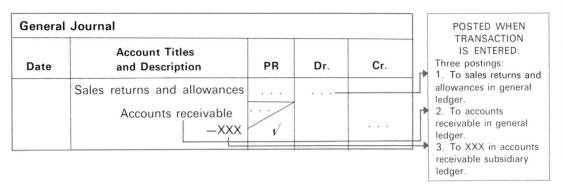

General Journal				
Date	Account Titles and Description	PR	Dr.	Cr.
	Sales returns and allowances	. . .	. . .	
	Accounts receivable —XXX	·.· ✓		. . .

POSTED WHEN TRANSACTION IS ENTERED:
Three postings:
1. To sales returns and allowances in general ledger.
2. To accounts receivable in general ledger.
3. To XXX in accounts receivable subsidiary ledger.

Situation 3: Issuing a Credit Memo with Sales Tax
Recorded in a General Journal

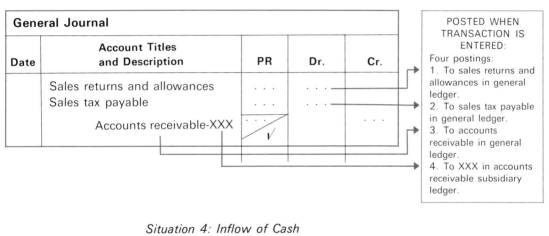

General Journal				
Date	Account Titles and Description	PR	Dr.	Cr.
	Sales returns and allowances	. . .	. . .	
	Sales tax payable	. . .	. . .	
	Accounts receivable-XXX	·.· ✓		. . .

POSTED WHEN TRANSACTION IS ENTERED:
Four postings:
1. To sales returns and allowances in general ledger.
2. To sales tax payable in general ledger.
3. To accounts receivable in general ledger.
4. To XXX in accounts receivable subsidiary ledger.

Situation 4: Inflow of Cash

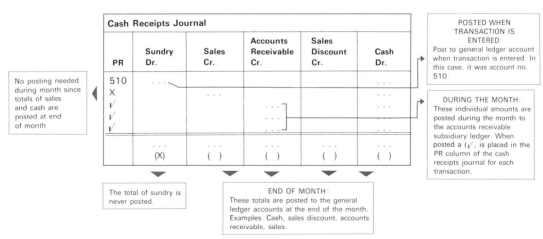

No posting needed during month since totals of sales and cash are posted at end of month

Cash Receipts Journal					
PR	Sundry Dr.	Sales Cr.	Accounts Receivable Cr.	Sales Discount Cr.	Cash Dr.
510	. . .				. . .
X		. . .			. . .
✓			. . .		. . .
✓			. . .		. . .
✓					. . .
	. . . (X)	. . . ( )	. . . ( )	. . . ( )	. . . ( )

POSTED WHEN TRANSACTION IS ENTERED:
Post to general ledger account when transaction is entered. In this case, it was account no. 510.

DURING THE MONTH:
These individual amounts are posted during the month to the accounts receivable subsidiary ledger. When posted a (✓, is placed in the PR column of the cash receipts journal for each transaction.

The total of sundry is never posted.

END OF MONTH:
These totals are posted to the general ledger accounts at the end of the month. Examples: Cash, sales discount, accounts receivable, sales.

Situation 5: Purchase of Merchandise or Other Items on Account

DURING THE MONTH:

These individual amounts are posted during the month to the accounts payable subsidiary ledger. When posted a (√) is placed in the PR column of the purchase journal for each transaction.

Purchase Journal

PR	Accounts Payable Cr.	Pur-chases Dr.	Sundry Dr.
√	. . .	. . .	
√	. . .		. . .
√	. . .	. . .	
	. . .	. . .	. . .
	( )	( )	(X)

POSTED WHEN TRANSACTION IS ENTERED:

Post to general ledger account when transaction is entered.

The total of sundry is never posted.

END OF MONTH:

These totals are posted to the general ledger accounts at end of the month.
Examples: Accounts payable, purchases.

Situation 6: Issuing a Debit Memo on Receiving a Credit Memo

General Journal

Date	Account Title and Description	PR	Dr.	Cr.
	Accounts payable-XXX	√	. . .	
	Purch. ret. and allow.	. . .		. . .

POSTED WHEN TRANSACTION IS ENTERED:

Three postings:
1. Post to accounts payable in the general ledger.
2. Post to XXX in the accounts payable subsidiary ledger. A (√) indicates posting to subsidiary ledger is complete.
3. Post to purchase returns and allowances in general ledger.

Situation 7: Outward Flow of Cash

No posting needed during month since totals of purchases and cash are posted at end of month.

Cash Payments Journal

PR	Sundry Dr.	Accounts Payable Dr.	Purchases Dr.	Cash Cr.
√		. . .		. . .
510	. . .			. . .
X			. . .	. . .
√		. . .		. . .
	. . .	. . .	. . .	. . .
	(X)	( )	( )	( )

DURING THE MONTH:

These individual amounts are posted during the month to the accounts payable subsidiary ledger. When posted a (√) is placed in the PR column of the cash payments journal for each transaction.

The total of sundry is never posted.

END OF MONTH:

These totals are posted to the general ledger accounts at end of month.
Examples: Cash, purchases, accounts payable.

SUMMARY OF NEW ACCOUNTING LANGUAGE TERMS

Learning Unit 22

Cash Payments Journal: A special journal that records all transactions involving the payment of cash.

Purchase Discount: An account in the general ledger that records discounts offered by suppliers of merchandise for prompt payment of purchases by customers.

Learning Unit 23

Schedule of Accounts Payable: A list of the creditors, in alphabetical order, from the accounts payable subsidiary ledger that have an outstanding balance. This total should be equal to the balance in accounts payable controlling account at the end of the month.

QUESTION INTERACTORS

1. What is the purpose of the cash payments journal?
2. Explain why the total of the cash column in the cash payments journal is posted only at the end of the month.
3. Why does the cash payments journal represent an "outward flow"?
4. Define purchases.
5. What is the relationship between purchases and purchase discounts?
6. What is the purpose of the sundry account in the cash payments journal?
7. Explain why purchase discount is usually a credit balance.
8. Purchases reduce the cost of merchandise for resale. Agree or disagree?
9. Explain how the cash payments journal saves journalizing and posting labor.
10. What is the purpose of cross-footing the cash payments journal?
11. Are the following statements true or false? (Based on the cash payments journal presented in this chapter.)
    a. The cash column is posted daily.
    b. The purchase discount column is a debit balance.
    c. The accounts payable column is posted only monthly.
    d. The total of the sundry account column is always posted.
    e. Cash purchases are recorded in the purchase journal.
    f. The sundry column is always needed in a special journal.
12. What is the difference between the accounts payable subsidiary ledger and the controlling account, accounts payable, in the general ledger?
13. Define what is meant by a schedule of accounts payable.
14. If sales tax is collected at the time of the sale, it represents an asset to the owner. Please comment.

15. Match the following. The first one is completed as a sample.

(1) __F__ Sales discount   A. Special journal recording only receipts of cash

(2) _____ Schedule of accounts payable   B. Miscellaneous

(3) _____ Issue a credit memo   C. List of customers owing money

(4) _____ Sales journal   D. Buying merchandise on account

(5) _____ Cash receipts journal   E. Debit memorandum

(6) _____ Purchase journal   F. A reduction in sales; it has a debit balance

(7) _____ Schedule of accounts receivable   G. List of amount owed suppliers from purchases on account

(8) _____ Accounts receivable   H. A decrease in cost of purchases

(9) _____ Purchase discount   I. Sales made on account

(10) _____ Sundry column   J. A controlling account in the general ledger

16. Assuming the use of the journals presented in the text on sales, purchases, cash receipts, cash payments, and general journal, please place the letters SJ, PJ, CRJ, CPJ, or GJ next to each transaction below, showing which journal it should be entered in.

(1) _____ Paid salaries $600.

(2) _____ Received merchandise and an invoice dated March 10, 19XX, from P. B. Bloom Company $500.

(3) _____ Sold merchandise on credit to B. Voig, invoice no. 1, $3,600.

(4) _____ Issued a credit memorandum to acknowledge receipt of defective merchandise to Ralph Sons $300.

(5) _____ Cash sales $300.

(6) _____ Cash purchases $500.

(7) _____ Received payment of $3,600 from B. Voig.

(8) _____ Purchased equipment $200 on account.

PROBLEM INTERACTORS

1. Smarty's Grocery Store utilizes a cash payments journal. The headings of the journal are as follows (note the slight variation from the cash payments journal presented in the text).

Cash Payments Journal   Page 2

Cash Cr.	Check No.	Date	Account Description	PR	Sundry Dr.	Accounts Payable Dr.	Purchase Discount Cr.	Purchases Dr.

At the start of August the following accounts had balances as shown:

Accounts Payable Subsidiary Ledger

B. A. Wholesalers

Date	PR	Dr.	Cr.	Bal.
19XX Aug. 1	Bal.			50

M. A. Suppliers

Date	PR	Dr.	Cr.	Bal.
19XX Aug. 1	Bal.			50

N. A. R. Wholesalers

Date	PR	Dr.	Cr.	Bal.
19XX Aug. 1	Bal.			75

V. A. D. Wholesalers

Date	PR	Dr.	Cr.	Bal.
19XX Aug. 1	Bal.			100

General Ledger

Cash   110

Date	PR	Dr.	Cr.	Bal.
19XX Aug. 1	Bal.			10,000

Accounts Payable   210

Date	PR	Dr.	Cr.	Bal.
19XX Aug. 1	Bal.			275

Purchases   510

Date	PR	Dr.	Cr.	Bal.

Purchase Discount   511

Date	PR	Dr.	Cr.	Bal.

Advertising Expense   610

Date	PR	Dr.	Cr.	Bal.

Utilities Expense   613

Date	PR	Dr.	Cr.	Bal.

Salaries Expense   614

Date	PR	Dr.	Cr.	Bal.

Your task, as Smarty's accountant, is to:

a. Record the following transactions into the cash payments journal.

b. Total and rule the columns of the journal.

c. Post to the general ledger and accounts payable subsidiary ledger as appropriate.

19XX, AUG. 5: Paid advertising expense $50, check no. 1.

7: Paid V. A. D. Wholesalers $98 ($100 less a 2% discount) for previous purchases made on account, check no. 2.

8: Paid M. A. Suppliers $50 for merchandise purchased on account, no discount, check no. 3.

19: Purchased merchandise for cash $500, check no. 4.

22: Paid B. A. Wholesalers amount owed from purchases of $50 on account, less discount of 2%, check no. 5.

24: Paid utilities expense of $100, check no. 6.

26: Purchased merchandise for $200, check no. 7.

28: Paid salaries expense of $100, check no. 8.

* 2. John Allen operates a wholesale lumber yard utilizing a cash payments journal of the following type.

Cash Payments Journal   Page 2

Date	Check Payable To	Check No.	Cash Cr.	Accounts Payable Dr.	Lumber Merchandise Dr.	Lumber Purchase Discount Cr.	Sundry Dr. Amount	PR	Discount

The account balances as of December 1 are as follows:

Accounts Payable Subsidiary Ledger

B & M Company

Date	PR	Dr.	Cr.	Bal.
19XX Dec. 1	Bal.			50

David Corp.

Date	PR	Dr.	Cr.	Bal.
19XX Dec. 1	Bal.			200

Ben Pierce Company

Date	PR	Dr.	Cr.	Bal.
19XX Dec. 1	Bal.			100

General Ledger

Cash   110

Date	PR	Dr.	Cr.	Bal.
19XX Dec. 1	Bal.			5,000

Delivery Truck   150

Date	PR	Dr.	Cr.	Bal.

Accounts Payable   210

Date	PR	Dr.	Cr.	Bal.
19XX Dec. 1	Bal.			375

J. Thomas Corp.

Date	PR	Dr.	Cr.	Bal.
19XX Dec. 1	Bal.			25

Lumber Purchase   **510**

Date	PR	Dr.	Cr.	Bal.

Lumber Purchase Discount   **511**

Date	PR	Dr.	Cr.	Bal.

Rent Expense   **610**

Date	PR	Dr.	Cr.	Bal.

Telephone Expense   **611**

Date	PR	Dr.	Cr.	Bal.

Your task is to:

a. Journalize the following transactions.

b. Total and rule the journal.

c. Post to accounts payable subsidiary ledger and general ledger where appropriate.

d. Prepare a schedule of accounts payable. Does it equal accounts payable in the controlling account at the end of December?

19XX, DEC.   1: Bought a new delivery truck for $3,000 from John's Garage, check no. 1.

      4: Paid half of amount owed B & M Company from previous purchases on account, no discount, check no. 2.

      6: Bought lumber merchandise for $150 from Smiles Company, check no. 3.

     10: Paid J. Thomas Corp. amount owed less a 10% discount, check no. 4.

     15: Paid $100 for lumber, check no. 5 to J. Clo.

     18: Paid $200 for lumber merchandise, check no. 6 to B. Blum.

     28: Paid telephone bill, $15, check no. 7 to New Maine Telephone.

     29: Paid rent expense, $100, check no. 8 to B. Realty.

     29: Paid Ben Pierce $50 less a $5 purchase discount, check no. 9.

** 3. Abby Ellen decided to open up a wholesale company as of March 1, 19XX, utilizing five journals in recording business transactions. The journals and their headings are as follows (all journals are page 1):

Sales Journal

Date	Account Debited	Invoice No.	Terms	PR	Accounts Receivable Dr.	Toy Sales Cr.

Purchases Journal

Date	Account Credited	PR	Accounts Payable Cr.	Toy Purchases Dr.	Sundry Accounts Dr.		
					Account	PR	Amount

Cash Receipts Journal

Date	Account Credited	PR	Sundry Account Cr.	Sales Cr.	Accounts Receivable Cr.	Sales Discount Dr.	Cash Dr.

Cash Payment Journal

Date	Check No.	Account Debited	PR	Sundry Account Dr.	Accounts Payable Dr.	Purchase Discount Cr.	Cash Cr.

General Journal

Date	Account Titles and Descriptions	PR	Debit	Credit

As the newly hired accountant, your task is to:

a. Set up ledger accounts from the chart of accounts.

b. Journalize the transaction for the month of March.

c. Total and rule the journal.

d. Post to accounts payable and accounts receivable subsidiary ledgers as appropriate.

e. Prepare a schedule of accounts receivable and schedule of accounts payable.

The chart of accounts of the Abby Ellen Toy Store is:

ASSETS	*REVENUE*
110 Cash	410 Sales
112 Accounts Receivable	412 Sales Returns and
114 Prepaid Rent	Allowances
116 Delivery Truck	414 Sales Discount

Chart continued on next page.

LIABILITIES	COST OF MERCHANDISE—TOYS
210 Accounts Payable	510 Purchases
212 Notes Payable	512 Purchases Returns and Allowances
	514 Purchases Discounts

OWNER'S EQUITY	EXPENSES
310 A. Ellen Investment	610 Salaries Expense
320 Income Summary	612 Cleaning Expense

19XX, MAR.

1: Abby Ellen invested $4,000 into the toy store.

2: Paid three months rent in advance $60, check no. 1.

2: Purchased merchandise from Earl Miller Company on account $1,000, terms 2/10, n/30.

3: Sold merchandise to Bill Burton on account $700, invoice no. 1, terms 2/10, n/30.

6: Sold merchandise to Jim Rex on account $500, invoice no. 2, terms 2/10, n/30.

9: Purchased merchandise from Earl Miller Co. on account $800, terms 2/10, n/30.

9: Sold merchandise to Bill Burton on account $300, invoice no. 3, terms 2/10, n/30.

9: Paid cleaning service $30, check no. 2.

10: Jim Rex returned merchandise that cost $100 to Abby Ellen Toy Store. Abby Ellen issued credit memorandum no. 1 to Jim Rex for $100.

11: Purchased merchandise from Minnie Katz on account $1,000, terms 1/15, n/60.

12: Paid Earl Miller Co. invoice dated March 2, check no. 3.

13: Sold $700 of toy merchandise for cash.

13: Paid salaries $240, check no. 4.

14: Returned merchandise to Minnie Katz in the amount of $200. Abby Ellen Toy Store issued debit memorandum no. 1 to Minnie Katz.

15: Sold merchandise for $300 cash.

16: Received payment from Jim Rex for invoice no. 2 (less returned merchandise) less discount.

16: Bill Burton paid invoice no. 1 $700.

16: Sold toy merchandise to Amy Rose on account, invoice no. 4, $1,600, terms 2/10, n/30.

21: Purchased delivery truck $720 on account from Sam Katz Garage.

22: Sold to Bill Burton merchandise on account $400, invoice no. 5, terms 2/10, n/30.

23: Paid Minnie Katz balance owed, check no. 5.

19XX, MAR. 24: Sold toy merchandise on account to Amy Rose $400, invoice no. 6, terms 1/10, n/30.

25: Purchased toy merchandise for cash $150, check no. 6.

27: Purchased toy merchandise from Woody Smith on account $1,200, terms 2/10, n/30.

28: Bill Burton paid invoice no. 5 dated March 22 less discount.

28: Amy Rose paid invoice no. 6 dated March 24.

29: Borrowed $2,000 from a local bank, interest not due for one year.

29: Purchased merchandise from Earl Miller Co. $1,200, terms 2/10, n/30.

30: Paid Earl Miller Co. March 29 transaction, check no. 7.

30: Sold merchandise to Bonnie Flow Company on account $1,000, invoice no. 7, terms 2/10, n/30.

ADDITIONAL PROBLEM INTERACTORS

1-A. Phil Jones utilizes a cash payments journal for his local bookstore. The headings of the journal are as follows (note the slight variations from the cash payments journal presented in the text)

Cash Payments Journal   Page 2

Cash Cr.	Check No.	Date	Account Description	PR	Sundry Dr.	Accounts Payable Dr.	Purchase Discount Cr.	Purchases Dr.

At the beginning of April the following accounts had balances as shown:

Accounts Payable Subsidiary Ledger

Jones Publishing Co.

Date	PR	Dr.	Cr.	Bal.
19XX April 1	Bal.			50

Macy Publisher

Date	PR	Dr.	Cr.	Bal.
19XX April 1	Bal.			100

General Ledger

Cash   110

Date	PR	Dr.	Cr.	Bal.
19XX April 1	Bal.			20,000

Accounts Payable   210

Date	PR	Dr.	Cr.	Bal.
19XX April 1	Bal.			650

Accounts Payable Subsidiary Ledger (Cont.)   General Ledger (Cont.)

Mike's Press Co.

Date	PR	Dr.	Cr.	Bal.
19XX April 1	Bal.			200

Smith & Sons Publishers

Date	PR	Dr.	Cr.	Bal.
19XX April 1	Bal.			300

Purchases   **510**

Date	PR	Dr.	Cr.	Bal.

Purchase Discount   **511**

Date	PR	Dr.	Cr.	Bal.

Advertising Expense   **610**

Date	PR	Dr.	Cr.	Bal.

Telephone Expense   **612**

Date	PR	Dr.	Cr.	Bal.

Wage Expense   **614**

Date	PR	Dr.	Cr.	Bal.

Your task is to:
a. Record the following transactions into the cash payments journal.
b. Total and rule the columns of the journal.
c. Post to the general ledger and accounts payable subsidiary ledger as appropriate.

19XX, APR.   7: Paid Smith & Sons Publishers $294 ($300 less a 2% discount) for previous purchases made on account, check no. 1.

9: Paid advertising expense $100, check no. 2.

15: Purchased merchandise for cash $300, check no. 3.

18: Paid Mike's Press Co. $200 for merchandise purchased on account, check no. 4, no discount.

23: Paid Jones Publishing Co. amount owed from purchases of $50 on account less the 2% discount, check no. 5.

25: Paid telephone expense for the month $25, check no. 6.

28: Purchased merchandise for cash $150, check no. 7.

29: Paid wage expense $200, check no. 8.

*2-A. Ken Sorkin operates a wholesale appliance center. The following cash payments journal is used to record all payments of cash (by check)

						Appliance Merchandise Discount Cr.	Sundry Dr.		
Date	Check Payable To	PR	Check No.	Cash Cr.	Appliance Merchandise Dr.		Amount	PR	Account

Cash Payments Journal — Page 5

The account balances as of April 1, 19XX, are as follows:

Accounts Payable Subsidiary Ledger

ABC Corp.

Date	PR	Dr.	Cr.	Bal.
19XX April 1	Bal.			500

Ben Benson Corp.

Date	PR	Dr.	Cr.	Bal.
19XX April 1	Bal.			400

Barry Katz Corp.

Date	PR	Dr.	Cr.	Bal.
19XX April 1	Bal.			300

Small Corp.

Date	PR	Dr.	Cr.	Bal.
19XX April 1	Bal.			600

General Ledger

Cash 110

Date	PR	Dr.	Cr.	Bal.
19XX April 1	Bal.			10,000

Delivery Truck 150

Date	PR	Dr.	Cr.	Bal.

Accounts Payable 210

Date	PR	Dr.	Cr.	Bal.
19XX April 1	Bal.			1,800

Appliance Purchase 510

Date	PR	Dr.	Cr.	Bal.

Appliance Purchase Discount 511

Date	PR	Dr.	Cr.	Bal.

Rent Expense 610

Date	PR	Dr.	Cr.	Bal.

Utilities Expense 620

Date	PR	Dr.	Cr.	Bal.

Your task is to:

a. Journalize the following transactions.

b. Total and rule the journal.

c. Post to accounts payable subsidiary ledger when appropriate.

d. Prepare a schedule of accounts payable. Does it equal accounts payable in the controlling account at the end of April?

19XX, APR. 1: Paid half of amount owed Ben Benson Corp. from previous purchases of appliances on account, $200 less a $4 discount, check no. 1.

3: Purchased a delivery truck for $5,000 cash, check no. 2 payable to Jim Smith.

5: Bought appliance merchandise for cash $500 from B. Motas, check no. 3.

8: Bought additional appliance merchandise $100 cash from B. Motas, check no. 4.

15: Paid Small Corp. amount owed less a 5% purchase discount, check no. 5.

28: Paid utilities expense $100, check no. 6, to B. P. Utility Co.

29: Paid rent expense to Realty Trust $50, check no. 7.

30: Paid half of amount owed Barry Katz Co., no discount, check no. 8.

** 3-A. Howard King decided to open up on May 1, 19XX, as a distributor of car parts to auto dealers. The journals and their headings are as follows:

Sales Journal

Date	Account Debited	Invoice No.	PR	Accounts Receivable Dr.	Sales Cr.	Terms

Purchase Journal

Date	Amount Dr.	PR	Accounts Payable Cr.	Auto Parts Purchases Dr.	Sundry Dr. Account	PR	Amount

Cash Receipts Journal

Date	Account Cr.	PR	Sundry Accounts Cr.	Auto Parts Sales Cr.	Accounts Receivable Cr.	Auto Parts Sales Discount Dr.	Cash Dr.

Cash Payments Journal

Date	Check No.	Account Debited	PR	Sundry Accounts Dr.	Accounts Payable Dr.	Purchase Discount Cr.	Cash Cr.

General Journal

Date	Account Title and Description	PR	Debit	Credit

As the newly hired accountant, your task is to:

a. Set up ledger accounts from the chart of accounts.

b. Journalize the transactions for the month of May.

c. Total and rule journals.

d. Open and post to accounts payable and accounts receivable subsidiary ledger as appropriate,

e. Prepare a schedule of accounts receivable and a schedule of accounts payable.

The chart of accounts for Howard King's Auto Parts is as follows:

ASSETS	REVENUE
110 Cash	410 Auto Parts Sales
112 Accounts Receivable	412 Sales Returns and Allowances
114 Prepaid Rent	414 Sales Discounts
116 Delivery Truck	

LIABILITIES	COST OF MERCHANDISE— AUTO PARTS
210 Accounts Payable	510 Purchases
212 Notes Payable	512 Purchase Returns and Allowances
	514 Purchase Discounts

OWNER'S EQUITY	EXPENSES
310 H. King Investment	610 Wage Expense
320 Income Summary	612 Janitorial Expense

19XX, MAY   1: Howard King invested $1,000 into the auto parts business.

2: Paid three months rent in advance $300, check no. 1.

2: Purchased auto parts from Ed Newburgh Co. on account $250, terms 2/10, n/30.

3: Sold merchandise to Tom Grant Co. on account $200, invoice no. 1, terms 2/10, n/30.

6: Sold merchandise to Belle Flynn Co. on account $100, invoice no. 2, terms 2/10, n/30.

9: Purchased merchandise from Ed Newburgh Co. on account $200, terms 2/10, n/30.

9: Sold merchandise to Tom Grant Co. on account $70, invoice no. 3, terms 2/10, n/30.

9: Paid janitorial expense $10, check no. 2.

19XX, MAY 10: Belle Flynn Co. returned auto merchandise that cost $50 to Howard King Auto Co. Howard King issued a credit memorandum no. 1 to Belle Flynn Co., for $50.

11: Purchased merchandise from Denton Crews Co. on account $300, terms 1/15, n/60.

12: Paid Ed Newburgh Co. invoice dated May 2, check no. 3.

13: Sold $150 of auto parts merchandise for cash.

13: Paid wages of $50, check no. 4.

14: Returned merchandise to Denton Crews Co. in the amount of $100. Howard King Auto Parts issued debit memorandum no. 1 to Denton Crews Co.

15: Sold auto parts merchandise for $100 cash.

16: Received payment from Belle Flynn for invoice no. 2 (less returned merchandise less discount) dated May 6.

16: Tom Grant paid invoice no. 1 $200, no discount.

16: Sold auto parts merchandise to Jay Reef on account, invoice no. 4, $400, terms 2/10, n/30.

21: Purchased a delivery truck $150 on account from Joan Peabody's Garage.

22: Sold to Tom Grant Co. auto parts merchandise on account $100, invoice no. 5, terms 2/10, n/30.

23: Paid balance owed Denton Crews Co., check no. 5 (beware).

24: Sold auto parts merchandise to Jay Reef Co. on account $100, invoice no. 6 terms 1/10, n/30.

25: Purchased auto parts from J. P. Car for cash $300, check no. 6.

27: Purchased auto parts merchandise from Neila Moore Co. on account $400, terms 2/10, n/30.

28: Jay Reef Co. paid invoice no. 6 dated May 24.

29: Borrowed $1,000 from a local bank, interest due in two years.

29: Purchased auto parts merchandise from Ed Newburgh Co. $400 on account, terms 2/10, n/30.

30: Paid Ed Newburgh Co. May 29 transaction, check no. 7.

30: Sold auto parts merchandise to Sue Beef Co. on account, invoice no. 7, terms 2/10, n/30, $1,000.

CHALLENGE PROBLEM INTERACTOR

The Doughy Baking Company uses: five journals, and general and subsidiary ledgers to record all transactions. Using the code given for the journals and ledgers, indicate the journal and ledger(s) in which each of the following transactions would be recorded:

CODE:

AP—Accounts Payable Subsidiary Ledger   GJ—General Journal

AR—Accounts Receivable Subsidiary Ledger   GL—General Ledger

CPJ—Cash Payments Journal   PJ—Purchase Journal

CRJ—Cash Receipts Journal   SJ—Sales Journal

TRANSACTION	JOURNAL	LEDGER(S)
Example: Sold merchandise for cash	CRJ	GI
1. Salaries accrued at the end of the accounting period.		
2. Owner withdrew cash for personal use.		
3. Sold merchandise on account.		
4. Paid a creditor within the discount for a purchase on account.		
5. Paid rent expense for the month.		
6. Purchased merchandise on account for resale.		
7. Received a check from a customer for a sale on account paid within the discount period.		
8. Returned damaged merchandise purchased on account.		
9. Purchased office supplies on account.		
10. Recorded the net income on the books.		
11. Purchased office equipment on account.		
12. Owner made additional investment in the business.		

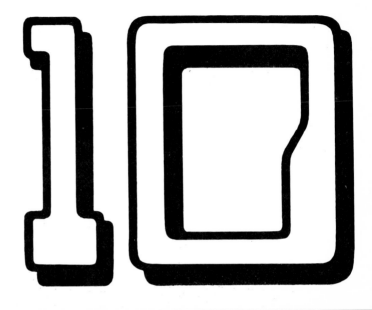

accounting control

In previous chapters we have developed the special journals of Ralph's Sporting Goods. As Ralph finds his business increasing, he is becoming quite concerned about developing a system of procedures and records for close control over the cash receipts and cash payments of the business.

THE CONTROL OF CASH

Ralph is concerned both about detecting possible thefts and about increasing the store's efficiency. The control he wants to develop over the store's assets, as well as the monitoring of its operations, is known as *internal control*.

Ralph, his accountant, and a consultant Ralph hired to study internal control questions, sat down together and developed the following company policies:

1. Responsibilities and duties of employees will be divided. For example, the person receiving the cash, whether at the register or by opening mail will not record this information into the accounting records. The accountant, for his part, will not be handling the cash receipts.
2. All cash receipts of Ralph's Sporting Goods will be deposited into the bank the same day.
3. All cash payments will be made by check.
4. Employees will be rotated. This allows workers to become acquainted with the work of others as well as to prepare for a possible changeover in jobs.

5. Ralph Jones will sign all checks after receiving authorization to pay from respective departments.
6. At time of payment, all supporting invoices or documents will be stamped paid. That will show when the invoice or document is paid as well as the number of the check used.
7. All checks will be pre-numbered (1, 2, 3, 4, 5, etc.). This will control the use of checks and make it difficult to use a check fraudulently without its being revealed at some point.
8. The above policies of Ralph's Sporting Goods will be continually reevaluated and modified as needed.

As he considered the control of both cash receipts and cash payments, Ralph realized how time-consuming and expensive it would be to write checks for small amounts to pay for postage, small supplies, etc. What was needed for these small expenses was an *imprest fund* or *petty cash fund*.

LEARNING UNIT 25

The Establishment of a Petty Cash Fund

It was decided that for the month of February Ralph's Sporting Goods would need a fund of $20 to cover small expenditures. This petty cash was expected to last no longer than one month.

SETTING UP THE FUND

The following is the mind-process chart for the establishment of a $20 petty cash fund, which would be entered in the cash payments journal on February 1, 19XX.

Petty cash is an asset, which is established by writing new checks.

Accounts Affected	Category	↑ ↓	Rule
Petty Cash	Asset	↑	Dr.
Cash (checks)	Asset	↓	Cr.

Cash Payments Journal							Page 1
Date	Check No.	Accounts Debited	PR	Sundry Dr.	Accounts Payable Dr.	Purchase Discount Cr.	Cash Cr.
19XX Feb. 1	8	Petty Cash	115	20			20

The establishment of a fund creates a new asset called petty cash; this new asset was created by writing check no. 8, thereby reducing the asset cash. In reality, the total assets stay the same; what has occurred is *a shift from the asset cash (check no. 8) to a new asset account called petty cash.*

But who is responsible for controlling the petty cash fund? Ralph gives his office manager, Joe Bloom, the responsibility and the authority to make payments from the petty cash fund, which is kept in the office safe in a small tin box. In other companies the cashier or secretary may be in charge of petty cash.

MAKING PAYMENTS FROM THE PETTY CASH FUND

The office manager of Ralph's Sporting Goods, Joe Bloom, has the responsibility of filling out a petty cash voucher for each cash payment made from the petty cash fund.

Petty Cash Voucher No. 1

Date: _____   Amount: _____

Paid To: _____

For: _____

Approved By: _____

Payment Received By: _____

Debit Account No. _____

Note that this simple voucher when completed will include:

1. The voucher number (which will be in sequence).
2. The date.
3. The person or organization to whom the payment was made.
4. The amount of the payment.
5. The reason for the payment.
6. The initials of the person who approved the payment.
7. The signature of the person who received the payment.
8. The account to which the expense will be charged. (This point we will be dealing with next.)

The completed vouchers are placed in the petty cash box. No matter how many vouchers Joe Bloom fills out, the total of (*1*) *the vouchers in the box and* (*2*) *the cash not paid should equal the original amount of petty cash with which the fund was established.*

Before going on, assume you are Joe Bloom and fill out a petty cash voucher for a payment to Charlie Smith using the facts listed below.

Facts: On February 2, 19XX, Charlie Smith requested $1 to pay for the cleaning of a package sold to a local customer, as delivery was urgent. This expense is to be charged to account no. 612, cleaning expense. Have a classmate sign for Charlie.

SOLUTION to Unit Interactor **25A**

Petty Cash Voucher No. 1

Date: _____ 2/2/XX _____   Amount: _____ $1.00 _____

Paid To: _____ Charlie Smith _____

For: _____ Cleaning Package _____

Approved By: _____ J. B. _____

Payment Received By: _____ Charlie Smith _____

Debit Account No: _____ 612, Cleaning Expense _____

Now the petty cash box has $19 cash and a $1 petty cash voucher. The sum of $19 and a $1 voucher equals the beginning amount in petty cash, $20.

HOW TO REPLENISH THE PETTY CASH FUND

Assume that at the end of February the following items are documented by petty cash vouchers in the petty cash box as having been paid by Joe Bloom:

19XX, FEB. 2: Cleaning package, $1.00
            5: Postage stamps, $3.00
            8: First aid supplies, $5.00
            9: Delivery expense, $2.00
           14: Delivery expense, $5.00
           27: Postage stamps, $2.00

Information about each expense recorded in the auxiliary has yet to be journalized and posted to the ledger. The auxiliary will aid us in gathering information for the journal entry.

Joe keeps this information in a separate petty cash receipts and payments book. It is not a special journal, but an aid to Joe—an auxiliary record that is not essential, but quite helpful as part of the petty cash system.

No postings will be done from the following auxiliary book. At some point the information found in the auxiliary petty cash record will be journalized into the cash payments journal and posted to the appropriate ledger accounts to reflect up-to-date balances.

Auxiliary Petty Cash Record

Date	Voucher No.	Description	Receipts	Pay- ments	Postage 614 Dr.	Delivery 616 Dr.	Sundry Dr. Account	Amount
19XX								
Feb. 1		Establishment	20					
2	1	Cleaning		1.00			Cleaning 612	1.00
5	2	Postage		3.00	3.00			
8	3	First Aid		5.00			Miscellaneous 618	5.00
9	4	Delivery		2.00		2.00		
14	5	Delivery		5.00		5.00		
27	6	Postage		2.00	2.00			
		Total	20	18.00	5.00	7.00		6.00

This $18 of expenses is recorded in the cash payments journal and the new check no. 20 for $18 is cashed and returned to Joe Bloom. The petty cash box now once again reflects $20 cash. The old vouchers that were used are stamped to indicate they have been processed and the fund replenished.

A new check is written in the replenishment process.

If at some point the petty cash fund is to be greater than $20, a check can be written that will increase petty cash and decrease cash. If the petty cash account balance is to be reduced, we can credit or reduce petty cash. But for our present purpose petty cash will remain at $20.

SUMMARY: In summary, here are the key points to remember:

Establishment

Cash Payments Journal Page 1

Date	Check No.	Accounts Debited	PR	Sundry Dr.	Accounts Payable Dr.	Purchase Discount Cr.	Cash Cr.
19XX							
Feb. 1	8	Petty Cash	115	20			20

28		Postage Expense	614	5			
		Delivery Expense	616	7			
		Cleaning Expense	612	1			
	20	Miscellaneous Expense	618	5			18*

*This requires writing a new check that will allow the petty cash box to be replenished and the old vouchers to be taken out and recorded in appropriate expense accounts.

The auxiliary petty cash record after replenishment would look as follows:

Auxiliary Petty Cash Record

Date	Voucher No.	Description	Receipts	Pay-ments	Postage 614 Dr.	Delivery 616 Dr.	Sundry Dr. Account	Sundry Dr. Amount
19XX								
Feb. 1		Establishment	20.00					
2	1	Cleaning		1.00			Cleaning 612	1.00
5	2	Postage		3.00	3.00			
8	3	First Aid		5.00			Miscellaneous 618	5.00
9	4	Delivery		2.00		2.00		
14	5	Delivery		5.00		5.00		
27	6	Postage		2.00	2.00			
		Total	20.00	18.00	5.00	7.00		6.00
		Ending Balance		2.00				
			20.00	20.00				
		Ending Balance	2.00					
28		Replenishment	18.00					
28		Balance (New)	20.00					

At this time you should be able to:

1. Define internal control.
2. State five possible internal control policies.
3. State the purpose for a petty cash fund.
4. Prepare a journal entry for the cash payments journal to record the establishment of petty cash.

5. Prepare a petty cash voucher for payment.
6. Prepare in the cash payments journal the entry to replenish petty cash.
7. Differentiate between the cash payments journal and the auxiliary petty cash record.
8. Explain why no postings result from the auxiliary petty cash record.
9. Explain why the replenishment of petty cash doesn't affect the petty cash account.
10. Explain why a new check is needed in the replenishment process.

UNIT INTERACTOR 25B

MINI REVIEW: A petty cash fund helps avoid the writing of checks for small amounts. To establish the petty cash fund a check is drawn and money is turned over to the person responsible for petty cash.

Keep in mind that the actual amount of cash in petty cash *plus* the total of the receipts (vouchers) should be equal to the amount of petty cash that was originally established.

A misconception many students have is that the petty cash record is part of the special journal. In fact it is an auxiliary record that supplements the normal accounting records.

As the custodian of the petty cash fund it is your task to prepare entries to establish the fund on November 1, as well as to replenish the fund on November 30. Please keep an auxiliary petty cash record.

19XX, NOV. 1: Established petty cash fund for $30, check no. 5.
           5: Voucher 11, Delivery Expense, $7.
           9: Voucher 12, Delivery Expense, $5.
          10: Voucher 13, Office Repair Expense, $8.
          17: Voucher 14, General Expense, $4.
          25: Voucher 15, General Expense, $2.
          30: Replenishment of petty cash fund, $26, check no. 106.

SOLUTION to Unit Interactor 25B

Cash Payments Journal

Date	Check No.	Accounts Debited	PR	Sundry Dr.	Accounts Payable Dr.	Purchase Discount Cr.	Cash Cr.
19XX Nov. 1	5	Petty Cash	*	30			30
30		Delivery Expense		12			
		General Expense		6			
	106	Office Repair Expense		8			26

*The PR would show posting. Deleted for simplicity at this point.

Auxiliary Petty Cash Record

Date	Voucher No.	Description	Receipts	Payments	Delivery No. 612	General No. 614	Sundry Dr. Account	Amount
19XX								
Nov. 1		Establishment	30.00					
5	11	Delivery		7.00	7.00			
9	12	Delivery		5.00	5.00			
10	13	Repairs		8.00			Office Repair	8.00
17	14	General		4.00		4.00		
25	15	General		2.00		2.00		
		Total	30.00	26.00	12.00	6.00		8.00
		Ending Balance		4.00				
			30.00	30.00				
30		Ending Balance	4.00					
30		Replenishment	26.00					
Dec. 1		New Balance	30.00					

As we saw in the last unit, Ralph realizes the importance of cash control and is a firm believer in rotating his personnel within the company. At the end of each month he is planning to conduct a training session for selected personnel on various phases of the business of Ralph's Sporting Goods, so that his workers gain insight into as many aspects of the business as possible. He feels this will foster greater understanding and cooperation among workers in the company.

The following learning unit is based on the workshop he presented to his employees on the control of cash, specifically in terms of the bank's relationship to Ralph's Sporting Goods.

LEARNING UNIT 26

Bank Procedures and Structure for Checking Accounts and Bank Reconciliations

THE TRAINING SESSION

Before his shop opened on January 1, 19XX, Ralph had a meeting at Security National Bank to discuss the steps in opening up and using a checking account for Ralph's Sporting Goods. The following is a summary of that meeting:

The manager of the bank gave Ralph a signature card to fill out.

The signature card

AUTHORIZED SIGNATURES OF

SECURITY NATIONAL BANK, Lynn, Mass.

_____ SS #

_____ SS #

_____ SS #

Write address on other side   Date

PO&CT 235

Home Address	Res. Phone
Business Address	Bus. Phone
Bank Reference	
	Officer Amt. $

When Ralph asked what it was for, the manager told him that he must sign it (since Ralph would be signing checks) so that the bank could check and validate his signature when checks were presented for payment. The signature card would be kept in the bank's files so that possible forgeries could be spotted.

At the meeting Ralph received deposit tickets and a checkbook. The deposit tickets were to be used when Ralph's Sporting Goods received cash or checks from any source and deposited them into the checking account. The amounts of cash and checks that are deposited in the bank are entered on this form. Don't be concerned about the technicalities of filling it out; we will be doing it later. It is important to understand that one copy stays with the bank and a duplicate copy remains with the company, so they can verify that items in the cash receipts journal that make up the deposit have actually been deposited correctly.

310

SECURITY NATIONAL BANK

DEPOSIT TICKET

FOR DEPOSIT TO THE ACCOUNT OF

_____

DO NOT WRITE IN THIS SPACE ▼

PLEASE BE SURE THAT ALL ITEMS ARE PROPERLY ENDORSED.   LIST EACH CHECK SEPARATELY.

Checks and other items are received for deposit subject to the terms and conditions of this bank's collection agreement.

DATE_____

DEPOSITOR PLEASE ENTER ACCOUNT NUMBER IN THESE BLOCKS

	DOLLARS	CENTS
CURRENCY		
COIN		
CHECKS LIST EACH SEPARATELY		
1		
2		
3		
4		
5		
6		
7		
8		
9		
10		
11		
12		
13		
14		
15		
16		
17		
18		
19		
20		
TOTAL		

PO & CT 205

The checks that Ralph will deposit require his signature on the reverse side. This endorsement by Ralph could look as follows:

Ralph Jones	Pay to the order of Security National Bank *Ralph Jones*	Pay to the order of Security National Bank for Deposit Only *Ralph Jones*
Blank Endorsement	Full Endorsement	Restrictive Endorsement

Ralph has chosen the restrictive endorsement, since he is concerned with safety and this type of endorsement restricts or limits any further negotiation of the check(s).

The checkbook contained checks of the type illustrated here. These checks would be used to inform the bank by a written order (the check) that a specific amount of money was to be paid to the person or company indicated on the check. Once again, don't worry about filling out the form; we will see how to do this soon.

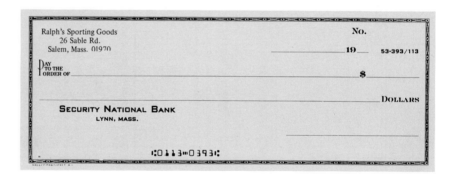

The manager indicated that at the end of each month the bank would send Ralph's Sporting Goods a statement that would indicate (1) the balance of the cash on deposit at the bank based on the bank's records to start the month, (2) a list of deposits that the store made during the month, (3) the checks that were received by the bank for payment and thus deducted from the store's account balance, (4) the ending cash balance, according to the bank records for the store at the end of the month.

Let us look at the transactions of Ralph's Sporting Goods for the month of January that affect the checking account. Remember, all payments of money are by written check (except petty cash), and all money (checks) received is deposited in the bank account.

DATE OF DEPOSIT	AMOUNT	RECEIVED FROM
Jan. 2, 19XX	$20,000	R. Jones Investment

DATE OF DEPOSIT	AMOUNT	RECEIVED FROM
Jan. 13, 19XX	$3,500	Cash Sales

Deposit Ticket No. 1

Deposit Ticket No. 2

SECURITY NATIONAL BANK

DEPOSIT TICKET

FOR DEPOSIT TO THE ACCOUNT OF

Ralph's Sporting Goods

DO NOT WRITE IN THIS SPACE ▼

PLEASE BE SURE THAT ALL ITEMS ARE PROPERLY ENDORSED. LIST EACH CHECK SEPARATELY.

Checks and other items are received for deposit subject to the terms and conditions of this bank's collection agreement.

DATE 1/2/XX

	DOLLARS	CENTS
CURRENCY		
COIN		
CHECKS LIST EACH SEPARATELY		
1 15-111	20,000	00
2		
3		
4		
5		
6		
7		
8		
9		
10		
11		
12		
13		
14		
15		
16		
17		
18		
19		
20		
PO & CT 205 **TOTAL**	20,000	00

DEPOSITOR PLEASE ENTER ACCOUNT NUMBER IN THESE BLOCKS

1 8 2 8 8 1

SECURITY NATIONAL BANK

DEPOSIT TICKET

FOR DEPOSIT TO THE ACCOUNT OF

Ralph's Sporting Goods

DO NOT WRITE IN THIS SPACE ▼

PLEASE BE SURE THAT ALL ITEMS ARE PROPERLY ENDORSED. LIST EACH CHECK SEPARATELY.

Checks and other items are received for deposit subject to the terms and conditions of this bank's collection agreement.

DATE 1/13/XX

	DOLLARS	CENTS
CURRENCY	3,500	00
COIN		
CHECKS LIST EACH SEPARATELY		
1		
2		
3		
4		
5		
6		
7		
8		
9		
10		
11		
12		
13		
14		
15		
16		
17		
18		
19		
20		
PO & CT 205 **TOTAL**	3,500	00

DEPOSITOR PLEASE ENTER ACCOUNT NUMBER IN THESE BLOCKS

1 8 2 8 8 1

* All entries are based on transactions found in Chapters 6-9.

DATE OF DEPOSIT	AMOUNT	RECEIVED FROM
Jan. 15, 19XX	$1,500	Cash Sales

DATE OF DEPOSIT	AMOUNT	RECEIVED FROM	
Jan. 16, 19XX	$5,460	D. Adams Corp.	$1,960
		B. Baker Corp.	$3,500

Deposit Ticket No. 3

Deposit Ticket No. 4

SECURITY NATIONAL BANK

DEPOSIT TICKET

FOR DEPOSIT TO THE ACCOUNT OF

Ralph's Sporting Goods

DO NOT WRITE IN THIS SPACE ▼

PLEASE BE SURE THAT ALL ITEMS ARE PROPERLY ENDORSED. LIST EACH CHECK SEPARATELY.

Checks and other items are received for deposit subject to the terms and conditions of this bank's collection agreement.

DATE 1/15/XX

DEPOSITOR PLEASE ENTER ACCOUNT NUMBER IN THESE BLOCKS

1 8 2 8 8 1

	DOLLARS	CENTS
CURRENCY	1,500	00
COIN		
CHECKS 1		
2		
3		
4		
5		
6		
7		
8		
9		
10		
11		
12		
13		
14		
15		
16		
17		
18		
19		
20		
PO & CT 205 **TOTAL**	1,500	00

SECURITY NATIONAL BANK

DEPOSIT TICKET

FOR DEPOSIT TO THE ACCOUNT OF

Ralph's Sporting Goods

DO NOT WRITE IN THIS SPACE ▼

PLEASE BE SURE THAT ALL ITEMS ARE PROPERLY ENDORSED. LIST EACH CHECK SEPARATELY.

Checks and other items are received for deposit subject to the terms and conditions of this bank's collection agreement.

DATE 1/16/XX

DEPOSITOR PLEASE ENTER ACCOUNT NUMBER IN THESE BLOCKS

1 8 2 8 8 1

	DOLLARS	CENTS
CURRENCY		
COIN		
CHECKS 1 18-111	1,960	00
2 22-114	3,500	00
3		
4		
5		
6		
7		
8		
9		
10		
11		
12		
13		
14		
15		
16		
17		
18		
19		
20		
PO & CT 205 **TOTAL**	5,460	00

Deposit Ticket No. 5

Deposit Ticket No. 6

SECURITY NATIONAL BANK

DEPOSIT TICKET

FOR DEPOSIT TO THE ACCOUNT OF

Ralph's Sporting Goods

DO NOT WRITE IN THIS SPACE

PLEASE BE SURE THAT ALL ITEMS ARE PROPERLY ENDORSED. LIST EACH CHECK SEPARATELY.

Checks and other items are received for deposit subject to the terms and conditions of this bank's collection agreement.

DATE 1/28/XX

	DOLLARS	CENTS
CURRENCY		
COIN		
CHECKS LIST EACH SEPARATELY		
1 22-114	1,960	00
2 18-111	1,600	00
3		
4		
5		
6		
7		
8		
9		
10		
11		
12		
13		
14		
15		
16		
17		
18		
19		
20		
TOTAL	3,560	00

DEPOSITOR PLEASE ENTER ACCOUNT NUMBER IN THESE BLOCKS

1 8 2 8 8 1

PO & CT 205

SECURITY NATIONAL BANK

DEPOSIT TICKET

FOR DEPOSIT TO THE ACCOUNT OF

Ralph's Sporting Goods

DO NOT WRITE IN THIS SPACE

PLEASE BE SURE THAT ALL ITEMS ARE PROPERLY ENDORSED. LIST EACH CHECK SEPARATELY.

Checks and other items are received for deposit subject to the terms and conditions of this bank's collection agreement.

DATE 1/29/XX

	DOLLARS	CENTS
CURRENCY		
COIN		
CHECKS LIST EACH SEPARATELY		
1 15-22	10,000	00
2		
3		
4		
5		
6		
7		
8		
9		
10		
11		
12		
13		
14		
15		
16		
17		
18		
19		
20		
TOTAL	10,000	00

DEPOSITOR PLEASE ENTER ACCOUNT NUMBER IN THESE BLOCKS

1 8 2 8 8 1

PO & CT 205

In summary, the following chart could be prepared from the cash receipts journal:

BANK DEPOSITS MADE FOR JANUARY

DATE OF DEPOSIT	AMOUNT	RECEIVED FROM
January 2	$20,000	R. Jones Investment
13	3,500	Cash Sales
15	1,500	Cash Sales
16	5,460	Check/D. Adams Corp. $1,960
		Check/B. Baker Corp. $3,500
28	3,560	Check/B. Baker Corp. $1,960
		Check/A. Sling Corp. $1,600
29	10,000	Bank Loan
Total deposits for month	$44,020	

Notice that Ralph's Sporting Goods deposited a total of $44,020 into the company checking account. Each deposit will be reflected on the stubs in Ralph's checkbook.

Now that we have looked at the inward flow of money, let's turn to the outward flow.

CHECKS WRITTEN BY RALPH'S SPORTING GOODS IN JANUARY

CHECK	DATE	PAYMENT TO	AMOUNT	DESCRIPTION
No. 1	Jan. 2	J. Landlord	$300	Rent in Advance

Ralph's Sporting Goods
26 Sable Rd.
Salem, Mass. 01970

No. 1

January 2 19XX   53-393/113

PAY TO THE ORDER OF J. Landlord $ 300. XX/100

Three Hundred and XX/100   DOLLARS

SECURITY NATIONAL BANK
LYNN, MASS.

Ralph Jones

⑈0113⑈0393⑈ 18288।

CHECK	DATE	PAYMENT TO	AMOUNT	DESCRIPTION
No. 2	Jan. 9	Bob's Cleaning	$150	Cleaning

Ralph's Sporting Goods
26 Sable Rd.
Salem, Mass. 01970

No. 2

January 9 19XX 53-393/113

PAY TO THE ORDER OF *Bob's Cleaning Service* $ *150* XX/100

One Hundred and Fifty and XX/100 —————— DOLLARS

SECURITY NATIONAL BANK
LYNN, MASS.

Ralph Jones

⑆0113⑉0393⑆ 182881

CHECK	DATE	PAYMENT TO	AMOUNT	DESCRIPTION
No. 3	Jan. 12	Pete Regan Co.	$4,900	Purchases on Account

Ralph's Sporting Goods
26 Sable Rd.
Salem, Mass. 01970

No. 3

January 12 19XX 53-393/113

PAY TO THE ORDER OF *P. Regan Company* $ *4900* XX/100

Four Thousand Nine Hundred and XX/100 —————— DOLLARS

SECURITY NATIONAL BANK
LYNN, MASS.

Ralph Jones

⑆0113⑉0393⑆ 182881

CHECK	DATE	PAYMENT TO	AMOUNT	DESCRIPTION
No. 4	Jan. 13	J. Bloom	$1,200	Salary, Office Manager*

Ralph's Sporting Goods
26 Sable Rd.
Salem, Mass. 01970

No. 4

January 13 19XX 53-393/113

PAY TO THE ORDER OF *J. Bloom* $ *1200* XX/100

One Thousand Two Hundred and XX/100 —————— DOLLARS

SECURITY NATIONAL BANK
LYNN, MASS.

Ralph Jones

⑆0113⑉0393⑆ 182881

* We will talk about payroll deductions in Chapters 14 and 15.

CHECK	DATE	PAYMENT TO	AMOUNT	DESCRIPTION
No. 5	Jan. 23	Russell Slater	$3,960	Purchases on Account

Ralph's Sporting Goods
26 Sable Rd.
Salem, Mass. 01970

No. *5*

January 23 19XX   53-393/113

PAY TO THE ORDER OF *Russell Slate Corp.* $ 3960 XX/100

Three thousand Nine Hundred and Sixty and XX/100   DOLLARS

SECURITY NATIONAL BANK
LYNN, MASS.

Ralph Jones

⑆0113⑉0393⑆   182881

CHECK	DATE	PAYMENT TO	AMOUNT	DESCRIPTION
No. 6	Jan. 25	T. Jones Co.	$750	Cash Purchases

Ralph's Sporting Goods
26 Sable Rd.
Salem, Mass. 01970

No. *6*

January 25 19XX   53-393/113

PAY TO THE ORDER OF *T. Jones Co.* $ 750 XX/100

Seven Hundred and Fifty and XX/100 ———   DOLLARS

SECURITY NATIONAL BANK
LYNN, MASS.

Ralph Jones

⑆0113⑉0393⑆   182881

CHECK	DATE	PAYMENT TO	AMOUNT	DESCRIPTION
No. 7	Jan. 30	Pete Regan Co.	$5,880	Purchase on Account

Ralph's Sporting Goods
26 Sable Rd.
Salem, Mass. 01970

No. 7

January 30 19XX   53-393/113

PAY TO THE ORDER OF   *P. Regan Company* $*5,880* XX/100

Fine Thousand Eight Hundred and Eighty and XX/100   DOLLARS

SECURITY NATIONAL BANK
LYNN, MASS.

Ralph Jones

⑈0113⑈0393⑈ 18288ı

In summary, the checks that were written for the month of January are as follows:

CHECKS WRITTEN FOR MONTH OF JANUARY

DATE	CHECK NO.	PAYMENT TO	AMOUNT	DESCRIPTION
Jan. 2	1	J. Landlord	$300	Rent in Advance
9	2	Bob's Cleaning	150	Cleaning
12	3	Pete Regan Co.	4,900	Purchases on Account
13	4	J. Bloom	1,200	Salary, Office Manager
23	5	Russell Slater	3,960	Purchases on Account
25	6	T. Jones Co.	750	Cash Purchase
30	7	Pete Regan Co.	5,880	Purchases on Account
Total amount of checks written			$17,140	

This information is on the stubs of the checkbook. The cash payments journal has the same information.

To this point:

Cash/checks deposited was	$44,020
Cash paid by check	17,140
Balance in company checkbook	$26,880

At the end of January the bank notifies us that the balance of the cash account is $19,947. How can this be? The following section deals with whether the bank is incorrect, the company is incorrect, or both the bank and the company are incorrect. What adjustments are needed?

At the end of January the bank sent Ralph's Sporting Goods the following report:

Bank statement

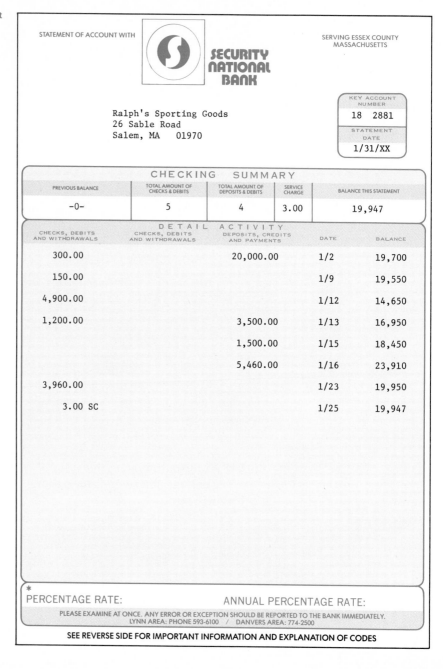

STATEMENT OF ACCOUNT WITH

SECURITY NATIONAL BANK

SERVING ESSEX COUNTY
MASSACHUSETTS

Ralph's Sporting Goods
26 Sable Road
Salem, MA   01970

KEY ACCOUNT NUMBER
18   2881
STATEMENT DATE
1/31/XX

CHECKING SUMMARY

PREVIOUS BALANCE	TOTAL AMOUNT OF CHECKS & DEBITS	TOTAL AMOUNT OF DEPOSITS & DEBITS	SERVICE CHARGE	BALANCE THIS STATEMENT
-0-	5	4	3.00	19,947

DETAIL ACTIVITY

CHECKS, DEBITS AND WITHDRAWALS	CHECKS, DEBITS AND WITHDRAWALS	DEPOSITS, CREDITS AND PAYMENTS	DATE	BALANCE
300.00		20,000.00	1/2	19,700
150.00			1/9	19,550
4,900.00			1/12	14,650
1,200.00		3,500.00	1/13	16,950
		1,500.00	1/15	18,450
		5,460.00	1/16	23,910
3,960.00			1/23	19,950
3.00 SC			1/25	19,947

*
PERCENTAGE RATE: ANNUAL PERCENTAGE RATE:

PLEASE EXAMINE AT ONCE. ANY ERROR OR EXCEPTION SHOULD BE REPORTED TO THE BANK IMMEDIATELY.
LYNN AREA: PHONE 593-6100   /   DANVERS AREA: 774-2500

SEE REVERSE SIDE FOR IMPORTANT INFORMATION AND EXPLANATION OF CODES

This statement shows the beginning balance of the cash at the start of the month, along with the checks the bank has paid, along with any deposits received. Any other charges or additions to the bank balance are indicated by codes found on the statement. All checks that have been paid by the bank are sent back to Ralph's Sporting Goods.

The problem is that this ending bank balance of $19,947 does not agree with the amount in Ralph's checkbook, $26,880, or the balance in the cash account in the ledger, $26,880.

The task of Ralph's accountant is to find out why there is a difference between the bank's balance and Ralph's balance and how the records can be brought into balance. This process of reconciling the bank balance vs. the company's balance is called *bank reconciliation*. To prepare the bank reconciliation, Ralph's accountant takes the following steps:

Relationship of cash receipts journal to bank reconciliation

In comparing the list of deposits received by the bank with the cash receipts journal, the accountant notices that the two deposits made on Jan. 28 and 29 for $3,560 and $10,000 were not on the bank's statement. The accountant realizes that in order to prepare this statement, the bank only included information about Ralph's Sporting Goods up to Jan. 25. These two deposits made by Ralph were not shown on the monthly bank statement, since they arrived at the bank after the statement was printed. The deposits not yet added onto the bank balance are called deposits in transit. These two deposits need to be added to the bank balance shown on the bank statement. Ralph's checkbook is not affected, since the two deposits already have been added to its balance. The bank has no way of knowing that the deposits are coming until they are received.

Relationship of cash payments journal to bank reconciliation

The accountant places the checks returned by the bank in numerical order (1, 2, 3, etc.). He opens the cash payments journal and places a checkmark (✓) next to each payment check that was returned by the bank. This indicates that the amount shown in the cash payments

Cash Payments Journal							Page 1
Date	Check No.	Account Debited	PR	Sundry Dr.	Accounts Payable Dr.	Pur- chases Cr.	Cash Cr.
19XX							
Jan. 2	1 ✓	Prepaid Rent	114	300			300
9	2 ✓	Cleaning Expense	612	150			150
12	3 ✓	P. Regan Co.	✓		5,000	100	4,900
13	4 ✓	Salaries	610	1,200			1,200
23	5 ✓	R. Slater Co.	✓		4,000	40	3,960
25	6	Purchases	510	750			750
30	7	P. Regan Co.	✓		6,000	120	5,880

journal has been paid and the bank has returned the checks processed (or cancelled after payment). The accountant notices in the cash payments journal that two payments were not made by the bank and these checks were not returned by the bank. On Ralph's books these two checks had been deducted from the checkbook balance; therefore, these outstanding checks, or checks that had not been presented to the bank for payment, are deducted from the bank balance. At some point these checks will reach the bank. Keep in mind that Ralph's checkbook balance has already subtracted the amount of these two checks; it is the bank that has no idea these checks have been written. When they are presented for payment, then the bank will reduce the amount of the balance.

The accountant notices a bank service charge of $3. In effect, Ralph's checkbook balance should be lowered by $3.

The accountant is continually on the lookout for NSF (Non-sufficient Fund) checks. This means that when Ralph's deposits a check, occasionally it will bounce from lack of sufficient funds. If this happens, it will result in Ralph's having less money than it thought and thus having to (1) lower its book balance, (2) try to collect the amount from the customer.

The following is the bank reconciliation prepared by the account-ant:

RALPH'S SPORTING GOODS

Bank Reconciliation
January 31, 19XX

Balance per Bank			Balance per Ralph's Books	
		$19,947	Less bank service charge	$26,880
Add deposits not received (in transit)				3
Jan. 28	$ 3,560			
29	10,000	13,560		
		$33,507		
Less checks outstanding				
Check no. 6	$ 750			
Check no. 7	5,880	6,630		
Adjusted bank balance		$26,877	*Adjusted book balance*	$26,877

This same work can be done on the back of the bank statement as follows:

Bank reconciliation prepared

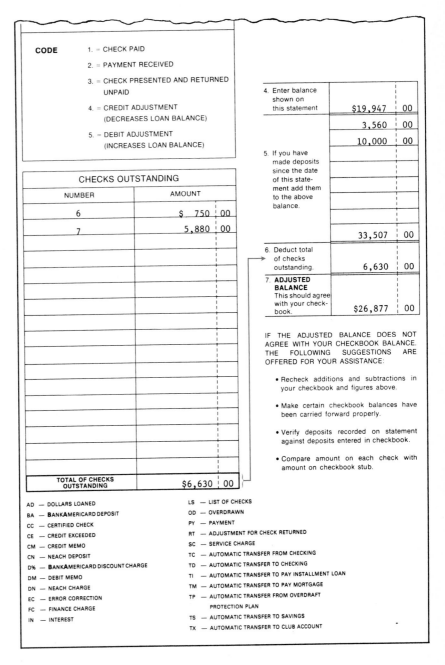

CODE	
1. = CHECK PAID	
2. = PAYMENT RECEIVED	
3. = CHECK PRESENTED AND RETURNED UNPAID	
4. = CREDIT ADJUSTMENT (DECREASES LOAN BALANCE)	
5. = DEBIT ADJUSTMENT (INCREASES LOAN BALANCE)	

4. Enter balance shown on this statement	$19,947	00
	3,560	00
	10,000	00
5. If you have made deposits since the date of this statement add them to the above balance.		
	33,507	00
6. Deduct total of checks outstanding.	6,630	00
7. **ADJUSTED BALANCE** This should agree with your checkbook.	$26,877	00

CHECKS OUTSTANDING		
NUMBER	AMOUNT	
6	$ 750	00
7	5,880	00
TOTAL OF CHECKS OUTSTANDING	$6,630	00

IF THE ADJUSTED BALANCE DOES NOT AGREE WITH YOUR CHECKBOOK BALANCE. THE FOLLOWING SUGGESTIONS ARE OFFERED FOR YOUR ASSISTANCE:

• Recheck additions and subtractions in your checkbook and figures above.

• Make certain checkbook balances have been carried forward properly.

• Verify deposits recorded on statement against deposits entered in checkbook.

• Compare amount on each check with amount on checkbook stub.

AD — DOLLARS LOANED
BA — BANKAMERICARD DEPOSIT
CC — CERTIFIED CHECK
CE — CREDIT EXCEEDED
CM — CREDIT MEMO
CN — NEACH DEPOSIT
D% — BANKAMERICARD DISCOUNT CHARGE
DM — DEBIT MEMO
DN — NEACH CHARGE
EC — ERROR CORRECTION
FC — FINANCE CHARGE
IN — INTEREST

LS — LIST OF CHECKS
OD — OVERDRAWN
PY — PAYMENT
RT — ADJUSTMENT FOR CHECK RETURNED
SC — SERVICE CHARGE
TC — AUTOMATIC TRANSFER FROM CHECKING
TD — AUTOMATIC TRANSFER TO CHECKING
TI — AUTOMATIC TRANSFER TO PAY INSTALLMENT LOAN
TM — AUTOMATIC TRANSFER TO PAY MORTGAGE
TP — AUTOMATIC TRANSFER FROM OVERDRAFT PROTECTION PLAN
TS — AUTOMATIC TRANSFER TO SAVINGS
TX — AUTOMATIC TRANSFER TO CLUB ACCOUNT

When next month's bank statement comes in, the accountant, after putting checks in numerical order, will check off the ones outstanding (check nos. 6 and 7) that had not been processed the previous month.

Also, a journal entry is needed to bring the ledger accounts of cash and service charges up to date. The following entry was prepared.

| Feb. 1 | Service Charge* | 3.00 | |
| | Cash | | 3.00 |

*Could be recorded as miscellaneous expense.

Notice that it will decrease Ralph's checkbook balance by $3.00 as well as reduce the ledger account cash. All adjustments that affect cash will have to be journalized and posted to the ledger. Why? If the cash balance in our ledger is indeed equal to the cash in the checkbook, all adjustments to the cash balance must be reflected in the ledger. Service charges and bounced checks are good examples of this.

You will notice in the problems section of this chapter that other variations may occur in preparing a bank reconciliation.

At this point you should be able to:

1. Define and state the purpose of a signature card.
2. Explain the function of the deposit ticket.
3. Explain the purpose of a duplicate deposit ticket.
4. Explain what may be attached to a deposit ticket.
5. Explain the relationship between Ralph's checkbook and the cash receipts and payments journal.
6. Be able to prepare deposit tickets and write checks.
7. Define and state the purpose of a bank statement.
8. Be able to prepare a bank reconciliation.
9. Differentiate between outstanding checks and deposits in transit.
10. Summarize the steps needed to prepare a bank reconciliation.

UNIT INTERACTOR 26

From the following information construct a bank reconciliation for Morse Co. as of June 30, 19XX. Then prepare journal entries if needed.

Beginning checkbook balance	$110
Beginning bank balance	135
Deposits (in transit)	50
Checks outstanding	80
Bank service charge (debit memo)	5

MORSE CO.

Bank Reconciliation
June 30, 19XX

Book		Bank	
Balance	$110	Balance	$135
Less service charge	5	Add deposits	50
		Less checks outstanding	80
Ending book balance	$105	*Ending bank balance*	$105

Service charge	5.00
Cash	5.00

PETTY CASH; BANK RECONCILIATION—A BLUEPRINT

PETTY CASH. Since it is inconvenient to write checks for small amounts, a petty cash fund can be established. To set it up, a check is written payable to petty cash. Assuming an auxiliary petty cash record is used, the establishment of petty cash is recorded in both the cash payments journal and the auxiliary petty cash record.

As money is spent out of the petty cash fund, the auxiliary record is updated. No entries are made into the cash payments journal until time of replenishment. At time of replenishment, the expenses will be debited in the cash payments journal and a new check will be written to replenish the petty cash fund. The information for the debit portion of the replenishment is needed, since the ledger accounts have not been updated to show individual petty cash expenses. Remember, information entered in the auxiliary petty cash record is not posted to the ledger. Therefore, a journal entry to replenish does the following: (1) records expenses, (2) shows a new check is needed to refill the petty cash fund. Before replenishment, the petty cash fund contained cash and vouchers. After replenishment, the voucher information is recorded and the vouchers are replaced with cash.

PETTY CASH

Date	Description	New Check Written	Recorded in Cash Payments Journal	Petty Cash Voucher Prepared	Recorded in Auxiliary Petty Cash Record
19XX					
Jan. 1	Establishment of petty cash for $50.	X	X		X
2	Paid salaries $1000.	X	X		
13	Paid $5. from petty cash for Band-aids			X	X
19	Paid $2. from petty cash for postage			X	X
24	Paid light bill $100.	X	X		
29	Replenishment petty cash to $50.	X	X		X

BANK RECONCILIATION. During a given period a company writes many checks and makes numerous deposits into its checking account. The bank, at the end of a period of time (usually a month), sends a bank statement indicating the balance of the account. The process of adjusting the bank's balance in relationship to the company's checkbook balance results in a bank reconciliation. Factors involved are checks outstanding, deposits in transit, service charges, etc. The cash receipts journal and cash payments journal will help the company in the bank reconciliation process to verify checks or deposits processed in relation to the records of the cash payments and receipts journal.

Adjustments that affect a company's checkbook balance will have to be recorded by a journal entry or entries.

Checkbook	Bank
— Service charge	— Checks outstanding
— NSF (bounced checks)	+ Deposits in transit
± Bank errors	± Bank errors

SUMMARY OF NEW ACCOUNTING LANGUAGE TERMS

Learning Unit 25

Auxiliary Petty Cash Record: A *supplementary* record for summarizing petty cash information. Postings do not occur from the auxiliary petty cash record. This information provides the basis for journalizing our replenishment entry into cash payments journal.

Imprest Fund (Petty Cash Fund): A fund (source) that allows payment of *small* amounts without the writing of checks.

Internal Control: A system of procedures and methods to control a firm's assets as well as monitor its operations.

Petty Cash Voucher: A petty cash form to be completed that indicates the date, voucher number, who will receive payment from petty cash fund, amount of payment, reason for payment, account to be charged, as well as authorization to receive money.

Learning Unit 26

Bank Reconciliation: This is the process of reconciling the checkbook balance with the bank balance given on the bank statement.

Bank Statement: A report sent by a bank to a customer indicating the previous balance, individual checks processed, individual deposits received, service charges, and ending bank balance. The customer needs this information to complete the bank reconciliation.

Checks: A form used to indicate a specific amount of money that is to be paid to a named person or company. Appropriate signatures are needed.

Deposits in Transit: Deposits that were made by customers of a bank but did not reach, or were not processed by, the bank before the preparation of the bank statement.

Deposit Ticket: A form provided by a bank for use in depositing money or checks into a checking account.

Outstanding Checks: Checks written by a company or person that were not received or not processed by the bank before the preparation of the bank statement.

NSF (Nonsufficient Funds): Notation indicating that a check has been written on an account that lacks sufficient funds to back it up.

QUESTION INTERACTORS

1. Define internal control.
2. What are the advantages of having checks prenumbered?
3. Explain the purpose of having a petty cash fund.
4. What is the difference between establishing a petty cash fund and replenishing it?
5. Explain the purpose of a petty cash voucher.
6. A petty cash box contains only cash. Please comment.
7. Who has authority in controlling the petty cash fund?
8. Be sure to post from the auxiliary petty cash record weekly. Agree or disagree?
9. All businesses using petty cash must have an auxiliary petty cash record. True or false? Please explain.
10. Why would someone total the columns of the auxiliary petty cash record?
11. Why isn't petty cash an asset updated at time of replenishment?
12. Define an imprest petty cash fund.
13. What is the purpose of signature cards, checks, and deposit tickets?
14. Explain what is meant by check outstanding. Does it have any relationship to deposit in transit?
15. Explain the steps that need to be taken to prepare a bank reconciliation.
16. It is quite uncommon for a company checkbook to be out of balance with the bank balance. Please comment.
17. What role could a cash payments or cash receipts journal have in the preparation of a bank reconciliation?

18. Outstanding checks are added to the checkbook balance. Please comment.

19. Deposits in transit are always added to the checkbook balance. Please comment.

20. The service charge is an increase to a checkbook balance. Please comment.

PROBLEM INTERACTORS

1. Bob Smith's company wishes to establish a petty cash fund on December 1, 19XX, for $40, check no. 1. Petty cash is account no. 125. Could you provide the entry that is needed in the cash payments journal? Assume no auxiliary petty cash record for this company.

Cash Payments Journal

Date	Account Debited Description	PR	Sundry Dr.	Accounts Payable Dr.	Cash Cr.	Check No.

By the end of the month the following items were paid from petty cash:

Account	Amount	Account No.
Donations	$ 5.00	610
Store Supplies	10.00	620
Advertising Expense	5.00	630
Office Expense	2.00	640
Freight	10.00	650

Could you now record the entry to replenish the petty cash fund back to $40 in the cash payments journal dated December 31, 19XX? Assume check no. 8 is written to replenish.

2. John Jay has opened up a country grocery store. To record business transactions he utilizes a cash payments journal and auxiliary petty cash record as shown below. Your task is to record the appropriate entries in the cash payments journal as well as the auxiliary petty cash record.

Auxiliary Petty Cash Record

Date	Description	Voucher No.	Receipt	Payment	Donations Expense	Advertising Expense	Sundry	
							Account	Amount

From the chart of accounts: petty cash (130), office supplies (140), donation expense (610), advertising expense (620), miscellaneous expense (630).

Cash Payments Journal							
Date	Payment to	PR	Sundry Dr.	Account Payable Dr.	Purchase Discount Cr.	Cash Cr.	Check No.

19XX, JUL. 2: Check no. 3 for $20 was issued to establish a petty cash fund.

4: Paid from petty cash $1 donation to aid the poor, voucher no. 1.

5: Check no. 4 for $100 was issued to pay for office supplies.

7: Paid $2 from petty cash for advertising stickers, voucher no. 2.

15: Paid $3 from petty cash to aid-the-elderly luncheon, voucher no. 3 (this is not considered a donation; it is placed under Miscellaneous).

17: Paid $1 from petty cash for a local advertisement, voucher no. 4.

20: Check no. 5 was issued to Ron Rose Co. for $100 less a 2% purchase discount for previous purchase on account.

21: Check no. 6 was issued to B. Baker Corp. for $200, no discount, for past purchases on account.

24: Paid $2 from petty cash for a donation to the blind, voucher no. 5.

24: Replenished petty cash to original establishment, check no. 7.

3. John Smith received the bank statement from Jones Bank indicating a bank balance of $1,000. Based on Smith's check stubs, the ending checkbook balance was $1,200. Your task is to prepare a bank reconciliation for John Smith as of July 31, 19XX, from the following information:

1. Checks outstanding: no. 110, $50; no. 115, $30; no. 118, $25.
2. Deposit in transit, $300.
3. Bank service charge, $5.

4. From the following bank statement, please (1) complete the bank reconciliation found on the reverse of the bank statement, (2) journalize the appropriate entries as needed.

HAPPY VALLEY NATIONAL BANK Rio Mean Brand Bugna, Texas					
Ron's Shoe Store 8811 2nd St. Bugna, Texas					
Old Balance	Checks in Order of Payment		Deposits	Date	New Balance
1,000.00				2/2	1,000.00
	15.00	35.00		2/3	950.00
	25.00		50.00	2/10	975.00
	100.00		100.00	2/15	975.00
	50.00 NSF		50.00	2/20	975.00
	200.00		200.00	2/24	975.00
	100.00	5.00 sc	30.00	2/28	900.00

The NSF means that a check (from Ralph Small) deposited by Ron's Shoe Store is returned by the bank because of *nonsufficient funds.* In effect this reduces the cash balance of Ron's Shoe Store, and now Ralph Small owes Ron's Shoe. The following information is provided for you.

1. A deposit of $500 is in transit.
2. The following checks were outstanding: no. 101, $100; no. 108, $200; no. 109, $55.
3. The checkbook of Ron's Shoe Store shows an ending balance of $1,100.

ADDITIONAL PROBLEM INTERACTORS

1-A. Bill Ron opened a local drugstore. Bill wishes to establish a petty cash fund, account no. 130, on May 1, 19XX, of $30, check no. 1. Prepare the journal entry in the cash payments journal of Ron's Drugstore. (Assume this company does not use an auxiliary petty cash record.)

Cash Payments Journal							
Date	Payment to	PR	Sundry Dr.	Account Payable Dr.	Purchase Discount Cr.	Cash Cr.	Check No.

During the month of May the following were paid from petty cash:

Account	Amount	Account No.
Delivery	$5.00	610
Advertising	4.00	620
Donations	4.00	630
Postage	3.00	640
Drug Supplies	4.00	650

Now record the entry to replenish the petty cash fund back to $30.00 in the cash payments journal dated May 31, 19XX. Assume check no. 5 to replenish.

2-A. The following transactions occurred that were related to the cash payments journal and petty cash:

19XX, APR. 1: Issued check no. 4 for $50 to establish a petty cash fund.

5: Paid from petty cash $5 for a postage, voucher no. 1.

8: Paid $10 from petty cash for office supplies, voucher no. 2.

15: Issued check no. 5 to Raisin Corp. for $200 less a 2% discount for past purchase on account.

17: Paid $5 from petty cash for office supplies, voucher no. 3.

20: Issued check no. 6 to Ribben Corp. $100 less a 5% discount from past purchases on account.

24: Paid from petty cash $10 for postage, voucher no. 4.

26: Paid from petty cash $5 for local church donation, voucher no. 5 (this is a miscellaneous payment).

28: Issued check no. 7 to John Lefave to pay for office equipment $300.

From the chart of accounts: petty cash (120), postage expense (610), office supplies expense (620), miscellaneous expense (630). The heading of the cash payments and auxiliary petty cash records are as follows:

Cash Payments Journal

Date	Payment to	PR	Sundry Dr.	Accounts Payable Dr.	Purchase Discount Cr.	Cash Cr.	Check No.

Auxiliary Petty Cash Record

Date	Description	Voucher No.	Receipt	Payment	Postage Expense	Office Supplies Expense	Sundry	
							Account	Amount

Your task is to:

a. Record the appropriate entries in the cash payments journal as well as the auxiliary petty cash record as needed.

b. Be sure to replenish the petty cash fund on April 30 (check no. 8).

3-A. John Brown Co. recently received a bank statement from the Sunshine Valley Bank indicating a bank balance of $3,000. Based on the company's check stubs the ending checkbook balance was $2,800. Your task is to prepare a bank reconciliation for John Brown Co. as of April 30, 19XX, from the following information:

1. Deposits in transit, $500.
2. Checks outstanding: no. 105, $400; no. 125, $200; no. 140, $125.
3. Bank service charges, $25.

4-A. From the accompanying bank statement (a) complete the bank reconciliation, (b) journalize the appropriate entries as needed. Notice the NSF, which means that a check (from Abe Long) deposited by Ranger Hardware is returned by the bank because of nonsufficient funds. In effect this reduces the cash balance of Ranger Hardware, and now Abe Long owes Ranger Hardware.

The following information is provided for you:

1. Checks outstanding: no. 140, $20; no. 150, $40; no. 160, $13.
2. A deposit of $104 is in transit.
3. The checkbook balance of Ranger Hardware shows an ending balance of $200.

RYAN COUNTY BANK
1 Rainy Road
Storybrook, Mass.

Ranger Hardware
2224 Heavy Street
Storybrook, Mass.

Old Balance	Checks in Order of Payment		Deposits	Date	New Balance
180				4/2	180.00
	3.00	9.00		4/3	168.00
	5.00		10.00	4/10	173.00
	20.00		20.00	4/15	173.00
	10.00 NSF		10.00	4/20	173.00
	40.00		40.00	4/24	173.00
	20.00	1.00 sc	6.00	4/28	158.00

Select one of the five answers below that applies to the situations listed for P.A.Y. Co. Also encircle the number of each situation that would require an entry to adjust the cash account to the corrected balance after bank reconciliation.

A—Add to the company's book balance
B—Deduct from the company's book balance
C—Add to the bank's balance
D—Deduct from the bank's balance
E—None of these

The situations are:

1. Outstanding checks amounted to $922.37. _____
2. An error was made when recording a check written for $57. It was recorded for $75. _____
3. An NSF check was included with the bank statement. _____
4. The bank service charge amounted to $3.75. _____
5. The bank charged the P. A. Y. Co. bank account with a check written by the B. A. Y. Co. _____
6. A check written for $52.96 to pay a creditor within the discount period was recorded as $52.69. _____
7. A deposit in transit amounted to $1,866.23. _____
8. The bank collected a note receivable for $500 and charged a collection fee of $6.00. _____
9. The bank incorrectly credited the account with a deposit from the D. A. Y. Co. _____
10. The bookkeeper discovered that a creditor had been overpaid. _____

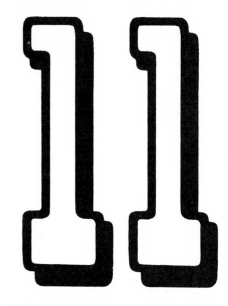

11

the combined
journal

$\mathbf{P}$art Two of this text has focused on the special journals of Ralph's Sporting Goods. We have developed the sales journal, purchase journal, cash payments journal, and cash receipts journal, as well as utilizing a general journal for sales returns and allowances and purchase returns and allowances.

LEARNING UNIT 27

The Combined Journal:
Its Structure and Purpose

Many small businesses that are concerned with saving journalizing and posting labor, however, are not concerned about division of labor (having a bookkeeper working on each special journal), since a small company has only one bookkeeper. Such businesses may want the advantages provided by special journals but would like to reduce the

Purpose of combined journal

number of journals needed. This chapter will develop a journal, a book of original entry, that dispenses with the special journals, yet gains their advantages in journalizing and posting.

One journal, a *combined journal*, containing many columns, can replace Ralph's special journals. If Ralph believes his business will remain small and would like to reduce the number of bookkeepers, it is conceivable that he may find the combined journal approach efficient. Let's look first at the five journals Ralph used to record his January transactions.

Sales Journal — Page 1

Date	Invoice No.	Description of Accounts Receivable	Terms	PR	Account Receivable—Dr. Sales—Cr.
19XX					
Jan. 3	1	B. Baker Corp.	2/10, n/30	✓	3,500
6	2	D. Adams Corp.	2/10, n/30	✓	2,500
9	3	B. Baker Corp.	2/10, n/30	✓	1,500
16	4	A. Sling Co.	2/10, n/30	✓	1,600
22	5	B. Baker Co.	2/10, n/30	✓	2,000
24	6	A. Sling Co.	1/10, n/30	✓	2,000
30	7	J. Keen Co.	2/10, n/30	✓	5,000
31		Total		112	18,100
				410	

Purchase Journal — Page 1

Date	Account Credited	PR	Accounts Payable Cr.	Purchases Dr.	Sundry—Dr. Account	PR	Amount
19XX							
Jan. 2	Pete Regan Co.	✓	5,000	5,000			
9	Pete Regan Co.	✓	4,000	4,000			
11	Russell Slater	✓	5,000	5,000			
21	Mike's Garage	✓	3,600		Delivery truck	116	3,600
27	King Co.	✓	6,000	6,000			
29	Pete Regan Co.	✓	6,000	6,000			
31	Total		29,600	26,000			3,600
			(210)	(510)			(X)

Cash Payments Journal — Page 1

Date	Check No.	Account Debited	PR	Sundry Dr.	Accounts Payable Dr.	Purchase Discount Cr.	Cash Cr.
19XX							
Jan. 2	1	Prepaid Rent	114	300			300
9	2	Cleaning Expense	612	150			150
12	3	Pete Regan Co.	✓		5,000	100	4,900
13	4	Salaries	610	1,200			1,200
23	5	Russell Slater	✓		4,000	40	3,960
25	6	Purchases	510	750			750
30	7	Pete Regan Co.	✓		6,000	120	5,880
31		Total		2,400	15,000	260	17,140
				(X)	(210)	(514)	(110)

Cash Receipts Journal   Page 1

Date	Account Credited	PR	Sundry Cr.	Sales Cr.	Accounts Receivable Cr.	Sales Discount Dr.	Cash Dr.
19XX							
Jan. 2	R. Jones Investment	310	20,000				20,000
13	Cash Sales	X		3,500			3,500
15	Cash Sales	X		1,500			1,500
16	D. Adams Corp.	√			2,000	40	1,960
16	B. Baker Corp.	√			3,500		3,500
28	B. Baker Corp.	√			2,000	40	1,960
28	A. Sling Co.	√			1,600		1,600
29	Notes Payable	212	10,000				10,000
31	Total		30,000	5,000	9,100	80	44,020
			(X)	(410)	(112)	(414)	(110)

General Journal   Page 1

Date	Account Explanation	PR	Dr.	Cr.
19XX				
Jan. 10	Sales Returns and Allowances	412	500	
	Accounts Receivable—D. Adams Corp.	√/112		500
	Credit Memo No. 1			
14	Accounts Payable—Russell Slater	√/210	1,000	
	Purchase Return and Allowances	512		1,000
	Debit Memo			

STRUCTURE OF COMBINED JOURNAL

Our goal in this chapter is to place all of the above information for Ralph's Sporting Goods into the following combined journal:

Combined Journal   Month: January   Page 1

Date	Explanation	Check No.	PR	Sundry Dr.	Sundry Cr.	Cash Dr.	Cash Cr.	Accounts Receivable Dr.	Accounts Receivable Cr.	Accounts Payable Dr.	Accounts Payable Cr.	Sales* Cr.	Sales Discount Dr.	Purchases Dr.	Purchase Discount Cr.

* Ralph's Sporting Goods did not involve sales tax. If it did, we would need to establish a column for sales tax payable.

CHOOSING THE HEADINGS FOR THE COMBINED JOURNAL

If Ralph decided to use the combined journal, he and the account-ant would go over the chart of accounts. They would be concerned with setting up columns in the combined journal for accounts in which transactions would occur frequently. Based on their analysis, Ralph and the accountant agreed to set up the following special columns in a combined journal.*

Cash Dr.—This column records increases in cash.

Cash Cr.—This column records decreases in cash.

Accounts Receivable Dr.—This column records amounts owed from sales on account.

Accounts Receivable Cr.—This column records amounts paid by customers from past sales on account.

Accounts Payable Dr.—This column reflects amount paid creditors.

Accounts Payable Cr.—This column reflects amounts owed creditors.

Columns of combined journal explained

Sales Cr.—This column records all sales made for cash or on account. The cash or accounts receivable column will record the inflow of assets from the sale.

Sales Discount Dr.—This column records the amounts of discounts taken by customers.

Purchases Dr.—All purchases of merchandise for resale are recorded in this column. Keep in mind that this column records purchases for cash or on account; the cash or accounts payable column will record the other parts of the purchase entry.

Purchase Discount Cr.—This column records the amounts of discounts Ralph receives by paying for purchases before the discount period expires.

Sundry Dr., Cr.—These two columns record transactions that do not occur too frequently. If a transaction occurs and no special columns are set up to record part or all of it, it can be recorded in the sundry columns.

Before filling out the combined journal for Ralph's Sporting Goods for the month of January, let's review the mind process chart for analyzing the transactions, including the column headings of the combined journal needed for each part of the transaction.

MIND PROCESS CHART: RALPH'S SPORTING GOODS TRANSACTIONS

Transaction	Accounts Affected	Category	↑ ↓	Rules	Combined Journal Headings
Jan. 2—Invested $20,000 cash in opening Ralph's Sporting Goods	Cash Investment	Asset Owner's Equity	↑ ↑	Dr. Cr.	Cash Sundry
Jan. 2—Paid three months' rent in advance, $300	Prepaid Rent Cash	Asset Asset	↑ ↓	Dr. Cr.	Sundry Cash
Jan. 2—Purchased merchandise from Pete Regan Co. on account, $5,000, terms 2/10, n/30	Purchases Accounts Payable	Cost of Merchandise for Resale Liability	↑ ↑	Dr. Cr.	Purchases Accounts Payable

*The columns are located in the order that is most convenient for Ralph. For example, the sundry column comes before cash. Other companies may wish to list cash first.

Ralph's Sporting Goods Transactions (*cont.*)

Transaction	Accounts Affected	Category	↑ ↓	Rules	Combined Journal Headings
Jan. 3—Sold merchandise to Robert Baker on account, $3,500, invoice no. 1, terms 2/10, n/30	Accounts Receivable Sales	Asset Revenue	↑ ↑	Dr. Cr.	Accounts Receivable Sales
Jan. 6—Sold merchandise to D. Adams Corp. on account, $2,500, invoice no. 2, terms 2/10, n/30	Accounts Receivable Sales	Asset Revenue	↑ ↑	Dr. Cr.	Accounts Receivable Sales
Jan. 9—Purchased merchandise from Pete Regan Co. on account, $4,000, terms 2/10, n/30	Purchases Accts. Payable	Cost of Merchandise for Resale Liability	↑ ↑	Dr. Cr.	Purchases Accounts Payable
Jan. 9—Sold merchandise to Robert Baker on account, $1,500, invoice no. 3, terms 2/10, n/30	Accounts Receivable Sales	Asset Revenue	↑ ↑	Dr. Cr.	Accounts Receivable Sales
Jan. 9—Paid cleaning service $150	Cleaning Expense Cash	Expense Asset	↑ ↓	Dr. Cr.	Sundry Cash
Jan. 10—D. Adams Corp. returned merchandise costing $500; Ralph's issued credit memo no. 1 to Adams for $500	Sales Returns and Allowances Accounts Receivable	Revenue Reduction Asset	↑ ↓	Dr. Cr.	Sundry Accounts Receivable
Jan. 11—Purchased merchandise from R. Slater on account, $5,000, terms 1/15, n/60	Purchases Accounts Payable	Cost of Merchandise for Resale Liability	↓ ↑	Dr. Cr.	Purchases Accounts Payable
Jan. 12—Paid P. Regan Co., invoice dated Jan. 2	Accounts Payable Purchase Discount Cash	Liability ↓ Cost of Merchandise for Resale Asset	↓ ↑ ↓	Dr. Cr. Cr.	Accounts Payable Purchase Discount Cash
Jan. 13—Sold $3,500 of merchandise for cash	Cash Sales	Asset Revenue	↑ ↑	Dr. Cr.	Cash Sales
Jan. 13—Paid salaries $1,200	Salary Expense Cash	Expense Asset	↑ ↓	Dr. Cr.	Sundry Cash

Ralph's Sporting Goods Transactions (*cont.*)

Transaction	Accounts Affected	Category	↑ ↓	Rules	Combined Journal Headings
Jan. 14—Returned merchandise to R. Slater in amount of $1,000. Ralph's issued debit memo no. 1 to Slater	Accounts Payable	Liability	↓	Dr.	Accounts Payable
	Purchase Returns and Allowances	↓ Cost of Merchandise for Resale	↑	Cr.	Sundry
Jan. 15—Sold merchandise for $1,500	Cash	Asset	↑	Dr.	Cash
	Sales	Revenue	↑	Cr.	Sales
Jan. 16—Received payment from D. Adams Corp. for invoice no. 2, less discount	Cash	Asset	↑	Dr.	Cash
	Sales Discount	Revenue Reduction	↑	Dr.	Sales Discount
	Accounts Receivable	Asset	↓	Cr.	Accounts Receivable
Jan. 16—Robert Baker paid invoice no. 1, $3,500, no discount	Cash	Asset	↑	Dr.	Cash
	Accounts Receivable	Asset	↓	Cr.	Accounts Receivable
Jan. 16—Sold merchandise to A. Sling Co. on account, invoice no. 4, $1,600, terms 2/10, n/30	Accounts Receivable	Asset	↑	Dr.	Accounts Receivable
	Sales	Revenue	↑	Cr.	Sales
Jan. 21—Purchased delivery truck, $3,600, on account, from Mike's Garage	Delivery Truck	Asset	↑	Dr.	Sundry
	Accounts Payable	Liability	↑	Cr.	Accounts Payable
Jan. 22—Sold to Robert Baker on account, $2,000, invoice no. 5, terms 2/10, n/30	Accounts Receivable	Asset	↑	Dr.	Accounts Receivable
	Sales	Revenue	↑	Cr.	Sales
Jan. 23—Paid R. Slater balance owed	Accounts Payable	Liability	↓	Dr.	Accounts Payable
	Purchase Discount	↓ Cost of Merchandise for Resale	↑	Cr.	Purchase Discount
	Cash	Asset	↓	Cr.	Cash
Jan. 24—Sold merchandise to A. Sling Co. $2,000, invoice no. 6, terms 1/10, n/30	Accounts Receivable	Asset	↑	Dr.	Accounts Receivable
	Sales	Revenue	↑	Cr.	Sales

Ralph's Sporting Goods Transactions (*cont.*)

Transaction	Accounts Affected	Category	↑ ↓	Rules	Combined Journal Headings
Jan. 25—Purchased merchandise for cash $750	Purchases	Cost of Merchandise for Resale	↑	Dr.	Purchases
	Cash	Asset	↓	Cr.	Cash
Jan. 27—Purchased merchandise from King Co. on account $6000, terms 2/10, n/30	Purchases	Cost of Merchandise for Resale	↑	Dr.	Purchases
	Accounts Payable	Liability	↑	Cr.	Accounts Payable
Jan. 28—Robert Baker paid invoice no. 5, dated Jan. 22, less discount	Cash	Asset	↑	Dr.	Cash
	Sales Discount	Revenue Reduction	↑	Dr.	Sales Discount
	Accounts Receivable	Asset	↓	Cr.	Accounts Receivable
Jan. 28—A. Sling Co. paid invoice no. 4, dated Jan. 16, no discount	Cash	Asset	↑	Dr.	Cash
	Accounts Receivable	Asset	↓	Cr.	Accounts Receivable
Jan. 29—Borrowed $10,000 from bank. Interest not due for five years	Cash	Asset	↑	Dr.	Cash
	Notes Payable	Liability	↑	Cr.	Sundry
Jan. 29—Purchased merchandise from Pete Regan Co. $6,000, terms 2/10, n/30	Purchases	Cost of Merchandise for Resale	↑	Dr.	Purchases
	Accounts Payable	Liability	↑	Cr.	Accounts Payable
Jan. 30—Sold merchandise to J. Keen Co. on account, invoice no. 7, terms 2/10, n/30, $5,000	Accounts Receivable	Asset	↑	Dr.	Accounts Receivable
	Sales	Revenue	↑	Cr.	Sales
Jan. 30—Paid Pete Regan Co. $5,880 from purchase on Jan. 29	Accounts Payable	Liability	↓	Dr.	Accounts Payable
	Cash	Asset	↓	Cr.	Cash
	Purchase Discount	↓ Cost of Merchandise for Resale	↑	Cr.	Purchase Discount

From the above chart, the completed combined journal for Ralph's Sporting Goods for January would look like this. (Don't worry about postings and reference numbers; we will be analyzing the posting of each column in a moment.) Use this chart as reference for the remainder of chapter. Don't memorize.

Combined Journal Month: January   Page 1

Date	Explanation	Check No	PR	Sundry Dr.	Sundry Cr.	Cash Dr.	Cash Cr.	Accounts Receivable Dr.	Accounts Receivable Cr.	Accounts Payable Dr.	Accounts Payable Cr.	Sales Cr.	Sales Disc. Dr.	Pur. Dr.	Pur. Disc. Cr.
19XX															
Jan. 2	R. Jones Investment		310		20,000	20,000									
2	Prepaid Rent	1	114	300			300								
2	Pete Regan Co.		✓								5,000			5,000	
3	B. Baker Corp.		✓					3,500				3,500			
6	D. Adams Corp.		✓					2,500				2,500			
9	Pete Regan Co.		✓								4,000			4,000	
9	B. Baker Corp.		✓					1,500				1,500			
9	Cleaning Expense	2	612	150			150								
10	Sales Returns and Allowances—D. Adams Corp.		412 / ✓	500					500						
11	Russell Slater	3	✓				4,900			5,000					100
12	Pete Regan Co.		✓								5,000			5,000	
13	Cash Sales		X			3,500						3,500			
13	Salaries	4	610	1,200			1,200								
14	Purchase Return—Russell Slater		512 / ✓		1,000					1,000					
15	Cash Sales		X			1,500						1,500			
16	D. Adams Corp.		✓			1,960			2,000				40		
16	B. Baker Corp.		✓			3,500			3,500						
16	A. Sling Co.		✓					1,600				1,600			
21	Delivery Truck—Mike's Garage		116	3,600							3,600				
22	B. Baker Corp.		✓					2,000				2,000			
23	Russell Slater		✓					2,000				2,000			
24	A. Sling Co.		✓			1,960			2,000				40		
25	Purchases—Cash	5	X				750							750	
27	King Co.	6	✓				3,960			4,000					40
28	B. Baker Corp.		✓								6,000			6,000	
28	A. Sling Co.		✓			1,600			1,600						
29	Notes Payable		212		10,000	10,000									
29	Pete Regan Co.		✓								6,000			6,000	
30	Pete Regan Co.	7	✓				5,880			6,000					120
30	J. Keen Co.		✓					5,000				5,000			
	Total			5,750	31,000	44,020	17,140	18,100	9,600	16,000	29,600	23,100	80	26,750	260
				(X)	(X)	(110)	(110)	(112)	(112)	(210)	(210)	(410)	(414)	(510)	(514)

1. Sales, Sales Discount, Purchases, and Purchase Discount Columns

POSTING RULES—SALES (Cr.). The total of sales. $23,100, is posted to sales account 410 in the general ledger at the end of the month. When this is posted, the account number, 410, is placed at the bottom of the sales column. No daily postings are needed.

SALES DISCOUNT (Dr.)—$80. The total of sales discount, $80, is posted to sales discount account no. 414 in the general ledger at the end of the month. When this is posted, the account number, 414, is placed at the bottom of the sales discount column. No daily postings are needed.

PURCHASES (Dr.). The total of purchases, $26,750, is posted to the purchases account no. 510 in the general ledger at the end of the month. When this is posted, the account number, 510, is placed at the bottom of the purchases column. No daily postings are needed.

PURCHASES DISCOUNT (Cr.). The total of purchase discounts, $260, is posted to the purchases discount account no. 514 in the general ledger at the end of the month. When this is posted, the account number, 514, is placed at the bottom of the purchases discount column. No daily postings are needed.

Sales Cr.	Sales Discount Dr.	Purchases Dr.	Purchase Discount Cr.
		5,000	
3,500			
2,500			
		4,000	
1,500			
		5,000	
			100
3,500			
1,500			
	40		
1,600			
2,000			
			40
2,000			
		750	
		6,000	
	40		
		6,000	
			120
5,000			
23,100	80	26,750	260
(410)	(414)	(510)	(514)

2. Accounts Payable

POSTING RULES: TOTAL. At the end of the month the total of the debit column of accounts payable and the total of the credit column are posted to accounts payable in the general ledger account no. 210. When this is done, the account number 210 is entered below the totals of the debit and credit columns.

Accounts Payable   **210**

Date		PR	Dr.	Cr.	Bal.
19XX					
Jan.	31	CJ1*	16,000		16,000 Dr.
	31	CJ1		29,600	13,600

*CJ: Combined journal

SUBSIDIARY LEDGER POSTING RULES. The debit or credit to the individual suppliers in the accounts payable subsidiary ledger is posted daily. When this is posted a ($\checkmark$) is placed in the PR column of a combined journal.

Accounts Payable Subsidiary Ledger

King Co.

Date		PR	Dr.	Cr.	Bal.
19XX					
Jan.	27	CJ1		6,000	6,000

Mike's Garage

Date		PR	Dr.	Cr.	Bal.
19XX					
Jan.	27	CJ1		3,600	3,600

Pete Regan Co.

Date		PR	Dr.	Cr.	Bal.
19XX					
Jan.	2	CJ1		5,000	5,000
	9	CJ1		4,000	9,000
	12	CJ1	5,000		4,000
	29	CJ1		6,000	10,000
	30	CJ1	6,000		4,000

Russell Slater

Date		PR	Dr.	Cr.	Bal.
19XX					
Jan.	11	CJ1		5,000	5,000
	14	CJ1	1,000		4,000
	23	CJ1	4,000		0

Date	Explanation	Check No.	PR	Accounts Payable Dr.	Accounts Payable Cr.
19XX					
Jan. 2	R. Jones Investment		310		
2	Prepaid Rent	1	114		
2	Pete Regan Co.		✓		5,000
3	B. Baker Corp.		✓		
6	D. Adams Corp.		✓		
9	Pete Regan Co.		✓		4,000
9	B. Baker Corp.		✓		
9	Cleaning Expense	2	612		
10	Sales Returns and Allowances D. Adams Corp.		✓ 412		
11	Russell Slater		✓		5,000
12	Pete Regan Co.	3	✓	5,000	
13	Cash Sales		X		
13	Salaries	4	610		
14	Purchase Returns— Russell Slater		✓ 512	1,000	
15	Cash Sales		X		
16	D. Adams Corp.		✓		
16	B. Baker Corp.		✓		
16	A. Sling Co.		✓		
21	Delivery Truck—Mike's Garage		116		3,600
22	B. Baker Corp.		✓		
23	Russell Slater	5	✓	4,000	
24	A. Sling Co.		✓		
25	Purchases—Cash	6	X		
27	King Co.		✓		6,000
28	B. Baker Corp.		✓		
28	A. Sling Co.		✓		
29	Notes Payable		212		
29	Pete Regan Co.		✓		6,000
30	Pete Regan Co.	7	✓	6,000	
30	J. Keen Co.		✓		
	Total			16,000	29,600
				(210)	(210)

Notice that the total of the individual suppliers in the accounts payable ledger does indeed equal the balance of accounts payable at the end of the month in the general ledger.

Date		PR	Dr.	Cr.	Bal.
19XX					
Jan.	31	CJ1	16,000		16,000 Dr.
	31	CJ1		29,600	13,600

King Co.	$6,000
Mike's Garage	3,600
Pete Regan Co.	4,000
	$13,600

Now let's look at the accounts receivable columns, which should follow the same basic rules as accounts payable, except that we are now dealing with amounts customers owe from sales on account instead of amounts we owe from purchases on account.

3. Accounts Receivable Columns

POSTING RULES: TOTALS. At the end of the month the total of the debit as well as the credit columns of accounts receivable are posted to accounts receivable in the general ledger account no. 112. When this is done, the account number 112 is entered below the totals of the debit and credit columns.

Accounts Receivable 112

Date		PR	Dr.	Cr.	Bal.
19XX					
Jan.	31	CJ1	18,100		18,100
	31	CJ1		9,600	8,500

Accounts Receivable Subsidiary Ledger

D. Adams Corp.

Date		PR	Dr.	Cr.	Bal.
19XX					
Jan.	6	CJ1	2,500		2,500
	10	CJ1		500	2,000
	16	CJ1		2,000	0

B. Baker Corp.

Date		PR	Dr.	Cr.	Bal.
19XX					
Jan.	3	CJ1	3,500		3,500
	9	CJ1	1,500		5,000
	16	CJ1		3,500	1,500
	22	CJ1	2,000		3,500
	28	CJ1		2,000	1,500

J. Keen Co.

Date		PR	Dr.	Cr.	Bal.
19XX					
Jan.	30	CJ1	5,000		5,000

Accounts Receivable Subsidiary Ledger (cont.)

A. Sling Co.

Date		PR	Dr.	Cr.	Bal.
19XX					
Jan.	16	CJ1	1,600		1,600
	24	CJ1	2,000		3,600
	28	CJ1		1,600	2,000

Date	Explanation	Check No.	PR	Accounts Receivable Dr.	Accounts Receivable Cr.
19XX					
Jan. 2	R. Jones Investment		310		
2	Prepaid Rent	1	114		
2	Pete Regan Co.		✓		
3	B. Baker Corp.		✓	3,500	
6	D. Adams Corp.		✓	2,500	
9	Pete Regan Co.		✓		
9	B. Baker Corp.		✓	1,500	
9	Cleaning Expense	2	612		
10	Sales Returns and Allowances		✓		
	D. Adams Corp.		412		500
11	Russell Slater		✓		
12	Pete Regan Co.	3	✓		
13	Cash Sales		X		
13	Salaries	4	610		
14	Purchase Returns—		✓		
	Russell Slater		512		
15	Cash Sales		X		
16	D. Adams Corp.		✓		2,000
16	B. Baker Corp.		✓		3,500
16	A. Sling Co.		✓	1,600	
21	Delivery Truck—Mike's Garage		116		
22	B. Baker Corp.		✓	2,000	
23	Russell Slater	5	✓		
24	A. Sling Co.		✓	2,000	
25	Purchases—Cash	6	X		
27	King Co.		✓		
28	B. Baker Corp.		✓		2,000
28	A. Sling Co.		✓		1,600
29	Notes Payable		212		
29	Pete Regan Co.		✓		
30	Pete Regan Co.	7	✓		
30	J. Keen Co.		✓	5,000	
	Total			18,100	9,600
				(112)	(112)

The debit or credit to the individual customer's account in the accounts receivable subsidiary ledger is posted daily. When this is done, a ($\checkmark$) is placed in the PR column of the combined journal.

Once again, notice that the sum of what the individual customers owe Ralph will be equal to the balance of accounts receivable in the general ledger at the end of the month.

Accounts Receivable — 112

Date		PR	Dr.	Cr.	Bal.
19XX					
Jan.	31	CJ1	18,100		18,100
	31	CJ1		9,600	8,500

SCHEDULE OF ACCOUNTS RECEIVABLE

R. Baker Corp.	$1,500
J. Keen Corp.	5,000
A. Sling Corp.	2,000
Total Accounts Receivable	$8,500

4. Cash and Sundry Columns

Totals of sundry columns are never posted.

Each account that is recorded in the sundry column is posted to the general ledger account as soon as possible. When this is done the account number to which it was posted in the general ledger is then placed in the PR column of the combined journal.

Partial General Ledger Postings of Sundry

Prepaid Rent — 114

Date		PR	Dr.	Cr.	Bal.
19XX					
Jan.	2	CJ1	300		300

Delivery Truck — 116

Date		PR	Dr.	Cr.	Bal.
19XX					
Jan.	21	CJ1	3,600		3,600

Notes Payable — 212

Date		PR	Dr.	Cr.	Bal.
19XX					
Jan.	29	CJ1		10,000	10,000

Jones Investment — 310

Date		PR	Dr.	Cr.	Bal.
19XX					
Jan.	2	CJ1		20,000	20,000

Sales Returns and Allowances — 412

Date		PR	Dr.	Cr.	Bal.
19XX					
Jan.	10	CJ1	500		500

Purchase Returns 512

Date		PR	Dr.	Cr.	Bal.
19XX					
Jan.	14	CJ1		1,000	1,000

Salary Expense 610

Date		PR	Dr.	Cr.	Bal.
19XX					
Jan.	13	CJ1	1,200		1,200

Cleaning Expense 612

Date		PR	Dr.	Cr.	Bal.
19XX					
Jan.	9	CJ1	150		150

Date	Explanation	Check No.	PR	Sundry Dr.	Sundry Cr.	Cash Dr.	Cash Cr.
19XX							
Jan. 2	R. Jones Investment		310		20,000	20,000	
2	Prepaid Rent	1	114	300			300
2	Pete Regan Co.		✓				
3	B. Baker Corp.		✓				
6	D. Adams Corp.		✓				
9	Pete Regan Co.		✓				
9	B. Baker Corp.		✓				
9	Cleaning Expense	2	612	150			150
10	Sales Returns and Allowances		✓				
	D. Adams Corp.		412	500			
11	Russell Slater		✓				
12	Pete Regan Co.	3	✓				4,900
13	Cash Sales		X			3,500	
13	Salaries	4	610	1,200			1,200
14	Purchase Returns—		✓				
	Russell Slater		512		1,000		
15	Cash Sales		X			1,500	
16	D. Adams Corp.		✓			1,960	
16	B. Baker Corp.		✓			3,500	
16	A. Sling Co.		✓				
21	Delivery Truck—Mike's Garage		116	3,600			
22	B. Baker Corp.		✓				
23	Russell Slater	5	✓				3.960
24	A. Sling Co.		✓				
25	Purchases—Cash	6	X				750
27	King Co.		✓				
28	B. Baker Corp.		✓			1,960	
28	A. Sling Co.		✓			1,600	
29	Notes Payable		212		10,000	10,000	
29	Pete Regan Co.		✓				
30	Pete Regan Co.	7	✓				5,880
30	J. Keen Co.		✓				
	Total			5,750	31,000	44,020	17,140
				(X)	(X)	(110)	(110)

CASH. The totals of the cash column, $44,020 and $17,140, are posted at the end of the month to cash account no. 110 in the general ledger. When the totals of cash are posted, the account number is placed below the total column of cash in the combined journal.

Cash					110
Date	PR	Dr.	Cr.	Bal.	
19XX					
Jan. 31	CJ1	44,020		44,020	
31	CJ1		17,140	26,880	

PROVING THE COLUMNS OF THE COMBINED JOURNAL

Notice that the total amount of the debit columns, $110,700, is equal to the total amount of the credit columns, $110,700:

Checking the accuracy of the combined journal

ACCOUNT TITLE	Dr.	Cr.
Sundry	$5,750	$31,000
Cash	44,020	17,140
Accounts Receivable	18,100	9,600
Accounts Payable	16,000	29,600
Sales		23,100
Sales Discount	80	
Purchase/Discount	26,750	260
	$110,700	$110,700

You will see that dates 13, 15, and 25 have (X) in the PR column.* This means no posting is to occur. The information recorded is posted from other columns. For example, the cash sales involves no subsidiary ledgers; therefore, there is no (✓) in the PR column. The information about cash sales is found in the cash column and sales column, thus creating the (X) to show not to post. This information is not part of the sundry column.

In summation, the combined journal represents another option to small businesses that do not have many transactions. Lawyers, doctors, dentists, and other professionals may utilize a combined journal, which may be modified in many ways to suit individual needs.

As the business grows, the volume of transactions may increase, possibly creating the need for more specialized journals than the combined journal can offer. Remember, if a company adds bookkeepers to its

*See combined journal on page 349.

accounting department, management must be prepared to provide a system of dividing the work to be done. This division of labor may play an important part in determining the types of special journals that are needed.

At this time you should be able to:

1. State and define the purpose of a combined journal.
2. Explain why Ralph's Sporting Goods may decide to utilize a combined journal instead of a special journal.
3. Post information from a combined journal into the accounts receivable subsidiary ledger, accounts payable subsidiary ledger, and general ledger as appropriate.
4. Prove the combined journals columns.
5. Prepare a schedule of accounts payable as well as a schedule of accounts receivable from the accounts payable and accounts receivable subsidiary ledgers.
6. Explain when the combined journal may become inefficient for Ralph's Sporting Goods.

UNIT INTERACTOR 27

Based on the combined journal presented in this chapter, classify each statement as true or false.

1. Combined journals are less efficient than other types of special journals.
2. The total of the cash column is posted daily.
3. The total of the sundry column is not posted.
4. The total of the sales column is not posted.
5. All combined journals have the same headings.
6. Combined journals cannot be proved.
7. Subsidiary ledgers are posted from the cash column.
8. The combined journal is used for large companies.
9. A dentist could possibly use a combined journal.
10. A lawyer will always use a combined journal.

SOLUTION to Unit Interactor 27

1. False. 2. False. 3. True. 4. False. 5. False. 6. False. 7. False. 8. False. 9. True. 10. False.

If a company does not wish to record business transactions in four special journals and a general journal but wishes to maintain many of their advantages, a combined journal may be the best alternative. Either way results in the same schedules, as shown in the accompanying illustration.

When a combined journal is utilized, there will still be a need to develop an accounts receivable subsidiary ledger and accounts payable subsidiary ledger. As information is entered into the combined journal about accounts receivable or accounts payable, the individual customer or supplier will have to be immediately updated. As in the other special journals, the totals of many columns of the combined journal need to be posted to accounts in the general ledger at the end of the month. The combined journal in many ways represents a multipurpose special journal.

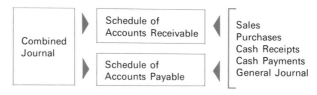

SUMMARY OF NEW ACCOUNTING LANGUAGE TERMS

Learning Unit 27

Combined Journal: A special journal that combines the features of the sales, cash payments, cash receipts, purchase, and general journals into one special journal. This journal is used by smaller firms that do not conduct numerous transactions requiring specific individual special journals.

QUESTION INTERACTORS

Answer true or false to the statements related to the letters on the combined journal opposite.

A. The (X) means to post the total.

B. The total of cash, $44,020, is posted to account no. 110 in the general ledger during the month.

C. The total of accounts receivable, $9,600, is posted to account no. 112 in the general ledger at end of month.

D. Sales, $23,100, shouldn't be posted.

E. Purchase of $26,750 is only posted once, the total at the end of the month to account no. 510 in the general ledger.

F. Cleaning expense is posted to the subsidiary ledger.

G. The (X) means no daily posting needed.

H. The (√) means the accounts payable subsidiary ledger of Russell Slater has been updated from this transaction.

I. The number 310 means no posting to the general ledger is needed.

J. The diagonal line in the posting reference (PR) column means only one posting is needed.

Combined Journal — Month: January — Page 1

Date	Explanation	Check No.	PR	Sundry Dr.	Sundry Cr.	Cash Dr.	Cash Cr.	Accounts Receivable Dr.	Accounts Receivable Cr.	Accounts Payable Dr.	Accounts Payable Cr.	Sales Cr.	Sales Disc. Dr.	Pur. Dr.	Purchase Disc. Cr.
19XX Jan. 2	R. Jones Investment	(I)	310		20,000	20,000									
2	Prepaid rent		114	300			300								
2	Pete Regan & Co.		✓								5,000			5,000	
3	B. Baker Corp.		✓					3,500				3,500			
6	D. Adams Corp.		✓					2,500				2,500			
9	Pete Regan Co.		✓								4,000			4,000	
9	B. Baker Corp.		✓					1,500				1,500			
9	Cleaning Expense	(F)	612	150			150								
10	Sale Returns and Allowances D. Adams Corp.	(J)	412 ✓	500					500						
11	Russell Slater		✓				4,900			5,000					100
12	Pete Regan Co.		✓				3,960			4,000					40
13	Cash Sales		X			3,500						3,500			
13	Salaries		610	1,200			1,200								
14	Purchase Returns— Russell Slater		512 ✓		1,000					1,000					
15	Cash Sales	(G)	X			1,500						1,500			
16	D. Adams Corp.		✓			1,960			2,000				40		
16	B. Baker Corp.		✓			3,500			3,500						
16	A. Sling Co.		✓					1,600				1,600			
21	Delivery Truck— Mike's Garage		116	3,600							3,600				
22	B. Baker Corp.	(H)	✓					2,000				2,000			
23	Russell Slater		✓					2,000				2,000			
24	A. Sling Co.		✓								5,000			5,000	
25	Purchases—Cash		X				750							750	
27	King Co.		✓			1,960			2,000				40		
28	B. Baker Corp.		✓								6,000			6,000	
28	A. Sling Co.		✓			1,600			1,600						
29	Notes Payable		212		10,000	10,000									
29	Pete Regan Co.		✓								6,000			6,000	
30	Pete Regan Co.		✓				5,880			6,000					120
30	J. Keen Co.		✓					5,000				5,000			
Total				5,750	31,000	44,020	17,140	18,100	9,600	16,000	29,600	23,100	80	26,750	260
				(X) (A)	(X)	(110) (B)	(110)	(112)	(112) (C)	(210)	(210)	(410) (D)	(414)	(510) (E)	(514)

353

1. Bill Budd, a recent graduate of a leading dental school, decided to open his own dental office. After talking with his accountant, he decided to record all business transactions in a combined journal. The following is the chart of accounts for the dental office.

ASSETS	REVENUE
110 Cash	410 Dental Fees
120 Accounts Receivable	
130 Prepaid Rent	
140 Dental Equipment	

LIABILITIES	EXPENSES
210 Accounts Payable	510 Salary Expenses
	520 Telephone Expenses
	530 Utilities Expense

OWNER'S EQUITY
320 B. Budd Investments
330 Income Summary

Your task is to:

a. Record the following transactions in the combined journal. Complete the PR column as if you were completing the postings.

b. Prove the combined journal.

Combined Journal													Month	Page 1
				Sundry		Cash		Acc. Rec.		Acc. Pay.		Dental Equip.	Dental Fees	
Date	Explanation	Check No.	PR	Dr.	Cr.	Dr.	Cr.	Dr.	Cr.	Dr.	Cr.	Dr.	Cr.	

19XX, APR. 1: Bill Budd invested $20,000 cash and $8,000 of dental equipment into the practice.

1: Paid three months, rent in advance $600, check no. 1.

10: Purchased dental equipment on account $5,000 from Ring Corp.

12: Purchased dental equipment on account from Ron Suppliers $3,000.

15: Received $100 cash for the extraction of a tooth.

18: Completed dental work on account for the Go Football Club $5,000.

20: Completed dental work on account $100 for John Smith.

19XX, APR. 24: Paid Ring Corp. one-half amount owed from April 10 transaction, check no. 2.

26: Paid telephone bill $100, check no. 3.

28: Paid salaries $500, check no. 4.

29: Paid utilities bill $18, check no. 5.

29: Received one-half amount owed from John Smith on April 20 transaction.

*2. John Sullivan opened a cleaning store that also sold accessories. The following is the chart of accounts for the Sullivan Cleaning Company.

ASSETS	REVENUE
110 Cash	410 Cleaning Sales
120 Accounts Receivable	420 Sales Discount
130 Prepaid Insurance	
140 Cleaning Equipment	

LIABILITIES	COST OF PURCHASES
210 Accounts Payable	510 Purchases
220 Notes Payable	520 Purchase Returns and Allowances
	530 Purchase Discounts

OWNER'S EQUITY	EXPENSES
310 J. Sullivan Investment	610 Utilities Expense
320 Income Summary	620 Advertising Expense

Here are the transactions for the month of January:

19XX, JAN. 1: John Sullivan invested $10,000 cash into the business.

8: Paid for a five-year company insurance policy in advance, check no. 1, $500.

10: Purchased merchandise on account from Jim Company $600.

12: Cleaned shirts for cash $725.

15: Cleaned suits on account for A. Ling $500.

17: Purchased cleaning equipment on account from B. Bang Company $700.

20: Borrowed $5,000 from Valley Frank National Bank.

21: Cleaned shirts for A. Ling $100 on account.

24: Received payment from A. Ling for $500 less a 2% discount from January 15 transaction.

25: Purchased merchandise on account from Bomb Company $50.

26: Cleaned pants for Ron Smith on account $10.

27: Paid Jim Company $600 less a 2% discount for merchandise that was purchased on January 10, check no. 2.

19XX, JAN. 28: Returned $100 of cleaning equipment to B. Bang Company for faulty workmanship.

29: Paid Bomb Company $50 less a 10% discount on purchases made on account on January 25, check no. 3.

30: Cash sales $1,000.

30: Received payment from Ron Smith $10 less a 20% sales discount.

Your task is to:

a. Set up ledger accounts in the general ledger (some accounts may not be used in January).

b. Set up accounts in the accounts payable and accounts receivable subsidiary ledgers as needed (don't worry here about alphabetical order).

c. Journalize the above transactions into the combined journal.

d. Post to the accounts payable and accounts receivable subsidiary ledgers as appropriate.

e. Post to the general ledger as appropriate.

f. Prove the combined journal.

g. Verify the subsidiary ledgers to the controlling accounts.

The heading of the combined journal of the Sullivan Cleaning Company is as follows:

Combined Journal																Month		Page 1
Date	Expla-nation	Check No.	PR	Sundry		Cash		Accounts Receivable		Accounts Payable		Cleaning Sales Disc. Dr.	Cleaning Sales Cr.	Purchases Dr.	Purchases Discount Cr.			
				Dr.	Cr.	Dr.	Cr.	Dr.	Cr.	Dr.	Cr.							

ADDITIONAL PROBLEM INTERACTORS

1-A. Ron Avery, a recent graduate of medical school, has decided to open his own office. Based on the advice of his accountant, he decided to use a combined journal. The following is the chart of accounts for Dr. Avery's office.

ASSETS	REVENUE
110 Cash	410 Medical Fees
120 Accounts Receivable	
130 Prepaid Insurance	
140 Office Equipment	

LIABILITIES	EXPENSES
210 Accounts Payable	510 Telephone Expense
	520 Cleaning Expense
	530 Utilities Expense

OWNER'S EQUITY

310 R. Avery Investment
320 Income Summary

The heading of the combined journal is:

Combined Journal													Month	Page 1
		Check		Sundry		Cash		Acc. Rec.		Acc. Pay.		Office Equip.	Medical Fees
Date	Explanation	No.	PR	Dr.	Cr.	Dr.	Cr.	Dr.	Cr.	Dr.	Cr.	Dr.	Cr.

Your task is to:

a. Record the following transactions in the combined journal. Complete the PR column as if you were posting.

b. Prove the combined journal.

19XX, JUL.

1: Ron Avery invested $15,000 cash and $2,000 of office equipment into the practice.

1: Paid insurance on the office for one year in advance $1,200, check no. 1.

9: Purchased office equipment on account from Blum Stationery Co. $100.

12: Purchased office equipment on account from S. M. Stationery Co. $500.

18: Completed on account physical examinations on each school child at Fairview Elementary School, $4,000.

18: Received $500 cash for medical fees earned.

19: Performed on account a complete examination for Jim Smith's son $100.

20: Paid Blum Stationery one-half the amount owed from July 9 transaction, check no. 2.

26: Paid telephone bill $50, check no. 3.

27: Paid utilities $25, check no. 4.

28: Paid John Toby Cleaning Co. $50 for cleaning service performed, check no. 5.

29: Paid one-half the amount owed S. M. Stationery Company from July 12 transaction, check no. 6.

* 2-A. Jan Smith opened up a new hardware store. The following chart of accounts was developed.

ASSETS	REVENUE
110 Cash	410 Hardware Sales
120 Accounts Receivable	420 Hardware Sales Discount
130 Prepaid Rent	
140 Store Equipment	

LIABILITIES	COST OF PURCHASES
210 Accounts Payable	510 Purchases
220 Notes Payable	520 Purchase Returns and Allowances
	530 Purchase Discount

OWNER'S EQUITY	EXPENSES
310 J. Smith Investment	610 Advertising Expense
320 Income Summary	620 Salaries Expense
	630 Repairs Expense

19XX, JUL. 1: Jan Smith invested $20,000 cash into the business.
1: Paid three months' rent in advance $500.
8: Purchase merchandise on account from Ron's Wholesalers $500.
12: Sold merchandise for cash $1,000.
15: Sold merchandise on account to John's Garden Center, $1,000.
18: Borrowed $500 from Sun Valley Bank.
19: Purchased store equipment for $1,000 cash.
20: Sold merchandise on account to John's Garden Center for $500.
22: Sold merchandise on account to J. Slow $50.
23: Received payment from John's Garden Center for $500 less a 10% discount from July 20 transaction.
25: Purchased merchandise on account from V. P. Suppliers $100.
27: Paid Ron's Wholesalers $500 less a 5% discount for merchandise purchased on July 8, check no. 1.
29: Paid V. P. Suppliers $100 less a 10% discount on purchase made on account on July 25, check no. 2.
30: Received $5,000 from cash sales.
30: Received payment from J. Slow less a 10% sales discount from July 22 transaction.

Your task is to:

a. Set up ledger accounts in the general ledger as needed (not all may be used).

b. Set up accounts in the accounts payable and accounts receivable subsidiary ledgers as needed.

c. Journalize the above transactions into the combined journal.

d. Post to the accounts payable and accounts receivable subsidiary ledgers as appropriate.

e. Post to the general ledger as appropriate.

f. Prove the combined journal.

g. Determine the balance in the controlling accounts receivable and payable.

The heading of the combined journal of the hardware company is as follows:

Combined Journal														Month		Page 1
Date	Expla-nation	Check No.	PR	Sundry Dr.	Sundry Cr.	Cash Dr.	Cash Cr.	Accounts Receivable Dr.	Accounts Receivable Cr.	Accounts Payable Dr.	Accounts Payable Cr.	Hardware Sales Cr.	Hardware Sales Discount Dr.	Purchases Dr.	Purchases Discount Cr.

CHALLENGE PROBLEM INTERACTOR

Below are the headings that might appear in a combined journal. Indicate which columns would be affected by each of the transactions listed below.

Date	PR	Sundry Dr.	Sundry Cr.	Cash Dr.	Cash Cr.	Acc. Rec. Dr.	Acc. Rec. Cr.	Acc. Pay. Dr.	Acc. Pay. Cr.	Sales Cr.	Sales Discount Dr.	Pur-chases Dr.	Purchase Discount Cr.

Transaction

0. (Example)
   Cash Sale————*Cash Dr.; Sales Cr.*
1. Paid semimonthly wages
2. Sold merchandise on account
3. Owner withdrew cash for personal use
4. Purchased merchandise for resale on account
5. Paid for a year's insurance in advance
6. Customer returned merchandise for credit

7. Paid creditor within discount period
8. Borrowed cash from the local bank
9. Customer paid account within discount period
10. Purchased office equipment, making a partial down payment with cash and balance on account

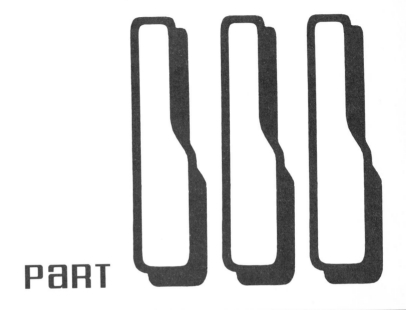

PART

The Accounting Cycle Completed for a Merchandise Firm

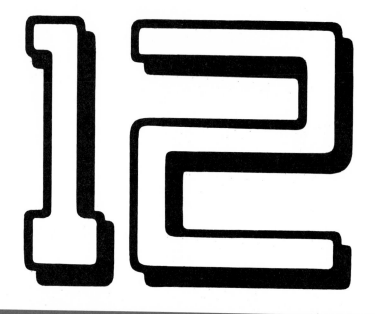

the
accounting cycle
continued

In Part Two we developed the special journals of Ralph's Sporting Goods. Step by step we followed the transactions of Ralph's company for January and decided which journals the information should be recorded in. Remember all those posting rules for the columns? But no matter which combination of journals Ralph's Sporting Goods uses:

Sales Journal
Purchase Journal   or   Combined Journal
Cash Receipts Journal   - - - - - - - - - - - -
Cash Payments Journal   General Ledger
General Journal   - - - - - - - - - - - -
- - - - - - - - - - - - - - - - - -
General Ledger   Subsidiary Ledgers
- - - - - - - - - - - - - - - - - -
Subsidiary Ledgers

after the postings are complete, the trial balance will look as follows:

RALPH'S SPORTING GOODS

Trial Balance
January 31, 19XX

	Dr.	Cr.
Cash	26,880	
Accounts Receivable	8,500	
Prepaid Rent	300	
Delivery Truck	3,600	
Accounts Payable		13,600
Notes Payable		10,000
R. Jones Investment		20,000
Sales		23,100
Sales Returns and Allowances	500	
Sales Discount	80	
Purchases	26,750	
Purchase Returns and Allowances		1,000
Purchase Discounts		260
Salary Expense	1,200	
Cleaning Expense	150	
	67,960	67,960

In Part Two of this book we completed the first three stages of the accounting cycle:

1. Business transactions occurred for Ralph's Sporting Goods for January.
2. Business transactions analyzed and recorded into journals.
3. Information posted from journals to ledger.

Also covered was how and when to post to the subsidiary ledgers.

Part Three will begin with the trial balance of Ralph's Sporting Goods for the end of January and complete the accounting cycle for the month of January:

4. Prepare a trial balance.
5. Prepare a worksheet.
6. Prepare financial statements.
7. Journalize and post adjusting entries.
8. Journalize and post closing entries.
9. Prepare a post-closing trial balance.

LEARNING UNIT 28

Worksheet Primer

Students often ask for a primer to help them understand better how to complete a worksheet before they attempt it. Looking at Ralph's trial balance for January 31, 19XX, let us begin by reviewing the purpose of each account.

PARTIAL ANALYSIS OF A TRIAL BALANCE

RALPH'S SPORTING GOODS

Trial Balance
January 31, 19XX

		Dr.	Cr.
	⋮	⋮	⋮
1	Sales		23,100
2	Sales Returns and Allowances	500	
3	Sales Discount	80	
4	Purchases	26,750	
5	Purchase Returns and Allowances		1,000
6	Purchase Discount		260
	Salary Expense	1,200	
	Cleaning Expense	150	

Sales

Dr.	Cr.
−	+

Sales Returns and Allowances

Dr.	Cr.
+	−

Sales discount defined

1. *Sales.* The $23,100 is the total amount of cash and or charge sales made to customers before any sales discount or sales returns and allowances. This sales account is usually described as *gross sales.* Sales have a credit balance and will be shown on the income statement.
2. *Sales Returns and Allowances.* The $500 indicates that customers have (1) returned merchandise to Ralph's and/or (2) received a reduction in the selling price that doesn't relate to any cash discount for prompt payment. For example, a defect in a ski may be found by the customer, who wants to keep the ski but get a reduction in price. In either case the effect of a sales return and allowance will be to reduce the total amount of sales. In this case, sales returns and allowances reduce Ralph's gross sales by $500. Keep in mind that sales have a credit balance and sales returns and allowances have a debit balance. A sales returns and allowances ↑, total earned sales ↓.
3. *Sales Discounts.* This balance of $80 represents savings to Ralph's customers who decided to take advantage of cash discounts he offered for prompt payment. For example, 2/10, n/30 means that if a customer pays

Dr.	Cr.
+	−

within ten days, Ralph will give him a 2% sales discount. This sales discount will also reduce the amount of gross sales earned. But early payment also means that Ralph will have the use of the money earlier. Keep in mind that sales discount is a debit balance that reduces earned gross sales.

$$GROSS\ SALES - SRA - SALES\ DISCOUNTS = NET\ SALES$$
$$1 \qquad\qquad 2 \qquad\qquad 3$$

Sales
− SRA
− Sales Discounts
= Net Sales

How do we find Ralph's actually earned sales for the month? By beginning with gross sales and subtracting sales returns and allowances and sales discounts, we will get a clear picture of the total amount of earned sales or what is called *net sales*.

GROSS SALES		$23,100
LESS: SALES RETURNS AND ALLOWANCES	$500	
SALES DISCOUNT	80	580
NET SALES		$22,520

Analysis of Costs

Ralph's Sporting Goods earned net sales of $22,520 during January. But what about costs? How much did it cost Ralph to make or earn those net sales? Let's look first at purchases.

Purchases defined

Purchases

Dr.	Cr.
+	−

4. *Purchases.* This account on the trial balance of Ralph's Sporting Goods has a debit balance of $26,750, which is the cost of bringing merchandise into Ralph's store for resale to the customers (this figure has not been adjusted for purchase returns and allowances or purchase discounts). For example, Ralph may purchase a football for $7 in hopes of reselling it for $12; the $7 represents a cost to Ralph. The purchases account of Ralph's Sporting Goods has a debit balance which shows the total cost of merchandise purchased during January for resale to customers.

Purchase returns and allowances defined

Purchase Returns and Allowances

Dr.	Cr.
−	+

5. *Purchase Returns and Allowances.* This account has a balance of $1,000, derived from (1) unsalable merchandise that Ralph sent back to suppliers because of defects, and/or (2) price reductions that Ralph received from suppliers because of defective merchandise that he could resell if he reduced the price. The normal balance of purchases returns and allowances is a credit. For example, if Ralph ordered 200 bowling balls and found small cracks in them, but felt they still could be sold at a reduced price, a purchase allowance could be granted by the supplier. In either case, the

effect of a purchase returns and allowance account is to reduce the amount of purchase costs to Ralph.

COST OF PURCHASES	$26,750
LESS: PURCHASE RETURNS AND ALLOWANCES	1,000
COST OF PURCHASES BEFORE PURCHASE DISCOUNTS ARE CONSIDERED	$25,750

Purchase discounts defined

6. *Purchase Discounts.* Because Ralph was willing and able to pay within a specified period for certain merchandise that he bought on account, he received purchase discounts. For example, if terms of a purchase on account were 2/15, n/30, Ralph would receive a purchase discount of 2% if he paid within fifteen days. Purchase discounts, therefore—amounting to $260 during January—reduce the cost of merchandise purchased for resale by Ralph's Sporting Goods.

Purchase Discount

Dr.	Cr.
−	+

Let's now summarize how Ralph determines the actual cost of purchase for resale.

PURCHASES		$26,750
LESS: PURCHASE RETURNS		
AND ALLOWANCES	$1,000	
PURCHASE DISCOUNTS	260	1,260
COST OF NET PURCHASES		$25,490

Net Purchase

= Purchases

− Purchase Discounts

− PRA

This figure for net purchases indicates the actual cost of buying merchandise for resale to customers. But in most stores, such as supermarkets, clothing stores, auto dealerships, not all merchandise that is bought for resale during a given month, year, etc. is sold before that period ends. Some merchandise is left over to be sold the following month, year, etc. For Ralph's Sporting Goods on January 1, however, there was no merchandise in the store for resale; the store was just beginning operations. We would say that *beginning merchandise inventory was zero.* During the month Ralph purchased merchandise that could be resold. From the analysis above we see that Ralph had net purchases of $25,490.

At the end of January Ralph wanted to know what merchandise was not sold as well as its dollar cost. The accountant gave him the following update of the cost of merchandise (goods) unsold at the end of the month, summarizing (1) what was left in ending inventory (items of unsold merchandise) and (2) the cost amount of each inventory (cost of unsold goods to Ralph).

RALPH'S SPORTING GOODS

Ending Inventory Sheet
As of January 31, 19XX

Amount	Explanation	Unit Cost	Total
200	Bowling balls	$10.00	$2,000.00
50	Ski jackets	8.00	400.00
3	Ski mobiles	1,000.00	3,000.00
30	Baseball bats	1.00	30.00
30	Hockey sticks	1.00	30.00
10	Footballs	1.00	10.00
20	Tennis rackets	1.00	20.00
			$5,490.00

Counted by: _____ Checked and priced by: _____

Earned revenue ← Incurred cost, expense that helped earn revenue

Since ending inventory has not yet created earned revenue, it will not be included in the cost of merchandise sold until it is sold.

Ralph realized that the cost of merchandise unsold, $5,490, should not be included in the cost of merchandise that was sold, since these unsold items *did not help create earned sales* for January.

He could now calculate the cost to the store for the merchandise sold during January as follows:

Cost of Merchandise (Goods) Sold for January:

1. Merchandise Inventory, Jan. 1, 19XX			$0
2. Purchases		$26,750	
3. Less: Purchase Returns and Allowances	$1,000		
4. Purchase Discount	260	1,260	
5. Cost of Net Purchases			25,490
6. Less Merchandise Inventory, Jan. 31, 19XX			5,490
7. Cost of Merchandise (Goods) Sold during January			$20,000

1. There was no merchandise on hand for resale to customers, since business was just prepared to open.
2. Bought $26,750 of merchandise that hopefully would be resold to customers.
3. Received price reductions or sent back merchandise due to defects $1,000.
4. Received a cash discount by paying within contracted period of time $260.
5. Difference between cost of purchases, less returns and allowances, and discounts $25,490.
6. Cost of unsold merchandise that remains for resale to customers during the next period $5,490.
7. It cost Ralph $20,000 to sell the merchandise to customers before looking at heat, lights, wages, etc.

The $20,000 represents the cost of bringing the merchandise into the store. This is not the price charged to customers.

Now let's look at and put together Ralph's earned sales in relation to the actual cost of selling the merchandise.

Gross profit

RALPH'S SPORTING GOODS

Income Statement
For Month Ended January 31, 19XX

Revenue			
Gross Sales		$23,100	
Less: Sales Returns and Allow-	$500		
ances			
Sales Discount	80	580	
Net Sales			$22,520
Cost of Merchandise (Goods) Sold			
Merchandise Inventory,			
Jan. 1, 19XX		$0	
Purchases	$26,750		
Less: Purchase Returns			
and Allowances $1,000			
Purchase Discount 260	1,260		
Cost of Net Purchases		25,490	
Cost of Merchandise (Goods)			
Available for Sale		25,490	
Less Merchandise Inventory,			
Jan. 31		5,490	
Cost of Merchandise (Goods)			
Sold			20,000
Gross Profit from Sales			$ 2,520

This figure of $2,520 is called gross profit. It represents the difference between the price Ralph pays for his merchandise and the price at which it is sold to customers.

This figure of $2,520 is not the same as net income. What about heat, lights, wages, telephone, advertising, and other expenses? In simplistic **Net income** terms, net income could be calculated as follows:

NET SALES	NET SALES
− COST OF MERCHANDISE SOLD	− COST OF GOODS SOLD
= GROSS PROFIT ON SALES *OR*	= GROSS PROFIT ON SALES
− EXPENSES	− EXPENSES
= NET INCOME	= NET INCOME

At this time you should be able to:

1. Define (a) gross sales, (b) net sales, (c) net purchases, (d) gross profit, and explain the purpose of computing them.
2. Differentiate between sales discount and purchase discount.
3. Differentiate between sales returns and allowances and purchase returns and allowances.
4. Define and state the purpose of preparing an ending inventory sheet.
5. From a group of accounts calculate net sales and cost of goods sold and gross profit.
6. Differentiate between gross profit and net income.

UNIT INTERACTOR 28

From the following mixed list of accounts calculate: net sales, net purchases, cost of goods sold, gross profit.

Purchase Returns and Allowances	$ 4
Sales Returns and Allowances	10
Beginning Inventory	6
Sales Discount	5
Purchase Discount	5
Purchases	14
Ending Inventory	3
Gross Sales	100

SOLUTION to Unit Interactor 28

	GROSS SALES		SALES RETURNS AND ALLOWANCES		SALES DISCOUNT
NET SALES = $85:	100	−	10	−	5

	PURCHASES		PURCHASE RETURNS AND ALLOWANCES		PURCHASE DISCOUNT
NET PURCHASES = $5:	14	−	4	−	5

	BEGINNING INVENTORY		NET PURCHASES		ENDING INVENTORY
COST OF GOODS SOLD = $8:	6	+	5	−	3

	NET SALES		COST OF GOODS SOLD
GROSS PROFIT = $77:	85	−	8

LEARNING UNIT 29

Preparing the Worksheet

Before preparing the worksheet, we update the chart of accounts of Ralph's Sporting Goods as follows:

ASSETS	REVENUE
110 Cash	410 Sales
112 Accounts Receivable	412 Sales Returns and Allowances
113 Merchandise Inventory*	414 Sales Discounts
114 Prepaid Rent	
116 Delivery Truck	
116A Accumulated Depreciation—Truck	

LIABILITIES	COST OF GOODS SOLD
210 Accounts Payable	510 Purchases
212 Notes Payable	512 Purchase Returns and Allowances
214 Salaries Payable	514 Purchase Discounts

OWNER'S EQUITY	EXPENSES
310 R. Jones Investment	610 Salaries Expense
320 Income Summary	612 Cleaning Expense
	614 Depreciation Expense—Truck
	616 Rent Expense

*By the end of this unit the starred new addition will be explained.

Let's look first at a partial section of the worksheet:

Completing
the worksheet columns
of a merchandise company

Account Titles	Trial Balance Dr.	Trial Balance Cr.
Cash	2688000	
Accounts Receivable	850000	
Merchandise Inventory	0	
Prepaid Rent	30000	
Delivery Truck	360000	
Acc. Depr.—Delivery Truck		0
Accounts Payable		1360000
Notes Payable		1000000
R. Jones Investment		2000000
Sales		2310000
Sales Returns and Allowances	50000	
Sales Discount	8000	
Purchases	2675000	
Purchase Returns and Allow.		100000
Purchase Discount		26000
Salary Expense	120000	
Cleaning Expense	15000	
	6796000	6796000

Notice that the trial balance of Ralph's has been listed with two changes, indicated by arrows on page 371.

1. Merchandise inventory to begin in January is zero. This is shown as an asset called merchandise inventory.
2. Accumulated depreciation for the truck is listed below the truck to begin the month the truck was purchased. No depreciation has resulted.

These two accounts have been included with zero balances to make the preparation of the worksheet for a merchandise company easier to follow, especially for the first time. All of the figures were the result of the postings from Ralph's special and general journals.

COMPLETING THE ADJUSTMENTS COLUMNS

Account Titles	Trial Balance Dr.	Trial Balance Cr.	Adjustments Dr.	Adjustments Cr.
Cash	2688000			
Accounts Receivable	850000			
Merchandise Inventory	0			
Prepaid Rent	30000			Ⓐ 10000
Delivery Truck	360000			
Acc. Dep.—Delivery Truck		0		Ⓑ 5000
Accounts Payable		1360000		
Notes Payable		1000000		
R. Jones Investment		2000000		
Sales		2310000		
Sales Returns and Allowances	50000			
Sales Discount	8000			
Purchases	2675000			
Purchase Returns and Allow.		100000		
Purchase Discount		26000		
Salary Expense	120000		Ⓒ 2500	
Cleaning Expense	15000			
	6796000	6796000		
Rent Expense			Ⓐ 10000	
Dep. Exp.—Delivery Truck			Ⓑ 5000	
Salaries Payable				Ⓒ 2500
			17500	17500

At the end of January the following adjustment data are presented.

A. During January rent expired $100.

B. Truck depreciation $50 per month.

$$\left(\frac{\text{cost } \$3,600}{6 \text{ years}} = \$600 \text{ depreciation per year or } \frac{\$600}{12} = \$50 \text{ per month}\right)$$

C. Salaries earned but unpaid or not due until February $25.

A RENT EXPIRED. Since the asset prepaid rent has expired $100, the result is to increase rent expense by $100 and to reduce the amount of prepaid rent by $100. Notice that rent expense is added in the account titles column, since it was not found in the trial balance.

B DEPRECIATION. When depreciation on the delivery truck occurs, two steps need to be recorded:

1. Depreciation expense on the truck is increased ↑ (Dr.).
2. The contra-asset accumulated depreciation is increased ↑ (Cr.) to reflect the amount of depreciation taken on the truck.

On the worksheet notice that only depreciation expense had to be added to the account title list. The accumulated depreciation account, although not having a balance, was already placed below delivery truck.

C SALARIES. To reflect a true picture of salaries expense for January, Ralph adjusts or brings up to date salaries expense by $25, since the work was performed in January.

Although the salaries are not paid until February, they have helped create earned sales in January; therefore, they should be included as part of the expenses of Ralph's Sporting Goods in January.

Notice that salaries payable is added to the account title list. It was not necessary to add salary expense, since it was already in the trial balance. The totaling of the adjustment columns shows that the debit of $175 is equal to the credit of $175.

In summary, these three adjustments have helped to *update* the trial balance. Remember back to the accrual basis of accounting, which matches earned sales against the expenses incurred to make them. These adjustments for rent, salaries, and depreciation reflect actual costs that should be included in trying to match earned sales with expenses.

THE ADJUSTED TRIAL BALANCE

The adjustments and the beginning trial balance are summarized in the adjusted trial balance.

Account Titles	Trial Balance Dr.	Trial Balance Cr.	Adjustments Dr.	Adjustments Cr.	Adjusted Trial Balance Dr.	Adjusted Trial Balance Cr.
Cash	2688000				2688000	
Accounts Receivable	850000				850000	
Merchandise Inventory	0				0	
Prepaid Rent	30000			(A) 10000	20000	
Delivery Truck	360000				360000	
Acc. Dep.—Delivery Truck		0		(B) 5000		5000
Accounts Payable		1360000				1360000
Notes Payable		1000000				1000000
R. Jones Investment		2000000				2000000
Sales		2310000				2310000
Sales Returns and Allowances	50000				50000	
Sales Discount	8000				8000	
Purchases	2675000				2675000	
Purchase Returns and Allow.		100000				100000
Purchase Discount		26000				26000
Salary Expense	120000		(C) 2500		122500	
Cleaning Expense	15000				15000	
	6796000	6796000				
Rent Expense			(A) 10000		10000	
Dep. Exp.—Delivery Truck			(B) 5000		5000	
Salaries Payable				(C) 2500		2500
			17500	17500	6803500	6803500

ACCOUNTS	BEFORE ADJUSTMENTS	ADJUSTED TRIAL BALANCE	BALANCE
1. Prepaid Rent	$ 300	$ 200	(Dr.)
2. Accumulated Depreciation—Truck	0	50	(Cr.)
3. Salary Expense	1,200	1,225	(Dr.)
4. Rent Expense	0	100	(Dr.)
5. Depreciation Expense—Truck	0	50	(Dr.)
6. Salaries Payable	0	25	(Cr.)

The total of $68,035 for the debit and credit columns of the adjusted trial balance indicates that the debits and credits after adjustments still prove their equality.

The topics we now turn to require close attention, as students often find them confusing. Therefore, we shall develop each point thoroughly before proceeding to the next.

In Unit 28, the worksheet primer, much time was spent on how to calculate net sales, net purchases, cost of goods sold, and gross profit. If you feel uncertain on these points, please stop here and review Unit 28.

Now for those who have decided to continue, let's first review the major points of the worksheet primer (those points need constant review) as relates to the situation for Ralph's Sporting Goods at the end of January.

ACCOUNTS	FOUND ON
1. Sales	Income Statement
2. Sales Returns and Allowances	Income Statement
3. Sales Discount	Income Statement
4. Beginning Merchandise Inventory	Income Statement/ Balance Sheet*
5. Purchases	Income Statement
6. Purchase Returns and Allowances	Income Statement
7. Purchase Discount	Income Statement
8. Ending Merchandise Inventory	Income Statement/ Balance Sheet†

Now let's analyze this chart to see how the cost of merchandise inventory is calculated.

At the end of January which accounts add to the cost of the merchandise that is sold?

POINT A. If there had been a balance in merchandise inventory to start January, it would have to be assumed (1) to have been sold by the end of January, so that (2) it would then be part of cost of the merchandise sold. But, since Ralph had zero balance of merchandise inventory to begin January, it cannot be part of the cost of goods sold for January.

POINT B. The following add to the cost of merchandise sold for January (Dr. balance):

1. Beginning merchandise inventory (if there was a balance)
2. Purchases in January.

The following reduce the cost of merchandise for January (Cr. balance):

3. Purchase returns and allowances
4. Purchase discount

*Found on the balance sheet from the prior accounting.

†Found on the balance sheet on the current balance sheet.

5. Unsold merchandise inventory at the end of January (ending inventory).

Note that points B-1 and B-5 are not combined. Each inventory is listed in the cost of merchandise sold separately.

POINT C. Merchandise inventory on income statements and balance sheets:

1. The beginning merchandise inventory is assumed to be sold by the end of the month; therefore, it is no longer an asset to a company (on the balance sheet). It is placed on the income statement as part of the cost of merchandise sold (point B-1).

2. The ending merchandise inventory is goods that are unsold and therefore are not part of the cost of merchandise (cost of goods sold). This ending merchandise inventory is placed on the balance sheet as an asset to begin February (point B-5). The ending inventory each month becomes the beginning inventory for the next month. Do not combine the figures for beginning and ending inventory!

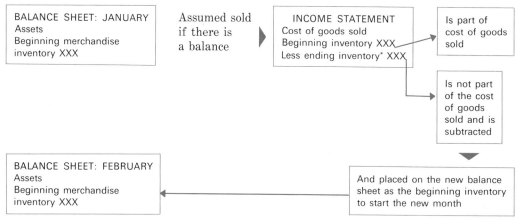

*This figure is based on the inventory sheet shown on page 368.

Here is a quick review of the main points so far.

1. If Ralph had beginning merchandise inventory it would
   a. be assumed to be sold by the end of the month.
   b. be part of the cost of merchandise sold found on the income statement.
   c. no longer be recorded as an asset on the balance sheet.*

2. Purchases represent a cost of the merchandise sold before considering reductions that result from:
   a. purchase returns and allowances (Cr.)
   b. purchase discounts (Cr.)

3. Ending merchandise inventory
   a. represents goods not sold.
   b. is not part of the cost of goods sold and therefore is subtracted from the cost of goods sold on the income statement.
   c. is the balance of unsold goods and is shown on the balance sheet as an

*The next chapter will explain how the beginning inventory is removed from the account.

asset (Dr.). This ending inventory becomes the beginning inventory for the next period.

4. Figures for beginning and ending inventory are not combined.

You should now be ready to proceed. If you don't feel ready, please go back to the beginning of the chapter or review the student interactor in the study guide.

COMPLETING THE WORKSHEET INCOME STATEMENT COLUMNS

The worksheet income statement column is completed as follows:

Account Titles	Income Statement	
	Dr.	Cr.
Cash		
Accounts Receivable		
Merchandise Inventory	0*	549000
Prepaid Rent		
Delivery Truck		
Acc. Dep. — Delivery Truck		
Accounts Payable		
Notes Payable		
R. Jones Investment		
Sales		2310000
Sales Returns and Allowances	50000	
Sales Discount	8000	
Purchases	2675000	
Purchase Returns and Allow.		100000
Purchase Discount		26000
Salary Expense	122500	
Cleaning Expense	15000	
Rent Expense	10000	
Dep. Exp. — Delivery Truck	5000	
Salaries Payable		
	2885500	2985000
Net Income	99500	
	2985000	2985000

$5,490 is the cost of ending inventory. It is assumed to be unsold and therefore not part of the cost of goods sold. By placing it in the credit column, we reduce the cost of the goods sold. Any costs will be recorded in the debit column. Remember, ending inventory will be subtracted from cost of goods sold on the income statement.

$23,100 is the *credit* balance of sales. The sales returns and allowances $500 and sales discount $80 are placed on the debit side, which represents a reduction to total sales:

(Cr.) Sales
(Dr.) Less: Sales returns and allowances
(Dr.) Less: Sales discount

The purchase account $26,750 is on the debit side, reflecting an increase in costs to Ralph.
The purchase returns and allowances $1,000 and purchase discount $260 are on the credit side, which reduces cost of purchases:

(Dr.) Purchases
(Cr.) Less: Purchase returns and allowances
(Cr.) Less: Purchase discount

* If there had been beginning inventory, it would have been recorded here, since it would have been assumed to be sold and thus a cost. For example, the *following* month the $5,490 would end up in the debit column of the income statement since it would be assumed to be sold and thus a cost.

Explanation is given for each item that is new or involves a merchandise company. The net income and the totals of the income statement columns are calculated the same way as in past worksheets.

Remember, the worksheet is not the formal income statement. It presents an informal source of information for the accountant. If the ending inventory of $5,490 is not subtracted from the cost of the merchandise, the figure for gross profit as well as net income will be inaccurate.

THE BALANCE SHEET COLUMNS

The only new point in this chapter that affects the balance sheet columns is that of merchandise inventory. Below we see the balance sheet columns filled out. Notice the explanation for placing the ending merchandise inventory of $5,490 as a debit in the balance sheet columns.

Account Titles	Balance Sheet Dr.	Balance Sheet Cr.
Cash	26 880 00	
Accounts Receivable	8 500 00	
Merchandise Inventory	5 490 00	
Prepaid Rent	200 00	
Delivery Truck	3 600 00	
Acc. Dep.—Delivery Truck		50 00
Accounts Payable		13 600 00
Notes Payable		10 000 00
R. Jones Investment		20 000 00
Sales		
Sales Returns and Allowances		
Sales Discount		
Purchases		
Purchase Returns and Allow.		
Purchase Discount		
Salary Expense		
Cleaning Expense		
Rent Expense		
Dep. Exp.—Delivery Truck		
Salaries Payable		25 00
	44 670 00	43 675 00
Net Income		995 00
	44 670 00	44 670 00

At the end of January the inventory sheet revealed $5,490 of merchandise inventory that was not sold. This inventory was subtracted from the cost of goods sold on the income statement (shown by placing the $5,490 in the credit columns of the income statement).

This ending inventory, $5,490, now becomes the beginning inventory of Ralph's Sporting Goods to begin on February 1. When this beginning inventory is sold, it will be subtracted from the cost of goods sold in February.

The following is the completed worksheet of Ralph Jones for January:

RALPH'S SPORTING GOODS

Worksheet

For Month Ended January 31, 19XX

Account Titles	Trial Balance Dr.	Trial Balance Cr.	Adjustments Dr.	Adjustments Cr.	Adjusted Trial Balance Dr.	Adjusted Trial Balance Cr.	Income Statement Dr.	Income Statement Cr.	Balance Sheet Dr.	Balance Sheet Cr.
Cash	2688000				2688000				2688000	
Accounts Receivable	850000				850000				850000	
Merchandise Inventory	0				0		0	549000	549000	
Prepaid Rent	30000			Ⓐ10000	20000				20000	
Delivery Truck	360000				360000				360000	
Acc. Dep.—Delivery Truck		0		Ⓑ5000		5000				5000
Accounts Payable		1360000				1360000				1360000
Notes Payable		1000000				1000000				1000000
R. Jones Investment		2000000				2000000				2000000
Sales		2310000				2310000		2310000		
Sales Returns and Allowances	50000				50000		50000			
Sales Discount	8000				8000		8000			
Purchases	2675000				2675000		2675000			
Purchase Returns and Allow.		100000				100000		100000		
Purchase Discount		26000				26000		26000		
Salary Expense	120000		Ⓒ2500		122500		122500			
Cleaning Expense	15000				15000		15000			
	6796000	6796000								
Rent Expense			Ⓐ10000		10000		10000			
Dep. Exp.—Delivery Truck			Ⓑ5000		5000		5000			
Salaries Payable				Ⓒ2500		2500				2500
			17500	17500	6803500	6803500	2885500	2985000	4467000	4367500
Net Income							99500			99500
							2985000	2985000	4467000	4467000

From this worksheet the financial statement can be completed quickly by Ralph's accountant. First, however, let's review. At this time you should be able to:

1. Prepare a worksheet for a merchandise company.
2. Explain why sales discounts and sales returns and allowances are placed in the debit columns of the income statement on the worksheet instead of with sales on the credit side of the income statement column.
3. Explain why purchase returns and allowances and purchase discounts

are located in the credit column of the income statement columns on the worksheet.

4. State the reasons why ending merchandise inventory is subtracted from cost of goods sold.
5. Name which statement ending inventory will be found on and define it.
6. Explain the difference in preparing a worksheet for a service company vs. a worksheet for a merchandise company.

UNIT INTERACTOR 29

Fill in the X's where appropriate for each account. Be sure to note that this company, unlike Ralph's, has a beginning inventory. Use an (X-B) for beginning inventory and an (X-E) for the ending inventory. All accounts have no unusual balances. The first two accounts are filled out as examples; the solution and explanation will follow the problem.

Account Titles	Adjusted Trial Balance		Income Statement		Balance Sheet	
	Dr.	Cr.	Dr.	Cr.	Dr.	Cr.
Cash	X				X	
Accounts Receivable	X				X	
Merchandise Inventory						
Office Supplies						
Prepaid Insurance						
Office Equipment						
Accumulated Depreciation—Office Equipment						
Accounts Payable						
S. Katz Investment						
S. Katz Withdrawal						
Sales						
Sales Returns and Allowances						
Sales Discount						
Purchases						
Purchase Returns and Allowances						
Purchase Discount						
Office Salaries						
Insurance Expense						
Depreciation Expense—Office Equipment						

Account Titles	Adjusted Trial Balance	Income Statement Dr.	Income Statement Cr.	Balance Sheet Dr.	Balance Sheet Cr.
Cash	X			X	
Accounts Receivable	X			X	
Merchandise Inventory	X-B	X-B	X-E	X-E	
Office Supplies	X			X	
Prepaid Insurance	X			X	
Office Equipment	X			X	
Acc. Dep.—Office Equipment		X			X
Accounts Payable		X			X
S. Katz Investment		X			X
S. Katz Withdrawal	X			X	
Sales		X	X		
Sales Returns and Allowances	X		X		
Sales Discount	X		X		
Purchases	X		X		
Purchase Returns and Allow.		X		X	
Purchase Discounts		X		X	
Office Salaries	X		X		
Insurance Expense	X		X		
Dep. Exp.—Office Equipment	X		X		

X-B. The beginning inventory is assumed to be sold and therefore is part of the cost of merchandise sold. Costs are shown on the debit column of the income statement columns on the worksheet.

X-E. The ending inventory is not yet sold; therefore it is *not* a cost of merchandise sold. This ending inventory becomes the beginning inventory of the next period shown on the balance sheet columns.

Do not take the difference between beginning and ending inventory. Each figure is calculated separately on the income statement.

Transactions Occur

▼

Record in Special Journals

▼

Post to Subsidiaries (Accounts Receivable and Accounts Payable)

▼

Post to General Ledger

▼

Prepare Trial Balance

▼

Prepare Worksheet

Whether a combined journal or a set of special journals is used to record transactions, the posting and balancing process will result in the same trial balance.

A merchandise firm will require an expanded makeup of items on the income statement and balance sheet. For example, a new section entitled cost of goods sold is subtracted from net sales to arrive at gross profit. Gross profit less expenses gives net income. A service company does not have to worry about recording beginning inventory, purchases, etc., since it sells a service and not merchandise.

The merchandise company will also have to show on its balance sheet a figure for beginning inventory. It will be calculated by tallying inventory at the end of a period of time.

The key points in completing a worksheet for a merchandise company are the following:

1. The beginning inventory will be assumed to be sold by the end of the period. Thus, it is a cost, which is shown as a debit on the income statement columns of a worksheet.
2. By taking an inventory, the cost of ending inventory is determined. This ending inventory, which is not sold, is not a cost; therefore, it must be recorded as a credit on the income statement column of the worksheet (to show it is not a cost) as well as on the debit column of the balance sheet columns of the worksheet. This ending merchandise inventory will indeed become the beginning inventory to start the next month.
3. Sales   Credit balance

      Sales discount   Debit balance

      Sales returns and allowances   Debit balance

      Purchases   Debit balance

      Purchase returns and allowances   Credit balance

      Purchase discount   Credit balance
4. Do not combine beginning and ending inventory.

This chapter has presented a great deal of information, so please be sure to reread it.

BEGINNING INVENTORY
+ NET PURCHASES
= COST OF GOODS AVAILABLE TO SELL
− ENDING INVENTORY
= COST OF GOODS SOLD

SUMMARY OF NEW ACCOUNTING LANGUAGE TERMS

Learning Unit 28

Beginning Merchandise Inventory: The cost of goods on hand in a company to begin an accounting period. This merchandise inventory is an asset. At the end of the accounting period it is assumed to be sold and thus becomes part of the cost of goods sold. This amount will be placed in the debit column of the income statement column on the worksheet.

Cost of Goods Sold: Cost of beginning inventory plus net purchases (purchases minus purchase returns minus purchase discounts) minus cost of unsold ending inventory equals cost of the goods sold.

Ending Merchandise Inventory: The cost of goods that remain unsold at the end of the accounting period. These unsold goods represent a decrease to the total cost of goods sold.

This ending inventory will become the beginning inventory to begin the next accounting period.

Gross Profit: Net sales minus cost of goods sold.

Gross Sales: Sales before considering any sales returns and allowances or sales discounts.

Net Income: Net sales minus cost of goods sold equals gross profit minus operating expenses equals net income.

Net Purchases: Gross purchases minus purchases returns and allowances minus purchase discounts.

Net Sales: Gross sales minus sales returns and allowances minus sales discounts equals net sales.

QUESTION INTERACTORS

1. Define gross sales, sales returns and allowances. What are their usual balances?
2. Define purchases, purchase returns and allowances. What are their usual balances?
3. How are net sales calculated?
4. On which financial statement will net sales be found?
5. What is the difference between buying merchandise and buying equipment?
6. Purchase discounts are increased by debits. Agree or disagree?
7. How are net purchases calculated?
8. Beginning merchandise inventory is found only on the balance sheet. Please explain your support or rebuttal.
9. The ending merchandise inventory of an accounting period never becomes the beginning inventory for the next accounting period. Agree or disagree?
10. Ending inventory is added as part of the cost of merchandise sold. True or false?
11. The cost of merchandise unsold is reduced from the cost of goods sold. True or false?
12. Define the purpose of the ending inventory sheet.
13. How is gross profit calculated?
14. Once gross profit is calculated, net income will be the same. Please comment.

15. Please fill in the following, using the sample (line A) as a guide:

Account	Usual Balance	Statement Found On
A. Cash	Debit	Balance Sheet
1. Purchases		
2. Accumulated Depreciation		
3. Purchase Returns and Allowances		
4. Sales		
5. Accounts Receivable		
6. Sales Discount		
7. Rent Expense		
8. Accounts Payable		
9. Beginning Merchandise Inventory		
10. Ending Merchandise Inventory		
11. Prepaid Rent		
12. Equipment		
13. Salaries Payable		

PROBLEM INTERACTORS

1. For the worksheet below, your task is to bring the account amounts across to their proper columns. On December 1, merchandise inventory was $5,000. Ending merchandise inventory was $6,000 on December 31.

SHELDON COMPANY

Worksheet

For Year Ended December 31, 19XX

Account Titles	Trial Balance Dr.	Trial Balance Cr.	Adjustments Dr.	Adjustments Cr.	Adjusted Trial Balance Dr.	Adjusted Trial Balance Cr.	Income Statement Dr.	Income Statement Cr.	Balance Sheet Dr.	Balance Sheet Cr.
⋮										
Merchandise Inventory	500000									
⋮										
Sales		997500								
Sales Returns and Allowances	1000									
Sales Discount	500									
Purchases	850000									
Purchase Returns and Allow.		10000								
Purchase Discounts		5000								
⋮										

2. From the mixed accounts below, calculate

a. Net sales.   c. Gross profit.

b. Cost of goods sold.   d. Net income.

Cash	$ 4.00
Purchase Discount	5.00
Sales Returns and Allowances	10.00
Beginning Inventory Jan. 1	50.00
Accounts Payable	10.00
Sales Discount	5.00
Purchase Returns and Allowances	20.00
Accounts Receivable	2.00
Sales	200.00
Ending Inventory Jan. 31	15.00
Purchases	50.00
J. Ring Investment	100.00
Operating Expense	5.00

*3. The following is the trial balance of John Harris Company.

JOHN HARRIS COMPANY

Trial Balance
December 31, 19XX

	Dr.	Cr.
Cash	1,620.00	
Accounts Receivable	3,840.00	
Beginning Merchandise Inv. Dec. 1	2,080.00	
Prepaid Rent	200.00	
Equipment	7,200.00	
Accumulated Depreciation—Equipment		1,200.00
Accounts Payable		1,720.00
J. Harris Investment		6,440.00
Sales		36,800.00
Sales Returns and Allowances	1,820.00	
Sales Discount	720.00	
Purchases	17,520.00	
Purchase Returns and Allowances		560.00
Purchase Discounts		340.00
Salaries Expense	6,720.00	
Miscellaneous Expense	4,640.00	
Insurance Expense	320.00	
Utilities Expense	380.00	
	47,060.00	47,060.00

Your task is to prepare a worksheet for John Harris based on the following data:*

1. On December 31 ending merchandise inventory is calculated from the inventory sheet as having a cost of $1,840.
2. Rent expired is $100.
3. Depreciation expense for December is $100.
4. Salaries of $140 were earned but not paid in December.

*4. The owner of J. Roberts Stationery has asked you to prepare a worksheet from the following trial balance:

J. ROBERTS COMPANY

Trial Balance
July 31, 19XX

	Dr.	Cr.
Cash	804.00	
Petty Cash	20.00	
Accounts Receivable	1,276.00	
Beginning Merchandise Inv. July 1	2,546.00	
Prepaid Rent	108.00	
Office Supplies	172.00	
Office Equipment	4,640.00	
Accumulated Depreciation—Equipment		2,320.00
Accounts Payable		1,982.00
J. Roberts Investment		3,738.00
J. Roberts Withdrawal	2,400.00	
Sales		26,322.00
Sales Returns and Allowances	48.00	
Sales Discount	1,200.00	
Purchases	14,658.00	
Purchase Discount		8.00
Purchase Returns and Allowances		174.00
Office Salaries Expense	4,704.00	
Insurance Expense	1,200.00	
Advertising Expense	480.00	
Utilities Expense	288.00	
	34,544.00	34,544.00

Additional data are as follows:

1. Ending merchandise inventory on July 31 is $1,362.
2. Office supplies used up are $50.

*Not all items here represent adjustments.

3. Rent expired is $100.

4. Depreciation expense for office equipment is $200.

5. Salaries earned but not paid are $100.

ADDITIONAL PROBLEM INTERACTORS

1-A. For the worksheet below, your task is to bring the account amounts across to their proper columns. On July 1 merchandise inventory was $8,000. Ending merchandise inventory on July 31 was $10,000.

JIM CO.
Worksheet
For Month Ended July 31, 19XX

Account Titles	Trial Balance Dr.	Trial Balance Cr.	Adjustments Dr.	Adjustments Cr.	Adjusted Trial Balance Dr.	Adjusted Trial Balance Cr.	Income Statement Dr.	Income Statement Cr.	Balance Sheet Dr.	Balance Sheet Cr.
Merchandise Inventory	800000									
Sales		2100000								
Sales Returns and Allowances	20000									
Sales Discount	10000									
Purchases	2440000									
Purchase Returns and Allow.		10000								
Purchase Discount		5000								

2-A. Based upon the accounts below, calculate:

a. Net sales.

b. Cost of goods sold.

c. Gross profit.

d. Net income.

Operating Expense	$ 15.00
J. Small Investment	1,000.00
Purchases	100.00
Ending Investment June 30	20.00
Sales	300.00
Accounts Receivable	150.00
Cash	3,000.00
Purchase Discount	5.00
Sales Returns and Allowances	50.00
Beginning Merchandise Inventory June 1	40.00
Purchase Returns and Allowances	5.00
Sales Discounts	10.00
Accounts Payable	950.00

* 3-A. The following is the trial balance of the Janet Rose Hardware store.

J. ROSE HARDWARE

Trial Balance
December 31, 19XX

	Dr.	Cr.
Cash	324.00	
Accounts Receivable	768.00	
Beginning Merchandise Inv. Dec. 1	416.00	
Prepaid Insurance	40.00	
Store Equipment	1,440.00	
Acc. Dep.—Store Equipment		240.00
Accounts Payable		344.00
J. Rose Investment		1,288.00
Hardware Sales		7,360.00
Hardware Sales Returns and Allow.	364.00	
Hardware Sales Discounts	144.00	
Purchases	3,504.00	
Purchase Discounts		112.00
Purchase Returns and Allowances		68.00
Wage Expense	1,344.00	
Rent Expense	928.00	
Miscellaneous Expense	64.00	
Telephone Expense	76.00	
	9,412.00	9,412.00

Your task is to prepare a worksheet for J. Rose Hardware based on the following data:

1. On December 31 ending merchandise inventory shows a cost of $368 from the inventory sheet.
2. Insurance expired is $20.
3. Depreciation on store equipment for December is $100.
4. Wages earned but not paid in December is $100.

* 4-A. The owner of Bob's Clothing Company has asked you to prepare a worksheet from the following trial balance.

BOB'S CLOTHING COMPANY

Trial Balance
May 31, 19XX

	Dr.	Cr.
Cash	402.00	
Petty Cash	10.00	
Accounts Receivable	638.00	
Beginning Merchandise Inv. May 1	1,273.00	
Prepaid Insurance	54.00	
Clothing Supplies	86.00	
Store Equipment	2,320.00	
Acc. Dep.—Store Equipment		1,160.00
Accounts Payable		991.00
B. Bob Investment		1,869.00
B. Bob Withdrawal	1,200.00	
Sales		13,161.00
Sales Returns and Allowances	24.00	
Sales Discount	600.00	
Purchases	7,329.00	
Purchase Discount		4.00
Purchase Returns and Allowances		87.00
Store Salaries	2,352.00	
Rent Expense	600.00	
Advertising Expense	240.00	
Miscellaneous Expense	144.00	
	17,272.00	17,272.00

Additional data are as follows:

1. Ending merchandise inventory on May 31 is $681.
2. Clothing supplies used up are $20.
3. Insurance expired is $10.
4. Depreciation expense for store equipment is $100.
5. Salaries earned but not paid are $50.

CHALLENGE PROBLEM INTERACTORS

1. Merchandise Inventory on December 31, 1983, is $90,000. *Gross purchases* for 1984 are $130,000. *All* two percent cash discounts were taken on the purchases during 1984. The cost of goods sold is

$137,000 for 1984. Determine:

a. Cost of goods available for sale. _____
b. Merchandise inventory, December 31, 1984. _____

2. Using the information in problem 1, if the total operating expenses were $85,000 and the net income was $65,000, determine net sales for 1984. _____

3. If cost of goods sold is understated—check the correct answer: (Note: Overstated is too high; understated is too low)

a. Ending inventory is overstated _____ Understated _____ No effect _____
b. Net income is overstated_____ Understated_____ No effect_____

4. If net purchases are overstated—check one:

a. Ending inventory is overstated_____ Understated_____ No effect_____
b. Cost of goods sold is overstated_____ Understated_____ No effect_____
c. Net income is overstated_____ Understated_____ No effect_____

5. If net sales amount to $200,000; operating expenses $70,000; net income $10,000; beginning merchandise inventory $40,000; ending merchandise inventory $26,000; determine:

a. Gross profit on sales _____
b. Cost of goods sold _____
c. Net purchases _____

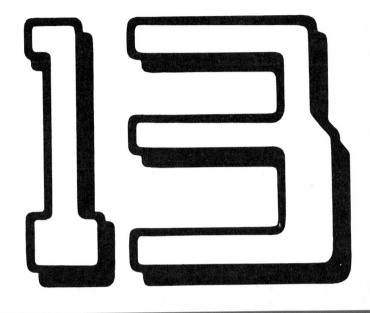

completion
of the
accounting cycle

In the last unit we prepared the worksheet of Ralph's Sporting Goods. We have thus accomplished the following steps in the accounting cycle:

1, 2. Transactions of Ralph's Sporting Goods for January have occurred and have been analyzed and recorded into various journals.

3. This information has been posted from the journals to the ledger.

4. The trial balance has been prepared.

5. The worksheet has been completed.

LEARNING UNIT 30

Preparing the Financial Statements

Now we move on to step 6, the preparation of the income statement and balance sheet.

THE INCOME STATEMENT

The income statement prepared for a merchandise firm

Ralph is interested in knowing how well his sporting goods shop performed for January. What were its sales? Were many customers unhappy with their purchases? What is the cost of the merchandise brought into the store versus the selling price received? How much merchandise is being returned to suppliers? What is the cost of the merchandise that has not been sold?

The following income statement is prepared from the worksheet. A detailed explanation of each section will follow:

Account Titles	Income Statement	
	Dr.	Cr.
Cash		
Accounts Receivable		
Merchandise Inventory		5,490
Prepaid Rent		
Delivery Truck		
Accumulated Depreciation—Delivery Truck		
Accounts Payable		
Notes Payable		
R. Jones Investment		
Sales		23,100
Sales Returns and Allowances	500	
Sales Discount	80	
Purchases	26,750	
Purchase Returns and Allowances		1,000
Purchase Discount		260
Salary Expense	1,225	
Cleaning Expense	150	
Rent Expense	100	
Depreciation Expense—Delivery Truck	50	
	28,855	29,850
Net Income	995	
	29,850	29,850

RALPH'S SPORTING GOODS

Income Statement
For Month Ended January 31, 19XX

Revenue			
Gross Sales		$23,100	
Less: Sales Returns and Allowances	$500		
Sales Discount	80	580	
Net Sales			$22,520
Cost of Merchandise (Goods) Sold			
Merchandise Inventory, Jan. 1, 19XX		$ 0	
Purchases	$26,750		
Less: Purchase Returns and Allowances	$1,000		
Purchase Discount	260	1,260	
Cost of Net Purchases*		25,490	
Cost of Merchandise (Goods) Available for Sale		$25,490	
Less Merchandise Inventory, Jan. 31, 19XX		5,490	
Cost of Merchandise Sold			20,000
Gross Profit from Sales			$ 2,520
Operating Expenses			
Salary Expense		$1,225	
Cleaning Expense		150	
Rent Expense		100	
Depreciation Expense—Delivery Truck		50	
Total Operating Expenses			1,525
Net Income			$ 995

*Cost of goods available for sales = beginning inventory and net purchases.

First let's analyze the revenue section repeated below.

A. Ralph's Sporting Goods has earned $23,100 of sales—partially cash sales and partially sales on account. Remember in the accrual basis of accounting, a sale occurs when it is earned, whether or not payment is received at the time. This figure of $23,100 is called gross sales, since it represents total sales earned before any sales returns, allowances, or discounts.

B, C. Since Ralph is very concerned about keeping his customers satisfied, accounts have been set up to record sales returns and allowances as well as sales discounts. In the month of January sales returns and allowances was $500 and sales discounts was $80.

D. Total gross sales of $23,100 is reduced by $580, the total of sales returns and allowances and sales discounts.

E. The actual, or net, sales of Ralph's Sporting Goods for January is $22,520. This figure was calculated by:

> GROSS SALES
> LESS: SALES RETURNS AND ALLOWANCES
>   SALES DISCOUNTS
> = NET SALES

Keep in mind that this net sales figure of $22,520 doesn't represent only cash sales. The accountant and Ralph have not chosen to keep separate accounts for cash and charge sales.

RALPH'S SPORTING GOODS

Income Statement
For Month Ended January 31, 19XX

Revenue			
Gross Sales		(A) $23,100	
Less: Sales Returns and			
Allowances	(B) $500		
Sales Discount	(C) 80	(D) 580	
Net Sales			(E) $22,520

We look next at the cost of goods merchandise sold section.

A. At the beginning of January Ralph's Sporting Goods had zero merchandise inventory. Notice that if there had been a beginning merchandise inventory it would have to (1) be assumed to be sold, (2) be a part of the cost of the goods sold.

B. During the month Ralph made purchases on account, as well as for cash, for $26,750. This was the total cost of purchases before considering any merchandise that was returned or any purchase price adjustments that were made.

C, D, E. In reality the actual cost of purchases, or what is called net purchases, is calculated by subtracting the cost of purchase returns and allowances as well as any purchase discounts from the cost of purchases.

F. The cost to Ralph of the merchandise that is available to sell to customers is $25,490 (remember, this is not our selling price). If there was a beginning inventory, it would have been added to the $25,490. Cost of goods available for sale is equal to beginning inventory and net purchases.

G, H. What is the cost of the merchandise not sold? This figure, which will reduce the cost of the merchandise sold, because unsold merchandise is not part of the cost of the goods sold, is calculated by taking an ending inventory, which is summarized on the inventory sheet. Subtracting ending merchandise inventory $5,490 from the cost of merchandise available to sell to customers will give us the cost of merchandise sold by Ralph to his customers. The cost to Ralph is $20,000 for the merchandise that is sold. What is his profit?

I. Taking the net sales of $22,520 and subtracting the cost of the merchandise sold $20,000 shows a gross profit for Ralph's Sporting Goods on sales, or profit before any operating expenses, of $2,520.

Net Sales			$22,520
Cost of Merchandise (Goods) Sold			
A. Merchandise Inventory Jan. 1, 19XX		$ 0	
B. Purchases		$26,750	
C. Less: Purchase Returns and Allowances	$1,000		
D. Purchase Discounts	260	1,260	
E. Cost of Net Purchases		25,490	
F. Cost of Merch. (Goods) Avail. for Sale		$ 25,490	
G. Less Merch. Inventory, Jan. 31, 19XX		5,490	
H. Cost of Merchandise Sold			20,000
I. *Gross Profit from Sales*			$ 2,520

But what about Ralph's other expenses?

J, K. Besides the cost of merchandise Ralph also has incurred salary expense, cleaning expense, and rent expense. Depreciation expense on the truck is also shown. In reality Ralph's Sporting Goods has additional expenses of $1,525.

J. Expenses		
Salary Expense	$1,225	
Cleaning Expense	150	
Rent Expense	100	
Depreciation Expense—Truck	50	
Total Operating Expenses		1,525
K. Net Income		$ 995

Taking gross profit of $2,520 and subtracting expenses of $1,525, we find that Ralph shows a net income of $995. That is, earned revenue is greater than expenses incurred to earn it by $995. As we will see, this $995 will increase Ralph Jones's equity in the business.

PREPARING THE BALANCE SHEET: A CLASSIFIED APPROACH

Up to this point you have prepared balance sheets in an *account form*, assets on the left and liabilities and owner's equity on the right. Now let's look at another form for preparing a balance sheet. This form, which presents the assets on the top of the page and the liabilities and owner's equity beneath them, is called the *report form*. The account form and report form are equally acceptable; our choice depends on how we want to arrange the balance sheet accounts. We have been classifying assets as cash, accounts receivable, equipment, and the like; now we will subgroup these classifications in more detail.

The assets section on Ralph's balance sheet will be broken down into:

Current assets   (a) Assets of the firm that will be used up in the daily operation of Ralph's business. Examples include cash, accounts receivable, prepaid insurance, and merchandise inventory. These will be called *current assets*.

Fixed assets   (b) Assets of the firm that help in producing earned revenue whose life extends beyond one year. Examples could be land, buildings, equipment, etc. These will be called *fixed assets*. (Some texts call these assets plant and equipment.)

The liabilities section on Ralph's balance sheet will be broken down into:

Current liabilities   (a) Amount owed (debts) that will come due within one year. Examples could include accounts payable and salaries payable. These are called *current liabilities.*

(b) Amounts owed (debts) that will not come due within one year. Examples could include notes payable and mortgage payable. These are called *long-term liabilities.*

There will be no change in the owner's equity section. Many other subgroupings may be used in preparing a "classified balance sheet"; however, the one we have set up is sufficient for Ralph. It is prepared from the worksheet of Ralph's business as follows:

Account Titles	Income Statement		Balance Sheet	
	Dr.	Cr.	Dr.	Cr.
Cash			26,880	
Accounts Receivable			8,500	
Merchandise Inventory		5,490	5,490	
Prepaid Rent			200	
Delivery Truck			3,600	
Acc. Dep. Delivery Truck				50
Accounts Payable				13,600
Notes Payable				10,000
R. Jones Investment				20,000
Sales		23,100		
Sales Returns and Allowances	500			
Sales Discount	80			
Purchases	26,750			
Purchase Returns and Allow.		1,000		
Purchase Discount		260		
Salary Expense	1,225			
Cleaning Expense	150			
Rent Expense	100			
Dep. Exp.—Delivery Truck	50			
Salaries Payable				25
	28,855	29,850	44,670	43,675
Net Income	995			995
	29,850	29,850	44,670	44,670

RALPH'S SPORTING GOODS

Balance Sheet
January 31, 19XX

Assets

Current Assets:			
Cash		$26,880	
Accounts Receivable		8,500	
Merchandise Inventory		5,490	
Prepaid Rent		200	
Total Current Assets			$41,070
Fixed Assets:			
Delivery Truck	$3,600		
Less: Accumulated Depreciation	50		3,550
Total Assets			$44,620

Notice delivery truck is listed under fixed assets.

Liabilities

Current Liabilities:			
Accounts Payable	$13,600		
Salaries Payable	25		
Total Current Liabilities		$13,625	
Long Term Liabilities:			
Notes Payable		10,000	
Total Liabilities			$23,625

Owner's Equity

R. Jones Investment 1/1/XX		$20,000	
Net Income for Jan.		995	
R. Jones Investment 1/31/XX			20,995
Total Liabilities and Owner's Equity			$44,620

Let's review the construction of the balance sheet. Notice that the balance sheet shown above is the vertical report form instead of the horizontal account type.

RALPH'S SPORTING GOODS

Balance Sheet
January 31, 19XX

Assets

Current Assets:		
Cash	$26,880	
Accounts Receivable	8,500	
Merchandise Inventory	5,490	
Prepaid Rent	200	
Total Current Assets		$41,070
Fixed Assets:		
Delivery Truck	$3,600	
Less Accumulated Depreciation	50	3,550
Total Assets		$44,620

The assets are listed from the worksheet. Note that the ending merchandise inventory of $5,490 is now listed as the beginning merchandise inventory for the next accounting period. Once again, notice how the assets are grouped into current and fixed. The accumulated depreciation $50 is subtracted from the value of the delivery truck $3,600 to arrive at $3,550, the amount of unexpired depreciation of the delivery truck on the books of Ralph's Sporting Goods. By adding the total current assets $41,070 and the total fixed assets $3,550, we find that total assets equals $44,620. Based on the accounting equation, let's see now whether the total of the liabilities and ending owner's equity does equal the total of the assets.

Liabilities		
Current Liabilities:		
Accounts Payable	$13,600	
Salaries Payable	25	
Total Current Liabilities	$13,625	
Long-Term Liabilities:		
Notes Payable	10,000	
Total Liabilities		$23,625
Owner's Equity		
R. Jones Investment 1/1/XX	$20,000	
Net Income for January	995	
R. Jones Investment, 1/31/XX		20,995
Total Liabilities and Owner's Equity		$44,620

From the worksheet, the current liabilities accounts payable and salaries payable give total current liabilities of $13,625. Adding the note payable, which is not due for more than a year and therefore is a long-term liability, gives total liabilities of $23,625. These are obligations of Ralph's that are to be paid at a future date—some within a year.

From the worksheet, Ralph's beginning investment is $20,000. At the end of January the income statement showed net income of $995. This net income figure is extracted from the worksheet and added to Ralph's beginning investment. In effect, his equity in the sporting goods shop has increased:

R. Jones Investment

$20,000 $20,995
JANUARY 2 ⟶ $995 NET INCOME ⟶ JANUARY 31

As we see in the owner's equity section of the balance sheet, the new or ending figure for R. Jones Investment ($20,995) is added to the total of the liabilities ($23,625), giving a total of liabilities and owner's equity of $44,620. This is equal to the total of the assets $44,620. This balance sheet indicates the financial position of Ralph's Sporting Goods at the end of January. By analyzing it you will be able to answer the following questions:

1. What is its cash position? ⟶ $26,880
2. Are any notes owed? ⟶ $10,000
3. What is the amount of accounts receivable? ⟶ $ 8,500
4. Have Jones's rights increased or decreased as of January 31, 19XX? ⟶ $ +995
5. What is the total amount of current liabilities of the business? ⟶ $13,625

At this point you should be able to:

1. Prepare, in proper form, an income statement from a worksheet for a merchandise firm.
2. Differentiate between a classified and an unclassified balance sheet.
3. Prepare in proper form a *classified balance* sheet from a worksheet for a merchandise firm.
4. Compare the structure and purposes of the income statement vs. the balance sheet for a merchandise firm.

Your task is to fill in the amounts of each account on the income statement and balance sheet statements in the study guide. A worksheet is provided for you.

BALL CO.

Worksheet
For Month Ended December 31, 19XX

Account Titles	Trial Balance Dr.	Trial Balance Cr.	Adjustments Dr.	Adjustments Cr.	Adjusted Trial Balance Dr.	Adjusted Trial Balance Cr.	Income Statement Dr.	Income Statement Cr.	Balance Sheet Dr.	Balance Sheet Cr.
Cash	48600				48600				48600	
Merchandise Inventory	62400				62400		(62400)	80000	80000	
Prepaid Rent	115200			3000	112200				112200	
Prepaid Insurance	6000				6000				6000	
Office Equipment	216000				216000				216000	
Accu. Dep.—Office Equipment		36000		6000		42000				42000
Accounts Payable		51600				51600				51600
B. Ball Investment		193200				193200				193200
Sales		1104000				1104000		1104000		
Sales Returns and Allowances	54600				54600		54600			
Sales Discount	21600				21600		21600			
Purchases	525600				525600		525600			
Purchase Ret. and Allow.		16800				16800		16800		
Purchase Discount		10200				10200		10200		
Salaries Expense	201600		15000		216600		216600			
Insurance Expense	139200				139200		139200			
Utilities Expense	9600				9600		9600			
Plumbing Expense	11400				11400		11400			
	1411800	1411800								
Rent Expense			3000		3000		3000			
Dep. Exp.—Office Equipment			6000		6000		6000			
Salaries Payable				15000		15000				15000
			24000	24000	1432800	1432800	1050000	1211000	462800	301800
Net Income							161000			161000
							1211000	1211000	462800	462800

*Please notice once again how the beginning inventory of $624 has been assumed to be sold and thus is entered as a cost on the debit column of the income statement on the worksheet.

BALL COMPANY

Income Statement
For Month Ended December 31, 19XX

Revenue				
Gross Sales			$11,040	
Less: Sales Returns and Allowances		$ 546		
Sales Discount		216	762	
Net Sales				$10,278
Cost of Merchandise (Goods) Sold				
Merchandise Inventory, Dec. 1. 19XX			$ 624	
Purchases		$5,256		
Less: Purchase Returns and Allowances	$168			
Purchase Discount	102	270		
Cost of Net Purchases			4,986	
Cost of Merchandise (Goods) Available for Sale			$5,610	
Less: Merchandise Inv. Dec. 31, 19XX			800	
Cost of Merchandise (Goods) Sold				4,810
Gross Profit from Sales				$ 5,468
Operating Expenses:				
Salary Expense			$2,166	
Insurance Expense			1,392	
Utilities Expense			96	
Plumbing Expense			114	
Rent Expense			30	
Depreciation Expense—Office Equipment			60	
Total Operating Expense				3,858
Net Income				$ 1,610

BALL COMPANY

Balance Sheet
December, 31, 19XX

Assets

Current Assets:			
Cash		$ 486	
Merchandise Inventory, Dec. 31, 19XX		800	
Prepaid Rent		1,122	
Prepaid Insurance		60	
Total Current Assets			$2,468
Fixed Assets:			
Office Equipment	$2,160		
Less Accumulated Depreciation	420		1,740
Total Assets			$4,208

Liabilities

Current Liabilities:			
Accounts Payable		$ 516	
Salaries Payable		150	
Total Current Liabilities			$ 666

Owner's Equity

B. Ball Investment, Dec. 1, 19XX		$1,932	
Net Income for December		1,610	
B. Ball Investment, Dec. 31, 19XX			3,542
Total Liabilities and Owner's Equity			$4,208

LEARNING UNIT 31

Adjusting Entries, Closing Entries, Journalized and Posted: Steps 7, 8 of Cycle

ADJUSTING ENTRIES

Adjusting entries   From the worksheet of Ralph's Sporting Goods the adjustments for rent, depreciation, and salaries are brought up to date at the end of January. We copy the information in the adjustments column of the worksheet in the form of journal entries. The journalized and posted adjusting entries are illustrated as follows:

General Journal: Ralph's Sporting Goods   Page 1

Date	Description	PR	Dr.	Cr.
19XX	*Adjusting Entries*			
Jan. 31	Rent Expense	616	100|00	
	Prepaid Rent	114		100|00
	Rent Expired			
31	Depreciation Expense—Truck	614	50|00	
	Accumulated Depreciation—Truck	116A		50|00
	Depreciation on Truck			
31	Salary Expense	610	25|00	
	Salaries Payable	214		25|00
	Salaries Owed But Not Paid			

Partial Ledger of Accounts Adjusted

Prepaid Rent   Account No. 114

Date	Item	PR	Dr.	Cr.	Bal.
19XX					
Jan. 2		CPJ1	300|00		300|00
31	Adjustment	GJ1		100|00	200|00

Accumulated Depreciation—Truck   Account No. 116A

Date	Item	PR	Dr.	Cr.	Bal.
19XX					
Jan. 31	Adjustment	GJ1		50|00	50|00

Salaries Payable   Account No. 214

Date	Item	PR	Dr.	Cr.	Bal.
19XX					
Jan. 31	Adjustment	GJ1		25|00	25|00

Salaries Expense   Account No. 610

Date	Item	PR	Dr.	Cr.	Bal.
19XX					
Jan. 13		CPJ1	1200|00		1200|00
31	Adjustment	GJ1	25|00		1225|00

404

Partial Ledger of Accounts Adjusted (cont.)

Depreciation Expense—Truck   **Account No. 614**

Date		Item	PR	Dr.	Cr.	Bal.
19XX Jan.	31	Adjustment	GJ1	5000		5000

Rent Expense   **Account No. 616**

Date		Item	PR	Dr.	Cr.	Bal.
19XX Jan.	31	Adjustment	GJ1	10000		10000

CLOSING ENTRIES

At the beginning of the text we studied closing entries. Although Ralph's merchandise company has additional accounts, the same principles and procedures apply here.

STEP 1. Costs, expenses, and reductions to revenue are transferred to the income summary.

Beginning Inventory (if sold)
Sales Returns and Allowances
Sales Discount ▶ Income Summary
Purchases
Expenses

STEP 2. Revenues and reductions to costs are transferred to the income summary.

Ending Inventory
Sales
Purchase Returns and Allowances ▶ Income Summary
Purchase Discount

The balance of the income summary is transferred to owner's investment.

	Income Summary		Owner's Equity
	Beginning Inventory (sold)	Ending Inventory (not sold)	
	Sales Returns and Allowances	Revenues	
	Sales Discount	Purchase Discount	
All items in debit column	Purchases	Purchase Returns and	
of income statement	Expenses	Allowances	
on worksheet will be closed			
by crediting them in journal			
and then posting.			

All items in debit column of income statement on worksheet will be closed by crediting them in journal and then posting.

All items in credit column of income statement on worksheet will be closed by debiting them in journal and then posting.

Notice on the worksheet that all the accounts on the debit side of the above income summary account are located in the debit columns of the income statement. All the credits in the income summary are located in the credit columns of the income statement.

Account Titles	Adjusted Trial Balance Dr.	Adjusted Trial Balance Cr.	Income Statement Dr.	Income Statement Cr.	Balance Sheet Dr.	Balance Sheet Cr.
Cash	268800				268800	
Accounts Receivable	85000				85000	
Merchandise Inventory	0		0	54900	54900	
Prepaid Rent	2000				2000	
Delivery Truck	36000				36000	
Acc. Depr.—Delivery Truck		500				500
Accounts Payable		136000				136000
Notes Payable		100000				100000
R. Jones Investment		200000				200000
Sales		231000		231000		
Sales Returns and Allowances	5000		5000			
Sales Discount	800		800			
Purchases	267500		267500			
Purchase Returns and Allow.		10000		10000		
Purchase Discount		2600		2600		
Salary Expense	12250		12250			
Cleaning Expense	1500		1500			
Rent Expense	1000		1000			
Depr. Exp.—Delivery Truck	500		500			
Salaries Payable		250				250
	680350	680350	288550	298500	446700	436750
Net Income			9950			9950
			298500	298500	446700	446700

406

The following are the journalized and posted closing entries:

General Journal: Ralph's Sporting Goods				Page 2	
Date	Description	PR	Dr.	Cr.	
19XX					
Jan. 31	Income Summary	320	28,855 00		
	Sales Returns and Allowances*	412		500 00	
	Sales Discount	414		80 00	
	Purchase	510		26,750 00	
	Salary Expense	610		1,225 00	
	Cleaning Expense	612		150 00	
	Rent Expense	616		100 00	
	Depreciation Expense—Delivery Truck	614		50 00	
	Records the transfer of all expenses and reductions to revenue to Income Summary				
	Merchandise Inventory	113	5,490 00		
	Sales	410	23,100 00		
	Purchase Returns and Allowances	512	1,000 00		
	Purchase Discounts	514	260 00		
	Income Summary	320		29,850 00	
	Records the transfer of credit account balances on Income Statement columns of worksheet; records ending inventory as now the beginning inventory for February.				
	Income Summary	320	995 00		
	R. Jones Investment	310		995 00	
	Records the transfer of profit to R. Jones from Income Summary.				

*If Ralph's had had a beginning inventory, it would have been closed here by a credit.

Notice that by using the columns of the worksheet, we debit all items in the credit column of the income statement and transfer them to income summary.

All balances on the debit columns of the income statement are credited and transferred to income summary.

The profit $995 is debited to reduce income summary to zero and is transferred to owner's investment as an increase.

The partial ledger after the postings looks as follows:

Merchandise Inventory					Account No. 113	
Date	Item	PR	Dr.	Cr.	Bal.	
19XX						
31	Closing	GJ2	5490 00		5490 00	

Ralph Jones Investment   **Account No. 310**

Date		Item	PR	Dr.	Cr.	Bal.
19XX						
Jan.	2		CRJ1		20,000 00	20,000 00
	31	Closing	GJ2		995 00	20,995 00

Income Summary   **Account No. 320**

Date		Item	PR	Dr.	Cr.	Bal.
19XX						
Jan.	31	Closing	GJ2		29,850 00	29,850 00
	31	Closing	GJ2	28,855 00		995 00
	31	Closing	GJ2	995 00		0

Sales   **Account No. 410**

Date		Item	PR	Dr.	Cr.	Bal.
19XX						
Jan.	31		SJ1		18,100 00	18,100 00
	31		CRJ1		5,000 00	23,100 00
	31	Closing	GJ2	23,100 00		0

Sales Returns and Allowances   **Account No. 412**

Date		Item	PR	Dr.	Cr.	Bal.
19XX						
Jan.	10		GJ1	500 00		500 00
	31	Closing	GJ2		500 00	0

Sales Discount   **Account No. 414**

Date		Item	PR	Dr.	Cr.	Bal.
19XX						
Jan.	31		CRJ1	80 00		80 00
	31	Closing	GJ2		80 00	0

Purchases   **Account No. 510**

Date		Item	PR	Dr.	Cr.	Bal.
19XX						
Jan.	31		PJ1	26,000 00		26,000 00
	31		CPJ1	750 00		26,750 00
	31	Closing	GJ2		26,750 00	0

Purchase Returns and Allowances   Account No. 512

Date		Item	PR	Dr.	Cr.	Bal.
19XX						
Jan.	14		GJ1		1000|00	1000|00
	31	Closing	GJ2	1000|00		0

Purchase Discount   Account No. 514

Date		Item	PR	Dr.	Cr.	Bal.
19XX						
Jan.	31		CPJ1		260|00	260|00
	31	Closing	GJ2	260|00		0

Salaries Expense   Account No. 610

Date		Item	PR	Dr.	Cr.	Bal.
19XX						
Jan.	13		CPJ1	1200|00		1200|00
	31	Adjustment	GJ1	25|00		1225|00
	31	Closing	GJ2		1225|00	0

Cleaning Expense   Account No. 612

Date		Item	PR	Dr.	Cr.	Bal.
19XX						
Jan.	9		CPJ1	150|00		150|00
	31	Closing	GJ2		150|00	0

Depreciation Expense   Account No. 614

Date		Item	PR	Dr.	Cr.	Bal.
19XX						
Jan.	31	Adjustment	GJ1	50|00		50|00
	31	Closing	GJ2		50|00	0

Rent Expense   Account No. 616

Date		Item	PR	Dr.	Cr.	Bal.
19XX						
Jan.	31	Adjustment	GJ1	100|00		100|00
	31	Closing	GJ2		100|00	0

Once the closing entries have been posted, the accounts are ruled as explained earlier. What accounts are left? The $995 or net income summarizes the income statement in owner's equity. Remaining to be carried over to the next accounting period are assets, liabilities, and the ending figure for owner's investment.

At this point you should be able to:

1. Journalize and post adjusting entries for a merchandising company.
2. Journalize and post closing entries for a merchandising company.

UNIT INTERACTOR 31

From the following worksheet fill in the amounts required for the journalizing of the closing entries, and update the merchandise inventory.

If there were a withdrawal account, it would have been closed as in previous chapters.

BALL COMPANY
Worksheet
For Month Ended December 31, 19XX

Account Titles	Trial Balance Dr.	Trial Balance Cr.	Adjustments Dr.	Adjustments Cr.	Adjusted Trial Balance Dr.	Adjusted Trial Balance Cr.	Income Statement Dr.	Income Statement Cr.	Balance Sheet Dr.	Balance Sheet Cr.
Cash	48600				48600				48600	
Merchandise Inventory	62400				62400		62400	80000	80000	
Prepaid Rent	115200			3000	112200				112200	
Prepaid Insurance	6000				6000				6000	
Office Equipment	216000				216000				216000	
Acc. Dep.—Office Equipment		36000		6000		42000				42000
Accounts Payable		51600				51600				51600
B. Ball Investment		193200				193200				193200
Sales		1104000				1104000		1104000		
Sales Returns and Allowances	54600				54600		54600			
Sales Discount	21600				21600		21600			
Purchases	525600				525600		525600			
Purchase Returns and Allow.		16800				16800		16800		
Purchase Discount		10200				10200		10200		
Salaries Expense	201600		15000		216600		216600			
Insurance Expense	139200				139200		139200			
Utilities Expense	9600				9600		9600			
Plumbing Expense	11400				11400		11400			
	1411800	1411800								
Rent Expense			3000		3000		3000			
Dep. Exp.—Office Equipment			6000		6000		6000			
Salaries Payable				15000		15000				15000
			24000	24000	1432800	1432800	1050000	1211000	462800	301800
Net Income							161000			161000
							1211000	1211000	462800	462800

Fill in the amounts:	Dr.	Cr.
Income Summary	_____	
Merchandise Inventory* (beginning)		_____
Sales Returns and Allowance		_____
Sales Discount		_____
Purchases		_____
Salary Expense		_____
Insurance Expense		_____
Utilities Expense		_____
Plumbing Expense		_____
Rent Expense		_____
Depreciation Expense—Office Equipment		_____
Merchandise Inventory (ending)	_____	
Sales	_____	
Purchase Returns and Allowances	_____	
Purchase Discount	_____	
Income Summary		_____
Income Summary	_____	
B. Ball Investment		_____

Merchandise Inventory   Account No. 113

Date	Item	PR	Dr.	Cr.	Bal.
19XX Dec. 1	Balance	√			624

SOLUTION to Unit Interactor **31**

Income Summary	10,500	
Merchandise Inventory		624
Sales Returns and Allowance		546
Sales Discount		216

*Notice that the Ball Company does indeed have a beginning inventory on December 1, 19XX.

SOLUTION (cont.)	Dr.	Cr.
Purchases		5,256
Salary Expense		2,166
Insurance Expense		1,392
Utilities Expense		96
Plumbing Expense		114
Rent Expense		30
Depreciation Expense—Office Equip.		60
Merchandise Inventory	800	
Sales	11,040	
Purchase Returns and Allowances	168	
Purchase Discount	102	
Income Summary		12,110
Income Summary	1,600	
B. Ball Investment		1,610

Merchandise Inventory					Account No. 113	
Date	Item	PR	Dr.	Cr.	Bal.
19XX					
Dec. 1	Balance	√			624
31	Closing	GJ2		624	0
31	Closing	GJ2	800		800

LEARNING UNIT 32

Post-Closing Trial Balance

PREPARING THE POST-CLOSING TRIAL BALANCE:
FINAL STEP OF THE CYCLE

After the adjusting and closing entries were posted, the temporary accounts were summarized to reflect a net profit of $995. What remain are the permanent accounts—assets, liabilities, and the ending figure for owner's investment. We can see this by analyzing the balance sheet columns of the worksheet:

Account Titles	Balance Sheet Dr.	Balance Sheet Cr.
Cash	26 880 00	
Accounts Receivable	8 500 00	
Merchandise Inventory	5 490 00	
Prepaid Rent	200 00	
Delivery Truck	3 600 00	
Acc. Dep.—Delivery Truck		50 00
Accounts Payable		13 600 00
Notes Payable		10 000 00
R. Jones Investment		20 000 00
Sales		
Sales Returns & Allowances		
Sales Discount		
Purchases		
Purchase Returns & Allow.		
Purchase Discount		
Salary Expense		
Cleaning Expense		
Rent Expense		
Dep. Exp.—Delivery Truck		
Salaries Payable		25 00
	44 670 00	43 675 00
Net Income		995 00
	44 670 00	44 670 00

The data in the ledger accounts are the balances shown on the worksheet except for R. Jones Investment, which is $20,995 instead of $20,000, because the worksheet uses Jones's beginning investment figure before net income is added to it. The post-closing trial balance of R. Jones Sporting Goods is as follows:

Post-closing trial balance

RALPH'S SPORTING GOODS		
Post-Closing Trial Balance		
January 31, 19XX		
	Dr.	**Cr.**
Cash	2688000	
Accounts Receivable	850000	
Merchandise Inventory	549000	
Prepaid Rent	20000	
Delivery Truck	360000	
Acc. Dep.—Delivery Truck		5000
Accounts Payable		1360000
Notes Payable		1000000
Salaries Payable		2500
R. Jones Investment		2099500
	4467000	4467000

Notice all temporary accounts have been closed, and are not shown on this post-closing trial balance.

This figure was updated in the ledger by posting the closing entries.

At this point you should be able to:

1. Explain how temporary accounts have been summarized.
2. Prepare a post-closing trial balance.
3. Explain why beginning owner's equity has changed.

UNIT INTERACTOR 32

From the following worksheet prepare a post-closing trial balance.

B. BALL COMPANY
Worksheet
For Month Ended December 31, 19XX

Account Titles	Trial Balance Dr.	Trial Balance Cr.	Adjustments Dr.	Adjustments Cr.	Adjusted Trial Balance Dr.	Adjusted Trial Balance Cr.	Income Statement Dr.	Income Statement Cr.	Balance Sheet Dr.	Balance Sheet Cr.
Cash	48600				48600				48600	
Merchandise Inventory	62400				62400		62400	80000	80000	
Prepaid Rent	115200			3000	112200				112200	
Prepaid Insurance	6000				6000				6000	
Office Equipment	216000				216000				216000	
Acc. Dep.—Office Equipment		36000		6000		42000				42000
Accounts Payable		51600				51600				51600
B. Ball Investment		193200				193200				193200
Sales		1104000				1104000		1104000		
Sales Returns and Allow.	54600				54600		54600			
Sales Discount	21600				21600		21600			
Purchases	525600				525600		525600			
Purchases Returns and Allow.		16800				16800		16800		
Purchase Discount		10200				10200		10200		
Salaries Expense	201600		15000		216600		216600			
Insurance Expense	139200				139200		139200			
Utilities Expense	9600				9600		9600			
Plumbing Expense	11400				11400		11400			
	1411800	1411800								
Rent Expense			3000		3000		3000			
Dep. Exp.—Office Equipment			6000		6000		6000			
Salaries Payable				15000		15000				15000
			24000	24000	1432800	1432800	1050000	1211000	462800	301800
Net Income							161000			161000
							1211000	1211000	462800	462800

B. BALL COMPANY

Post-Closing Trial Balance
January 31, 19XX

	Dr.	Cr.
Cash	486	
Merchandise Inventory	800	
Prepaid Rent	1,122	
Prepaid Insurance	60	
Office Equipment	2,160	
Acc. Dep.—Office Equipment		420
Salaries Payable		150
Accounts Payable		516
B. Ball Investment		3,542
Total	4,628	4,628

COMPLETION OF THE ACCOUNTING CYCLE—A BLUEPRINT

Prepare Income Statement

⯆

Prepare Balance Sheet

⯆

Journalize and Post Adjusting Entries

⯆

Journalize and Post Closing Entries

⯆

Prepare a Post-Closing Trial Balance

Once the worksheet of the merchandise company is prepared, the next step is preparing the financial statements. The income statement columns of the worksheet provide the information necessary to complete the income statement. It is up to you to organize these data in the following categories:

For the income statement: = Net Sales
    − Cost of Goods Sold
    = Gross Profit
    − Expenses
    = Net Income

For the balance sheet: The balance sheet columns of the worksheet provide the information needed to complete the statement.* Please keep in mind that the ending merchandise inventory is now an asset in the beginning inventory on the balance sheet. The worksheet contains the beginning figure for owner's investment; it is up to you to calculate the ending figure.

The preparation of the income statement and balance sheet for a merchandise company involves more details, but the process is the same as for a service company except for the impact of cost of goods sold and its relationship to merchandise inventory, etc.

The completion of the worksheet and preparation of financial statements still does not complete the cycle. Why? The ledger has not been updated to reflect (1) adjustments and (2) an ending figure for owner's

---

* It is up to you to take the information from the worksheet and prepare a classified balance sheet, subgrouping assets into current and fixed, as well as liabilities into current and long term.

investment. Also, the temporary accounts have not been cleared in the ledger to prepare for the next period. Therefore, from the adjustment columns of the worksheet, the adjustments are journalized and posted to the ledger.

In order to clear all temporary accounts and arrive at an ending figure for owner's investment, we can obtain closing entries by going to the income statement columns of the worksheet and proceeding as follows:

1. All items in the credit column must be debited to be cleared. These items are journalized and the total credited to income summary.
2. All items in the debit column must be credited to be cleared. These items are journalized and the total debited to income summary.
3. The balance of the temporary account, income summary, is cleared to owner's investment.

Once the closing entries are journalized and posted, the owner's investment account will reveal a balance for ending owner's investment, and all temporary accounts will have a zero balance.

The last step of the cycle is the post-closing trial balance, or a list of the ledger. This list is made up of assets, liabilities, and an ending figure for owner's equity.

SUMMARY OF NEW ACCOUNTING LANGUAGE TERMS

Learning Unit 30

Classified Balance Sheet: A balance sheet that lists assets divided into current and fixed, as well as liabilities grouped into current and long-term. It is a more detailed balance sheet than in previous chapters.

Current Assets: Assets that will be turned into cash or sold or used up within a year through the regular operations of the firm.

Current Liabilities: Bills that will come due within one year or less.

Fixed Assets: Revenue producing assets that have a life of greater than one year.

Long-Term Liabilities: Debts that are not due for at least one year.

QUESTION INTERACTORS

1. How is the cost of goods sold section calculated?
2. Purchase discount is an operating expense. Agree or disagree? Why?
3. Net purchases always equals gross purchases. Please comment.
4. Define current asset, fixed asset, current liability, and long-term liability.
5. List the items making up owner's equity on the balance sheet.
6. Explain what the following journal entries accomplish:
   a. Income Summary
      Merchandise Inventory
      Sales Returns and Allowances
      Sales Discount

Purchase Returns and Allowances
Salary Expense
Depreciation Expense—Car

b. Merchandise Inventory
Sales
Purchase Discounts
Purchase Returns and Allowances
Income Summary

c. Income Summary
R. Jones Investment

7. Closing entries can be prepared from the worksheet. Agree or disagree?

8. What categories make up a post-closing trial balance? Why?

9. Which of the following accounts will be closed?

a. Sales Discount.
b. Prepaid Rent.
c. Accumulated Depreciation.
d. Purchases.
e. Accounts Payable.
f. Salaries Payable.
g. Sales Returns and Allowances.
h. Investment.
i. Supplies.
j. Rent Expense.

10. Complete the following chart:

	Account	Normal Balance	Statement Found On
a.	Sales		
b.	Sales Discount		
c.	Sales Returns and Allowances		
d.	Purchase		
e.	Purchase Discount		
f.	Purchase Returns and Allowances		
g.	Beginning Merchandise Inventory		
h.	Prepaid Rent		
i.	Supplies		
j.	Rent Expense		
k.	Accounts Payable		
l.	Insurance Expense		
m.	Accumulated Depreciation		

11. Compare the post-closing trial balance to the balance sheet.

PROBLEM INTERACTORS

1. Fill in the following chart:

Account	Category	Dec. ↓	Inc. ↑	Normal Balance	Temporary	Permanent	Statement Found On
Cash							
Accounts Receivable							
Merchandise Inventory							
Prepaid Rent							
Delivery Truck							
Accumulated Depreciation—Delivery Truck							
Accounts Payable							
Notes Payable							
R. Jones Investment							
Sales							
Sales Returns and Allowances							
Sales Discount							
Purchases Returns and Allowances							
Purchase Discount							
Salary Expense							
Cleaning Expense							
Rent Expense							
Depreciation Expense—Delivery Truck							
Salaries Payable							

2. From the following worksheet for J. Mills Co. your task is to prepare in proper form (a) an income statement and (b) a classified balance sheet.

J. MILLS CO.

Worksheet
For Month Ended December 31, 19XX

Account Titles	Trial Balance Dr.	Trial Balance Cr.	Adjustments Dr.	Adjustments Cr.	Adjusted Trial Balance Dr.	Adjusted Trial Balance Cr.	Income Statement Dr.	Income Statement Cr.	Balance Sheet Dr.	Balance Sheet Cr.
Cash	8100				8100				8100	
Accounts Receivable	19200				19200				19200	
Merchandise Inventory	10400				10400		10400	20000	20000	
Prepaid Rent	1000			400	600				600	
Store Equipment	36000				36000				36000	
Acc. Dep.—Store Equipment		6000		6000		12000				12000
Accounts Payable		8600				8600				8600
J. Mills Investment		32200				32200				32200
Sales		184000				184000		184000		
Sales Returns and Allowances	9100				9100		9100			
Sales Discount	3600				3600		3600			
Purchases	87600				87600		87600			
Purchase Returns and Allow.		2800				2800		2800		
Purchase Discount		1700				1700		1700		
Salary Expense	33600		6400		40000		40000			
Advertising Expense	3500				3500		3500			
Insurance Expense	23200				23200		23200			
	235300	235300								
Rent Expense			400		400		400			
Dep. Exp.—Store Equipment			6000		6000		6000			
Salaries Payable				6400		6400				6400
			12800	12800	247700	247700	183800	208500	83900	59200
Net Income							24700			24700
							208500	208500	83900	83900

3. Journalize the closing entries for R. Smith Co.

R. SMITH CO.
Partial Worksheet
For Month Ended December 31, 19XX

Account Titles	Trial Balance Dr.	Trial Balance Cr.	Adjustments Dr.	Adjustments Cr.	Adjusted Trial Balance Dr.	Adjusted Trial Balance Cr.	Income Statement Dr.	Income Statement Cr.	Balance Sheet Dr.	Balance Sheet Cr.
Merchandise Inventory	5200				5200		5200	20000	20000	
Sales		92000				92000		92000		
Sales Returns and Allowances	2000				2000		2000			
Sales Discount	4000				4000		4000			
Purchases	43800				43800		43800			
Purchase Returns and Allow.		1400				1400		1400		
Purchase Discount		1200				1200		1200		
Rent Expense			1000		1000		1000			
Dep. Exp.—Equipment			2000		2000		2000			
							58000	114600		
Net Income							56600			
							114600	114600		

4. Prepare a post-closing trial balance for J. Roff Co.

J. ROFF CO.
Partial Worksheet
For Month Ended December 31, 19XX

Account Titles	Trial Balance Dr.	Trial Balance Cr.	Adjustments Dr.	Adjustments Cr.	Adjusted Trial Balance Dr.	Adjusted Trial Balance Cr.	Income Statement Dr.	Income Statement Cr.	Balance Sheet Dr.	Balance Sheet Cr.
Cash									8100	
Petty Cash									19200	
Accounts Receivable									500	
Merchandise Inventory									5000	
Office Equipment									36000	
Acc. Dep.—Office Equipment										7000
Notes Payable										8600
J. Roff Investment										32200
Salaries Payable										2500
									68800	50300
Net Income										18500
									68800	68800

ADDITIONAL PROBLEM INTERACTORS

1-A. Fill in the blanks (don't use the same account more than once).

Possible Account	Category	Normal Balance	Statement Found On
a. _____	Asset	Dr.	Balance sheet
b. _____	Contra-revenue	Dr.	Income statement
c. _____	Increases costs of goods sold	Dr.	Income statement
d. _____	Contra-revenue	Dr.	Income statement
e. _____	Decrease in cost of purchase	Cr.	Income statement
f. _____	Liability	Cr.	Balance sheet
g. _____	Result of established petty cash	Dr.	Balance sheet
h. _____	Contra-asset	Cr.	Balance sheet
i. _____	Gross revenue	Cr.	Income statement
j. _____	Decrease in cost of purchase	Cr.	Income statement

2-A. From the worksheet for Ben's Wholesale your task is to prepare in proper form (1) an income statement, and (2) a classified balance sheet.

BEN'S WHOLESALE

Worksheet

For Month Ended December 31, 19XX

Account Titles	Trial Balance Dr.	Trial Balance Cr.	Adjustments Dr.	Adjustments Cr.	Adjusted Trial Balance Dr.	Adjusted Trial Balance Cr.	Income Statement Dr.	Income Statement Cr.	Balance Sheet Dr.	Balance Sheet Cr.
Cash	16200				16200				16200	
Accounts Receivable	38400				38400				38400	
Merchandise Inventory	20800				20800		20800	10000	10000	
Prepaid Rent	2000			1000	1000				1000	
Office Equipment	72000				72000				72000	
Acc. Dep.—Office Equipment		12000		2000		14000				14000
Accounts Payable		17200				17200				17200
J. Ben Investment		64400				64400				64400
Sales		368000				368000		368000		
Sales Returns and Allowances	18200				18200		18200			
Sales Discount	7200				7200		7200			
Purchases	175200				175200		175200			
Purchase Returns and Allow.		5600				5600		5600		
Purchase Discount		3400				3400		3400		
Salaries Expense	67200		5000		72200		72200			
Insurance Expense	46400				46400		46400			
Utilities Expense	3200				3200		3200			
Advertising Expense	3800				3800		3800			
	470600	470600								
Rent Expense			1000		1000		1000			
Dep. Exp.—Office Equipment			2000		2000		2000			
Salaries Payable				5000		5000				5000
			8000	8000	477600	477600	350000	387000	137600	100600
Net Income							37000			37000
							387000	387000	137600	137600

3-A. Journalize the closing entries for James Co.

JAMES CO.

Partial Worksheet
For Month Ended December 31, 19XX

Account Titles	Trial Balance Dr.	Cr.	Adjustments Dr.	Cr.	Adjusted Trial Balance Dr.	Cr.	Income Statement Dr.	Cr.	Balance Sheet Dr.	Cr.
Merchandise Inventory	10400				10400		10400	5000	5000	
Sales		184000				184000		184000		
Sales Returns and Allowances	9100				9100		9100			
Sales Discount	3600				3600		3600			
Purchases	87600				87600		87600			
Purchase Returns and Allow.		2800				2800		2800		
Purchase Discount		1700				1700		1700		
Rent Expense			500		500		500			
Depreciation Expense—Truck			1000		1000		1000			
							112200	193500		
Net Income							81300			
							193500	193500		

4-A. Prepare a post-closing trial balance for Lavy Co.

LAVY CO.

Partial Worksheet
For Month Ended December 31, 19XX

Account Titles	Trial Balance Dr.	Cr.	Adjustments Dr.	Cr.	Adjusted Trial Balance Dr.	Cr.	Income Statement Dr.	Cr.	Balance Sheet Dr.	Cr.
Cash									32400	
Petty Cash									76800	
Accounts Receivable									2000	
Merchandise Inventory									20000	
Office Equipment									144000	
Acc. Dep.—Office Equipment										28000
Accounts Payable										34400
J. Lavy Investment										128800
Wages Payable										10000
									275200	201200
Net Income										74000
									275200	275200

Classify, using the code symbols, in which category or categories each of the following items would appear.

If the accounts are closed at the end of an accounting period, or used in the closing process, circle your answer.

Code

A. Current Assets

B. Fixed Assets

C. Contra-fixed Assets

D. Current Liabilities

E. Long-term Liabilities

F. Owner's Equity

G. Contra-owner's Equity

1. Operating Revenue

2. Contra-operating Revenue

3. Cost of goods sold

4. Contra-cost of Goods Sold

5. Operating Expenses

a. _____ Accounts Payable

b. _____ Prepaid Insurance

c. _____ Land

d. _____ H. Smith Withdrawals

e. _____ Purchase Discounts

f. _____ Sales

g. _____ Merchandise Inventory (ending 12/31, Year 2)

h. _____ Accumulated Depreciation— Building

i. _____ Merchandise Inventory (beginning 1/1, Year 2)

j. _____ Wages Payable

k. _____ Purchases

l. _____ Purchase Returns and Allowances

m. _____ Office Equipment

n. _____ Interest Payable

o. _____ Petty Cash

p. _____ Mortgage Payable

q. _____ H. Smith Investment

r. _____ Sales Returns and Allowances

s. _____ Rent Payable (due within one year)

t. _____ Advertising Expense

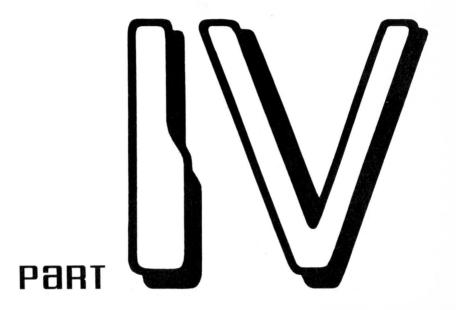

PART **IV**

Payroll

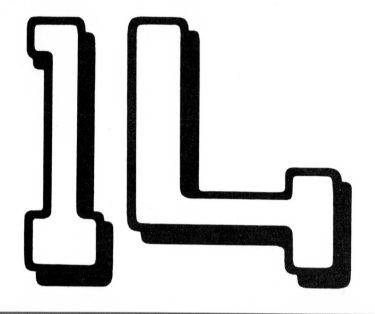

payroll procedures and concepts

Many small businesses require the bookkeeper or accountant to compute, record, pay, as well as complete the related state and federal reports connected with payroll. We shall attempt to be as realistic as possible in our analysis, which centers on completing aspects of payroll for Morse Market for a one-year cycle. At various points in the year you will be asked to complete the payroll requirements. Explanations at each step of the payroll cycle will indicate the "whys" in terms of payroll concepts, procedures, and regulations.

LEARNING UNIT 33

The Morse Market Payroll

On January 1, 19XX, John Morse decided to revamp the operations of Morse Market. After interviewing potential workers (employees), John let go all past employees and hired the following people:

	Mary Blake—Clerk
	Abby Katz—Secretary
Employees	Morris Lester—Office Manager
	Burton Pound—Truck Driver
	James Ryan—Stock Room Manager

Mary Blake would receive a salary of $125 per week. Morris Lester agreed to work for a weekly salary of $300, and Jim Ryan for $250. The other two workers were hired on an hourly basis. Abby Katz would receive $3 per hour, while Burton Pound would be paid $4.50 per hour to drive the delivery truck. John Morse, the owner, will not be receiving salary from the business but he plans eventually to draw out portions of the profits.

OVERTIME: THE WAGE AND HOUR LAW

Calculating overtime   Morse believes no overtime will be necessary. If employees worked more than 40 hours, Morse Market would pay 1½ times the regular rate for the overtime. Those hired on an hourly basis will record hours worked in a daily log. (Some companies may use time cards. Inserted into a time clock, the card is punched to indicate hours on the job.)

Thinking back to a job you have held, whether part time or full time, you may remember trying to stretch the amount of hours worked. If you were paid $2.40 per hour and you worked 50 hours in one week, your pay would probably have been calculated as follows:

```
50 HOURS AT $2.40          = $120
10 HOURS AT $1.20          =   12
AMOUNT OF PAY RECEIVED  = $132
```

But why is overtime calculated on over 40 hours of work? The Wage and Hour Law states that a worker will receive a minimum hourly rate of pay* and that the maximum number of hours a worker will work during a week at the regular rate of pay is 40. Once 40 hours is reached, at least time and a half must be paid. This law, also known as the Fair Labor Standards Act, has many amendments that deal with minimum wage, child labor restrictions, and equal pay regardless of sex. It applies to employers who are involved directly or indirectly in interstate commerce. Not all employers must take 40 hours as the standard; restaurants, hotels, and the like have maximum hours of up to 44. Also, many high-level employees in administrative capacities are exempt. Check with proper authorities for specific details regarding state and federal requirements.

INCOME TAX WITHHOLDING CERTIFICATES

John Morse has asked his employees to fill out income tax withholding certificates, and he gets the forms back filled out as shown.

Form **W-4**
(Rev. April 19 XX)
Department of the Treasury
Internal Revenue Service

Employee's Withholding Allowance Certificate
(This certificate is for income tax withholding purposes only; it will remain in effect until you change it.)

Type or print your full name
Mary Blake

Your social security number
011–82–1514

Home address (Number and street or rural route)
15 Claremont St.

Marital status
☐ Single ☒ Married
(If married but legally separated, or spouse is a nonresident alien, check the single block.)

City or town, State and ZIP code
Ring, Mass. 01965

1 Total number of allowances you are claiming . . . . | 0

2 Additional amount, if any, you want deducted from each pay (if your employer agrees) . . . . | $

I certify that to the best of my knowledge and belief, the number of withholding allowances claimed on this certificate does not exceed the number to which I am entitled.

Signature ▶ Mary Blake   Date ▶ January 1, , 19 XX

16—83587-1

Form **W-4**
(Rev. April 19 XX)
Department of the Treasury
Internal Revenue Service

Employee's Withholding Allowance Certificate
(This certificate is for income tax withholding purposes only; it will remain in effect until you change it.)

Type or print your full name
Abby Katz

Your social security number
111–33–2281

Home address (Number and street or rural route)
87 Garfield Ave.

Marital status
☐ Single ☒ Married
(If married but legally separated, or spouse is a nonresident alien, check the single block.)

City or town, State and ZIP code
Richfield, Mass. 01910

1 Total number of allowances you are claiming . . . . | 0

2 Additional amount, if any, you want deducted from each pay (if your employer agrees) . . . . | $

I certify that to the best of my knowledge and belief, the number of withholding allowances claimed on this certificate does not exceed the number to which I am entitled.

Signature ▶ Abby Katz   Date ▶ January 1, , 19 XX

16—83587-1

---

* Current rate is $2.65 per hour.

Form **W-4**
(Rev. April 19XX)
Department of the Treasury
Internal Revenue Service

Employee's Withholding Allowance Certificate

(This certificate is for income tax withholding purposes
only; it will remain in effect until you change it.)

Type or print your full name
Morris Lester

Your social security number
021-36-9494

Home address (Number and street or rural route)
15 Bone Drive

Marital status
☐ Single ☒ Married

City or town, State and ZIP code
Appleyard, Mass. 01932

(If married but legally separated, or spouse is a nonresident alien, check the single block.)

1 Total number of allowances you are claiming   1

2 Additional amount, if any, you want deducted from each pay (if your employer agrees) . . . . $

I certify that to the best of my knowledge and belief, the number of withholding allowances claimed on this certificate does not exceed the number to which I am entitled.

Signature ▶ Morris Lester   Date ▶ January 1, _____, 19 XX

16—63587-1

Form **W-4**
(Rev. April 19 XX)
Department of the Treasury
Internal Revenue Service

Employee's Withholding Allowance Certificate

(This certificate is for income tax withholding purposes
only; it will remain in effect until you change it.)

Type or print your full name
Burton Pound

Your social security number
223-15-6655

Home address (Number and street or rural route)
18 Rivell Rd.

Marital status
☐ Single ☒ Married

City or town, State and ZIP code
Rawchester, Mass. 01933

(If married but legally separated, or spouse is a nonresident alien, check the single block.)

1 Total number of allowances you are claiming   4

2 Additional amount, if any, you want deducted from each pay (if your employer agrees) . . . . $

I certify that to the best of my knowledge and belief, the number of withholding allowances claimed on this certificate does not exceed the number to which I am entitled.

Signature ▶ Burton Pound   Date ▶ January 1, _____, 19 XX

16—63587-1

Form **W-4**
(Rev. April 19 XX)
Department of the Treasury
Internal Revenue Service

Employee's Withholding Allowance Certificate

(This certificate is for income tax withholding purposes
only; it will remain in effect until you change it.)

Type or print your full name
James Ryan

Your social security number
999-52-1681

Home address (Number and street or rural route)
10 Sable Rd.

Marital status
☐ Single ☒ Married

City or town, State and ZIP code
Salem, Mass. 01917

(If married but legally separated, or spouse is a nonresident alien, check the single block.)

1 Total number of allowances you are claiming   2

2 Additional amount, if any, you want deducted from each pay (if your employer agrees) . . . . $

I certify that to the best of my knowledge and belief, the number of withholding allowances claimed on this certificate does not exceed the number to which I am entitled.

Signature ▶ James Ryan   Date ▶ January 1, _____, 19 XX

16—63587-1

W-4 completed

These forms, commonly called W-4's, supply information that will be used in determining how much taxes will be deducted from the earnings of each employee. The social security number is used as the person's identification number. From the W-4's, Morse derives the following key information about his new employees:

Name of Employee	Number of Allowances Claimed	Marital Status
Mary Blake	0	Married
Abby Katz	0	Married
Morris Lester	1	Married
Burton Pound	4	Married
James Ryan	2	Married

Although all the workers are married, they claim different numbers of allowances.

Usually a worker is entitled to an allowance for self, one for the husband or wife (unless the husband or wife is working and claiming an allowance), and one for each dependent for which the worker is providing more than half the support in a given year. Other technicalities, such as extra allowances for being blind or over 65 years of age, need not be discussed here; you can find them when you need them on IRS information sheets.

Now let's follow how Morse Market handles its payroll for each month of the calendar year, January 1 to December 31.

JANUARY PAYROLL FOR MORSE MARKET*

Calendar year: January 1 thru December 31

Morse Market pays its employees on a weekly basis. The accompanying chart contains the payroll information for the first week. A detailed explanation of new terminology as well as the way the figures are arrived at will follow. *To keep it simple, the weekly payroll will be the same each week for the entire year for Morse Market.* (You will see that the chart gives us a detailed breakdown of payroll information. Please don't try to memorize the chart, since we will be explaining it column by column.)

Payroll register illustrated

Week	Employee	Allow- ance and Marital Status	Salary per Week	Wages per Hour	No. of Hours	Earnings			Deductions			Net Pay	Check No.
						Regular	Overtime	Gross	FICA	FWT	SWT		
19XX 1	Mary Blake	M-0	125.00			125.00		125.00	7.31	14.40	6.25	97.04	
	Abby Katz	M-0		3.00	10	30.00		30.00	1.76	–0–	–0–	28.24	
	Morris Lester	M-1	300.00			300.00		300.00	17.55	45.60	15.00	221.85	
	Burton Pound	M-4		4.50	25	112.50		112.50	6.58	32.60	12.50	99.19	
	Jim Ryan	M-2	250.00			250.00		250.00	14.63	32.60	12.50	190.27	
						817.50		817.50	47.83	93.70	39.38	636.59	

*For simplicity, assume January has exactly four weeks. This assumption will speed our analysis.

Notice that for Morse this summarized information represents a *special payroll journal,* called a *payroll register.** Let's look at the figures for Morris Lester, in order to understand this payroll register as well as the way calculations are arrived at:

The payroll register for Morse Market is considered to be a special journal.

Week	Employee	Allow-ance and Marital Status	Salary per Week	Wages per Hour	No. of Hours	Earnings			Deductions			Net Pay	Check No.
						Regular	Overtime	Gross	FICA	FWT	SWT		
19XX													
1	Mary Blake	M-0	125.00			125.00		125.00	7.31	14.40	6.25	97.04	
	Abby Katz	M-0		3.00	10	30.00		30.00	1.76	–0–	–0–	28.24	
	Morris Lester	M-1	300.00			300.00		300.00	17.55	45.60	15.00	221.85	
	Burton Pound	M-4		4.50	25	112.50		112.50	6.58	1.10	5.63	99.19	
	Jim Ryan	M-2	250.00			250.00		250.00	14.63	32.60	12.50	190.27	
						817.50		817.50	47.83	93.70	39.38	636.59	

Ⓐ   Ⓑ   Ⓒ Ⓓ   Ⓔ Ⓕ Ⓖ Ⓗ   Ⓘ

Ⓐ *ALLOWANCE AND MARITAL STATUS.* The information M-1 indicates that from the W-4 Lester is claiming one allowance and he is married. Keep in mind that payroll at Morse Market is recorded and paid weekly.

Ⓑ *SALARY PER WEEK.* Morris earned a salary of $300 per week (if he were paid on an hourly basis the other two columns could be used).

Ⓒ *REGULAR EARNINGS.* This salary of $300 represents his earnings for the week without overtime.

Ⓓ *OVERTIME EARNINGS.* Since there is no overtime, this is left blank.

Ⓔ *GROSS EARNINGS.* Morris Lester's earnings, before any taxes, is $300. This is called his *gross earnings.* But how do we know the amount of taxes that will be deducted to arrive at the actual pay he will take home?

Calculating FICA

Ⓕ *DEDUCTIONS: FICA 17.55.* This tax of $17.55 results from a law called the Federal Insurance Contributions Act (FICA), which helps fund the payments related to (1) monthly retirement benefits for those over

---

* Some companies prefer to use the payroll register as a supplementary record instead of as a special journal. When we learn how to post this information we will see why Morse chose to use his payroll register as a special journal and not as a supplementary record.

62 years of age, (2) medical benefits after age 65, (3) benefits for workers who have become disabled, (4) benefits for families of deceased workers who were covered by the Federal Social Security Act. But why is $17.55 deducted from Morris Lester's gross amount? The current FICA taxes both the employee (Morris) and the employer an equal amount. In this case each worker contributes 5.85% of the first $15,300 that is earned.* The maximum a worker can contribute in any one year is $895.05 (5.85% × $15,300). If a worker makes less than $15,300, he will not pay in the possible maximum of $895.05. If a worker earns $30,000, he will still contribute only $895.05, since only the first $15,300 is taxed by FICA.*

In Morris Lester's situation, his gross earnings is reduced by $17.55 (5.85% × $300) for FICA contributions. Morse Market will have to match Lester's contribution.

Charts to determine the amount of FICA contribution are provided by the IRS in Circular E of the Employer's Tax Guide. If they are used, the multiplication (percentage method) of 5.85% times gross pay is not needed.

G DEDUCTIONS: FWT 45.60. Recall that on the W-4 Morris Lester claimed one allowance and gave his status as married. Remember, too, that all payroll is recorded and paid weekly. Instead of trying to make complex calculations, we obtain this figure of $45.60 for FWT (Federal Withholding Tax) from a wage bracket table provided in Circular E of the Employer's Tax Guide.

Since all Morse's employees are paid weekly and are married, we shall turn our attention to the withholding tables for weekly and married. (There are other tables for biweekly, semimonthly, monthly, and other payroll periods for both single and married.) Let's see how the $45.60 Federal Withholding Tax was arrived at from the table.

---

*The following rates, base, and maximum tax for FICA are anticipated in the future:

Year	Rate	Base	Maximum Tax
1978	6.05%	17,700	1,070.85
1979	6.13%	22,900	1,403.77
1980	6.13%	25,900	1,587.67
1981	6.65%	29,700	1,975.05
1982	6.70%	31,800	2,130.60

Only a few years back the FICA rate was 5.85% on $10,800. The rate as well as the base is continually changing, but the theory and procedures remain. For Morse all FICA contributions will be at 5.85% of the first $15,300 of earnings. At the time of writing the current rate is 6.05% on the first $17,700. Please remember the case we will be looking at assumes a rate of 5.85% on the first $15,300.

MARRIED Persons — WEEKLY Payroll Period

And the wages are—		And the number of withholding allowances claimed is—										
At least	But less than	0	1	2	3	4	5	6	7	8	9	10 or more
		The amount of income tax to be withheld shall be—										
$0	$48	$0	$0	$0	$0	$0	$0	$0	$0	$0	$0	$0
48	49	.10	0	0	0	0	0	0	0	0	0	0
49	50	.20	0	0	0	0	0	0	0	0	0	0
50	51	.40	0	0	0	0	0	0	0	0	0	0
51	52	.60	0	0	0	0	0	0	0	0	0	0
52	53	.80	0	0	0	0	0	0	0	0	0	0
53	54	.90	0	0	0	0	0	0	0	0	0	0
54	55	1.10	0	0	0	0	0	0	0	0	0	0
55	56	1.30	0	0	0	0	0	0	0	0	0	0
56	57	1.40	0	0	0	0	0	0	0	0	0	0
57	58	1.60	0	0	0	0	0	0	0	0	0	0
58	59	1.80	0	0	0	0	0	0	0	0	0	0
59	60	1.90	0	0	0	0	0	0	0	0	0	0
60	62	2.20	0	0	0	0	0	0	0	0	0	0
62	64	2.50	.10	0	0	0	0	0	0	0	0	0
64	66	2.90	.40	0	0	0	0	0	0	0	0	0
66	68	3.20	.80	0	0	0	0	0	0	0	0	0
68	70	3.60	1.10	0	0	0	0	0	0	0	0	0
70	72	3.90	1.40	0	0	0	0	0	0	0	0	0
72	74	4.20	1.80	0	0	0	0	0	0	0	0	0
74	76	4.60	2.10	0	0	0	0	0	0	0	0	0
76	78	4.90	2.50	0	0	0	0	0	0	0	0	0
78	80	5.30	2.80	.40	0	0	0	0	0	0	0	0
80	82	5.60	3.10	.70	0	0	0	0	0	0	0	0
82	84	5.90	3.50	1.00	0	0	0	0	0	0	0	0
84	86	6.30	3.80	1.40	0	0	0	0	0	0	0	0
86	88	6.60	4.20	1.70	0	0	0	0	0	0	0	0
88	90	7.00	4.50	2.10	0	0	0	0	0	0	0	0
90	92	7.30	4.80	2.40	0	0	0	0	0	0	0	0
92	94	7.60	5.20	2.70	.30	0	0	0	0	0	0	0
94	96	8.00	5.50	3.10	.60	0	0	0	0	0	0	0
96	98	8.30	5.90	3.40	1.00	0	0	0	0	0	0	0
98	100	8.70	6.20	3.80	1.30	0	0	0	0	0	0	0
100	105	9.40	6.80	4.30	1.90	0	0	0	0	0	0	0
105	110	10.40	7.70	5.20	2.70	.30	0	0	0	0	0	0
110	115	11.40	8.60	6.00	3.60	1.10	0	0	0	0	0	0
115	120	12.40	9.60	6.90	4.40	2.00	0	0	0	0	0	0
120	125	13.40	10.60	7.70	5.30	2.80	.40	0	0	0	0	0
125	130	14.40	11.60	8.70	6.10	3.70	1.20	0	0	0	0	0
130	135	15.40	12.60	9.70	7.00	4.50	2.10	0	0	0	0	0
135	140	16.40	13.60	10.70	7.80	5.40	2.90	.50	C	0	0	0
140	145	17.40	14.60	11.70	8.80	6.20	3.80	1.30	0	0	0	0
145	150	18.40	15.60	12.70	9.80	7.10	4.60	2.20	0	0	0	0
150	160	19.90	17.10	14.20	11.30	8.40	5.90	3.50	1.00	0	0	0
160	170	21.90	19.10	16.20	13.30	10.40	7.60	5.20	2.70	.30	0	0
170	180	23.90	21.10	18.20	15.30	12.40	9.50	6.90	4.40	2.00	0	0
180	190	25.60	23.10	20.20	17.30	14.40	11.50	8.60	6.10	3.70	1.20	0
190	200	27.30	24.80	22.20	19.30	16.40	13.50	10.60	7.80	5.40	2.90	.50
200	210	29.00	26.50	24.10	21.30	18.40	15.50	12.60	9.80	7.10	4.60	2.20
210	220	30.70	28.20	25.80	23.30	20.40	17.50	14.60	11.80	8.90	6.30	3.90
220	230	32.40	29.90	27.50	25.00	22.40	19.50	16.60	13.80	10.90	8.00	5.60
230	240	34.10	31.60	29.20	26.70	24.30	21.50	18.60	15.80	12.90	10.00	7.30
240	250	35.80	33.30	30.90	28.40	26.00	23.50	20.60	17.80	14.90	12.00	9.10
250	260	37.50	35.00	32.60	30.10	27.70	25.20	22.60	19.80	16.90	14.00	11.10
260	270	39.20	36.70	34.30	31.80	29.40	26.90	24.50	21.80	18.90	16.00	13.10
270	280	41.70	38.40	36.00	33.50	31.10	28.60	26.20	23.70	20.90	18.00	15.10
280	290	44.20	40.60	37.70	35.20	32.80	30.30	27.90	25.40	22.90	20.00	17.10
290	300	46.70	43.10	39.50	36.90	34.50	32.00	29.60	27.10	24.70	22.00	19.10
300	310	49.20	45.60	42.00	38.60	36.20	33.70	31.30	28.80	26.40	23.90	21.10
310	320	51.70	48.10	44.50	40.90	37.90	35.40	33.00	30.50	28.10	25.60	23.10

The left-hand column of the table indicates wages. We know Morris Lester earned $300. Going down the wage column, we arrive at $300. He has claimed 1 allowance, therefore we move two columns over to the right and, under the heading of 1 allowance, find the figure of $45.60. The $45.60 indicates the amount of Federal Withholding Tax that should be deducted from the weekly pay of a married person earning between $300 and $310 and claiming 1 allowance.

H DEDUCTIONS: SWT 15.00. We are assuming a 5% State Withholding Tax (state income tax); therefore, $300 \times 5\% = \$15.00$. Various states also provide charts to lessen calculations.

I NET PAY. The net pay of $221.85 for Morris Lester shows what remains for him to take home after all deductions have been subtracted from gross earnings involving FICA, FWT, and SWT. In this case:

Gross Pay		$300.00
Less: FICA	$17.55	
FWT	45.60	
SWT	15.00	78.15
Net Pay		$221.85

Gross is what we earn and wish we took home—net pay is what we have to settle for.

Morse Market doesn't take out deductions for union dues, hospital insurance, savings bonds, life insurance, etc. These deductions are not required by law.

At this point you should be able to

1. Differentiate between an employee and an employer.
2. Calculate overtime pay.
3. Explain the purpose of the Wage and Hour Law.
4. Complete a W-4 form.
5. Explain "claiming an allowance."
6. Define a calendar year.
7. Define and state the purpose of a payroll register.
8. Define and state the purpose of FICA, FWT, SWT.
9. Calculate FICA deductions.
10. Utilize a wage bracket table to arrive at deduction of FWT.
11. Differentiate between gross pay and net pay.

Please answer true or false for the following:

1. Payroll is always based on a fiscal year beginning July 1.
2. Overtime is based on the FICA.
3. W-4's are used as an aid in payroll calculations.
4. FICA and FWT are the same tax.
5. Gross pay is really net pay.
6. FICA is paid only by the employer.
7. There is no maximum on FICA.
8. Wage bracket is a slow device compared to actual calculations.

SOLUTION to Unit Interactor **33**

1. False. 2. False. 3. True. 4. False. 5. False. 6. False. 7. False. 8. False.

LEARNING UNIT 34

Recording and Paying the Payroll

THE PAYROLL REGISTER

The payroll register for week no. 1 is given again for your convenience.

Week	Employee	Allow-ance and Marital Status	Salary per Week	Wages per Hour	No. of Hours	Earnings			Deductions			Net Pay	Check No.
						Regular	Overtime	Gross	FICA	FWT	SWT		
19XX													
1	Mary Blake	M-0	125.00			125.00		125.00	7.31	14.40	6.25	97.04	
	Abby Katz	M-0		3.00	10	30.00		30.00	1.76	–0–	–0–	28.24	
	Morris Lester	M-1	300.00			300.00		300.00	17.55	45.60	15.00	221.85	
	Burton Pound	M-4		4.50	25	112.50		112.50	6.58	1.10	5.63	99.19	
	Jim Ryan	M-2	250.00			250.00		250.00	14.63	32.60	12.50	190.27	
						817.50		817.50	47.83	93.70	39.38	636.59	

We can check the accuracy of this payroll register by cross-footing it:

TOTAL EARNINGS – DEDUCTIONS = NET PAY

or

TOTAL EARNINGS = NET PAY + DEDUCTIONS

Since the payroll register is a special journal for Morse, postings to the ledger from the payroll register will be done monthly. There will be no need to journalize a payroll entry to record payroll before posting.

Eventually we will post the information in the payroll register to accounts in the general ledger. Why? Morse uses the payroll register as a special journal; therefore he will post from it directly. If he used the payroll journal as a supplementary record, he would have to take information from the payroll register and journalize a payroll entry and then post to the ledger accounts. To avoid duplication of effort, Morse considers the payroll register as his special payroll journal. He will not post information from the payroll register until the end of the month.

Now, using the T-account form, let's see which accounts will receive information from the payroll register column totals at the *end of the month*.

Payroll Register

Week	Salary per Week	Wages per Hour	No. of Hours	Earnings			Deductions			Net Pay	Check No.
				Regular	Over-time	Gross	FICA	FWT	SWT		
1											
2											
3											
4						(605)	(203)	(204)	(205)	(206)	

Wage and Salary Expense 605		FICA Payable 203		FWT Payable 204	
Records the total gross earnings for payroll			Shows the amount deducted from gross earnings by Morse for FICA, which is now owed to the U.S. Treasury		Shows the amount deducted from gross earnings by Morse for FWT, which is now owed to the U.S. Treasury

Wages and Salary Payable 206		SWT Payable 205	
	Shows the amount of salaries owed employees before the checks are written		Shows the amount deducted from gross earnings by Morse for SWT which is now owed to the state

The Wage and Hour Law and other federal regulations require Morse to maintain records for each employee, including name, address, rate and amount of pay, and other data. For Morse, this required information will be included in individual earnings records. In the next section we will be analyzing the content of an individual earnings record. For now, keep in mind:

1. The payroll register is a special payroll journal for Morse.
2. Posting will occur from the payroll register to ledger accounts at end of month.

If the payroll register was a supplementary record:

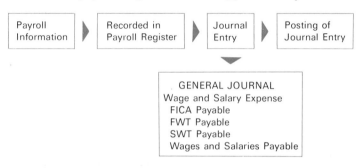

Keep in mind Morse doesn't use the payroll register as a supplementary record, but many companies do.

Remember that Morse Market does not make this journal entry, since it posts directly from the payroll register to the general ledger.

Morse Market has deducted money from the gross earnings of its employees; until these payments are made to the appropriate sources, Morse Market has created additional liabilities.

PAYING THE PAYROLL

Since Morse Market has only five employees, it pays payroll by check from its regular checking account.* The check form Morse uses provides space to list amounts earned along with deductions. Morse utilizes a cash payments (disbursements) journal to record the payment to each employee. As we see below, each entry reduces the amount of salaries and wages owed as well as showing:

1. Date of payment.
2. Amount of decrease in cash (check).
3. The payee, or person by whom payment is received.

---

*A larger firm may have a separate payroll checking account as well as a regular checking account. Often the checks are of different colors. A deposit for the full amount of the payroll is placed in this separate payroll account. When all the checks are written, the payroll account should be zero.

Cash Payments Journal

Date	Check No.	Payment To	PR	Sundry Dr.	Accounts Payable Dr.	Wages and Salaries Payable Dr.	Purchase Discount Cr.	Cash Cr.
Jan. 8	12	Mary Blake				97.04		97.04
8	13	Abby Katz				28.24		28.24
8	14	Morris Lester				221.85		221.85
8	15	Burton Pound				99.19		99.19
8	16	James Ryan				190.27		190.27

The total of wages and salaries payable will be posted at the end of the month as a debit in the general ledger. Notice that from the payroll register a credit figure for wages and salary payable is posted.

For example on January 8 Morris Lester is paid $221.85. The cash payments journal reveals a debit to wages and salaries payable and a credit to cash. Notice that the check number (14) is entered in the journal, and Morris Lester's name is placed in the payment to column. At the time of payment Morse Market furnishes each employee an earnings statement, indicating gross earnings for week 1 as well as deductions for net pay.

INDIVIDUAL EARNINGS RECORDS

When the employees of Morse Market were hired, an individual record for each person was set up. The one for Morris Lester is as follows:

NAME OF EMPLOYEE Morris Lester			SOCIAL SECURITY NUMBER 021-361-9494		
ADDRESS 15 Bone Drive			CITY OR TOWN Appleyard, MA 01932		
DATE OF BIRTH	MARRIED [x] OR SINGLE [ ]	NUMBER OF EXEMPTIONS 1	PHONE NO	CLOCK NO	
POSITION Office Mgr.	RATE $300/wk.	DATE	DATE STARTED 1/1/XX	DATE TERMINATED	
REMARKS			REASON		

		FIRST QUARTER 19									SECOND QUARTER 19							
WEEK #	LINE #	HOURS WORKED REG	OVER TIME	TOTAL EARNINGS	FED OLD AGE	WITH-HOLDING TAX	STATE TAX		NET PAY	WEEK #	LINE #	HOURS WORKED REG	OVER TIME	TOTAL EARNINGS	FED OLD AGE	WITH-HOLDING TAX	STATE TAX	NET PAY
1				300.00	17.55	45.60	15.00		221.85	14								
2										15								
3										16								

As each weekly payroll is summarized in the payroll register, the information about each employee is recorded in the employee's earning record.* Notice how the information about Morris Lester was entered.

* In the appendix on the "write-it-once" principle, you will see how to write the check and at the same time carbon-copy the information to the payroll register and the individual earnings card.

In the above form the individual earnings summary is broken down into four quarters, each made up of thirteen weeks ($13 \times 4 = 52$ weeks). These four quarters represent the calendar year.

Earnings and deductions totals can be calculated monthly or quarterly. This sheet, as we will see later, will assist Morse Market in meeting federal and state payroll information and requirements.

We now have an update in Morse Market's payroll recording process.

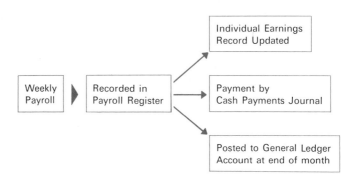

At this point you should be able to:

1. Cross-foot the payroll register.
2. Define and state the purpose of:
   a. Wage and Salary Expense.
   b. FICA Payable.
   c. FWT Payable.
   d. Wages and Salaries Payable.
   e. SWT Payable.
3. Differentiate a supplementary payroll register from a payroll register used as a special journal.
4. Prepare an entry in the cash payments journal to record payment of payroll to employees.
5. Define and state the purpose of the individual earnings record.

UNIT INTERACTOR 34

From the monthly payroll register, a special payroll journal, of Ball Co., fill in the blanks in the statements below.

1. The total at end of month of $500 will have to be posted to _____ .

2. Net pay is posted to _____ at end of month.

3. The totals of _____ , _____ ,
_____ all must be posted individually to accounts in
the general ledger at end of month.

4. A _____   _____
_____ does not require journal entries to be recorded
weekly in a general journal.

Week	Employee	Allowance and Marital Status	Salary per Week	Gross Earnings	Deductions			Net Pay
					FICA	FWT	SWT	
1 2 3 4								
Monthly Totals				500	29.75	131.40	25	314.35

SOLUTION to Unit Interactor **34**

1. Wage and Salary Expense.
2. Wages and Salaries Payable.
3. FICA, FWT, SWT.
4. Special Payroll Register.

LEARNING UNIT 35

Employer's Payroll Taxes

As each employee had to secure a proper identification number
(social security number) for purposes of reporting earnings, taxes, etc.,
Morse also secured an employer identification number. The form that
Morse completed in applying for the employer identification number is
SS-4. The SS-4 form asks for:

1. Name
2. Trade name
3. Address or place of business
4. County of business location
5. Type of organization
6. Ending month of accounting year
7. Reason for applying
8. Date starting business
9. First date wages will be paid
10. Number of employees
11. Nature of business

Morse sent the form back to the Internal Revenue Service and eventually received an employer identification number of 12134791.

Morse Market saw no need to prepare monthly financial statements. The balance sheet and income statement will be prepared semiannually. Therefore, Morse decided to record information about its payroll tax responsibilities at the *end of each month*.

So far we have been analyzing deductions from the worker. We have mentioned that Morse Market is required by law to match the 5.85% on the first $15,300 earned for each employee. Morse is also required to contribute to the federal unemployment compensation tax as well as the state unemployment compensation tax.

Keep in mind that 5.85% = .0585 in the decimal system.

FEDERAL UNEMPLOYMENT TAX ACT (FUTA)

Paid by employer; .5% is .005 in the decimal system.

This tax is used to provide temporary relief for those unemployed as well as to attempt to stabilize employment. This tax is paid only by the employer (Morse Market). The money reverts back to individual state unemployment programs. The rate for Morse is .5% (.005) on the first $4,200 of earnings for each employee.* (Actually, the rate is 3.2%, but a credit of 2.7% to the state leaves an effective balance of .5%.) Payment is due at the end of the year, unless the cumulative amount owed for the quarter is greater than $100, in which case quarterly payments are required.

STATE UNEMPLOYMENT TAX ACT (SUTA)

This tax is usually paid by the employer (only a few states require employees to contribute). The standard rate is 2.7% on the first $4,200 earned by each employee.† Morse Market, on the basis of unemployment claims made by its workers in the past, has received a state unemployment merit rating of 3.5%. State unemployment taxes will be paid quarterly, at the end of each 13-week period.

State unemployment paid by employer. State unemployment rates vary from state to state.

More will be said about these employers payroll taxes. For now, remember that Morse Market must pay:

1. State unemployment tax, 3.5% on $4,200, paid quarterly (end of three months) for each employee. All earnings in *excess* of $4,200 in a calendar year are exempt from state unemployment tax for the employer.
2. Federal unemployment tax, .5% on $4,200, paid annually if cumulative quarterly totals are less than $100 for the year. It is paid quarterly if any quarter exceeds a cumulative total of $100. Once again earnings in excess of $4,200 in a calendar year are exempt from federal employment tax for the employer.
3. FICA, 5.85% on $15,300. We will be discussing the timetable for FICA deposits for Morse in Chapter 15.

---

* At the time of writing the current rate is 3.4% on the first $6,000; with a state credit of 2.7%, the FUTA rate is an effective balance of .7%. These rates are continually in change. For our purpose we will assume for Morse Market 3.2% on $4,200 less 2.7% state credit, leaving an effective rate of .5% for FUTA.
† This may vary from state to state. For example, some states use a base of $4,800.

Since the payroll each week is the same, we refer to the information shown earlier.

Let's look now at the summary payroll information as well as the recording and payment of payroll taxes at the end of January (remember that January is assumed to be exactly four weeks). We will be looking at the federal taxes for Morse. State withholding taxes do vary from state to state, but the basic theory remains the same, although we are only discussing federal withholding and FICA.

FOR JANUARY

	GROSS	FICA	FWT
MARY BLAKE	$ 500.00	$ 29.24	$ 57.60
ABBY KATZ	120.00	7.04	0
MORRIS LESTER	1200.00*	70.20†	182.40‡
BURTON POUND	450.00	26.32	4.40
JAMES RYAN	1000.00	58.52	130.40
	$3270.00	$191.32	$374.80

*$300 per week x 4
†$17.55 x 4 weeks
‡$45.60 x 4 weeks

These summary figures were calculated from the employees' individual earnings records by adding the gross earnings of each employee, FICA withheld, and income tax withheld. If these figures are correct, they should match the total amounts that have been posted to the general ledger accounts from certain monthly column totals of the payroll register. We will record the journal entry for Morse Market's payroll taxes for the month of January and then look at the individual ledger accounts.

Since no employee during the first month has made more than $4,200 (or $15,300), the summary chart for January indicates gross earnings of $3,270. The employer payroll taxes can be calculated as follows:

1. $3,270 × 11.7% (5.85% + 5.85%) = $382.59 gross total FICA to be contributed.

   Total FICA to be contributed $382.59
   FICA contributed by employees   191.32
   Amount of FICA owed by Morse $191.27*

   Notice that Morse is matching the contribution of the employees.

2. State unemployment: 3.5% × $3,270 = $114.45.
3. Federal unemployment: .5% × $3,270 = $16.35.

*The FICA does not match exactly with $191.32 for FICA contributed by employees due to rounding.

The journal entry to record this payroll expense is as follows:†

19XX				
Jan. 31	Payroll Tax Expense		322.07	
	FICA Payable			191.27
	State Unemployment Tax Payable			114.45
	Federal Unemployment Tax Payable			16.35

322.07

PAYROLL TAX FOR THE MONTH OF JANUARY

Of course, the foregoing information is posted to the ledger accounts. Now let's look at the ledger, before any payroll deductions or payroll taxes are paid at the end of the month or quarter.

FICA Tax Payable   **203**

Date		PR	Dr.	Cr.	Bal.
19XX					
Jan.	31	PR1*		191.32	191.32
	31	GJ1		191.27	382.59

FWT Payable   **204**

Date		PR	Dr.	Cr.	Bal.
19XX					
Jan.	31	PR1		374.80	374.80

State Unemployment Tax Payable   **208**

Date		PR	Dr.	Cr.	Bal.
19XX					
Jan.	31	GJ1		114.45	114.45

Federal Unemployment Tax Payable   **310**

Date		PR	Dr.	Cr.	Bal.
19XX					
Jan.	31	GJ1		16.35	16.35

Payroll Tax Expense   **610**

Date		PR	Dr.	Cr.	Bal.
19XX					
Jan.	31	GJ1	322.07		322.07

*This amount, $191.32, was posted from the payroll register.

†	Account Affected	Category	↑ ↓	Rule
	Payroll Tax	Expense	↑	Dr.
	FICA	Liability	↑	Cr.
	State Unemployment	Liability	↑	Cr.
	Federal Unemployment	Liability	↑	Cr.

The FICA and FWT payable indicate amounts deducted from workers' earnings that are now liabilities for Morse. The employer's payroll tax liabilities of FICA, state unemployment, and federal unemployment have also occurred.

At this point you should be able to:

1. Differentiate between employee taxes and employer taxes.
2. Define and state the purpose of state unemployment and federal unemployment taxes.
3. Explain merit rating.
4. Calculate the amount of FICA the employer is to contribute.
5. Prepare a journal entry to record the employer's payroll taxes.

UNIT INTERACTOR 35

1. Fill in the blanks as of the end of June.

Weekly Wages Subject to
All Taxes, $3,000

5.85% FICA	_____
2.7% state unemployment	_____
.5% federal unemployment	_____

2. Prepare a journal entry to record the employer's payroll tax for the month of June.

Date	Account Titles	PR	Dr.	Cr.

SOLUTIONS to Unit Interactor 35

1. FICA, $175.50 (5.85% × $3,000); state unemployment, $81.00; federal unemployment, $15.00.

2.

Date	Account Titles	PR	Dr.	Cr.
19XX June 30	Payroll Tax Expense		271.50	
	FICA Payable			175.50
	State Unemployment			81.00
	Federal Unemployment			15.00
	Employer's Payroll Taxes			

The FWT payable is not part of the employer's payroll taxes. It represents deductions taken out of the employees' paycheck.

When a worker begins employment, a W-4 is completed. This gives the employer the information needed to calculate payroll deductions.

As the payroll period occurs, the information is recorded in the payroll register. When this is done, the individual earnings records of each employee should be updated. Some companies will then use the information in the payroll register to record a general journal entry, which will be posted to ledger accounts as usual. Some companies, if they choose to use the payroll register as the special journal, will not make a general journal entry but will post the total of the payroll register to specific ledger accounts. Either way, the end result will be the same. When payment of the payroll takes place, the transactions will be recorded in the cash payments journal.

The employer, besides matching the worker's FICA contributions, must pay state and federal unemployment. As of 1978 the employer pays unemployment tax based on the first $6,000 of earnings; the employees do not contribute. The times at which the employer's taxes are due depend upon the amount of deduction and the requirements of individual states for SUT and upon specific requirements by the federal government for FICA and FUT.

For Morse the payroll register is a special journal. If this were a supplementary record, it would require a journal entry to be made to record payroll and then to be posted to the ledger.

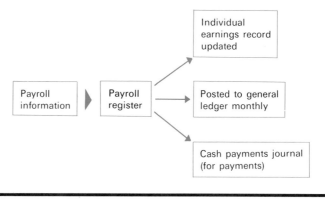

SUMMARY OF NEW ACCOUNTING LANGUAGE TERMS

Learning Unit 33

Calendar Year: A one-year period beginning on January 1 and ending on December 31, used to calculate payroll information.

FICA: Federal Insurance Contributions Act. A tax levied on both the employer and employee up to a certain maximum. FICA tax helps benefit persons retired, disabled, over 65 years of age, etc.

FWT: Federal Withholding Tax, commonly known as federal income tax.

Gross Earnings: Amount of pay received before any taxes. It is what the worker wishes he had.

Net Pay: Gross pay less deductions. Net pay is what the worker actually takes home.

Payroll Register: A multicolumn form that can be used either as a supplementary record payroll information or as a special payroll journal. If it is used as a special journal, posting will occur from the payroll register to the general ledger.

SWT: State Withholding Tax.

W-4 (Employee's withholding allowance certificate): A form filled out by employees to supply the employer needed information about the number of allowances claimed, marital status, etc., for determining deductions from an employee's paycheck.

Wage and Hour Law: This law prescribes a minimum hourly wage and a maximum number of work hours a week, beyond which, overtime must be paid.

Wage Bracket Table: Charts providing information about deductions for FWT or FICA, based on earnings and data supplied on the W-4.

Learning Unit 34

Employee Individual Earning Record: A record that summarizes the total amount of wages paid, as well as a deduction for a calendar year that will aid in preparing governmental reports.

Employer Payroll Taxes: The employer must match FICA and also must pay state and federal unemployment taxes.

FWT Payable: A liability account showing the amount an employer owes to the U.S. Treasury, after he has deducted FWT from employees' paychecks.

Federal Unemployment Tax: A tax paid by employers to the federal government. The rate in 1978 was .7% on the first $6,000 of earnings of each employee.

FICA Payable: A liability account showing the amount owed by an employer (comprising contributions of employer and employee) to the U.S. Treasury for FICA.

Merit Rating: A percentage rate assigned to a business by the state in calculating state unemployment tax. The lower the rating, the less tax must be paid. The rate is based upon the employment record of employer.

Payroll Quarters: Quarter 1—January, February, March; Quarter 2—April, May, June; Quarter 3—July, August, September; Quarter 4—October, November, December.

State Unemployment Tax: A tax paid by employers to the state.

Wage and Salary Expense: An account that records the total gross earnings for a payroll.

Wage and Salaries Payable: A liability account that shows net pay for payroll before payment is due.

QUESTION INTERACTORS

1. Differentiate between overtime and salary.
2. What is the purpose of the Wage and Hour Law?
3. Define and state the purpose of completing a W-4 (Employee's Withholding Certificate).
4. Usually, claiming more allowances on a W-4 results in receiving money sooner in a paycheck. Please comment.
5. *All* payroll registers must be supplementary records. True or false? Please comment.
6. Define and state the purpose of FICA.
7. The employer is the only person responsible for paying FICA. Agree or disagree?
8. Explain FWT and SWT.
9. What is a calendar year?

10. Define the purpose of a wage bracket table.
11. What purposes does the individual earnings record serve?
12. Why does payroll information center around 13-week quarters?
13. Draw a diagram showing how the following relate: (a) weekly payroll, (b) payroll register (assume to be a supplementary record), (c) individual earnings, (d) journal entries, (e) cash disbursement journal.
14. What payroll taxes usually involve the employer?
15. What is the purpose of federal unemployment tax? When is it paid?
16. Each state requires state unemployment taxes to be paid only once a year. Agree or disagree?
17. If you earned $120,000 this year, you would pay more FICA than your partner who earned $28,000. Agree or disagree?
18. Merit rating relates to FICA. Please comment.

PROBLEM INTERACTORS

1. As the bookkeeper of Jan's Flower Shop, please calculate the gross earnings for each of the following employees.

Employee	Hourly Rate	Regular Hours	Overtime	Gross Earnings
BEA FLOW	$3.00 per hour	40	4	
PAUL FLYNN	$6.00 per hour	40	2	
APPLES RONG	$8.00 per hour	40	8	
JAY WALKER	$2.50 per hour	40	6	

2. The Power Pack Company has five employees. Your task is to record the following information for Power Pack in a payroll register for payroll week 1. No overtime occurred.

Employee	Allowance and Marital Status	Weekly Salary
SAM BEAN	M-2	$250
EARL HITLER	M-3	$300
RON RALPH	M-0	$310
MARTHA RYE	M-1	$40
RUTH SLOAN	M-5	$220

FICA is 5.85%. All salaries are subject to FICA. Federal income tax is determined by the wage bracket table found in the text. State tax is assumed at 5%.

The heading of the payroll register is as follows:

Week No.	Employee	Allowance and Marital Status	Salary per Week	Earnings			Deductions			Net Pay	Check No.
				Regular	Overtime	Gross	FICA	FWT	SWT		

3. From the following payroll register, a supplementary record of Ron's Boutique, your task is to:
   a. Prepare the general journal entry to record the weekly payroll.
   b. Record in the cash disbursements journal the payment to each employee. Assume payment on January 10.
   c. If Ron utilized the payroll register as a special journal, what changes would be needed in (a) or (b) or both?

Payroll Register, Week Ended January 8, 19XX

Employees	Time Clock Card No.	Daily Time M T W T F S S	Total Hours	Overtime Hours	Regular Pay Rate	Regular Pay Before Overtime	Overtime Premium Pay	Gross Pay
Carl Bartlet	6	8 8 8 6 0 0 0	30		2.00	60		60
Pat Elario	3	8 8 8 8 8 0 0	40		2.50	100		100
John Riley	1	8 8 8 8 8 4 0	44	4	3.00	120	18	138
Jim Snively	15	8 8 8 8 8 0 0	40		2.50	100		100
Total						380	18	398

FICA Taxes	Federal Income Taxes	Medical Insurance	Labor Union Dues	Total Deductions	Net Pay (Take Home)	Check No.
3.00	5.20	4.00	2.50	14.70	45.30	103
5.00	9.10	4.00	2.50	20.60	79.40	104
6.90	10.70	4.00	2.50	24.10	113.90	105
5.00	7.00	2.50	4.00	18.50	81.50	106
19.90	32.00	14.50	11.50	77.90	320.10	

The heading of the journal is:

Date	Check No.	Payment To	Sundry Dr.	Accounts Payable Dr.	Wages Payable Dr.	Cash Cr.

4. For the month of June the following partial payment summary of Mo's Clothes is presented from the individual earnings records. Your task is, first, to complete the table, and second, to prepare a journal entry to record the payroll taxes for Mo. Please show all calculations.

Employee	Gross	FICA*	FWT†
JOAN FLING	$ 300		
PHILLIP JANGLES	400		
CINDY MONSELLO	400		
EDITH ROSE	900		
MIKE ROWE	1,100	_____	_____

*At 5.85%, and no one has earned more than $15,300, which is the base.
†Assume an 8% FWT instead of using the wage bracket table.

The state unemployment tax rate is 2.7%. The federal unemployment tax rate is .5%. Gross earnings have not exceeded $4,200 for any individual except Joan Fling, who has already earned a cumulative total of $4,200 before this payroll.

ADDITIONAL PROBLEM INTERACTORS

1-A. From the following information please complete the chart for gross earnings for the week.

Employee	Salary per 40-Hour Week	Hours of Overtime	Gross Earnings	
MARIA FLANDERS	$120	2	_____	A
LANE FORMAN	160	10	_____	B
SKIP HOPE	80	5	_____	C
JOE ROBERTS	200	3	_____	D

2-A. As the new bookkeeper of Ring Suppliers, your first task is to record the first week's payroll into the payroll register from the following information.

Employee	Allowance and Marital Status	Salary per Week
RON EAR	M-1	$260
JIM FERLON	M-3	300
SMITTY MOLL	M-0	50
NEILA MOORE	M-5	315
PETE RENEL	M-2	319

FICA tax rate is 5.85%; all salaries are subject to FICA. Federal income tax is determined from the table in the text. State tax is assumed to be 3%. The heading of the payroll register is as follows:

Payment Period	Allowance and Marital Status	Employee	Salary per Week	Earnings			Deductions			Net Pay
				Regular	Overtime	Gross	FICA	FWT	SWT	

3-A. The following payroll register is a *supplementary record* of Small's Market.

Payroll Register,
Week Ended January 8, 19XX

Employee	Time Card No.	Allowance and Marital Status	Daily Time M T W T F S S	Total Before Overtime	Overtime Hours	Regular Rate	Earnings Regular Rate	Overtime Rate	Gross Pay
King	5	M-5	6 10 8 8 8 8 0	40	8	3.60	144.00	43.20	187.20
Lovett	3	M-3	9 9 9 9 4 8 0	40	8	3.20	128.00	38.40	166.40
Morse	4	M-4	8 10 10 10 10 7 0	40	15	4.00	160.00	90.00	250.00
Sling	2	M-2	8 8 8 8 8 3 0	40	3	2.00	80.00	9.00	89.00
Slope	1	M-1	8 8 8 8 8 4 0	40	4	3.00	120.00	18.00	138.00
Total							632.00	198.60	830.60

Deductions

Employee	FICA Tax	Federal Income Tax	Life Insurance	Labor Union	Medical	Total Deductions	Net Pay	Check No.
King	0	34.00	2.00	10.00	5.00	51.00	136.20	111
Lovett	6.99	32.00	2.00	0	5.00	45.99	120.41	112
Morse	8.60	44.00	2.00	0	10.00	64.60	185.40	113
Sling	3.27	16.00	2.00	10.00	5.00	36.27	52.73	114
Slope	5.62	27.00	2.00	0	5.00	39.62	98.38	115
Total	24.48	153.00	10.00	20.00	30.00	237.48	593.12	

Your task is to:

a. Prepare the general entry to record the weekly payroll.
b. Record in the cash disbursements journal the payment to each employee. The heading of the journal is shown below.
c. If the payroll register was a special journal, would general journal entries be needed to record payroll? Please explain.

Date	Payment To	PR	Sundry	Accounts Payable Dr.	Wages Accrued Dr.	Cash Cr.	Check No.

4-A. For the month of April at Ray's Liquors the following partial payroll summary is taken from the individual earnings records. Both Mike Rice and Bill Salesman have earned more than $4,200 before this payroll. Your task is to:

a. Complete the table.
b. Prepare a journal entry to record the payroll taxes for Ray. Please show all calculations.

Employee	Gross	FICA*	FWT
Bill Barns	1,000		
Joe Bloom	300		
Jim Ready	600		
Mike Rice	200		
Bill Salesman	500		

*Assume that FICA is 5.85% and that no one has earned more than $15,300 on cumulative pay. FWT is assessed at 5%. The state unemployment tax rate is 1.5%. The federal unemployment tax rate is .5%.

CHALLENGE PROBLEM INTERACTOR

The following are the salaries and wages obligations of the Underneath Excavating Co. for the month of July, 198X.

	Gross Pay	Federal Income Tax Withheld	Union Dues Withheld
Salaries	30,000	6,000	0
Wages	70,000	14,000	1,500

Assume:

State income tax	4.6%—on total payroll
FICA tax	5.85%—Base—$16,500
Federal unemployment tax	0.5%—Base—$5,400
State unemployment tax	2.7%—Base—$5,400

90% of salaries and 60% of wages are subject to FICA tax. 70% of salaries and 40% of wages are subject to the unemployment tax.

In good general journal form, journalize the following payroll entries, assuming the payroll register is a supplementary record.

1. Record the salaries and wages for the month of July.
2. Record employer's payroll taxes.

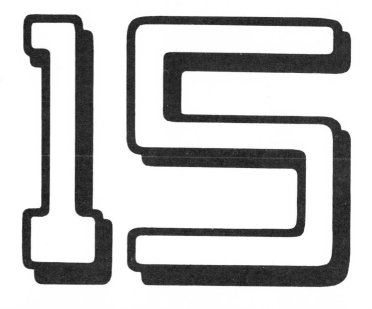

completing
the
payroll records

FICA of employee
+ FICA of employer
+ FWT of employee
= Amount owed

The last chapter analyzed Morse's basic payroll taxes. If at the end of any month (except the last month of the quarter) Morse's cumulative amount of undeposited *Federal Income Tax Withheld, Employees' FICA Taxes Withheld,* and *Employer's FICA Tax,* for the quarter, is $200 or more and less than $2,000, a deposit for the amount of the taxes withheld is due within 15 days after the end of the month (in this case by February 15*). This deposit of FICA (employee), FICA (employer), and federal income tax is made to an authorized commercial bank or a federal reserve bank. The Federal Tax Deposit ticket shown on the next page must accompany each deposit.

* The amount of taxes due determines the frequency of deposits. For Morse, deposits are due within 15 days of the following month. The following is a detailed breakdown of deposit requirements for other companies:

Deposit Requirements

Generally, you must deposit the income tax withheld and both the employer and employee social security taxes with an authorized commercial bank or a Federal Reserve bank. Deposits must be made in accordance with the instructions on the reverse of Federal Tax Deposit Form 501 which must accompany each deposit.

The amount of taxes determines the frequency of the deposits. The following rules show how often you must make deposits.

(1) If at the end of a quarter the total amount of undeposited taxes is less than $200, you are not required to make a deposit. You may either pay the taxes directly to Internal Revenue along with your quarterly Form 941 or make a deposit.

(2) If at the end of a quarter the total amount of undeposited taxes is $200 or more, you must deposit the entire amount on or before the last day of the first month after the end of the quarter. If $2,000 or more see rule 4 below.

(3) If at the end of any month (except the last month of a quarter) the cumulative amount of undeposited taxes for the quarter is $200 or more and less than $2,000, you must deposit the taxes

(Continued on next page)

Completion of First Quarter—
January, February, March

PAYROLL TAXES AT THE END OF JANUARY

Federal tax deposit card relates to FWT and FICA.

We are now looking at a situation where Morse's tax due for January is $757.39. Since this is greater than $200 but less than $2,000 Morse made the following deposit on February 15:

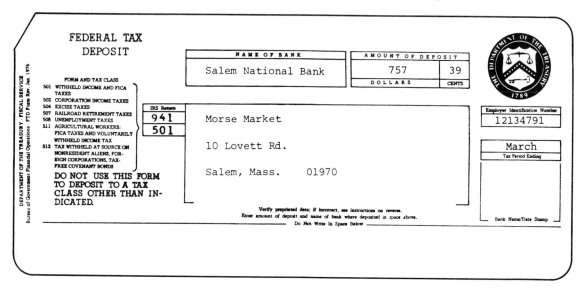

This form does not involve state or federal unemployment. Deposit No. 1 was calculated in this way:

Gross pay	$3,270	
Less excess over $15,300	0 = $3,270	
Times FICA rate	11.7%	(5.85% + 5.85%)
Total FICA	$382.59	(er) (ee)*
Add FWT	374.80	
Deposit	$757.39	*ee-employee; er-employer

within 15 days after the end of the month. (This does not apply if you made a deposit for a quarter-monthly period that occurred during the month under the $2,000 rule in 4 below.)

(4) If at the end of any quarter-monthly period the cumulative amount of undeposited taxes for the quarter is $2,000 or more, you must deposit the taxes within three banking days after the end of the quarter-monthly period. (A quarter-monthly period ends on the 7th, 15th, 22d, and last day of the month.) In determining banking days, exclude local banking holidays observed by authorized commercial banks, as well as Saturdays, Sundays, and legal holidays. The deposit requirements are considered met if: (a) you deposit at least 90 percent of the actual tax liability for the deposit period, and (b) if the quarter-monthly period occurs in a month other than the third month of a quarter, you deposit any underpayment with your first deposit that is required to be made after the 15th day of the following month. Any underpayment that is $200 or more for a quarter-monthly period that occurs during the third month of the quarter must be deposited on or before the last day of the next month.

The payroll summary for January was as follows:

EMPLOYEE	GROSS	FICA	FWT
MARY BLAKE	$ 500.00	$ 29.24	$ 57.60
ABBY KATZ	120.00	7.04	–0–
MORRIS LESTER	1,200.00	70.20	182.40
BURTON POUND	450.00	26.32	4.40
JAMES RYAN	1,000.00	58.52	130.40
	$3,270.00	$191.32	$374.80

ANALYSIS OF JANUARY PAYROLL SUMMARY. The gross pay for the month, $3,270, was taken from the monthly update presented at the end of the last chapter. Since no one earned in excess of $15,300, all of the wages are subject to FICA tax for both the employer and employee (5.85% + 5.85% = 11.7%). From the gross pay, total FICA tax is $382.59. Of the $382.59, $191.32 had been deducted from employees gross pay for the month of January leaving the FICA tax owed by Morse at $191.27.

$382.59   Total
– 191.32   FICA (ee)
$191.27   FICA (er) to be matched

Owing to rounding, the employee and employer contributions are not exactly equal, but it will all work out at the end.

The FICA (ee), FICA (er), and FWT now add up to $757.39. When this deposit is made, and we post from the cash payments journal to the ledger, we have the following results:

Notice that after deposit is made, FICA payable and FWT are reduced to a zero balance.

Before Deposit

FICA Payable

Date		PR	Dr.	Cr.	Bal.
19XX Jan.	31	PR1*		191.32	191.32
	31	GJ1		191.27	382.59

FWT Payable

Date		PR	Dr.	Cr.	Bal.
19XX Jan.	31	PR1		374.80	374.80

After Deposit

FICA Payable

Date		PR	Dr.	Cr.	Bal.
19XX Jan.	31	PR1		191.32	191.32
	31	GJ1		191.27	382.59
Feb.	15	CPJ1	382.59		–0–

FWT Payable

Date		PR	Dr.	Cr.	Bal.
19XX Jan.	31	PR1		374.80	374.80
Feb.	15	CPJ1	374.80		–0–

* Payroll register.

The liabilities for FICA and FWT payable are reduced by the deposit as shown.

Since the payroll is the same for January and February and both months are assumed to have exactly four weeks, the same deposit will be made on March 15. The February information is recorded in a payroll register, the individual employees' earnings records are updated, and so on. Before doing this let's calculate the employer's payroll tax expense for February. The employer's payroll expense for the month requires a general journal entry as shown in the previous chapter. Please also keep in mind that the Federal Tax Deposit Ticket only involves FICA (ee, er) and FWT. The state unemployment will be paid quarterly. Federal unemployment will be paid annually if cumulative quarterly totals are less than $100. If the cumulative total is greater than $100, quarterly payments will be needed, using deposit tickets similar to those used for FICA and FWT.

EMPLOYER'S PAYROLL TAX EXPENSE FOR FEBRUARY

Gross earnings for February is $3,270.
(Calculated from individual earnings records.)

1. FICA

$3,270 ×	11.7%	=	$382.59
(gross)	(FICA rate)		(total FICA due)
	(5.85% + 5.85%)		

Employer payroll tax expense

= FICA to be matched
+ state unemployment
+ federal unemployment

Total FICA due	$382.59	
Employees' contribution	191.32	
Amount owed by Morse	$191.27	(A)

2. STATE UNEMPLOYMENT

3.5% ×	$3,270	=	$114.45	(B)
(rate)	(gross taxable for State Unemployment) (no one has earned more than $4,200)		(amount owed)	

3. FEDERAL UNEMPLOYMENT

.5% ×	$3,270	=	$16.35	(C)
(rate)	(gross taxable for Federal Unemployment)		(amount owed)	

TOTAL PAYROLL TAX EXPENSE FOR MONTH OF FEBRUARY: $322.07

A + B + C

Now let's turn our attention to the completion of the Federal Tax Deposit Ticket paid on March 15.

The deposit for February (FICA + FWT) is exactly the same as January's:

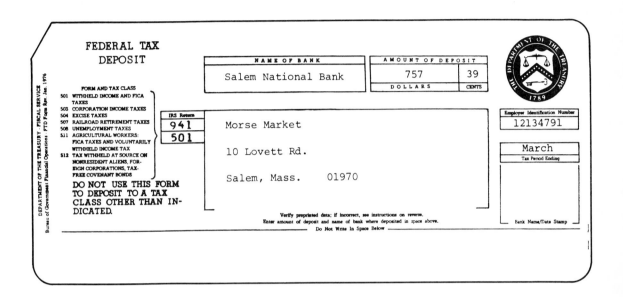

Remember: each deposit ticket involves only total FICA (employee and employer) and FWT.

Here is how Deposit No. 2 was calculated:

Gross pay	$3,270	
Less excess over $15,300	0	= $3,270
Times FICA rate:	.117	
Total FICA	$382.59	
Add FWT	374.80	
Deposit	$757.39	

Once again note that the $757.39 does not involve state or federal unemployment. Let's continue by looking at the employer's payroll taxes for March.

PAYROLL TAXES AT THE END OF MARCH

Each weekly payroll for Morse Market is the same. The only difference is that March has five weeks instead of four. The monthly summary for March from the individual earnings records is as follows:

EMPLOYEE	GROSS	FICA	FWT
MARY BLAKE	$ 625.00	$ 36.55	$ 72.00
ABBY KATZ	150.00	8.80	–0–
MORRIS LESTER	1,500.00*	87.75†	228.00‡
BURTON POUND	562.50	32.90	5.50
JAMES RYAN	1,250.00	73.15	163.00
	$4,087.50	$239.15	$468.50

*5 wks. × $300.

†5 wks. × $17.55.

‡5 wks. × $45.60.

EMPLOYER'S PAYROLL TAX EXPENSE FOR MARCH

Gross earnings for March is $4,087.50.

1. FICA

$4,087.50 ×	11.7%	=	$478.24
(gross)	(FICA rate)		(total due FICA)

Total FICA due $478.24

Employees' contribution   239.15

Amount owed by Morse $239.09

2. STATE UNEMPLOYMENT:

3.5% ×	$4,087.50	=	$143.06
(rate)	(gross taxable for State Unemployment)		(amount owed)

3. FEDERAL UNEMPLOYMENT

.5% ×	$4,087.50	=	$20.44
(rate)	(gross taxable for Federal Unemployment)		(amount owed)

Ⓒ

TOTAL PAYROLL EXPENSE FOR MONTH OF MARCH: $402.59

A + B + C

The following deposit is for FICA and FWT made on April 15:*

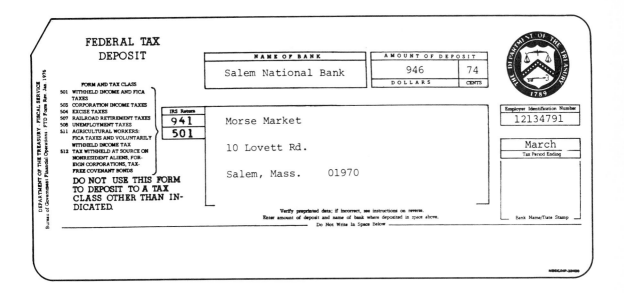

Deposit No. 3 was calculated this way:

Gross pay		$4,087.50
Less excess over $15,300	0	= $4,087.50
Times FICA rate		.117
Total FICA		$478.24
Add FWT		468.50
Deposit		$946.74

COMPLETION OF FORM 941

March ends the first quarter (13 weeks) of the calendar year (January 1–December 31). At the end of each quarter Morse Market is required to complete form 941, the Employer's Quarterly Federal Tax Return. This form must be filed by the end of the month that follows each quarter. In Morse's case, this report must be filed by April 30. Adding up the quarterly summary of each employee from the individual records gives the following results:

*This last deposit could be made at the same time Form 941 is completed (by April 30).

EMPLOYEE	TAXABLE FICA WAGES	FICA	FWT
BLAKE	$ 1,625.00	$ 95.03	$ 187.20
KATZ	390.00	22.88	–0–
LESTER	3,900.00	228.15	592.80
POUND	1,462.50	85.54	14.30
RYAN	3,250.00	190.19	423.80
	$10,627.50	$621.79	$1,218.10

Let's look at Lester to see how information was obtained before completing Form 941.

					FIRST QUARTER 19										SECOND QUARTER 19					
W E E K #	L I N E #	HOURS WORKED REG	HOURS WORKED OVER TIME	TOTAL EARNINGS	DED. FED OLD AGE	DED. WITH. HOLDING TAX	DED. STATE TAX			NET PAY	W E E K #	L I N E #	HOURS WORKED REG	HOURS WORKED OVER TIME	TOTAL EARNINGS	DED. FED OLD AGE	DED. WITH. HOLDING TAX	DED. STATE TAX			NET PAY
1				300.00	17.55	45.60	15.00			221.85	14										
2				300.00	17.55	45.60	15.00			221.85	15										
3				300.00	17.55	45.60	15.00			221.85	16										
4				300.00	17.55	45.60	15.00			221.85	17										
5				300.00	17.55	45.60	15.00			221.85	18										
6				300.00	17.55	45.60	15.00			221.85	19										
7				300.00	17.55	45.60	15.00			221.85	20										
8				300.00	17.55	45.60	15.00			221.85	21										
9				300.00	17.55	45.60	15.00			221.85	22										
10				300.00	17.55	45.60	15.00			221.85	23										
11				300.00	17.55	45.60	15.00			221.85	24										
12				300.00	17.55	45.60	15.00			221.85	25										
13				300.00	17.55	45.60	15.00			221.85	26										
TOTAL 1ST QTR				3,900.00	228.15	592.80	195.			2,884.05	TOTAL 2ND QTR										
TOTAL 3 MOS				3,900.00	228.15	592.80	195.			2,884.05	TOTAL 6 MOS										

			THIRD QUARTER 19							FOURTH QUARTER 19			
W E	L I	HOURS WORKED	TOTAL	DEDUCTIONS FED	DEDUCTIONS WITH		NET	W E	L I	HOURS WORKED	TOTAL	DEDUCTIONS FED WITH	NET

Note that we are only concerned for this report with FICA and FWT. Morse would be required to complete a separate report for SWT, and possibly FUT if the cumulative tax liability was greater than $100.

Periodically changes are made in tax laws and often tax forms are redesigned. Effective January 1978, form 941 was changed to speed up the reporting process. Schedule A was deleted and Schedule B was moved from the back of the form to the front. You will find a sample of the revised form 941 on the inside back cover of this text with instructions for its use. But for purposes of this chapter we will work with the older form in which Schedule A is used.

Form **941**
(Rev. April 19   )
Department of the Treasury
Internal Revenue Service

Employer's Quarterly Federal Tax Return

SSA Use Only

F ☐ 2 ☐ U ☐ E ☐
S ☐ 1 ☐ L ☐ T ☐
X ☐ 0 ☐ V ☐ A ☐

Schedule A—Quarterly Report of Wages Taxable under the Federal Insurance Contributions Act—FOR SOCIAL SECURITY

List for each nonagricultural employee the WAGES taxable under the FICA which were paid during the quarter. If you pay an employee more than $15,300 in a calendar year, report only the first $15,300 of such wages. In the case of "Tip Income," see instructions on page 4. IF WAGES WERE NOT TAXABLE UNDER THE FICA, MAKE NO ENTRIES IN ITEMS 1 THROUGH 9 AND 14 THROUGH 18.

1. Total pages of this return including this page and any pages of Form 941a ▶ 1	2. Total number of employees listed ▶ 5	3. (First quarter only) Number of employees (except household) employed in the pay period including March 12th ▶ 5

4. EMPLOYEE'S SOCIAL SECURITY NUMBER	5. NAME OF EMPLOYEE (Please type or print)	6. TAXABLE FICA WAGES Paid to Employee in Quarter (Before Deductions) Dollars / Cents	7. TAXABLE TIPS REPORTED (See page 4) Dollars / Cents
011 82 1514	Mary Blake	1,625.00	
111 33 2281	Abby Katz	390.00	
021 36 9494	Morris Lester	3,900.00	
223 15 6655	Burton Pound	1,462.50	
999 52 1681	James Ryan	3,250.00	

If you need more space for listing employees, use Schedule A continuation sheets, Form 941a.
Totals for this page—Wage total in column 6 and tip total in column 7 ⟶ | 10,627.50 | None

8. TOTAL WAGES TAXABLE UNDER FICA PAID DURING QUARTER. $ 10,627.50   ◁

(Total of column 6 on this page and continuation sheets.) Enter here and in item 14 below.

9. TOTAL TAXABLE TIPS REPORTED UNDER FICA DURING QUARTER. $ None   ◁

(Total of column 7 on this page and continuation sheets.) Enter here and in item 15 below. (If no tips reported, write "None.")

Employer's name, address, employer identification number, and calendar quarter. (If not correct, please change)

Name (as distinguished from trade name)
▶ John Morse
Date quarter ended
March 31, 19XX

Trade name, if any
▶ Morse Market
Employer Identification No.
12 134791

Address and ZIP code
10 Lovett Rd., Salem, Mass.   01970

Entries must be made both above and below this line; if address different from previous return, check here ☐

Name (as distinguished from trade name)
▶ John Morse
Date quarter ended
March 31, 19XX

Trade name, if any
▶ Morse Market
Employer Identification No.
12 134791

Address and ZIP code
10 Lovett Rd., Salem, Mass.   01970

T		FP	
FF		I	
FD		TOT	

10. Total Wages And Tips Subject to Withholding Plus Other Compensation . . . . . ⟶	10,627	50
11. Amount Of Income Tax Withheld From Wages, Tips, Annuities, etc. (See instructions)	1,218	10
12. Adjustment For Preceding Quarters Of Calendar Year		
13. Adjusted Total Of Income Tax Withheld . . . . ⟶	1,218	10
14. Taxable FICA Wages Paid (Item 8) . . $ 10,627.50 _____ multiplied by 11.7%=TAX	1,243	42
15. Taxable Tips Reported (Item 9) . . . $ _____ multiplied by 5.85%=TAX		
16. Total FICA Taxes (Item 14 plus Item 15) . . . . ⟶	1,243	42
17. Adjustment (See instructions)		
18. Adjusted Total Of FICA Taxes . . . . ⟶	1,243	42
19. Total Taxes (Item 13 plus Item 18) . . . . ⟶	2,461	52
20. TOTAL DEPOSITS FOR QUARTER (INCLUDING FINAL DEPOSIT MADE FOR QUARTER) AND OVERPAYMENT FROM PREVIOUS QUARTER LISTED IN SCHEDULE B (See instructions on page 4)	2,461	52

Note: If undeposited taxes at the end of the quarter are $200 or more, the full amount must be deposited with an authorized commercial bank or a Federal Reserve bank in accordance with instructions on the reverse of the Federal tax deposit form. This deposit must be entered in Schedule B and included in item 20.

21. Undeposited Taxes Due (Item 19 Less Item 20—This Should Be Less Than $200). Pay To Internal Revenue Service And Enter Here . . . .

22. If Item 20 is More Than Item 19, Enter Excess Here ▶ $ _____ And Check If You Want It ☐ Applied to Next Return, Or ☐ Refunded.

23. If not liable for returns in the future, write "FINAL" (See instructions) ▶ _____ Date final wages paid ▶

Under penalties of perjury, I declare that I have examined this return, including accompanying schedules and statements, and to the best of my knowledge and belief it is true, correct, and complete.

Date   April 15, 19XX _____ Signature   John Morse _____ Title (Owner, etc.) _____ Owner

Form 941 (4-76)

Notice that the employer's name is written twice. The form was perforated; the top half was sent to the Social Security Administration to update FICA contributions by employees, and the bottom half is for the Internal Revenue Service. Refer to the inside back cover for changes in procedure.

Notice how the summary information we have prepared is placed on the form.

SCHEDULE B—RECORD OF FEDERAL TAX DEPOSITS

Deposit period ending:	A. Tax liability for period	B. Amount deposited	C. Date of deposit
Overpayment from previous quarter	/////////		/////////
First month of quarter — 1st through 7th day			
First month of quarter — 8th through 15th day			
First month of quarter — 16th through 22d day			
First month of quarter — 23d through last day			
1 First month total . . . . [1]	757.39	757.39	2/15/XX
Second month of quarter — 1st through 7th day			
Second month of quarter — 8th through 15th day			
Second month of quarter — 16th through 22d day			
Second month of quarter — 23d through last day			
2 Second month total . . . . [2]	757.39	757.39	3/15/XX
Third month of quarter — 1st through 7th day			
Third month of quarter — 8th through 15th day			
Third month of quarter — 16th through 22d day			
Third month of quarter — 23d through last day			
3 Third month total . . . . [3]	946.74	946.74	4/15/XX
4 Total for quarter (total of items 1, 2, and 3)	2,461.52	2,461.52	/////////
5 Final deposit made for quarter. (Enter zero if the final deposit made for the quarter is included in item 4.)		−0−	
6 Total deposits for quarter (total of items 4 and 5)—enter here and in item 20, page 1		2,461.52	/////////

The deposits made by Morse equal the total amount due. Also notice that no employee for Morse has earned more than $15,300. Thus all wages and salaries were FICA taxable.

$ 757.39 for January
757.39 for February
946.74 for March
$2,461.52 for Quarter

At this point you should be able to:

1. Explain the purpose and contents of a federal tax deposit.
2. Explain how monthly earnings figures for earnings, FICA, FWT, and so on, are obtained for each employee to arrive at a monthly summary.
3. Explain the relationship of 11.7% to FICA.
4. Calculate state unemployment tax from the monthly summary.
5. Calculate federal unemployment tax.
6. List the months that make up each quarter of payroll.
7. At end of each quarter summarize each employee's earning records and complete Form 941, Employer's Quarterly Federal Tax Return.

UNIT INTERACTOR 36

Based on the following information, complete Form 941 (excluding the schedule on the back) for the first quarter for John's Flowers, 1 Main St., Salem, Mass. 01970.

1. Summary of employees' earnings and deductions:

EMPLOYEE	SOCIAL SECURITY NUMBER	EARNINGS FOR QUARTER	FICA	INCOME TAX WITHHELD
RAY BLESS	031 22 8132	$ 1,462.50	$ 85.54	$ 14.30
SMALL FRANK	666 55 4444	390.00	22.88	-0-
JOHN RIBLE	218 82 5491	1,625.00	95.03	187.20
BILL SMITH	023 33 4871	3,900.00	228.15	592.80
LESS SMOKE	810 29 2983	3,250.00	190.19	423.80
		$10,627.50*	$621.79	$1,218.10

*The total earnings of $10,627.50 were taxable FICA wages, since no individual employee earned more than $15,300.

2. Schedule of deposits by John's Flowers:

Month	Deposit	Amount
January	Feb. 15	$757.39
February	Mar. 15	757.39
March	Apr. 15	946.74

3. John Smith is the owner of John's Flowers. The employer's identification number is 18153891.

Form **941**
(Rev. April 19)
Department of the Treasury
Internal Revenue Service

Employer's Quarterly
Federal Tax Return

Schedule A—Quarterly Report of Wages Taxable under the Federal Insurance Contributions Act—FOR SOCIAL SECURITY

List for each nonagricultural employee the WAGES taxable under the FICA which were paid during the quarter. If you pay an employee more than $15,300 in a calendar year, report only the first $15,300 of such wages. In the case of "Tip Income," see instructions on page 4. IF WAGES WERE NOT TAXABLE UNDER THE FICA, MAKE NO ENTRIES IN ITEMS 1 THROUGH 9 AND 14 THROUGH 18.

SSA Use Only

F ☐ 2 ☐ U ☐ E ☐
S ☐ 1 ☐ L ☐ T ☐
X ☐ 0 ☐ V ☐ A ☐

1. Total pages of this return including this page and any pages of Form 941a ▶	2. Total number of employees listed ▶	3. (First quarter only) Number of employees (except household) employed in the pay period including March 12th ▶
1	5	5

4. EMPLOYEE'S SOCIAL SECURITY NUMBER 000 00 0000	5. NAME OF EMPLOYEE (Please type or print) ▼	6. TAXABLE FICA WAGES Paid to Employee in Quarter (Before Deductions) ▼ Dollars Cents	7. TAXABLE TIPS REPORTED (See page 4) Dollars Cents
031 22 8132	Ray Bless	1,462.50	
666 55 4444	Small Frank	390.00	
218 82 5491	John Rible	1,625.00	
023 33 4871	Bill Smith	3,900.00	
810 29 2983	Less Smoke	3,250.00	

If you need more space for listing employees, use Schedule A continuation sheets, Form 941a.
Totals for this page—Wage total in column 6 and tip total in column 7 ⟶ **10,627.50**   None

8. TOTAL WAGES TAXABLE UNDER FICA PAID DURING QUARTER. $ 10,627.50   ◁
(Total of column 6 on this page and continuation sheets.) Enter here and in item 14 below.

9. TOTAL TAXABLE TIPS REPORTED UNDER FICA DURING QUARTER. $ None   ◁
(Total of column 7 on this page and continuation sheets.) Enter here and in item 15 below. (If no tips reported, write "None.")

Employer's name, address, employer identification number, and calendar quarter. (If not correct, please change)

Name (as distinguished from trade name)
▶ John Smith
Trade name, if any
John's Flowers
Address and ZIP code
1 Main St., Salem, Mass. 01970

Date quarter ended
March 31, 19XX
Employer Identification No.
18 153891

Entries must be made both above and below this line; if address different from previous return, check here ☐

Name (as distinguished from trade name)
▶ John Smith
Trade name, if any
John's Flowers
Address and ZIP code
1 Main St., Salem, Mass. 01970

Date quarter ended
March 31, 19XX
Employer Identification No.
18 153891

	T		FP
FF		I	
FD		TOT	

10. Total Wages And Tips Subject to Withholding Plus Other Compensation . . . . . ⟶	10,627	50
11. Amount Of Income Tax Withheld From Wages, Tips, Annuities, etc. (See instructions)	1,218	10
12. Adjustment For Preceding Quarters Of Calendar Year		
13. Adjusted Total Of Income Tax Withheld . . . . ⟶	1,218	10
14. Taxable FICA Wages Paid (Item 8) . . $ 10,627.50 .... multiplied by 11.7% = TAX	1,243	42
15. Taxable Tips Reported (Item 9) . . . $ .... multiplied by 5.85% = TAX		
16. Total FICA Taxes (Item 14 plus Item 15) . . . . ⟶	1,243	42
17. Adjustment (See instructions)		
18. Adjusted Total Of FICA Taxes . . . . ⟶	1,243	42
19. Total Taxes (Item 13 plus Item 18) . . . . ⟶	2,461	52
20. TOTAL DEPOSITS FOR QUARTER (INCLUDING FINAL DEPOSIT MADE FOR QUARTER) AND OVERPAYMENT FROM PREVIOUS QUARTER LISTED IN SCHEDULE B (See instructions on page 4)	2,461	52

Note: If undeposited taxes at the end of the quarter are $200 or more, the full amount must be deposited with an authorized commercial bank or a Federal Reserve bank in accordance with instructions on the reverse of the Federal tax deposit form. This deposit must be entered in Schedule B and included in item 20.

21. Undeposited Taxes Due (Item 19 Less Item 20—This Should Be Less Than $200). Pay To Internal Revenue Service And Enter Here ▶

22. If Item 20 is More Than Item 19, Enter Excess Here ▶ $ And Check If You Want It ☐ Applied to Next Return, Or ☐ Refunded.

23. If not liable for returns in the future, write "FINAL" (See instructions) ▶   Date final wages paid ▶

Under penalties of perjury, I declare that I have examined this return, including accompanying schedules and statements, and to the best of my knowledge and belief it is true, correct, and complete.

Date April 15, 19XX   Signature John Smith   Title (Owner, etc.) Owner

Form 941 (4-76)

LEARNING UNIT 37

Second-Quarter Payroll

PAYROLL TAXES AT THE END OF APRIL

Here is the monthly payroll summary for April.

EMPLOYEE	GROSS	FICA	FWT
MARY BLAKE	$ 500.00	$ 29.24	$ 57.60
ABBY KATZ	120.00	7.04	–0–
MORRIS LESTER	1,200.00	70.20	182.40
BURTON POUND	450.00	26.32	4.40
JAMES RYAN	1,000.00	58.52	130.40
	$3,270.00	$191.32	$374.80

EMPLOYER'S PAYROLL TAX EXPENSE FOR APRIL

Gross earnings for April is $3,270.

1. FICA

$3,270 ×	11.7%	=	$382.59
(gross)	(FICA rate)		(total FICA due)

Total FICA due	$382.59
Employees' contribution	191.32
Amount owed by Morse	$191.27	Ⓐ

2. STATE UNEMPLOYMENT

| 3.5% × | $2,320 | = | $81.20 | Ⓑ
|---|---|---|---|
| (rate) | (gross taxable) | | (amount owed) |

Lester and Ryan over $4200 maximum

Gross earnings		$3,270
Exempt:		
Lester	$900	
Ryan	50	– 950
Gross taxable		$2,320

3. FEDERAL UNEMPLOYMENT

| .5% × | $2,320 | = | $11.60 | Ⓒ
|---|---|---|---|
| (rate) | (gross taxable for Federal Unemployment) | | (amount owed) |

TOTAL PAYROLL EXPENSE FOR MONTH OF APRIL: $284.07

A + B + C

Notice that Lester's earnings for the year thus far (17 weeks at $300) amount to $5,100, which is $900 over the $4,200 taxable for state and federal unemployment. Ryan has earned a total of $4,250, or $50 over the taxable amount. This does not affect the following federal tax deposit, which involves FICA and FWT. In this case, if some worker had earned cumulative wages of more than $15,300, both the employee and employer would have contributed less. Now let's complete the Federal Tax Deposit Ticket on May 15 for April FICA and FWT.

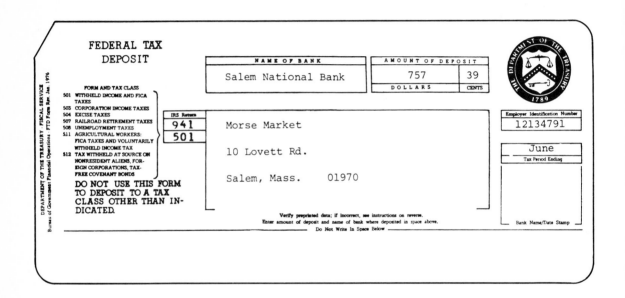

The calculation for Deposit No. 4 follows:

Gross pay	$3,270
Less excess over $15,300	0 = $3,270
Times FICA rate	.117
Total FICA	$382.59
Add FWT	374.80
Deposit	$757.39

Please note no employee for Morse has earned more than the maximum ($15,300). Thus all wages are FICA taxable ($3,270 × .117). Now let's go on to May.

The payroll summary for May follows.

EMPLOYEE	GROSS	FICA	FWT
MARY BLAKE	$ 500.00	$ 29.24	$ 57.60
ABBY KATZ	120.00	7.04	–0–
MORRIS LESTER	1,200.00	70.20	182.40
BURTON POUND	450.00	26.32	4.40
JAMES RYAN	1,000.00	58.52	130.40
	$3,270.00	$191.32	$374.80

EMPLOYER'S PAYROLL TAX EXPENSE FOR MAY

Gross earnings for May is $3,270.

1. FICA

$3,270 × 11.7% = $382.59
(gross   (FICA rate)   (total FICA due)
subject to
  FICA)

Total FICA due	$382.59
Employees' contribution	191.32
Amount owed by Morse	$191.27

Ⓐ———————————→

2. STATE UNEMPLOYMENT*

3.5% × $1,070 = $37.45   Ⓑ———————————→
(rate)   (gross)   (amount owed)

Total gross		$3,270
Exempt:		
Lester	$1,200	
Ryan	1,000	2,200
Gross taxable		$1,070

3. FEDERAL UNEMPLOYMENT*

.5% × $1,070 = $5.35   Ⓒ———————————→
(rate)   (gross)   (amount owed)

TOTAL PAYROLL EXPENSE FOR MONTH OF MAY: $234.07

A + B + C ←

*Note that state and federal unemployment taxes are decreasing for Morse, since Lester and Ryan have earned more than $4200.

The following tax ticket was paid on June 15.

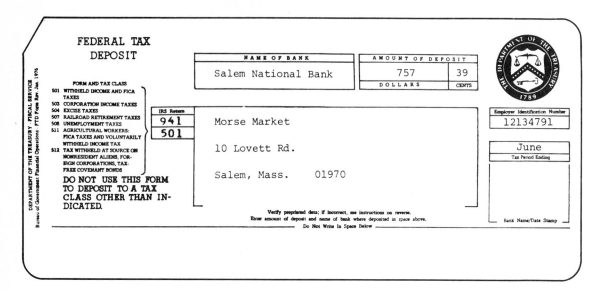

Here is the calculation for Deposit No. 5:

Gross pay	$3,270
Less excess over 15,300	0 = $3,270
Times FICA rate	.117
Total FICA	$382.59
Add FWT	374.80
Deposit	$757.39

Let's now move on to the employer's payroll taxes for June.

PAYROLL TAXES AT THE END OF JUNE

June is a five-week month. The payroll summary follows:

EMPLOYEE	GROSS	FICA	FWT
MARY BLAKE	$ 625.00	$ 36.55	$ 72.00
ABBY KATZ	150.00	8.80	–0–
MORRIS LESTER	1,500.00	87.75	228.00
BURTON POUND	562.50	32.90	5.50
JAMES RYAN	1,250.00	73.15	163.00
	$4,087.50	$239.15	$468.50

EMPLOYER'S PAYROLL TAX EXPENSE FOR JUNE

Gross earnings for June is $4,087.50.

1. FICA

$$\begin{array}{ccc} \$4,087.50 \times & 11.7\% & = & \$478.24 \\ \text{(gross)} & \text{(FICA rate)} & & \text{(total FICA due)} \end{array}$$

Total FICA due	$478.24
Employees' contribution	239.15
Amount owed by Morse	$239.09

(A) ─────────────────────────────→

2. STATE UNEMPLOYMENT

$$\begin{array}{ccc} 3.5\% \times & \$1,337.50 & = & \$46.81 \\ \text{(rate)} & \text{(gross)} & & \text{(amount owed)} \end{array}$$

(B) ─────────────────────────────→

Total gross		$4,087.50
Exempt:		
Lester	$1,500	
Ryan	1,250	2,750.00
Gross taxable		$1,337.50

3. FEDERAL UNEMPLOYMENT

$$\begin{array}{ccc} .5\% \times & \$1,337.50 & = & \$6.69 \\ \text{(rate)} & \text{(gross)} & & \text{(amount owed)} \end{array}$$

(C) ─────────────────────────────→

TOTAL PAYROLL EXPENSE FOR MONTH OF JUNE: $292.59

A + B + C ←

Now let's complete the deposit for FICA and FWT.

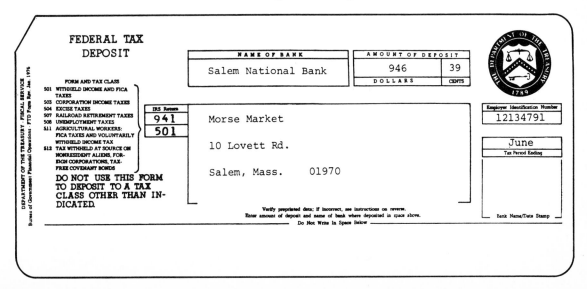

Employer's Quarterly Federal Tax Return

SSA Use Only

Schedule A—Quarterly Report of Wages Taxable under the Federal Insurance Contributions Act—FOR SOCIAL SECURITY

List for each nonagricultural employee the WAGES taxable under the FICA which were paid during the quarter. If you pay an employee more than $15,300 in a calendar year, report only the first $15,300 of such wages. In the case of "Tip Income," see instructions on page 4. IF WAGES WERE NOT TAXABLE UNDER THE FICA, MAKE NO ENTRIES IN ITEMS 1 THROUGH 9 AND 14 THROUGH 18.

F ☐ 2   ☐   E ☐
S ☐ 1   ☐ L   ☐ T ☐
X ☐ 0   ☐ V   ☐ A ☐

1. Total pages of this return including this page and any pages of Form 941a ▶	2. Total number of employees listed ▶	3. (First quarter only) Number of employees (except household) employed in the pay period including March 12th ▶
1	5	5

4. EMPLOYEE'S SOCIAL SECURITY NUMBER	5. NAME OF EMPLOYEE (Please type or print)	6. TAXABLE FICA WAGES Paid to Employee in Quarter (Before Deductions) Dollars / Cents	7. TAXABLE TIPS REPORTED (See page 4) Dollars / Cents
011 82 1514	Mary Blake	1,625.00	
111 33 2281	Abby Katz	390.00	
021 36 9494	Morris Lester	3,900.00	
223 15 6655	Burton Pound	1,462.50	
999 52 1681	James Ryan	3,250.00	

If you need more space for listing employees, use Schedule A continuation sheets, Form 941a.

Totals for this page—Wage total in column 6 and tip total in column 7 ⟶ **10,627.50** **None**

8. TOTAL WAGES TAXABLE UNDER FICA PAID DURING QUARTER. $ 10,627.50 ◁

(Total of column 6 on this page and continuation sheets.) Enter here and in item 14 below.

9. TOTAL TAXABLE TIPS REPORTED UNDER FICA DURING QUARTER. $ None ◁

(Total of column 7 on this page and continuation sheets.) Enter here and in item 15 below. (If no tips reported, write "None.")

Employer's name, address, employer identification number, and calendar quarter. (If not correct, please change)

Name (as distinguished from trade name)
John Morse
Trade name, if any
▶ Morse Market
Address and ZIP code
10 Lovett Rd., Salem, Mass 01970

Date quarter ended
June 30, 19XX
Employer Identification No.
12 134791

Entries must be made both above and below this line; if address different from previous return, check here ☐

Name (as distinguished from trade name)
John Morse
Trade name, if any
▶ Morse Market
Address and ZIP code
10 Lovett Rd., Salem, Mass. 01970

Date quarter ended
June 30, 19XX
Employer Identification No.
12 134791

T	FP
FF	I
FD	TOT

10. Total Wages And Tips Subject to Withholding Plus Other Compensation . . . . . ⟶	10,627	50
11. Amount Of Income Tax Withheld From Wages, Tips, Annuities, etc. (See instructions)	1,218	10
12. Adjustment For Preceding Quarters Of Calendar Year		
13. Adjusted Total Of Income Tax Withheld . . . . ⟶	1,218	10
14. Taxable FICA Wages Paid (Item 8) . . $ 10,627.50 . . . multiplied by 11.7% = TAX	1,243	42
15. Taxable Tips Reported (Item 9) . . . $ . . . . . . multiplied by 5.85% = TAX		
16. Total FICA Taxes (Item 14 plus Item 15) . . . . ⟶	1,243	42
17. Adjustment (See instructions)		
18. Adjusted Total Of FICA Taxes . . . . ⟶	1,243	42
19. Total Taxes (Item 13 plus Item 18)	2,461	52
20. TOTAL DEPOSITS FOR QUARTER (INCLUDING FINAL DEPOSIT MADE FOR QUARTER) AND OVERPAYMENT FROM PREVIOUS QUARTER LISTED IN SCHEDULE B (See instructions on page 4)	2,461	52

Note: If undeposited taxes at the end of the quarter are $200 or more, the full amount must be deposited with an authorized commercial bank or a Federal Reserve bank in accordance with instructions on the reverse of the Federal tax deposit form. This deposit must be entered in Schedule B and included in item 20.

21. Undeposited Taxes Due (Item 19 Less Item 20—This Should Be Less Than $200). Pay To Internal Revenue Service And Enter Here . . . .

22. If Item 20 is More Than Item 19, Enter Excess Here ▶ $ _____ And Check If You Want It ☐ Applied to Next Return, Or ☐ Refunded.

23. If not liable for returns in the future, write "FINAL" (See instructions) ▶ _____ Date final wages paid ▶ _____

Under penalties of perjury, I declare that I have examined this return, including accompanying schedules and statements, and to the best of my knowledge and belief it is true, correct, and complete.

Date July 15, 19XX   Signature John Morse   Title (Owner, etc.) Owner

The calculations for Deposit No. 6 follow:

Gross pay		$4,087.50
Less excess over $15,300		0 = $4,087.50
Times FICA rate		.117
Total FICA		$478.24
Add FWT		468.50
Deposit		$946.74

COMPLETION OF FORM 941

Form 941, completed for Morse Market for the second quarter, is shown on the opposite page.

Once again note that no employee has earned more than $15,300; thus lines 8 and 10 are the same.

At this point, you should be able to:

1. Calculate employer's payroll taxes for the second quarter.
2. Prepare federal tax deposit tickets.
3. Complete the Employer's Quarterly Federal Tax Return.
4. Identify when earnings for federal unemployment and state unemployment become exempt.

UNIT INTERACTOR 37

Reproduced here are the first two quarterly individual earnings records for Lester and Ryan. Please circle the point at which the earnings of each became exempt from state and federal unemployment taxes. Give a brief explanation for each.

NAME OF EMPLOYEE	Jim Ryan		SOCIAL SECURITY NUMBER	999-52-1681

ADDRESS	10 Sable Rd.	CITY OR TOWN	Salem, MA 01917

DATE OF BIRTH		MARRIED ☒ OR SINGLE ☐	NUMBER OF EXEMPTIONS 2	PHONE NO.	CLOCK NO.

POSITION	Stock Room	RATE $250/wk	DATE	DATE STARTED 1/1/XX	DATE TERMINATED

REMARKS		REASON	

FIRST QUARTER 19 / SECOND QUARTER 19

WEEK #	HOURS WORKED REG	OVER TIME	TOTAL EARNINGS	FED OLD AGE	WITH. HOLDING TAX	STATE TAX		NET PAY	WEEK #	HOURS WORKED REG	OVER TIME	TOTAL EARNINGS	FED OLD AGE	WITH. HOLDING TAX	STATE TAX		NET PAY
1			250.00	14.63	32.60	12.50		190.27	14			250.00	14.63	32.60	12.50		190.27
2			250.00	14.63	32.60	12.50		190.27	15			250.00	14.63	32.60	12.50		190.27
3			250.00	14.63	32.60	12.50		190.27	16			250.00	14.63	32.60	12.50		190.27
4			250.00	14.63	32.60	12.50		190.27	17			250.00	14.63	32.60	12.50		190.27
5			250.00	14.63	32.60	12.50		190.27	18			250.00	14.63	32.60	12.50		190.27
6			250.00	14.63	32.60	12.50		190.27	19			250.00	14.63	32.60	12.50		190.27
7			250.00	14.63	32.60	12.50		190.27	20			250.00	14.63	32.60	12.50		190.27
8			250.00	14.63	32.60	12.50		190.27	21			250.00	14.63	32.60	12.50		190.27
9			250.00	14.63	32.60	12.50		190.27	22			250.00	14.63	32.60	12.50		190.27
10			250.00	14.63	32.60	12.50		190.27	23			250.00	14.63	32.60	12.50		190.27
11			250.00	14.63	32.60	12.50		190.27	24			250.00	14.63	32.60	12.50		190.27
12			250.00	14.63	32.60	12.50		190.27	25			250.00	14.63	32.60	12.50		190.27
13			250.00	14.63	32.60	12.50		190.27	26			250.00	14.63	32.60	12.50		190.27
TOTAL 1ST QTR			3,250.00	190.19	423.80	162.50		2,473.51	TOTAL 2ND QTR			3,250.00	190.19	423.80	162.50		2,473.51
TOTAL 3 MOS			3,250.00	190.19	423.80	162.50		2,473.51	TOTAL 6 MOS			6,500.00	380.38	847.60	325.00		4,947.02

THIRD QUARTER 19 / FOURTH QUARTER 19

SOLUTION to Unit Interactor 37

NAME OF EMPLOYEE	Morris Lester		SOCIAL SECURITY NUMBER	021-36-9494

ADDRESS	15 Bone Drive	CITY OR TOWN	Appleyard, MA 01932

DATE OF BIRTH		MARRIED ☒ OR SINGLE ☐	NUMBER OF EXEMPTIONS 1	PHONE NO.	CLOCK NO.

POSITION	Office Mgr.	RATE $300/wk	DATE	DATE STARTED 1/1/XX	DATE TERMINATED

REMARKS		REASON	

FIRST QUARTER 19 / SECOND QUARTER 19

WEEK #	HOURS WORKED REG	OVER TIME	TOTAL EARNINGS	FED OLD AGE	WITH. HOLDING TAX	STATE TAX		NET PAY	WEEK #	HOURS WORKED REG	OVER TIME	TOTAL EARNINGS	FED OLD AGE	WITH. HOLDING TAX	STATE TAX		NET PAY
1			300.00	17.55	45.60	15.00		221.85	14			300.00	17.55	45.60	15.00		221.85
2			300.00	17.55	45.60	15.00		221.85	⑮			300.00	17.55	45.60	15.00		221.85
3			300.00	17.55	45.60	15.00		221.85	16			300.00	17.55	45.60	15.00		221.85
4			300.00	17.55	45.60	15.00		221.85	17			300.00	17.55	45.60	15.00		221.85
5			300.00	17.55	45.60	15.00		221.85	18			300.00	17.55	45.60	15.00		221.85
6			300.00	17.55	45.60	15.00		221.85	19			300.00	17.55	45.60	15.00		221.85
7			300.00	17.55	45.60	15.00		221.85	20			300.00	17.55	45.60	15.00		221.85
8			300.00	17.55	45.60	15.00		221.85	21			300.00	17.55	45.60	15.00		221.85
9			300.00	17.55	45.60	15.00		221.85	22			300.00	17.55	45.60	15.00		221.85
10			300.00	17.55	45.60	15.00		221.85	23			300.00	17.55	45.60	15.00		221.85
11			300.00	17.55	45.60	15.00		221.85	24			300.00	17.55	45.60	15.00		221.85
12			300.00	17.55	45.60	15.00		221.85	25			300.00	17.55	45.60	15.00		221.85
13			300.00	17.55	45.60	15.00		221.85	26			300.00	17.55	45.60	15.00		221.85
TOTAL 1ST QTR			3,900.00	228.15	592.80	195.		2,884.05	TOTAL 2ND QTR			3,900.00	228.15	592.80	195.		2,884.05
TOTAL 3 MOS			3,900.00	228.15	592.80	195.		2,884.05	TOTAL 6 MOS			7,800.00	456.30	1,185.60	390.		5,768.10

THIRD QUARTER 19 / FOURTH QUARTER 19

EXPLANATION: After week 14 Morris Lester has earned $4,200. All earnings over $4,200 are exempt from federal and state unemployment taxes.

NAME OF EMPLOYEE	Jim Ryan							SOCIAL SECURITY NUMBER	999-52-1681		
ADDRESS	10 Sable Rd.							CITY OR TOWN	Salem, MA 01917		
DATE OF BIRTH		MARRIED ☒ OR SINGLE ☐	NUMBER OF EXEMPTIONS 2					PHONE NO.		CLOCK NO.	
POSITION Stock Room		RATE $250/wk		DATE				DATE STARTED 1/1/XX		DATE TERMINATED	
REMARKS								REASON			

	FIRST QUARTER 19									SECOND QUARTER 19								
WEEK #	LINE #	HOURS WORKED REG	OVER TIME	TOTAL EARNINGS	FED OLD AGE	WITH. HOLDING TAX	STATE TAX			NET PAY	WEEK #	LINE #	HOURS WORKED REG	OVER TIME	TOTAL EARNINGS	FED OLD AGE	WITH. HOLDING TAX	STATE TAX			NET PAY
1				250 00	14.63	32 60	12.50			190 27	14				250 00	14.63	32 60	12.50			190 27
2				250 00	14.63	32 60	12.50			190 27	15				250 00	14.63	32 60	12.50			190 27
3				250 00	14.63	32 60	12.50			190 27	16				250 00	14.63	32 60	12.50			190 27
4				250 00	14.63	32 60	12.50			190 27	⑰				250 00	14.63	32 60	12.50			190 27
5				250 00	14.63	32 60	12.50			190 27	18				250 00	14.63	32 60	12.50			190 27
6				250 00	14.63	32 60	12.50			190 27	19				250 00	14.63	32 60	12.50			190 27
7				250 00	14.63	32 60	12.50			190 27	20				250 00	14.63	32 60	12.50			190 27
8				250 00	14.63	32 60	12.50			190 27	21				250 00	14.63	32 60	12.50			190 27
9				250 00	14.63	32 60	12.50			190 27	22				250 00	14.63	32 60	12.50			190 27
10				250 00	14.63	32 60	12.50			190 27	23				250 00	14.63	32 60	12.50			190 27
11				250 00	14.63	32 60	12.50			190 27	24				250 00	14.63	32 60	12.50			190 27
12				250 00	14.63	32 60	12.50			190 27	25				250 00	14.63	32 60	12.50			190 27
13				250 00	14.63	32 60	12.50			190 27	26				250 00	14.63	32 60	12.50			190 27
TOTAL 1ST QTR				3,250 00	190.19	423 80	162.50			2,473 51	TOTAL 2ND QTR				3,250 00	190.19	423 80	162.50			2,473 51
TOTAL 3 MOS				3,250 00	190.19	423 80	162.50			2,473 51	TOTAL 6 MOS				6,500 00	380.38	847 60	325.00			4,947 02
	THIRD QUARTER 19											FOURTH QUARTER 19									

EXPLANATION: In week 17, Jim's cumulative earnings reach $4,250; $50 of week 17 earnings is exempt. Weeks 18 and on are exempt from federal and state employment taxes.

LEARNING UNIT 38

Third-Quarter Payroll

PAYROLL TAXES AT THE END OF JULY

Again we use the payroll summary, calculating the needed FICA and FWT figures from the individual earnings records.

EMPLOYEE	GROSS	FICA	FWT
MARY BLAKE	$ 500.00	$ 29.24	$ 57.60
ABBY KATZ	120.00	7.04	–0–
MORRIS LESTER	1,200.00	70.20	182.40
BURTON POUND	450.00	26.32	4.40
JAMES RYAN	1,000.00	58.52	130.40
	$3,270.00	$191.32	$374.80

EMPLOYER'S PAYROLL TAX EXPENSE FOR JULY

Gross earnings for July is $3,270.

1. FICA

$3,270.00 ×	11.7%	=	$382.59
(gross)	(FICA rate)		(total FICA due)

Total FICA due	$382.59	
Employees' contribution	191.32	
Amount owed by Morse	$191.27	Ⓐ ⟶

2. STATE UNEMPLOYMENT

3.5% ×	$1,070	=	$37.45	Ⓑ ⟶
(rate)	(gross)		(amount owed)	

Gross		$3,270
Exempt:		
Lester	$1,200	
Ryan	1,000	2,200
Gross taxable		$1,070

3. FEDERAL UNEMPLOYMENT

.5% ×	$1,070	=	$5.35	Ⓒ ⟶
(rate)	(gross)		(amount owed)	

TOTAL PAYROLL EXPENSE FOR MONTH OF JULY: $234.07

A + B + C ⟵

Note the total state and federal unemployment paid by Morse is decreasing since Lester and Ryan have earned more than $4,200. Now let's make the deposit for FICA and FWT.

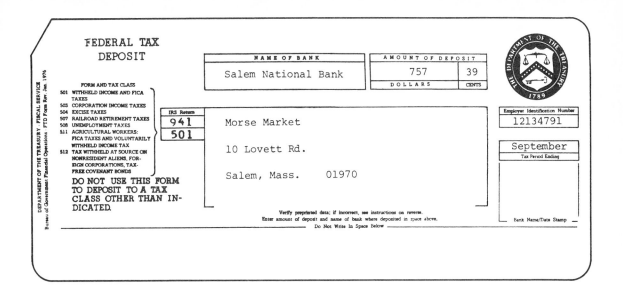

Here are the calculations for Deposit No. 7:

Gross pay	$3,270	
Less excess over $15,300	0 = $3,270	
Times FICA rate	.117	
Total FICA	$382.59	
Add FWT	374.80	
Deposit	$757.39	

On to August we go!

PAYROLL TAXES AT THE END OF AUGUST

The payroll summary for August follows:

EMPLOYEE	GROSS	FICA	FWT
MARY BLAKE	$ 500.00	$ 29.24	$ 57.60
ABBY KATZ	120.00	7.04	–0–
MORRIS LESTER	1,200.00	70.20	182.40
BURTON POUND	450.00	26.32	4.40
JAMES RYAN	1,000.00	58.52	130.40
	$3,270.00	$191.32	$374.80

EMPLOYER'S PAYROLL TAX EXPENSE FOR AUGUST

Gross earnings for August is $3,270.

1. FICA

$3,270.00 ×	11.7%	=	$382.59
(gross)	(FICA rate)		(total FICA due)

Total FICA due	$382.59
Employees' contribution	191.32
Amount owed by Morse	$191.27

(A) ⟶

2. STATE UNEMPLOYMENT

3.5% ×	$1,020	=	$35.70
(rate)	(gross)		(amount owed)

(B) ⟶

Gross		$3,270
Exempt:		
Lester	$1,200	
Ryan	1,000	
Blake	50	2,250
Gross taxable		$1,020

3. FEDERAL UNEMPLOYMENT

.5% ×	$1,020	=	$5.10
(rate)	(gross)		(amount owed)

(C) ⟶

TOTAL PAYROLL EXPENSE FOR MONTH OF AUGUST: $232.07

A + B + C ⟵

Now we will complete the deposit for FICA and FWT.

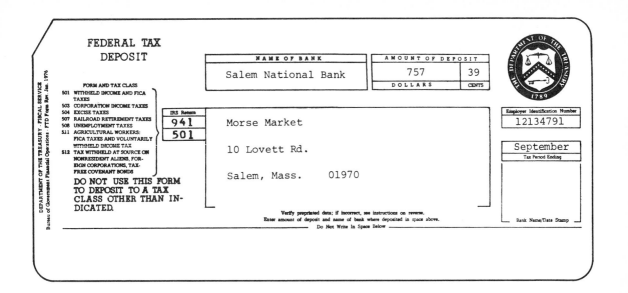

For Deposit No. 8:

Gross pay		$3,270
Less excess over $15,300		0 = $3,270
Times FICA rate		.117
Total FICA		$382.59
Add FWT		374.80
Deposit		$757.39

PAYROLL TAXES AT THE END OF SEPTEMBER

The payroll summary for September is as follows:

EMPLOYEE	GROSS	FICA	FWT
MARY BLAKE	$ 625.00	$ 36.55	$ 72.00
ABBY KATZ	150.00	8.80	–0–
MORRIS LESTER	1,500.00	87.75	228.00
BURTON POUND	562.50	32.90	5.50
JAMES RYAN	1,250.00	73.15	163.00
	$4,087.50	$239.15	$468.50

EMPLOYER'S PAYROLL TAX EXPENSE FOR SEPTEMBER

Gross earnings for September is $4,087.50

1. FICA

$4,087.50 ×	11.7%	=.	$478.24
(gross)	(FICA rate)		(total FICA due)

Total FICA due	$478.24
Employees' contribution	239.15
Amount owed by Morse	$239.09

2. STATE UNEMPLOYMENT

3.5% ×	$525.00	=	$18.38
(rate)	(gross)		(amount owed)

Gross		$4,087.50
Exempt:		
Blake	$ 625	
Lester	1,500	
Pound	187.50	
Ryan	1,250	3,562.50
Gross taxable		$ 525.00

3. FEDERAL UNEMPLOYMENT

.5% ×	$525.00	=	$2.63
(rate)	(gross)		(amount owed)

Ⓒ

TOTAL PAYROLL EXPENSE FOR MONTH OF SEPTEMBER: $260.10

↑

A + B + C ◄

Now let's complete the deposit for FICA and FWT.

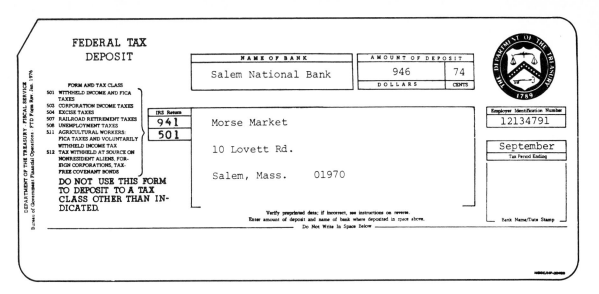

The Deposit No. 9 calculations are:

Gross pay	$4,087.50	
Less excess over $15,300	0	= $4,087.50
Times FICA rate	.117	
Total FICA	$478.24	
Add FWT	468.50	
Deposit	$946.74	

At this point, you should be able to:

1. Calculate employer's payroll taxes for the third quarter.
2. Prepare federal tax deposit tickets.
3. Complete the Employer's Quarterly Federal Tax Return.

UNIT INTERACTOR 38

From the information presented in this unit, as well as in other units in Chapter 15, your task is to complete Form 941, Employer's Quarterly Federal Tax Return, for the period ending September 30. Keep in mind that during the calendar year no employee of Morse has yet earned more than $15,300.

Form **941**
(Rev. April 19)
Department of the Treasury
Internal Revenue Service

Employer's Quarterly Federal Tax Return

Schedule A—Quarterly Report of Wages Taxable under the Federal Insurance Contributions Act—FOR SOCIAL SECURITY

List for each nonagricultural employee the WAGES taxable under the FICA which were paid during the quarter. If you pay an employee more than $15,300 in a calendar year, report only the first $15,300 of such wages. In the case of "Tip Income," see instructions on page 4. IF WAGES WERE NOT TAXABLE UNDER THE FICA, MAKE NO ENTRIES IN ITEMS 1 THROUGH 9 AND 14 THROUGH 18.

SSA Use Only

F ☐	2 ☐	U ☐	E ☐
S ☐	1 ☐	L ☐	T ☐
X ☐	0 ☐	V ☐	A ☐

| 1. Total pages of this return including this page and any pages of Form 941a ▶ 1 | 2. Total number of employees listed ▶ 5 | 3. (First quarter only) Number of employees (except household) employed in the pay period including March 12th ▶ 5 |

4. EMPLOYEE'S SOCIAL SECURITY NUMBER	5. NAME OF EMPLOYEE (Please type or print)	6. TAXABLE FICA WAGES Paid to Employee in Quarter (Before Deductions) Dollars	Cents	7. TAXABLE TIPS REPORTED (See page 4) Dollars	Cents
000 00 0000					
011 82 1514	Mary Blake	1,625.00			
111 33 2281	Abby Katz	390.00			
021 36 9494	Morris Lester	3,900.00			
223 15 6655	Burton Pound	1,462.50			
999 52 1681	James Ryan	3,250.00			

If you need more space for listing employees, use Schedule A continuation sheets, Form 941a.

Totals for this page—Wage total in column 6 and tip total in column 7 ➞ | 10,627.50 | None

8. TOTAL WAGES TAXABLE UNDER FICA PAID DURING QUARTER. $ 10,627.50 ◁

(Total of column 6 on this page and continuation sheets.) Enter here and in item 14 below.

9. TOTAL TAXABLE TIPS REPORTED UNDER FICA DURING QUARTER. $ None ◁

(Total of column 7 on this page and continuation sheets.) Enter here and in item 15 below. (If no tips reported, write "None.")

Employer's name, address, employer identification number, and calendar quarter. (If not correct, please change)

Name (as distinguished from trade name)
▶ John Morse
Trade name, if any
▶ Morse Market
Address and ZIP code
10 Lovett Rd., Salem, Mass. 01970

Date quarter ended
September 30, 19XX
Employer Identification No.
12 134791

Entries must be made both above and below this line; if address different from previous return, check here ☐

Name (as distinguished from trade name)
▶ John Morse
Trade name, if any
▶ Morse Market
Address and ZIP code
10 Lovett Rd., Salem, Mass. 01970

Date quarter ended
September 30, 19XX
Employer Identification No.
12 134791

	T		FP
	FF		I
	FD		

		TOT
10. Total Wages And Tips Subject to Withholding Plus Other Compensation ➞	10,627	50
11. Amount Of Income Tax Withheld From Wages, Tips, Annuities, etc. (See instructions)	1,218	10
12. Adjustment For Preceding Quarters Of Calendar Year		
13. Adjusted Total Of Income Tax Withheld	1,218	10
14. Taxable FICA Wages Paid (Item 8) . . $ 10,627.50 multiplied by 11.7% =TAX	1,243	42
15. Taxable Tips Reported (Item 9) . . . $ multiplied by 5.85% =TAX		
16. Total FICA Taxes (Item 14 plus Item 15) ➞	1,243	42
17. Adjustment (See instructions)		
18. Adjusted Total Of FICA Taxes	1,243	42
19. Total Taxes (Item 13 plus Item 18)	2,461	52
20. TOTAL DEPOSITS FOR QUARTER (INCLUDING FINAL DEPOSIT MADE FOR QUARTER) AND OVERPAYMENT FROM PREVIOUS QUARTER LISTED IN SCHEDULE B (See instructions on page 4)	2,461	52

Note: If undeposited taxes at the end of the quarter are $200 or more, the full amount must be deposited with an authorized commercial bank or a Federal Reserve bank in accordance with instructions on the reverse of the Federal tax deposit form. This deposit must be entered in Schedule B and included in item 20.

21. Undeposited Taxes Due (Item 19 Less Item 20—This Should Be Less Than $200). Pay To Internal Revenue Service And Enter Here

22. If Item 20 is More Than Item 19, Enter Excess Here ▶ $ And Check If You Want It ☐ Applied to Next Return, Or ☐ Refunded.

23. If not liable for returns in the future, write "FINAL" (See instructions) ▶ Date final wages paid ▶

Under penalties of perjury, I declare that I have examined this return, including accompanying schedules and statements, and to the best of my knowledge and belief it is true, correct, and complete.

Date October 15, 19XX Signature John Morse Title (Owner, etc.) Owner

Form 941 (4–76)

LEARNING UNIT 39

Fourth-Quarter Payroll

PAYROLL TAXES AT THE END OF OCTOBER

We begin again with the payroll summary, this time for October.

EMPLOYEE	GROSS	FICA	FWT
MARY BLAKE	$ 500.00	$ 29.24	$ 57.60
ABBY KATZ	120.00	7.04	–0–
MORRIS LESTER	1,200.00	70.20	182.40
BURTON POUND	450.00	26.32	4.40
JAMES RYAN	1,000.00	58.52	130.40
	$3,270.00	$191.32	$374.80

EMPLOYER'S PAYROLL TAX EXPENSE FOR OCTOBER

Gross earnings for October is $3,270.

1. FICA

$3,270.00 ×	11.7%	=	$382.59
(gross)	(FICA rate)		(total FICA due)

Total FICA due	$382.59
Employees' contribution	191.32
Amount owed by Morse	$191.27

 (A)

2. STATE UNEMPLOYMENT

3.5% ×	$120	=	$4.20
(rate)	(gross)		(amount owed)

 (B)

Gross		$3,270.00
Exempt:		
Blake	$ 500	
Lester	1,200	
Pound	450	
Ryan	1,000	3,150.00
Gross taxable		$ 120.00

3. FEDERAL UNEMPLOYMENT

.5% ×	$120	=	$.60
(rate)	(gross)		(amount owed)

(C)

TOTAL PAYROLL EXPENSE FOR MONTH OF OCTOBER: $196.07

A + B + C

Now let's complete the deposit for FICA and FWT, on Nov. 15 for the month of October.

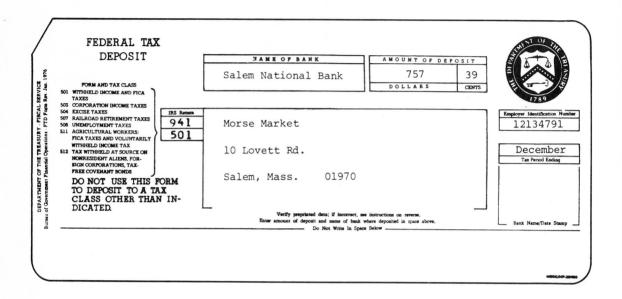

Deposit No. 10 calculations:

Gross pay	$3,270	
Less excess over $15,300	0 = $3,270	
Times FICA rate	.117	
Total FICA	$382.59	
Add FWT	374.80	
Deposit	$757.39	

Now we will work on the taxes for November.

PAYROLL TAXES AT THE END OF NOVEMBER

The payroll summary for November follows:

EMPLOYEE	GROSS	FICA	FWT
MARY BLAKE	$ 500.00	$ 29.24	$ 57.60
ABBY KATZ	120.00	7.04	–0–
MORRIS LESTER	1200.00	70.20	182.40
BURTON POUND	450.00	26.32	4.40
JAMES RYAN	1000.00	58.52	130.40
	$3270.00	$191.32	$374.80

EMPLOYER'S PAYROLL TAX EXPENSE FOR NOVEMBER

Gross earnings for November is $3,270.

1. FICA

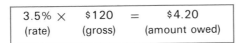

$$\underset{\text{(gross)}}{\$327.0} \times \underset{\text{(FICA rate)}}{11.7\%} = \underset{\text{(total FICA due)}}{\$382.59}$$

Total FICA due	$382.59
Employees' contribution	191.32
Amount owed by Morse	$191.27	Ⓐ

2. STATE UNEMPLOYMENT

$$\underset{\text{(rate)}}{3.5\%} \times \underset{\text{(gross)}}{\$120} = \underset{\text{(amount owed)}}{\$4.20}$$ Ⓑ

Gross		$3,270
Exempt:		
Blake	$ 500	
Lester	1,200	
Pound	450	
Ryan	1,000	3,150
Gross taxable		$ 120

3. FEDERAL UNEMPLOYMENT

$$\underset{\text{(rate)}}{.5\%} \times \underset{\text{(gross)}}{\$120} = \underset{\text{(amount owed)}}{\$.60}$$ Ⓒ

TOTAL PAYROLL EXPENSE FOR MONTH OF NOVEMBER: $196.07

A + B + C

Now let's complete the deposit for FICA and FWT on December 15.

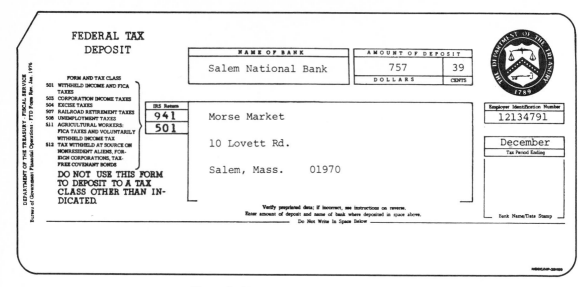

Deposit No. 11:

Gross pay	$3,270	
Less excess over $15,300	0 = $3,270	
Times FICA rate	.117	
Total FICA	$382.59	
Add FWT	374.80	
Deposit	$757.39	

We now come to the last month of the calendar year.

The payroll summary for December (five-week period) follows:

EMPLOYEE	GROSS	FICA	FWT
MARY BLAKE	$ 625.00	$ 36.55	$ 72.00
ABBY KATZ	150.00	8.80	–0–
MORRIS LESTER*	1,500.00	70.20	228.00
BURTON POUND	562.50	32.90	5.50
JAMES RYAN	1,250.00	73.15	163.00
	$4,087.50	$221.60	$468.50

* Notice that Morris Lester's last week salary of $300 is not taxable FICA wages. He has earned $15,300 before the last week's pay.

EMPLOYER'S PAYROLL TAX EXPENSE FOR DECEMBER

Gross earnings for December is $4,087.50.

1. FICA

$3,787.50 ×	11.7%	=	$443.14
(gross)	(FICA rate)		(total FICA due)

Total FICA due	$443.14	
Employees' contribution	221.60	
Amount owed by Morse	$221.54	Ⓐ

Gross	$4,087.50
Exempt	300.00
Gross Taxable	$3,787.50

2. STATE UNEMPLOYMENT

3.5% ×	$150	=	$5.25	Ⓑ
(rate)	(gross)		(amount owed)	

Gross		$4,087.50
Exempt:		
Blake	$ 625	
Lester	1,500	
Pound	562.50	
Ryan	1,250	3,937.50
Gross taxable		$ 150.00

3. FEDERAL UNEMPLOYMENT

.5% ×	$150	=	$.75	Ⓒ
(rate)	(gross)		(amount owed)	

TOTAL PAYROLL EXPENSE FOR MONTH OF DECEMBER: $227.54

A + B + C

Now let's complete the deposit for FICA and FWT.

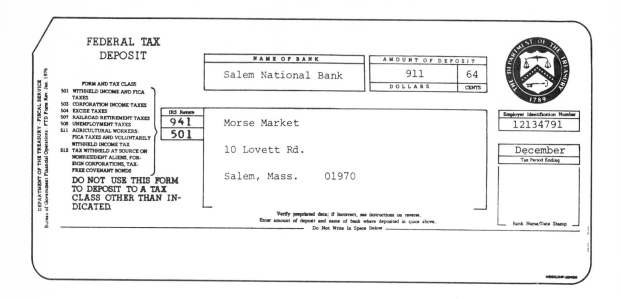

Deposit No. 12:

Gross pay	$4,087.50	
Less excess over $15,300	300.00 =	$3,787.50
Times FICA rate	.117	
Total FICA	$443.14	
Add FWT	468.50	
Deposit	$911.64	

At this point, you should be able to:

1. Calculate employer's payroll taxes for the fourth quarter.
2. Prepare federal tax deposit tickets.
3. Identify when wages are exempt regarding FICA.
4. Complete the Employer's Quarterly Federal Tax Return.

UNIT INTERACTOR 39

From the information in this and other units in this chapter your task is to prepare the quarterly Form 941 for Morse Market, dated January 31, 19XX.

Form **941**
(Rev. April 19   )
Department of the Treasury
Internal Revenue Service

Employer's quarterly Federal Tax Return

SSA·Use Only

Schedule A—Quarterly Report of Wages Taxable under the Federal Insurance Contributions Act—FOR SOCIAL SECURITY

List for each nonagricultural employee the WAGES taxable under the FICA which were paid during the quarter. If you pay an employee more than $15,300 in a calendar year, report only the first $15,300 of such wages. In the case of "Tip Income," see instructions on page 4. IF WAGES WERE NOT TAXABLE UNDER THE FICA, MAKE NO ENTRIES IN ITEMS 1 THROUGH 9 AND 14 THROUGH 18.

F ☐ 2	☐ U	☐ E ☐
S ☐ 1	☐ L	☐ T ☐
X ☐ 0	☐ V	☐ A ☐

1. Total pages of this return including this page and any pages of Form 941a ▶ **1**	2. Total number of employees listed ▶ **5**	3. (First quarter only) Number of employees (except household) employed in the pay period including March 12th ▶

4. EMPLOYEE'S SOCIAL SECURITY NUMBER	5. NAME OF EMPLOYEE (Please type or print)	6. TAXABLE FICA WAGES Paid to Employee in Quarter (Before Deductions) Dollars	Cents	7. TAXABLE TIPS REPORTED (See page 4) Dollars	Cents
000 00 0000	▼	▼			
011 82 1514	Mary Blake	1,625.00			
111 33 2281	Abby Katz	390.00			
021 36 9494	Morris Lester	3,600.00			
223 15 6655	Burton Pound	1,462.50			
999 52 1681	James Ryan	3,250.00			

If you need more space for listing employees, use Schedule A continuation sheets, Form 941a.

Totals for this page—Wage total in column 6 and tip total in column 7 ▶ | 10,327.50 | None

8. TOTAL WAGES TAXABLE UNDER FICA PAID DURING QUARTER. $ 10,327.50   ◁

(Total of column 6 on this page and continuation sheets.) Enter here and in item 14 below.

9. TOTAL TAXABLE TIPS REPORTED UNDER FICA DURING QUARTER. $ None   ◁

(Total of column 7 on this page and continuation sheets.) Enter here and in item 15 below. (If no tips reported, write "None.")

Employer's name, address, employer identification number, and calendar quarter. (If not correct, please change)

Name (as distinguished from trade name)
John Morse

Trade name, if any
▶ Morse Market

Address and ZIP code
10 Lovett Rd. Salem, Mass.   01970

Date quarter ended
Dec. 31, 19XX

Employer Identification No.
12 134791

Entries must be made both above and below this line; if address different from previous return, check here ☐ ....

Name (as distinguished from trade name)
John Morse

Trade name, if any
▶ Morse Market

Address and ZIP code
10 Lovett Rd., Salem, Mass.   01970

Date quarter ended
Dec. 31, 19XX

Employer Identification No.
12 134791

T	FP
FF	I
FD	TOT

10. Total Wages And Tips Subject to Withholding Plus Other Compensation . . . . . ▶	10,627	50
11. Amount Of Income Tax Withheld From Wages, Tips, Annuities, etc. (See instructions)	1,218	10
12. Adjustment For Preceding Quarters Of Calendar Year		
13. Adjusted Total Of Income Tax Withheld . . . . ▶	1,218	10
14. Taxable FICA Wages Paid (Item 8) . . $ 10,327.50 .... multiplied by 11.7% =TAX	1,208	32
15. Taxable Tips Reported (Item 9) . . . $ .... multiplied by 5.85% =TAX		
16. Total FICA Taxes (Item 14 plus Item 15)	1,208	32
17. Adjustment (See instructions)		
18. Adjusted Total Of FICA Taxes . . . . ▶	1,208	32
19. Total Taxes (Item 13 plus Item 18) . . . . ▶	2,426	42
20. TOTAL DEPOSITS FOR QUARTER (INCLUDING FINAL DEPOSIT MADE FOR QUARTER) AND OVERPAYMENT FROM PREVIOUS QUARTER LISTED IN SCHEDULE B (See instructions on page 4)	2,426	42

Note: If undeposited taxes at the end of the quarter are $200 or more, the full amount must be deposited with an authorized commercial bank or a Federal Reserve bank in accordance with instructions on the reverse of the Federal tax deposit form. This deposit must be entered in Schedule B and included in item 20.

21. Undeposited Taxes Due (Item 19 Less Item 20—This Should Be Less Than $200). Pay To Internal Revenue Service And Enter Here . . . . ▶   And Check If You Want It ☐ Applied to Next Return, Or ☐ Refunded.

22. If Item 20 is More Than Item 19, Enter Excess Here ▶ $

23. If not liable for returns in the future, write "FINAL" (See instructions) ▶   Date final wages paid ▶

Under penalties of perjury, I declare that I have examined this return, including accompanying schedules and statements, and to the best of my knowledge and belief it is true, correct, and complete.

Date   January 15, 19XX   Signature   John Morse   Title (Owner, etc.)   Owner

The difference in lines 8 and 10 is that Lester has earned more than $15,300 ($15,600), thus $300 is exempt from Social Security Tax.

LEARNING UNIT 40

Payroll Completion

UPDATED INDIVIDUAL EARNINGS RECORDS OF EMPLOYEES

NAME OF EMPLOYEE	Abby Katz				SOCIAL SECURITY NUMBER	111-33-2281	
ADDRESS	87 Garfield Ave.				CITY OR TOWN	Richfield, MA 01910	
DATE OF BIRTH		MARRIED [x] OR SINGLE [ ]	NUMBER OF EXEMPTIONS 0		PHONE NO.		CLOCK NO.
POSITION Secretary	RATE $3/hr.		DATE		DATE STARTED 1/1/XX		DATE TERMINATED
REMARKS					REASON		

FIRST QUARTER 19

WEEK #	LINE #	HOURS WORKED REG	HOURS WORKED OVER TIME	TOTAL EARNINGS	FED OLD AGE	WITH. HOLDING TAX	STATE TAX			NET PAY
1	10			30 00	1.76	-0-	-0-			28 24
2	10			30 00	1.76	-0-	-0-			28 24
3	10			30 00	1.76	-0-	-0-			28 24
4	10			30 00	1.76	-0-	-0-			28 24
5	10			30 00	1.76	-0-	-0-			28 24
6	10			30 00	1.76	-0-	-0-			28 24
7	10			30 00	1.76	-0-	-0-			28 24
8	10			30 00	1.76	-0-	-0-			28 24
9	10			30 00	1.76	-0-	-0-			28 24
10	10			30 00	1.76	-0-	-0-			28 24
11	10			30 00	1.76	-0-	-0-			28 24
12	10			30 00	1.76	-0-	-0-			28 24
13	10			30 00	1.76	-0-	-0-			28 24
TOTAL 1ST QTR				390 00	22.88	-0-	-0-			367 12
TOTAL 3 MOS				390 00	22.88	-0-	-0-			367 12

SECOND QUARTER 19

WEEK #	LINE #	HOURS WORKED REG	HOURS WORKED OVER TIME	TOTAL EARNINGS	FED OLD AGE	WITH. HOLDING TAX	STATE TAX			NET PAY
14	10			30 00	1.76	-0-	-0-			28 24
15	10			30 00	1.76	-0-	-0-			28 24
16	10			30 00	1.76	-0-	-0-			28 24
17	10			30 00	1.76	-0-	-0-			28 24
18	10			30 00	1.76	-0-	-0-			28 24
19	10			30 00	1.76	-0-	-0-			28 24
20	10			30 00	1.76	-0-	-0-			28 24
21	10			30 00	1.76	-0-	-0-			28 24
22	10			30 00	1.76	-0-	-0-			28 24
23	10			30 00	1.76	-0-	-0-			28 24
24	10			30 00	1.76	-0-	-0-			28 24
25	10			30 00	1.76	-0-	-0-			28 24
26	10			30 00	1.76	-0-	-0-			28 24
TOTAL 2ND QTR				390 00	22.88	-0-	-0-			367 12
TOTAL 6 MOS				780 00	45.76	-0-	-0-			734 24

THIRD QUARTER 19

WEEK #	LINE #	HOURS WORKED REG	HOURS WORKED OVER TIME	TOTAL EARNINGS	FED OLD AGE	WITH. HOLDING TAX	STATE TAX			NET PAY
27	10			30 00	1.76	-0-	-0-			28 24
28	10			30 00	1.76	-0-	-0-			28 24
29	10			30 00	1.76	-0-	-0-			28 24
30	10			30 00	1.76	-0-	-0-			28 24
31	10			30 00	1.76	-0-	-0-			28 24
32	10			30 00	1.76	-0-	-0-			28 24
33	10			30 00	1.76	-0-	-0-			28 24
34	10			30 00	1.76	-0-	-0-			28 24
35	10			30 00	1.76	-0-	-0-			28 24
36	10			30 00	1.76	-0-	-0-			28 24
37	10			30 00	1.76	-0-	-0-			28 24
38	10			30 00	1.76	-0-	-0-			28 24
39	10			30 00	1.76	-0-	-0-			28 24
TOTAL 3RD QTR				390 00	22.88	-0-	-0-			367 12
TOTAL 9 MOS				1,170 00	68.64	-0-	-0-			1,101 36

FOURTH QUARTER 19

WEEK #	LINE #	HOURS WORKED REG	HOURS WORKED OVER TIME	TOTAL EARNINGS	FED OLD AGE	WITH. HOLDING TAX	STATE TAX			NET PAY
40	10			30 00	1.76	-0-	-0-			28 24
41	10			30 00	1.76	-0-	-0-			28 24
42	10			30 00	1.76	-0-	-0-			28 24
43	10			30 00	1.76	-0-	-0-			28 24
44	10			30 00	1.76	-0-	-0-			28 24
45	10			30 00	1.76	-0-	-0-			28 24
46	10			30 00	1.76	-0-	-0-			28 24
47	10			30 00	1.76	-0-	-0-			28 24
48	10			30 00	1.76	-0-	-0-			28 24
49	10			30 00	1.76	-0-	-0-			28 24
50	10			30 00	1.76	-0-	-0-			28 24
51	10			30 00	1.76	-0-	-0-			28 24
52	10			30 00	1.76	-0-	-0-			28 24
TOTAL 4TH QTR				390 00	22.88	-0-	-0-			367 12
TOTAL YEAR				1,560 00	91.52	-0-	-0-			1,468 48

By January 31 of the new year (or usually within 30 days after an employee leaves a job) Morse Market furnishes a Form W-2 (withholding tax statement) for the previous year's earnings to each employee. This information is obtained from the individual earnings records; the records are reproduced here and the W-2 forms are shown on p. 495.

NAME OF EMPLOYEE	Mary Blake			SOCIAL SECURITY NUMBER	011-82-1514	
ADDRESS	15 Claremont St.			CITY OR TOWN	Ring, MA 01965	
DATE OF BIRTH		MARRIED [X] OR SINGLE [ ]	NUMBER OF EXEMPTIONS 0	PHONE NO.		CLOCK NO.
POSITION Clerk	RATE $125/wk.	DATE		DATE STARTED 1/1/XX		DATE TERMINATED
REMARKS				REASON		

FIRST QUARTER 19

WEEK #	LINE #	HOURS WORKED REG	OVER TIME	TOTAL EARNINGS	FED OLD AGE	WITH. HOLDING TAX	STATE TAX			NET PAY
1				125 00	7.31	14 40	6.25			97 04
2				125 00	7.31	14 40	6.25			97 04
3				125 00	7.31	14 40	6.25			97 04
4				125 00	7.31	14 40	6.25			97 04
5				125 00	7.31	14 40	6.25			97 04
6				125 00	7.31	14 40	6.25			97 04
7				125 00	7.31	14 40	6.25			97 04
8				125 00	7.31	14 40	6.25			97 04
9				125 00	7.31	14 40	6.25			97 04
10				125 00	7.31	14 40	6.25			97 04
11				125 00	7.31	14 40	6.25			97 04
12				125 00	7.31	14 40	6.25			97 04
13				125 00	7.31	14 40	6.25			97 04
TOTAL 1ST QTR				1,625 00	95.03	187 20	81.25			1,261 52
TOTAL 3 MOS				1,625 00	95.03	187 20	81.25			1,261 52

SECOND QUARTER 19

WEEK #	LINE #	HOURS WORKED REG	OVER TIME	TOTAL EARNINGS	FED OLD AGE	WITH. HOLDING TAX	STATE TAX			NET PAY
14				125 00	7.31	14 40	6.25			97 04
15				125 00	7.31	14 40	6.25			97 04
16				125 00	7.31	14 40	6.25			97 04
17				125 00	7.31	14 40	6.25			97 04
18				125 00	7.31	14 40	6.25			97 04
19				125 00	7.31	14 40	6.25			97 04
20				125 00	7.31	14 40	6.25			97 04
21				125 00	7.31	14 40	6.25			97 04
22				125 00	7.31	14 40	6.25			97 04
23				125 00	7.31	14 40	6.25			97 04
24				125 00	7.31	14 40	6.25			97 04
25				125 00	7.31	14 40	6.25			97 04
26				125 00	7.31	14 40	6.25			97 04
TOTAL 2ND QTR				1,625 00	95.03	187 20	81.25			1,261 52
TOTAL 6 MOS				3,250 00	190.06	374 40	162.50			2,523 04

THIRD QUARTER 19

WEEK #	LINE #	HOURS WORKED REG	OVER TIME	TOTAL EARNINGS	FED OLD AGE	WITH. HOLDING TAX	STATE TAX			NET PAY
27				125 00	7.31	14 40	6.25			97 04
28				125 00	7.31	14 40	6.25			97 04
29				125 00	7.31	14 40	6.25			97 04
30				125 00	7.31	14 40	6.25			97 04
31				125 00	7.31	14 40	6.25			97 04
32				125 00	7.31	14 40	6.25			97 04
33				125 00	7.31	14 40	6.25			97 04
34				125 00	7.31	14 40	6.25			97 04
35				125 00	7.31	14 40	6.25			97 04
36				125 00	7.31	14 40	6.25			97 04
37				125 00	7.31	14 40	6.25			97 04
38				125 00	7.31	14 40	6.25			97 04
39				125 00	7.31	14 40	6.25			97 04
TOTAL 3RD QTR				1,625 00	95.03	187 20	81.25			1,261 52
TOTAL 9 MOS				4,875 00	285.09	561 60	243.75			3,784 56

FOURTH QUARTER 19

WEEK #	LINE #	HOURS WORKED REG	OVER TIME	TOTAL EARNINGS	FED OLD AGE	WITH. HOLDING TAX	STATE TAX			NET PAY
40				125 00	7.31	14 40	6.25			97 04
41				125 00	7.31	14 40	6.25			97 04
42				125 00	7.31	14 40	6.25			97 04
43				125 00	7.31	14 40	6.25			97 04
44				125 00	7.31	14 40	6.25			97 04
45				125 00	7.31	14 40	6.25			97 04
46				125 00	7.31	14 40	6.25			97 04
47				125 00	7.31	14 40	6.25			97 04
48				125 00	7.31	14 40	6.25			97 04
49				125 00	7.31	14 40	6.25			97 04
50				125 00	7.31	14 40	6.25			97 04
51				125 00	7.31	14 40	6.25			97 04
52				125 00	7.31	14 40	6.25			97 04
TOTAL 4TH QTR				1,625 00	95.03	187 20	81.25			1,261 52
TOTAL YEAR				6,500 00	380.12	748 80	325.03			5,046 08

NAME OF EMPLOYEE	Morris Lester		SOCIAL SECURITY NUMBER	021-36-9494
ADDRESS	15 Bone Drive		CITY OR TOWN	Appleyard, MA 01932
DATE OF BIRTH		MARRIED ☒ OR SINGLE ☐ NUMBER OF EXEMPTIONS 1	PHONE NO.	CLOCK NO.
POSITION	Office Mgr.	RATE $300/wk DATE	DATE STARTED 1/1/XX	DATE TERMINATED
REMARKS			REASON	

FIRST QUARTER 19

WEEK #	LINE #	HOURS WORKED REG	OVER TIME	TOTAL EARNINGS	FED. OLD AGE	WITH. HOLDING TAX	STATE TAX			NET PAY
1				300 00	17.55	45 60	15.00			221 85
2				300 00	17.55	45 60	15.00			221 85
3				300 00	17.55	45 60	15.00			221 85
4				300 00	17.55	45 60	15.00			221 85
5				300 00	17.55	45 60	15.00			221 85
6				300 00	17.55	45 60	15.00			221 85
7				300 00	17.55	45 60	15.00			221 85
8				300 00	17.55	45 60	15.00			221 85
9				300 00	17.55	45 60	15.00			221 85
10				300 00	17.55	45 60	15.00			221 85
11				300 00	17.55	45 60	15.00			221 85
12				300 00	17.55	45 60	15.00			221 85
13				300 00	17.55	45 60	15.00			221 85
TOTAL 1ST QTR				3,900 00	228.15	592 80	195.			2,884 05
TOTAL 3 MOS				3,900 00	228.15	592 80	195.			2,884 05

SECOND QUARTER 19

WEEK #	LINE #	HOURS WORKED REG	OVER TIME	TOTAL EARNINGS	FED. OLD AGE	WITH. HOLDING TAX	STATE TAX			NET PAY
14				300 00	17.55	45 60	15.00			221 85
15				300 00	17.55	45 60	15.00			221 85
16				300 00	17.55	45 60	15.00			221 85
17				300 00	17.55	45 60	15.00			221 85
18				300 00	17.55	45 60	15.00			221 85
19				300 00	17.55	45 60	15.00			221 85
20				300 00	17.55	45 60	15.00			221 85
21				300 00	17.55	45 60	15.00			221 85
22				300 00	17.55	45 60	15.00			221 85
23				300 00	17.55	45 60	15.00			221 85
24				300 00	17.55	45 60	15.00			221 85
25				300 00	17.55	45 60	15.00			221 85
26				300 00	17.55	45 60	15.00			221 85
TOTAL 2ND QTR				3,900 00	228.15	592 80	195.			2,884 05
TOTAL 6 MOS				7,800 00	456.30	1185 60	390.			5,768 10

THIRD QUARTER 19

WEEK #	LINE #	HOURS WORKED REG	OVER TIME	TOTAL EARNINGS	FED. OLD AGE	WITH. HOLDING TAX	STATE TAX			NET PAY
27				300 00	17.55	45 60	15.00			221 85
28				300 00	17.55	45 60	15.00			221 85
29				300 00	17.55	45 60	15.00			221 85
30				300 00	17.55	45 60	15.00			221 85
31				300 00	17.55	45 60	15.00			221 85
32				300 00	17.55	45 60	15.00			221 85
33				300 00	17.55	45 60	15.00			221 85
34				300 00	17.55	45 60	15.00			221 85
35				300 00	17.55	45 60	15.00			221 85
36				300 00	17.55	45 60	15.00			221 85
37				300 00	17.55	45 60	15.00			221 85
38				300 00	17.55	45 60	15.00			221 85
39				300 00	17.55	45 60	15.00			221 85
TOTAL 3RD QTR				3,900 00	228.15	592 80	195.			2,884 05
TOTAL 9 MOS				11,700 00	684.45	1778 40	585.			8,652 15

FOURTH QUARTER 19

WEEK #	LINE #	HOURS WORKED REG	OVER TIME	TOTAL EARNINGS	FED. OLD AGE	WITH. HOLDING TAX	STATE TAX			NET PAY
40				300 00	17.55	45 60	15.00			221 85
41				300 00	17 55	45 60	15.00			221 85
42				300 00	17.55	45 60	15.00			221 85
43				300 00	17 55	45 60	15.00			221 85
44				300 00	17 55	45 60	15.00			221 85
45				300 00	17.55	45 60	15.00			221 85
46				300 00	17.55	45 60	15.00			221 85
47				300 00	17.55	45 60	15.00			221 85
48				300 00	17.55	45 60	15.00			221 85
49				300 00	17 55	45 60	15.00			221 85
50				300 00	17 55	45 60	15.00			221 85
51				300 00	17.55	45 60	15.00			221 85
52				300 00	-0-	45 60	15.00			239 40
TOTAL 4TH QTR				3,900 00	210.60	592 80	195.			2,901 60
TOTAL YEAR				15,600 00	895.05	2371 20	780.			11,553 75

492

NAME OF EMPLOYEE	Burton Pound							SOCIAL SECURITY NUMBER		223-15-6655		
ADDRESS	18 Rivell Rd							CITY OR TOWN		Ranchester, MA 01933		
DATE OF BIRTH		MARRIED [x] OR SINGLE [ ]		NUMBER OF EXEMPTIONS 4				PHONE NO			CLOCK NO.	
POSITION Truck Driver		RATE $4.50/hr.		DATE				DATE STARTED 1/1/XX			DATE TERMINATED	
REMARKS								REASON				

FIRST QUARTER 19 / SECOND QUARTER 19

WEEK #	LINE #	HOURS WORKED REG	OVER TIME	TOTAL EARNINGS	FED OLD AGE	WITH. HOLDING TAX	STATE TAX			NET PAY	WEEK #	LINE #	HOURS WORKED REG	OVER TIME	TOTAL EARNINGS	FED OLD AGE	WITH. HOLDING TAX	STATE TAX			NET PAY
1		25		112 50	6.58	1 10	5.63			99 19	14		25		112 50	6.58	1 10	5.63			99 19
2		25		112 50	6.58	1 10	5.63			99 19	15		25		112 50	6.58	1 10	5.63			99 19
3		25		112 50	6.58	1 10	5.63			99 19	16		25		112 50	6.58	1 10	5.63			99 19
4		25		112 50	6.58	1 10	5.63			99 19	17		25		112 50	6.58	1 10	5.63			99 19
5		25		112 50	6.58	1 10	5.63			99 19	18		25		112 50	6.58	1 10	5.63			99 19
6		25		112 50	6.58	1 10	5.63			99 19	19		25		112 50	6.58	1 10	5.63			99 19
7		25		112 50	6.58	1 10	5.63			99 19	20		25		112 50	6.58	1 10	5.63			99 19
8		25		112 50	6.58	1 10	5.63			99 19	21		25		112 50	6.58	1 10	5.63			99 19
9		25		112 50	6.58	1 10	5.63			99 19	22		25		112 50	6.58	1 10	5.63			99 19
10		25		112 50	6.58	1 10	5.63			99 19	23		25		112 50	6.58	1 10	5.63			99 19
11		25		112 50	6.58	1 10	5.63			99 19	24		25		112 50	6.58	1 10	5.63			99 19
12		25		112 50	6.58	1 10	5.63			99 19	25		25		112 50	6.58	1 10	5.63			99 19
13		25		112 50	6 58	1 10	5.63			99 19	26		25		112 50	6.58	1 10	5.63			99 19
TOTAL 1ST QTR				1,462 50	85 54	14 30	73.19			1,289 47	TOTAL 2ND QTR				1,462 50	85.54	14 30	73.19			1,289 47
TOTAL 3 MOS				1,462 50	85.54	14 30	73.19			1,289 47	TOTAL 6 MOS				2,925 00	171.08	28 60	146.38			2,578 94

THIRD QUARTER 19 / FOURTH QUARTER 19

WEEK #	LINE #	HOURS WORKED REG	OVER TIME	TOTAL EARNINGS	FED OLD AGE	WITH. HOLDING TAX	STATE TAX			NET PAY	WEEK #	LINE #	HOURS WORKED REG	OVER TIME	TOTAL EARNINGS	FED OLD AGE	WITH. HOLDING TAX	STATE TAX			NET PAY
27		25		112 50	6.58	1 10	5.63			99 19	40		25		112 50	6.58	1 10	5.63			99 19
28		25		112 50	6.58	1 10	5.63			99 19	41		25		112 50	6.58	1 10	5.63			99 19
29		25		112 50	6.58	1 10	5.63			99 19	42		25		112 50	6.58	1 10	5.63			99 19
30		25		112 50	6.58	1 10	5.63			99 19	43		25		112 50	6.58	1 10	5.63			99 19
31		25		112 50	6.58	1 10	5.63			99 19	44		25		112 50	6.58	1 10	5.63			99 19
32		25		112 50	6.58	1 10	5.63			99 19	45		25		112 50	6.58	1 10	5.63			99 19
33		25		112 50	6.58	1 10	5.63			99 19	46		25		112 50	6.58	1 10	5.63			99 19
34		25		112 50	6.58	1 10	5.63			99 19	47		25		112 50	6.58	1 10	5.63			99 19
35		25		112 50	6.58	1 10	5.63			99 19	48		25		112 50	6.58	1 10	5.63			99 19
36		25		112 50	6.58	1 10	5.63			99 19	49		25		112 50	6.58	1 10	5.63			99 19
37		25		112 50	6.58	1 10	5.63			99 19	50		25		112 50	6.58	1 10	5.63			99 19
38		25		112 50	6.58	1 10	5.63			99 19	51		25		112 50	6.58	1 10	5.63			99 19
39		25		112 50	6.58	1 10	5.63			99 19	52		25		112 50	6 58	1 10	5.63			99 19
TOTAL 3RD QTR				1,462 50	85.54	14 30	73.19			1,289 47	TOTAL 4TH QTR				1,462 50	85.54	14 30	73.19			1,289 47
TOTAL 9 MOS				4,387 50	256 62	42 90	219.57			3,868 41	TOTAL YEAR				5,850 00	342.16	57 20	292.76			5,157 88

493

NAME OF EMPLOYEE	Jim Ryan		SOCIAL SECURITY NUMBER	999-52-1681
ADDRESS	10 Sable Rd.		CITY OR TOWN	Salem, MA 01917
DATE OF BIRTH		MARRIED [x] OR SINGLE [ ]	NUMBER OF EXEMPTIONS 2	PHONE NO.	CLOCK NO.
POSITION Stockroom	RATE $250/wk	DATE	DATE STARTED 1/1/XX	DATE TERMINATED
REMARKS			REASON	

FIRST QUARTER 19

WEEK #	LINE #	REG	OVER TIME	TOTAL EARNINGS	FED OLD AGE	WITH. HOLDING TAX	STATE TAX			NET PAY
1				250 00	14.63	32 60	12.50			190 27
2				250 00	14.63	32 60	12.50			190 27
3				250 00	14.63	32 60	12.50			190 27
4				250 00	14.63	32 60	12.50			190 27
5				250 00	14.63	32 60	12.50			190 27
6				250 00	14.63	32 60	12.50			190 27
7				250 00	14.63	32 60	12.50			190 27
8				250 00	14.63	32 60	12.50			190 27
9				250 00	14.63	32 60	12.50			190 27
10				250 00	14.63	32 60	12.50			190 27
11				250 00	14.63	32 60	12.50			190 27
12				250 00	14.63	32 60	12.50			190 27
13				250 00	14.63	32 60	12.50			190 27
TOTAL 1ST QTR				3,250.00	190.19	423.80	162.50			2,473.51
TOTAL 3 MOS				3,250.00	190.19	423.80	162.50			2,473.51

SECOND QUARTER 19

WEEK #	LINE #	REG	OVER TIME	TOTAL EARNINGS	FED OLD AGE	WITH. HOLDING TAX	STATE TAX			NET PAY
14				250 00	14.63	32 60	12.50			190 27
15				250 00	14.63	32 60	12.50			190 27
16				250 00	14.63	32 60	12.50			190 27
17				250 00	14.63	32 60	12.50			190 27
18				250 00	14.63	32 60	12.50			190 27
19				250 00	14.63	32 60	12.50			190 27
20				250 00	14.63	32 60	12.50			190 27
21				250 00	14.63	32 60	12.50			190 27
22				250 00	14.63	32 60	12.50			190 27
23				250 00	14.63	32 60	12.50			190 27
24				250 00	14.63	32 60	12.50			190 27
25				250 00	14.63	32 60	12.50			190 27
26				250 00	14.63	32 60	12.50			190 27
TOTAL 2ND QTR				3,250.00	190.19	423.80	162.50			2,473.51
TOTAL 6 MOS				6,500.00	380.38	847.60	325.00			4,947.02

THIRD QUARTER 19

WEEK #	LINE #	REG	OVER TIME	TOTAL EARNINGS	FED OLD AGE	WITH. HOLDING TAX	STATE TAX			NET PAY
27				250 00	14.63	32 60	12.50			190 27
28				250 00	14.63	32 60	12.50			190 27
29				250 00	14.63	32 60	12.50			190 27
30				250 00	14.63	32 60	12.50			190 27
31				250 00	14.63	32 60	12.50			190 27
32				250 00	14.63	32 60	12.50			190 27
33				250 00	14.63	32 60	12.50			190 27
34				250 00	14.63	32 60	12.50			190 27
35				250 00	14.63	32 60	12.50			190 27
36				250 00	14.63	32 60	12.50			190 27
37				250 00	14.63	32 60	12.50			190 27
38				250 00	14.63	32 60	12.50			190 27
39				250 00	14.63	32 60	12.50			190 27
TOTAL 3RD QTR				3,250.00	190.19	423.80	162.50			2,473.51
TOTAL 9 MOS				9,750.00	570.57	1271.40	487.50			7,420.53

FOURTH QUARTER 19

WEEK #	LINE #	REG	OVER TIME	TOTAL EARNINGS	FED OLD AGE	WITH. HOLDING TAX	STATE TAX			NET PAY
40				250 00	14.63	32 60	12.50			190 27
41				250 00	14.63	32 60	12.50			190 27
42				250 00	14.63	32 60	12.50			190 27
43				250 00	14.63	32 60	12.50			190 27
44				250 00	14.63	32 60	12.50			190 27
45				250 00	14.63	32 60	12.50			190 27
46				250 00	14.63	32 60	12.50			190 27
47				250 00	14.63	32 60	12.50			190 27
48				250 00	14.63	32 60	12.50			190 27
49				250 00	14.63	32 60	12.50			190 27
50				250 00	14.63	32 60	12.50			190 27
51				250 00	14.63	32 60	12.50			190 27
52				250 00	14.63	32 60	12.50			190 27
TOTAL 4TH QTR				3,250.00	190.19	423.80	162.50			2,473.51
TOTAL YEAR				13,000.00	760.76	1695.20	650.00			9,894.04

494

For Official Use Only		Wage and Tax Statement 19XX
Morse Market 10 Lovett Rd. Salem, Mass. 01970	12134791	Type or print EMPLOYER'S name, address, ZIP code and Federal identifying number.	Copy A For Internal Revenue Service Center Employer's State identifying number

	Employee's social security number	1 Federal income tax withheld	2 Wages, tips, and other compensation	3 FICA employee tax withheld	4 Total FICA wages
21 ☐	011-82-1514	748.80	6,500.00	380.12	6,500.00

	Type or print Employee's name, address, and ZIP code below. (Name must aline with arrow)	5 Was employee covered by a qualified pension plan, etc.?	6 °	7 °
Name ▶	Mary Blake 15 Claremont St. Ring, Mass. 01965	8 State or local tax withheld	9 State or local wages	10 State or locality
		11 State or local tax withheld	12 State or local wages	13 State or locality

* See instructions on back of Copy D.

Form **W-2** See instructions on Form W-3 and back of Copy D. Department of the Treasury—Internal Revenue Service

---

For Official Use Only		Wage and Tax Statement 19XX
Morse Market 10 Lovett Rd. Salem, Mass. 01970	12134791	Type or print EMPLOYER'S name, address, ZIP code and Federal identifying number.	Copy A For Internal Revenue Service Center Employer's State identifying number

	Employee's social security number	1 Federal income tax withheld	2 Wages, tips, and other compensation	3 FICA employee tax withheld	4 Total FICA wages
21 ☐	111-33-2281	0	1,560.00	91.52	1,560.00

	Type or print Employee's name, address, and ZIP code below. (Name must aline with arrow)	5 Was employee covered by a qualified pension plan, etc.?	6 °	7 °
Name ▶	Abby Katz 87 Garfield Ave Richfield, Mass. 01910	8 State or local tax withheld	9 State or local wages	10 State or locality
		11 State or local tax withheld	12 State or local wages	13 State or locality

* See instructions on back of Copy D.

Form **W-2** See instructions on Form W-3 and back of Copy D. Department of the Treasury—Internal Revenue Service

---

For Official Use Only		Wage and Tax Statement 19XX
Morse Market 10 Lovett Rd. Salem, Mass. 01970	12134791	Type or print EMPLOYER'S name, address, ZIP code and Federal identifying number.	Copy A For Internal Revenue Service Center Employer's State identifying number

	Employee's social security number	1 Federal income tax withheld	2 Wages, tips, and other compensation	3 FICA employee tax withheld	4 Total FICA wages
21 ☐	021-36-9494	2,371.20	15,600.00	895.05	15,300.00

	Type or print Employee's name, address, and ZIP code below. (Name must aline with arrow)	5 Was employee covered by a qualified pension plan, etc.?	6 °	7 °
Name ▶	Morris Lester 15 Bone Drive Appleyard, Mass. 01932	8 State or local tax withheld	9 State or local wages	10 State or locality
		11 State or local tax withheld	12 State or local wages	13 State or locality

* See instructions on back of Copy D.

Form **W-2** See instructions on Form W-3 and back of Copy D. Department of the Treasury—Internal Revenue Service

Notice that boxes 2 and 4 are different. Box 2 shows Lester's total earnings while box 4 shows only the amount of FICA wages. Box 3 indicates he paid maximum for FICA.

For Official Use Only		Wage and Tax Statement 19XX

Form 1 (top)

Morse Market
10 Lovett Rd.
Salem, Mass. 01970

12134791

Type or print EMPLOYER'S name, address, ZIP code and Federal identifying number.

Copy A For Internal Revenue Service Center

Employer's State identifying number

21 ☐	Employee's social security number	1 Federal income tax withheld	2 Wages, tips, and other compensation	3 FICA employee tax withheld	4 Total FICA wages
	223-15-6655	57.20	5,850.00	342.16	5,850.00

Type or print Employee's name, address, and ZIP code below. (Name must aline with arrow)

Name ▶

Burton Pound
18 Rivell Rd.
Ranchester, Mass. 01933

5 Was employee covered by a qualified pension plan, etc.?	6 *	7 *
8 State or local tax withheld	9 State or local wages	10 State or locality
11 State or local tax withheld	12 State or local wages	13 State or locality

* See instructions on back of Copy D.

Form W-2   See instructions on Form W-3 and back of Copy D.   Department of the Treasury—Internal Revenue Service

---

Form 2 (bottom)

For Official Use Only		Wage and Tax Statement 19XX

Morse Market
10 Lovett Rd.
Salem, Mass. 01970

12134791

Type or print EMPLOYER'S name, address, ZIP code and Federal identifying number.

Copy A For Internal Revenue Service Center

Employer's State identifying number

21 ☐	Employee's social security number	1 Federal income tax withheld	2 Wages, tips, and other compensation	3 FICA employee tax withheld	4 Total FICA wages
	999-52-1681	1,695.20	13,000.00	760.76	13,000.00

Type or print Employee's name, address, and ZIP code below. (Name must aline with arrow)

Name ▶

James Ryan
10 Sable Rd.
Salem, Mass. 01917

5 Was employee covered by a qualified pension plan, etc.?	6 *	7 *
8 State or local tax withheld	9 State or local wages	10 State or locality
11 State or local tax withheld	12 State or local wages	13 State or locality

* See instructions on back of Copy D.

Form W-2   See instructions on Form W-3 and back of Copy D.   Department of the Treasury—Internal Revenue Service

---

These W-2 forms are prepared with at least four copies:*

Two copies (B and C) to employee—one to be attached to his federal tax return, one to keep for his own records.
One copy (D) for Morse's records.
One copy (A) sent to government by Morse.

If the W-2's cannot be delivered to the worker after a reasonable effort, Morse should keep them as part of its records for four years.

Many companies preprint their company name and address, along with identification numbers, on the W-2's before they are prepared.

---

* If city and state taxes are applicable six copies are prepared. Effective Jan. 1978, W-2 form is to be filed to Social Security Administration, since Schedule A of 941 has been deleted. Thus the FICA information is processed by Social Security from the W-2's and then the income tax information is sent to the IRS.

After the W-2's are prepared, Morse is required to complete Form W-3 to accompany the copies of the W-2's it sends to the federal government.*

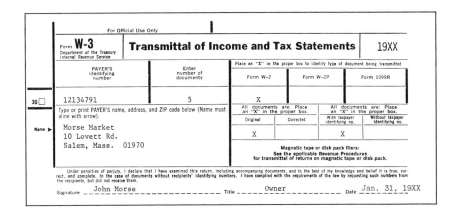

At this point, you should be able to:

1. Explain how individual earnings records are updated during the year.
2. Prepare wage and tax statements.
3. Explain the purpose of the W-3 form.

UNIT INTERACTOR 40

Using the following information, please fill out a W-2 for an employee of Mart Company, 331 Ring Rd., Salem, Mass. 01970, employer identification no. 181 66 892.

Employee:	Jim Rice
	23 Ron Rd.
	Binghamton, Mass. 01931
Social Security No.	021 39 9494
FWT	$2,000.00
Wages	15,300.00
FICA	895.05

* Effective Jan. 1978, W-3 is filed with the Social Security Administration with attached W-2's, since Schedule A in 941 has been deleted.

For Official Use Only		Wage and Tax Statement 19XX			
Mart Company 331 Ring Rd. Salem, Mass. 01970	18 166892	Type or print EMPLOYER'S name, address, ZIP code and Federal identifying number.	Copy A For Internal Revenue Service Center Employer's State identifying number		
Employee's social security number	1 Federal income tax withheld	2 Wages, tips, and other compensation	3 FICA employee tax withheld	4 Total FICA wages	
021 39 9494	2,000.00	15,300.00	895.05	15,300.00	
Type or print Employee's name, address, and ZIP code below. (Name must aline with arrow)		5 Was employee covered by a qualified pension plan, etc.?	6 *	7 *	
Jim Rice 23 Ron Rd. Binghamton, Mass. 01931		8 State or local tax withheld	9 State or local wages	10 State or locality	
		11 State or local tax withheld	12 State or local wages	13 State or locality	
		* See instructions on back of Copy D.			
Form **W-2**	See instructions on Form W-3 and back of Copy D.	Department of the Treasury—Internal Revenue Service			

21 ☐

Name ▶

LEARNING UNIT 41

Conclusion

PREPARATION OF FORM 940

The last form we shall deal with is the employer's annual federal unemployment tax return. Recall that each month we record the state and federal unemployment taxes. Morse pays the state unemployment tax at the end of each quarter.

The information needed to complete this form is gathered from the individual earnings records as well as the records of payment of the state unemployment taxes. Certain regulations on when to file for federal unemployment can be found on the reverse side of the form. If quarterly payments are needed deposit tickets are available similar to those for FICA and FWT.

Since the total federal unemployment tax due from Morse Market did not exceed $100 for the sum of the quarters of the calendar year, an annual payment is due by January 31. Here is an aid chart, followed by the completed Form 940. The key point is that all workers of Morse have earned cumulative wages of $4200 except Katz.

No. of Weeks in Month	Month	Amount of Earnings Exempt		Amount of Earnings Taxable		Federal Unemployment (.005)	
4	January		0	3,270		16.35	
4	February		0	3,270		16.35	
5	March		0	4,087.50		20.44	
4	April	Lester 900 Ryan 50	950	2,320		11.60	
4	May	Lester 1,200 Ryan 1,000	2,200	1.070		5.35	
5	June	Lester 1,500 Ryan 1,250	2,750	1,337.50		6.68	
4	July	Lester 1,200 Ryan 1,000	2,200	1,070		5.35	
4	August	Blake 50 Lester 1,200 Ryan 1,000	2,250	1.020		5.10	
5	September	Blake 625 Lester 1,500 Pound 187.50 Ryan 1,250	3,562.50	525		2.63	
4	October	Blake 500 Lester 1,200 Pound 450 Ryan 1,000	3,150	120		.60	
4	November	Blake 500 Lester 1,200 Pound 450 Ryan 1,000	3,150	120		.60	
5	December	Blake 625 Lester 1,500 Pound 562.50 Ryan 1,250	3,937.50	150		.75	
			24,150.00	18,360.00		91.80	

Notice that in the month of December only Abby Katz's wages are subject to federal and state unemployment, since she is the only one who has not earned more than $4,200.

| Form **940** Department of the Treasury Internal Revenue Service | | **Employer's Annual Federal Unemployment Tax Return** | | | | | | | **19XX** | |

Name of State 1	State reporting number as shown on employer's State contribution returns 2	Taxable payroll (As defined in State act) 3	Experience rate period 4 From—	To—	Experience rate 5	Contributions had rate been 2.7% (col. 3 × 2.7%) 6	Contributions payable at experience rate (col. 3 × col. 5) 7	Additional credit (col. 6 minus col. 7) 8	Contributions actually paid to State 9
Mass.	22418	18,360	1/1	12/31	3.5	495.72	642.60	----	642.60
Totals ▶		18,360							642.60

10 Total tentative credit (Column 8 plus column 9). . . . .   642 | 60

11 Total remuneration (including exempt remuneration) PAID during the calendar year for services of employees   42,510 | 00

Exempt Remuneration	Approximate number of employees involved	Amount paid
12 Exempt remuneration. (Explain each exemption shown, attaching additional sheet if necessary):		
13 Remuneration in excess of $4,200. (Enter only the excess over the first $4,200 paid to individual employees exclusive of exempt amounts entered on line 12)	4	24,150

14 Total exempt remuneration . . . .   24,150 | 00
15 Total taxable wages (line 11 less line 14) . . . .   18,360 | 00
16 Gross Federal tax (3.2% of line 15) . . . .   587 | 52
17 Enter 2.7% of the amount of wages shown on line 15 . . . .   495.72
18 Line 10 or line 17 whichever is smaller 495.72
19 Net Federal tax (line 16 less line 18) 91.80

Record of Federal Tax Deposits for Unemployment Tax (Form 508)

Quarter	Liability by period	Date of deposit	Amount of deposit
First			
Second			
Third			
Fourth			

20 Total Federal tax deposited . . . .

21 Balance due (line 19 less line 20—this should not exceed $100). Pay to "Internal Revenue Service" . . ▶   91.80
22 If no longer in business at end of year, write "FINAL" here ▶

Under penalties of perjury, I declare that I have examined this return, including accompanying schedules and statements, and to the best of my knowledge and belief it is true, correct, and complete, and that no part of any payment made to a State unemployment fund, which is claimed as a credit on line 18 above, was or is to be deducted from the remuneration of employees.

Date ▶   Signature ▶   Title (Owner, etc.) ▶

| T |
| FF |
| FD |
| FP |
| I |
| T |

(If incorrect make any necessary change.) ▶

Name (as distinguished from trade name)
John Morse
Trade name, if any
Morse Market
Address and ZIP code
10 Lovett Rd., Salem, Mass. 01970

Calendar Year
19XX
Employer Identification No.
12 134791

16—■—1

Morse Market also is required by state law to carry insurance for workman's compensation. For example, if someone is hurt on the job, this insurance provides some degree of financial protection. The rates differ for different jobs, risks, and other factors. The employer is usually responsible for paying all the premiums for workman's compensation. Often, it is paid in advance based upon payroll projection. At the end of the calendar year, if there is a difference between estimated and actual, the balance is rectified.

Although we have by no means covered all points about payroll, you should now have a sound basic understanding of payroll concepts and procedures. At this point, you should be able both to solve the question and problem interactors at the end of the chapter and to:

1. Identify wages exempt from federal unemployment taxes.
2. Prepare the Employer's Annual Federal Unemployment Tax Return (Form 940).

COMPLETION OF PAYROLL—A BLUEPRINT

At the end of each quarter, the federal government requires the employer to complete Form 941, the Employer's Quarterly Federal Tax Return. This form involves FICA paid by the worker and the employer as well as FWT, which was deducted from the worker's pay.

Depending upon how much FICA (employer and employee) is owed and how much deducted, the employer may have to make monthly (or more frequent) deposits. Cards are furnished to employers for making deposits before the end of the quarter (see the back of Form 941 for details.) At the end of each quarter, the amounts of deposits made are compared to the total amounts due; the difference is then sent along with Form 941.

Where do we get the information we need for Form 941? By going through each individual earnings record and adding up gross earnings and deductions for FICA and FWT, we can easily make the necessary calculations. Please remember that Form 941 does not involve any state or federal unemployment taxes.

At the end of the calendar year, the employer furnishes W-2's. This information also is calculated from the individual earnings record of each employee.

The whole process of payroll requires accuracy and an awareness of employee and employer responsibilities. Local state or federal offices can answer specific questions about due date.

The following is a sample tax calendar and timetable of a payroll cycle illustrated for Ron Company, an ongoing firm whose FICA and FWT fall between $200 and $2,000 per month.

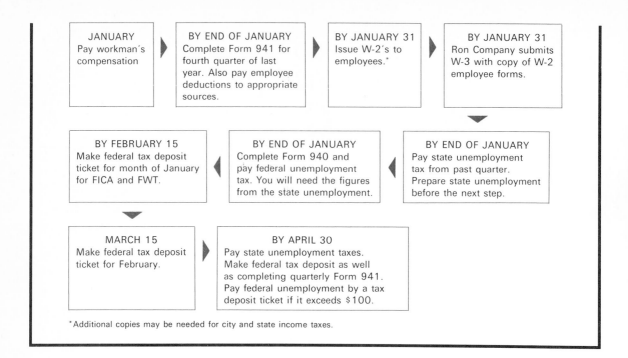

*Additional copies may be needed for city and state income taxes.

SUMMARY OF NEW ACCOUNTING LANGUAGE TERMS

Learning Unit 36

Form 941, Employer's Quarterly Federal Tax Return: A report due each quarter (three months) indicating total FICA owed plus FWT for the quarter. If federal tax deposits have been made correctly, the total deposit should equal the amount owed that is indicated on Form 941. If there is a difference, payment may be due.

Federal Tax Deposits: Cards sent to employers for making deposits (FWT and FICA of employer and employee). The amounts and timing of federal tax deposits depend on the amounts of FICA and FWT liabilities created. A list of regulations is found on the back of Form 941.

Learning Unit 40

Employer's Annual Federal Unemployment Tax Return (Form 940): A form used by employers at the end of the year to pay federal unemployment tax. If more than $100 is cumulatively owed in a quarter, it should be paid quarterly. Normally payment is by Jan. 31 after the calendar year, unless deposits have been made by an employer.

Form W-2, Wage and Tax Statement: A form completed by the employer at the end of the calendar year to provide a summary of gross earnings and deductions to each employee. At least two copies go to the employee, one copy to the IRS, and one copy into the records of the business.

Form W-3, Transmittal of Income and Tax Statement: A form completed by the employer to verify the number of W-2's. The W-2's are attached to the Form W-3.

1. A deposit can only be made once a month. Agree or disagree?
2. When a deposit is made, to whom is payment made?
3. The FICA rate directly affects the amount of state unemployment. Agree or disagree?
4. What months comprise the third quarter?
5. Compare and contrast how monthly payroll summaries can be prepared from the individual earnings records.
6. Why does Form 941 require the employer's address to be written twice?
7. What is the purpose of the schedule on the back of Form 941?
8. What does it mean when earnings are exempt?
9. Differentiate between a W-2 and a W-4.
10. State the purpose of a W-3.
11. Why would an employer consider preprinting his name, address, and identification on the W-4?
12. There is really no need to have more than one copy of the W-4. Please comment.
13. Workman's compensation is optional. Please discuss.
14. Form 940 is concerned only with FICA. Agree or disagree? Please comment.

PROBLEM INTERACTORS

1. The following is the payroll summary for the first three months for Mack Auto Shop, owned by Bill Mack.

Month	Social Security No.	Total Earned	FICA	FWT
(4 weeks) Jan.				
Marci Lowry	021-38-9432	$ 400.00	$ 23.40	$ 52.40
Mike Rice	119-71-2250	1,200.00	70.20	213.20
Bill Smith	181-62-6343	1,600.00	93.60	381.60
Jim Spoon	118-62-1820	800.00	46.80	108.00
		$4,000.00	$234.00	$755.20
(4 weeks) Feb.				
Marci Lowry		$ 400.00	$ 23.40	$ 52.40
Mike Rice		1,200.00	70.20	213.20
Bill Smith		1,600.00	93.60	381.60
Jim Spoon		800.00	46.80	108.00
		$4,000.00	$234.00	$755.20
(5 weeks) Mar.				
Marci Lowry		$ 500.00	$ 29.25	$ 69.00
Mike Rice		1,600.00	93.60	266.50
Bill Smith		2,000.00	117.00	477.00
Jim Spoon		1,000.00	58.50	135.00
		$5,100.00	$298.35	$947.50

Mack Auto Shop is located at 130 Rain Street, Swampscott, Mass. 01917.
Federal identification number 283256841.
FICA rate, 5.85%.
FWT was arrived at by wage bracket chart.
State unemployment is 2.7% on the first $4,200.
Federal unemployment is .5% on the first $4,200.

Your task is to:

a. Record the journal entry for the employer's payroll tax for *each month* and calculate the deposit for *each month*.

b. At the end of the quarter prepare Form 941, employer's quarterly federal tax return, for Mack Auto Shop.

2. From the following information related to Smith's Art Shop, please complete Form 940, the employer's annual federal unemployment tax return. Smith's Art Shop is located at 115 Ree Rd., Rye, Smithmont.

State identification number, 28413.
Experience rate, 2.2%.
Taxable payroll for year, $18,000.
Total payroll, $42,000.
Number of workers, 5.
Experience rating period, 1/1–12/31.
State, Smithmont.

ADDITIONAL PROBLEM INTERACTORS

1-A. The following is the payroll summary for the first three months of Ron's Flower Shop, owned by Ron Morin.

Month	Social Security No.	Total Earned	FICA	FWT
(4 weeks) Jan.				
Jim Dumont	282-03-9176	$ 600.00	$35.10	$102.00
Alice Fall	988-22-1142	1,400.00	81.90	309.60
Ranger Paul	918-22-7715	1,000.00	58.50	191.20
Ralph Slan	225-01-9862	200.00	11.70	16.40
		$3,200.00	$187.20	$619.20
(4 weeks) Feb.				
Jim Dumont		$ 600.00	$ 35.10	$102.00
Alice Fall		1,400.00	81.90	309.60
Ranger Paul		1,000.00	58.50	191.20
Ralph Slan		200.00	11.70	16.40
		$3,200.00	$187.20	$619.20
(5 weeks) March				
Jim Dumont		$ 750.00	$ 43.88	$127.50
Alice Fall		1,750.00	102.38	387.00
Ranger Paul		1,250.00	73.13	239.00
Ralph Slan		250.00	14.63	20.50
		$4,000.00	$234.02	$774.00

Ron's Flower Shop is located at 150 Ralph Road, Salem, Mass. 01917. Federal identification number 143116825.

FICA rate, 5.85%.

FWT was arrived at by wage bracket chart.

State unemployment is 3.5% on the first $4,200.

Federal unemployment is .5% on the first $4,200.

Your task for each month is to:

a. Record the journal entry for the employer's payroll taxes.

b. Prepare a deposit.

At the end of the quarter your task is to complete Form 941, the employer's quarterly federal tax return, for Ron's Flower Shop.

2-A. From the following information related to Burns Auto, please complete Form 940, the employer's annual federal unemployment tax return. Burns Auto is located at 225 Ras Road in Lowy, Avon, #01152.

State, Avon.

State identification number 22581

Experience rate, 2.6%.

Taxable payroll, $20,000.

Total payroll, $42,000.

Number of workers, 5.

Experience rating period 1/1–12/31.

CHALLENGE PROBLEM INTERACTOR

A portion of an incomplete payroll register is shown below. Complete the payroll register and answer the questions.

	Earnings		Deductions				Payment	Distribution	
Employee	Cumulative Pay	Gross Pay	FICA Taxes	Federal Income Taxes	Medical Insurance	Total Deductions	Net Pay	Office Salary	Shop Salary
Mary Adams	5,250	350		70	0			350	
John Marton	12,000	800		160	20				800
Sue Payner	4,200	280		56	0			280	
Craig Sayer	15,750	1,050		210	25				1,050
Alan Vanner	18,000	1,200		240	30				1,200
Total	55,200	3,680		736	75			630	3,050

PAYROLL REGISTER (Salaries for Second Half of August, 198X)

ASSUME

F.I.C.A. Tax	$16,500	Rate: 5.85%
Unemployment Tax:		
Federal	5,400	0.5%
State	5,400	2.7%

1. FICA tax payable for second half of August? _____
2. Salaries payable for second half of August? _____
3. Federal unemployment tax for second half of August? _____
4. State unemployment tax for second half of August? _____
5. If each employee earned his same salary *each month,* what is the amount of FICA tax that would be sent to the federal government at the end of the third quarter? _____

summary of the accounting process: a primer for the mini practice set

The first step in accounting is to analyze business transactions and to journalize them into their respective journals. Assuming that a company uses special journals, sales on account are recorded in a sales journal, purchases on account in a purchases journal, money received in a cash receipts journal, and payment of money in a cash payments journal. Entries that did not fit into these special journals are recorded in a general journal.

When information is placed into these journals, the accounts payable and accounts receivable subsidiary ledgers should be updated. This allows companies to respond to customers' requests for current balances as well as to determine amounts owed to creditors during the month. When information is posted to the subsidiary ledgers from the journals, a checkmark is used in the posting reference column of the individual journals.

If, during the month, transactions occurred involving petty cash, the transaction establishing petty cash needs to be entered in the cash payments journal. During the month money being paid out of petty cash is shown only in the auxiliary petty cash record. At the time of replenishment a compound entry must be placed into the cash payments journal to show individual expenses that were originally shown on the vouchers in the petty cash box as well as the new check that is written to replenish the fund.

At the end of the month the totals of the respective special journals are posted to the general ledger.

When a company records payroll during the month, it prepares this information in a payroll register* and from the totals of the register posts information to the ledger. At the same time, the individual earnings records of workers are updated. When the payroll is finally paid, it is reflected in the cash payments journal, which shows the individual checks that were written along with the reduction to salaries and wages payable.

As for the employer, he records his employer payroll taxes in the general journal. Of course, all information placed in general journals is posted to individual ledger accounts.

Once all the information about business transactions, particularly petty cash, payroll, and the like, is recorded in the journal and posted, a trial balance can be prepared on a worksheet, and then adjustments are prepared. The adjustment data on the worksheet are not placed into any journal or recorded in the ledger at this time. The worksheet provides a summary area for assembling information that will allow us to complete the accounting cycle.

From the worksheet the balance sheet and income statement are prepared. Next, in order to show ledger accounts up to the latest balances, we go to the adjustments column of the worksheet and journalize the adjusting entries. These adjusting entries are then posted to the ledger.

To clear the ledger of all temporary accounts, revenues, expenses, purchases, sales, sales discounts, etc., closing entries are journalized from the income statement column of the worksheet and posted to the ledger. Owner's investment will now be up to date with those latest and appropriate balances.

The last step is the preparation of the post-closing trial balance. This means going to the ledgers and listing accounts that have balances. You will find that the only accounts with balances are assets, liabilities, and owner's equity. All temporary accounts will have zero balances as a result of the closing process.

In conclusion, at the end of the accounting cycle you will have an up-to-date balance in your accounts receivable and accounts payable subsidiary ledgers. Your individual earnings recorded for payroll will be up to date, your special journals will be totaled and posted, and your petty cash auxiliary record will be up to date, showing the replenishment of petty cash to begin the next period in the ledger. Only assets, liabilities, and owner's equity will have a balance that will be brought forward to the next period. Each month, also, you will reconcile your checkbook balance to the bank balance.

---

* Assumed to be a special journal.

Before attempting to complete the mini practice set for J. Cling Dress Shop, test your readiness with this recall interactor. Then go back to specific parts of the text for the areas in which you need further review. Once you feel comfortable with each segment of the interactor, complete the accounting cycle for J. Cling Dress Shop in Appendix 2.

Answer true or false for each statement.

1. The establishment of petty cash does not affect the cash payments journal or the auxiliary petty cash record.
2. Withdrawal of owner could be recorded in the cash payments journal.
3. A debit or credit memo may be recorded in a general journal.
4. When money is paid from petty cash, it must be recorded immediately in the cash payments journal.
5. When payroll is recorded, the payroll register can never be used as a special journal.
6. The employer's payroll taxes do not include federal unemployment.
7. Closing entries are recorded in the adjustment columns of the worksheet.
8. Ending merchandise inventory is recorded as a cost in the income statement column of the worksheet.
9. The accounts payable and accounts receivable subsidiary ledgers are updated after a trial balance is prepared.
10. The result of paying payroll is to reduce cost and debit wages payable, assuming the payroll is not paid at the same time it was recorded.
11. The replenishment of petty cash affects the cash payment journal; also, the auxiliary record should be updated.
12. The post-closing trial balance usually contains purchases, purchase discounts, and sales discounts.

SOLUTION to Recall Interactor

1. False. 2. True. 3. True.   4. False.   5. False.   6. False.
7. False. 8. False. 9. False. 10. False. 11. True. 12. False.

APPENDIX

J. Cling
dress shop:
a mini practice set

Complete the accounting cycle:

19XX, JAN.   2: Invested $20,000 cash in opening the J. Cling Dress Shop.

  2: Established a petty cash fund $20, check no. 1.

  2: Paid three months rent in advance $300, check no. 2.

  2: Purchased merchandise from Morris Company on account $5,000, terms 2/10, n/30.

  2: Paid from the petty cash fund $1 for cleaning package voucher no. 1 (consider this a cleaning expense).

  3: Sold merchandise to Ronald Company on account $3,500, invoice no. 1, terms 2/10, n/30.

  5: Paid from petty cash fund for postage $3 voucher no. 2.

  6: Sold merchandise to Ronald Company on account $2,500, invoice no. 2, terms 2/10, n/30.

  8: Paid from the petty cash fund for First Aid emergency $5, voucher no. 3.

  9: Purchased merchandise from Morris Company on account $4,000, terms 2/10, n/30.

  9: Paid for delivery expense from petty cash fund $2, voucher no. 4.

  9: Sold merchandise to Ronald Company on account $1,500, invoice no. 3, terms 2/10, n/30.

  9: Paid cleaning service $150, check no. 3.

 10: Ronald Company returned merchandise costing $500,

from invoice no. 2. J. Cling issued credit memo no. 1 to Ronald Company for $500.

11: Purchased merchandise from Jones Company on account $5,000, terms 1/15, n/60.

12: Paid Morris Company invoice, date January 2, check no. 4.

13: Sold $3,500 of merchandise for cash.

14: Returned merchandise to Jones Company in amount of $1,000. J. Cling issued debit memo no. 1 to Jones Company.

14: Paid delivery expense from petty cash fund $5, voucher no. 5.

Employees of the J. Cling Dress Shop are paid bimonthly. The following is the payroll summary for January 14.* Pay will be received by employees on January 16.

Name	Gross	FWT	FICA	SWT	Net Pay
K. Mull	112.50	1.10	6.58	5.63	99.19
P. Pool	125.00	14.40	7.31	6.25	97.04
A. Run	30.00	—	1.76	—	28.24
J. Swan	300.00	45.60	17.55	15.00	221.85
J. Wing	250.00	32.60	14.63	12.50	190.27
	817.50	93.70	47.83	39.38	636.59

19XX, JAN. 15: Sold merchandise for $1,500 cash.

15: J. Cling withdrew $15 for her own personal satisfaction, check no. 5.

16: Received payment from Ronald Company for invoice no. 2, less discount.

16: Ronald Company paid invoice no. 1, $3,500.

16: Sold merchandise to Bing Company on account, invoice no. 4, $1,600, terms 2/10, n/30.

16: Issued check no. 6 to K. Mull, $99.19.
Issued check no. 7 to P. Pool, $97.04.
Issued check no. 8 to A. Run, $28.24.
Issued check no. 9 to J. Swan, $221.85.
Issued check no. 10 to J. Wing, $190.27.

21: Purchased delivery truck $3,600, on account from Moe's Garage.

22: Sold to Ronald Company merchandise on account $2,000, invoice no. 5, terms 2/10, n/30.

23: Paid Jones Company the balance owed, check no. 11.

* The employer's payroll taxes will be recorded monthly. Keep in mind that many companies record the taxes when the payroll is recorded. Also, J. Cling uses a payroll register as a special journal. For our purpose omit No. of Deductions, Marital Status, etc. in filling out the payroll register.

JAN. 24: Sold merchandise to Bing Company $2,000, invoice no. 6, terms 1/10, n/30.

25: Purchased merchandise for $750, check no. 12.

27: Purchased merchandise from Blew Company on account $6,000, terms 2/10, n/30.

27: Paid $2 postage from the petty cash fund, voucher no. 6.

28: Ronald Company paid invoice no. 5 dated January 22, less discount.

28: Recorded bimonthly payroll, exactly the same as two weeks ago.

28: Bing Company paid invoice no. 4 dated January 16.

29: Borrowed $10,000 from A. P. Bank.

29: Purchased merchandise from Morris Company on account $6,000, terms 2/10, n/30.

30: Issued check no. 13 to K. Mull, $99.19.
Issued check no. 14 to P. Pool, $97.04.
Issued check no. 15 to A. Run, $28.24.
Issued check no. 16 to J. Swan, $221.85.
Issued check no. 17 to J. Wing, $190.27.

30: Sold merchandise to Blew Company on account, invoice no. 7, terms 2/10, n/30, $5,000.

30: Issued check no. 18 to replenish the petty cash fund 18 dollars.

31: Recorded the following payroll tax expenses for J. Cling Dress Shop for January; payment is not due at this time: (1) FICA payable, (2) state unemployment, (3) federal unemployment.

Additional data needed:

1. During January, rent expired, $100.
2. Truck depreciates $50.
3. Salaries and wages earned but unpaid or not due yet, $100.
4. Ending merchandise inventory, $5,490.
5. SUTA, 3.5% on first $4,200.
6. FUTA, .5% on first $4,200.

Your task is to:

a. Set up a general ledger, accounts receivable subsidiary ledger and accounts payable subsidiary ledger, auxiliary petty cash, payroll register, and individual earnings records.

b. Journalize the transactions (don't forget to cross-foot the journals).

c. Update accounts payable and accounts receivable subsidiary ledgers.

d. Post to general ledger.

e. Prepare a trial balance on worksheet and complete worksheet.

f. Prepare an income statement and classified balance sheet.

g. Journalize adjusting and closing entries for worksheet.

h. Post adjusting and closing entries to the ledger.

i. Prepare a post-closing trial balance.

The chart of accounts for J. Cling Dress Shop is as follows:

ASSETS	LIABILITIES
110 Cash	210 Accounts Payable
111 Accounts Receivable	212 Wage and Salaries Payable
112 Petty Cash	214 FWT Payable
114 Merchandise Inventory	216 FICA Payable
116 Prepaid Rent	218 SWT Payable
118 Delivery Truck	220 SUTA Payable
120 Accumulated Depreciation—Truck	222 FUTA Payable
	224 Notes Payable

OWNER'S EQUITY	REVENUE
310 J. Cling Investment	410 Sales
320 J. Cling Withdrawal	412 Sales Returns and Allowances
330 Income Summary	414 Sales Discount

COST OF GOODS SOLD	EXPENSES
510 Purchases	610 Wage and Salary Expense
512 Purchases Returns and Allowances	611 Payroll Tax Expense
514 Purchases Discount	612 Cleaning Expense
	614 Depreciation Expense—Truck
	616 Rent Expense
	618 Postage Expense
	620 Delivery Expense
	622 Miscellaneous Expense

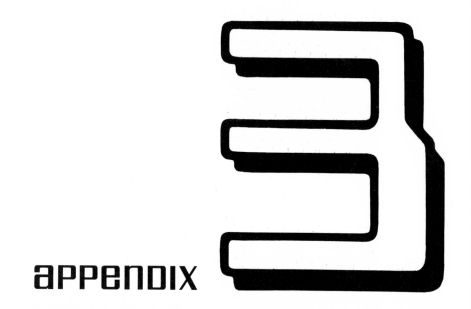

appendix 3

corporations

This course has centered on analyzing single proprietorships, but it is important to have some insight into another type of business organization, the *corporation*.

The owners of a corporation are known as stockholders. The corporation is a legal entity separate from the stockholders. In the eyes of the law a corporation is actually an artificial person, which may, for example, sue or be sued. But why would people want to establish a corporation instead of a single proprietorship or a partnership? (In a partnership, two or more people own the business.)

The advantages of a corporation are:

1. The stockholders are liable only to amount of the investment. For example, if a corporation goes bankrupt, the creditors can try to collect from the corporation but not from the personal assets of a stockholder.
2. In case of the death of the owners or managers, a business in the corporation form remains a going concern.
3. Banks and investors are more likely to lend money or invest in a business if it is a corporation.

The disadvantages of a corporation are:

1. Double taxation. The corporation itself is taxed, and when dividends or salaries are paid, the recipients also are taxed.

2. Cost of corporation.

3. Burden of compliance with the many state and federal regulations.

Let's compare two transactions to see how a single proprietorship and a corporation differ.

SINGLE PROPRIETORSHIP. Bill Book invests $100,000 into the business.

Cash	100,000	
B. Book Investment		100,000

CORPORATION. Bill Book buys 100,000 shares of stock at $1 per share.

Cash	100,000	
Common Stock		100,000

Notice that the proprietorship records B. Book investment, where the corporation increases an account called *common stock.*

Suppose that at the end of the accounting period, net income was $10,000. Let's look at the equity section of the balance sheet for both a corporation and a single proprietorship.

PROPRIETORSHIP		CORPORATION	
Owner's Equity		*Stockholder's Equity*	
B. Book Investment	$100,000	Common Stock, $1 per	$100,000
Net Income	10,000	share, 100,000 issued	
		Retained Earnings	10,000
B. Book Investment	$110,000	*Stockholder's Equity*	$110,000

The corporation has put its net income into an account called *retained earnings.* At this point, in the sole proprietorship B. Book has $110,000 worth of rights. In the corporation B. Book still owns 100,000 shares of stock. Whether the value of that stock will increase or decrease depends on how the company performs, what type of dividends or payments Book receives, and—most important—what other investors think the stock is worth in case Book wishes to sell.

In summary, the balance sheets involve the following:

PROPRIETORSHIP		CORPORATION	
Assets	**Liabilities**	**Assets**	**Liabilities**
	Owner's Equity		*Stockholder's Equity*
	Owner Investment		Stock
	Net Income		Retained Earnings

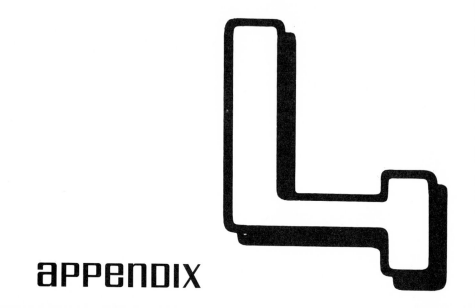

APPENDIX

the write-it-once principle: payroll simplified

In the text we have studied the interrelationships among payroll information, payroll register, cash payments journal, and individual earnings records. In this appendix, through the cooperation of Safeguard Business Systems,* we attempt to simplify the conventional payroll methods and to see how a write-it-once payroll system can save a bookkeeper a great deal of time.

The conventional payroll method may entail the following details and procedures:

1. You copy from the Time Card to the Payroll Journal, then prove the Payroll Journal.
2. Now copy from the Payroll Journal to the Earnings Record, and prove the Earnings Record.
3. Copy from the Earnings Record to the Employee Statement, and prove the Employee Statement.
4. Copy from Employee Statement to Check Stub, and prove the Check Stub.
5. Copy from the Check Stub to the Check, and prove the Check.
6. Copy the Check Number from the Check to the Payroll Journal.
7. Copy the employee's name from the Check to the Payroll Envelope.

*The Safeguard system allows a bookkeeper to lessen posting labor and develop a simple system of updating journals, ledgers, etc.

In the write-it-once system the check and the individual earnings card are inserted in the pegboard on top of the payroll register. When the check is written, that information is simultaneously entered on the individual earnings card as well as in the payroll register through carbons. There is no need to copy the information from the checks to the individual earnings card to the payroll register; it is all done in one writing.

The illustration on the opposite page shows how this could look.

CASH PAYMENTS

This write-it-once payroll system card indeed reduces clerical time. There are many write-it-once systems to handle payroll. Some systems combine a cash payments journal and payroll system. The entire conventional payroll system involves repetitive postings. By adapting this conventional method to a write-it-once principle, we can complete the payroll summary, individual earnings records, and payroll checks simultaneously. An example is shown in the illustration on pages 524 and 525. Notice that a column is set up for the company's bank balance.

ADVANTAGES OF WRITE-IT-ONCE SYSTEMS

Updating your accounts receivable and accounts payable subsidiary ledgers, as you learned to do in the text, can be time-consuming and tedious. The write-it-once principle adapts easily to either subsidiary ledger. For example, if you made a sale on account to Bo Cleaners, under the one-write system you would go to your accounts receivable subsidiary ledger to find the card on Bo Cleaners, or you would create a card. This card could be placed on the pegboard above the sales journal. As information about the sale was updated on the card (subsidiary), it would be carboned into the sales journal simultaneously. The same could be done for accounts payable.

The initial costs of setting up a write-it-once system are more than recouped by the time the bookkeeper saves, as well as by reductions in transpositions, slides, posting omissions, etc. The accounting theory remains the same, but the process becomes more efficient and economical.

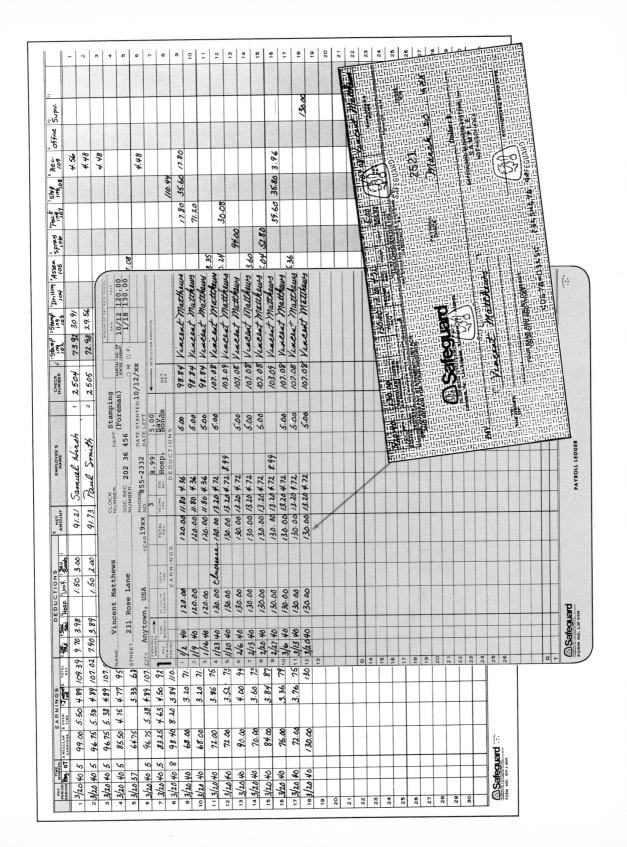

Safeguard Payroll Ledger (top form)

PAY PERIOD ENDING	TIME WORKED Reg	OT	EARNINGS Regular	Over Time	Earn. Amount	Total Pay	DEDUCTIONS W/H Tax	Soc. Sec.	Hosp.	Unif.	Sav. Bonds	NET AMOUNT	CHECK NUMBER	EMPLOYEE'S NAME	¹Stamp'ing 102	²Stamp'ing 103	Drilling 104	Assem 105	Spray 106	Pack'ing 107	Stmp Im'g 108	Rec. 109	Office Supv. 110	11
1	3/20 40	5	99.00	5.50	4.89	109.39	9.70	3.98	1.50	3.00		9.121	2504	Samuel Hirsch	73.92	30.91	120.00					4.56		1
2	3/20 40	5	96.75	5.38	4.89	107.02	7.60	3.89	1.50	2.00		9.173	2505	Paul Smith	71.98	29.56	130.00					4.48		2
3	3/20 40	5	96.75	5.38	4.89	107.																4.48		3
4	3/20 40	5	85.50	4.75	4.77	95																		4
5	3/20 37		64.75		3.33	63													1.08			4.48		5
6	3/20 40	5	96.75	5.38	4.89	107.																		6
7	3/20 40	5	83.25	4.63	4.50	92																		7
8	3/20 40	8	98.40	8.20	3.84	110.															110.44			8

Safeguard Payroll Ledger (lower form)

NAME: Vincent Matthews
STREET: 231 Rose Lane
CITY: Anytown, USA
YEAR 19xx

DEPT: Stamping (Foreman)
CLOCK NUMBER:
SOC. SEC. NUMBER: 202 36 456
PHONE NO: 855-2332
DATE STARTED 10/12/xx
DATE LEFT

MARITAL STATUS: ☐ M ☐ F.
RECORD OF PAY RATE CHANGE:
DATE	RATE
10/12	120.00
1/18	130.00

NO. OF EXEMPT: 3

PAY PERIOD ENDING	TIME WORKED	EARNINGS Regular	Over Time	Earn. Amount	TOTAL PAY	DEDUCTIONS Income Tax	Soc. Sec.	Hosp. 8.99	Sav. Bonds 5.00	NET PAY		Spray	Pack'ing	Stmp Im'g	Rec.	Office Supv.	
1	1/2 40	120.00			120.00	11.80	4.36		5.00	98.84	Vincent Matthews						1
2	1/9 40	120.00			120.00	11.80	4.36		5.00	98.84	Vincent Matthews						2
3	1/16 40	120.00			120.00	11.80	4.36		5.00	98.84	Vincent Matthews		71.20	17.80			3
4	1/23 40	130.00	Increase		130.00	13.20	4.72		5.00	102.08	Vincent Matthews	5.35					4
5	1/30 40	130.00			130.00	13.20	4.72	8.99	5.00	103.09	Vincent Matthews	0.24	30.08				5
6	2/6 40	130.00			130.00	13.20	4.72		5.00	107.08	Vincent Matthews		94.00				6
7	2/13 40	130.00			130.00	13.20	4.72		5.00	107.08	Vincent Matthews	3.60					7
8	2/20 40	130.00			130.00	13.20	4.72	8.99	5.00	103.09	Vincent Matthews						8
9	2/27 40	130.00			130.00	13.20	4.72		5.00	107.08	Vincent Matthews	1.04 52.80	39.60	35.60	17.80		9
10	3/6 40	130.00			130.00	13.20	4.72		5.00	107.08	Vincent Matthews	5.36	36.80	3.96			10
11	3/13 40	130.00			130.00	13.20	4.72		5.00	107.08	Vincent Matthews				130.00		11
12	3/20 40	130.00			130.00	13.20	4.72		5.00	107.08	Vincent Matthews						12

PAYROLL LEDGER

Safeguard · FORM NO. LW-46N

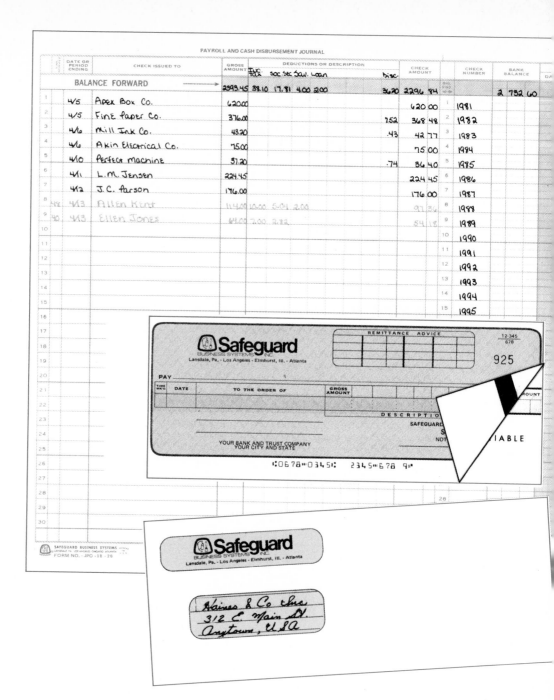

PAYROLL AND CASH DISBURSEMENT JOURNAL

	DATE OR PERIOD ENDING	CHECK ISSUED TO	GROSS AMOUNT	INC. TAX	SOC. SEC.	SAV.	LOAN	Disc.	CHECK AMOUNT		CHECK NUMBER	BANK BALANCE	
		BALANCE FORWARD ⟶	2595.45	38.10	17.81	4.00	2.00	3620	2296	84		2 732 60	
1	4/5	Apex Box Co.	620.00						620	00	1981		
2	4/5	Fine Paper Co.	376.00					7.52	368	48	1982		
3	4/6	Mill Ink Co.	43.20					.43	42	77	1983		
4	4/6	Akin Electrical Co.	75.00						75	00	1984		
5	4/10	Perfect Machine	37.20					.74	36	40	1985		
6	4/11	L. M. Jensen	224.45						224	45	1986		
7	4/12	J. C. Parson	176.00						176	00	1987		
8	4/13	Allen Kent	114.00	10.00	5.04	2.00			97	36	1988		
9	4/13	Ellen Jones	64.00	7.00	2.82				54	18	1989		
10											1990		
11											1991		
12											1992		
13											1993		
14											1994		
15											1995		

REMITTANCE ADVICE

⚠️ Safeguard
BUSINESS SYSTEMS INC.
Lansdale, Pa. - Los Angeles - Elmhurst, Ill. - Atlanta

12-345
678

925

PAY

TIME W/CO	DATE	TO THE ORDER OF	GROSS AMOUNT		AMOUNT

DESCRIPTION

SAFEGUARD
NOT ... IABLE

YOUR BANK AND TRUST COMPANY
YOUR CITY AND STATE

⑈0678⑈0345⑈ 2345⑈678 9⑈

⚠️ Safeguard
BUSINESS SYSTEMS INC.
Lansdale, Pa. - Los Angeles - Elmhurst, Ill. - Atlanta

Haines & Co. Inc.
312 E. Main St.
Anytown, USA

SAFEGUARD BUSINESS SYSTEMS
LANSDALE PA. LOS ANGELES CHICAGO ATLANTA
FORM NO. - JPO -18 - 76

eight n	Truck Exp.	Purchases	Ins.	Repairs	Office Supplies		Postage	Travel	Ent.	Advert.	Auto	Office Payroll	
						BAL. FWD.	100 00			478 15	48 25	242 50	
12 50	36 20	1 286 85											
		620 00				1							
		376 00				2							
		43 20				3							
				75 00		4							
				37 20		5							
3 20		221 25				6							
			176 00			7							
						8						114 40	
						9						64 00	
						10						78 00	
						11							
						12							

NAME	Allen Kent	CLOCK NUMBER	DEPT.	Manager	MARITAL STATUS	NO. OF EXEMPT.		RECORD OF PAY RATE CHANGES	
					M	3	DATE		RATE
STREET	231 Rose Lane	SOC. SEC. NUMBER	202 36 456		☒ M. ☐ F.		6/1/7X		2.10
CITY	Lansdale, Pa.	PHONE NO.	855-6811	DATE STARTED DATE LEFT			3/30/7X		2.20

TIME WORKED	DATE PAY PERIOD ENDING	YEAR	ENCIRCLE QUARTERS 1 2 3 4		GROSS PAYROLL	INC. TAX	Soc. Sec.	Sav.	DEDUCTION AMOUNTS	NET PAY	
			TIME WORKED					DEDUCTIONS			
		SU M T W T F SA									
		BROUGHT FORWARD ➡									
48	1/5	Allen Kent			109.20	9.30	4.80	2.00		93.10	1
48	1/12	Allen Kent			109.20	9.30	4.80	2.00		93.10	2
48	1/19	Allen Kent			109.20	9.30	4.80	2.00		93.10	3
48	1/26	Allen Kent			109.20	9.30	4.80	2.00		93.10	4
48	2/2	Allen Kent			109.20	9.30	4.80	2.00		93.10	5
48	2/9	Allen Kent			109.20	9.30	4.80	2.00		93.10	6
48	2/16	Allen Kent			109.20	9.30	4.80	2.00		93.10	7
48	2/23	Allen Kent			109.20	9.30	4.80	2.00		93.10	8
32	3/2	Allen Kent			69.20	3.20	2.96			61.04	9
48	3/9	Allen Kent			109.20	9.30	4.80	2.00		93.10	10
48	3/16	Allen Kent			109.20	9.30	4.80	2.00		93.10	11
48	3/23	Allen Kent			109.20	9.30	4.80	2.00		93.10	12
48	3/30	Allen Kent			109.20	9.30	4.80	2.00		93.10	13
					1377.60	114.80	60.56	24.00		1178.24	
48	4/6	Allen Kent			114.40	10.00	5.04	2.00		97.36	
48	4/13	Allen Kent			114.40	10.00	5.04	2.00		97.36	

If you are going to use this section for daily hours, write employees name on face of check before inserting this earnings record under the check.

SAFEGUARD BUSINESS SYSTEMS
GLENDALE PA. LOS ANGELES CHICAGO ATLANTA
FORM NO. LW-18-20

APPENDIX 5

use of
the cash basis
for
a service company

Many small service companies utilize a cash-basis system, recognizing revenue when cash is received and recording expenses when cash is paid. This system tends to distort the financial reports, since some revenues are recognized in years when they were not earned and some expenses are shown in years when not incurred. Some of the small service businesses using the cash basis make adjustments for depreciation, supplies, and to aid in presenting consistent financial statements from year to year.*

EXAMPLE OF A CASH-BASIS SYSTEM

For a cash-basis system utilized for the dental practice of Dr. B. A. Wheeler, his accountant designed four accounting books: a cash journal, general ledger, payroll record, and petty cash payments book. Of these, the cash journal is the only type we have not discussed in the text; therefore, an example of Dr. Wheeler's cash journal is shown here. Having studied the accrual basis of accounting, you will see that the cash basis is quite simple.

---

* For some companies utilizing the cash-basis system, actual revenue and expenses are quite close to those that accrue and, therefore, are quite acceptable for their needs. Those companies that do make some adjustments are really using what is called the modified cash basis.

Date	Account Description	PR	Cash Dr. (deposits made)	Cash Cr. (checks written)	Check No.	Dental Revenue Cr.	Dental Supplies Dr.	General Dr.	General Cr.
19XX									
April 1	Dental Fees	X	100			100			
5	Rent Expense	115		50	18			50	
8	Dental Fees	X	500			500			
9	Salary Expense	611		100	19			100	
14	Dental Equipment—Birn Co.	117		250	20			250	
18	Dental Supplies—Bring Co.	X		90	21		90		
19	Dr. Wheeler Withdrawal	311		80	22			80	
28	Dental Fees	X	400			400			
			1,000	570		1,000	90	480	
			(110)	(110)		(310)	(115)	(X)	(X)

Dr.: $1,570; Cr.: 1,570

Dr. Wheeler's cash journal does not involve columns for accounts receivable and accounts payable, since dental fees are recorded when money is received and expenses are recorded when paid. To see how much more detailed the accrual-basis combined journal is than the cash-basis combined cash journal, look at the combined journal in Chapter 11.

index